D1579998

£120

THE PLANE MAKERS

THE PLANE MAKERS

BILL GUNSTON

NEW ENGLISH LIBRARY
TIMES MIRROR

Copyright © 1980 by Basinghall Books Limited

First published in Great Britain by New English Library,
Barnard's Inn, Holborn, London EC1N 2JR in 1980

All rights reserved. No part of this publication may be
reproduced or transmitted, in any form or by any means,
without permission of the publishers.

Printed in Hong Kong
by South China Printing Co

Produced by
Basinghall Books Limited
59 Cambridge Road
Kings Heath, Birmingham

Picture research and captions: E. L. Cornwell
Index: Don Slater
Design Lawrence Bradbury

ISBN: 0-450-04754-7

CONTENTS

INTRODUCTION

Today the manufacture of aircraft is one of the world's largest industries. It is one of the most technically challenging occupations and can be accomplished by only a handful of countries. More than almost any other industry, it is a place for people with long-term vision and nerves of steel. Planemaking is not for the investor who wants a fast buck. A few months ago the British Treasury "leaked" an official report criticizing Britain's decision to rejoin the Airbus partnership, claiming that over a period of "three or four years" it could cause a loss of up to £500 ($1250) million. However, anyone who knows anything about aerospace will know that the initial three or four years is the time when one must simply pour in the money. But, if one has solved every one of the millions of calculations correctly (including many which cannot be predicted in advance) then after seven years one should have one's investment returned. After ten years one ought to be $2500 million or so in profit, and this quadruples after 20.

So a planemaker has to be prepared to remain at the job for quite a time, unlike the election-motivated government minister who knows he will long since have departed when the results of his actions come home to roost. Even so planemaking is such a big-scale business that governments have to be involved with the planemaker in various ways. The two sides are often mutually essential, and in a sensible country can work in harmony within a structure that brings out the best in both. But occasionally, notably in France in 1936 and in Britain from 1957 to 1965, the whole industry is rent asunder by foolish politicians. After both those traumas most of the industry ended up nationalized; in other words the top management suddenly tended to be civil servants.

This book is not meant to be partisan, but there are many examples in history which show that the "private" way is faster and surer than the nationalized way. For example, Dipl-Ing Wilhelm Gundermann, who designed the installation of the first jet engine, states "How was it that von Ohain was able to see his engine in the air $1\frac{3}{4}$ years before Sir Frank Whittle in England, who had registered his basic patent five years ahead of von Ohain? It was because he worked for Ernst Heinkel who, like his two chief engineers, was obsessed with producing faster and higher-flying aircraft. Whittle, on the other hand, was a serving officer who had to rely on government departments and committees of experts, and so had no chance of matching the personal initiative of an entrepreneur." In fact Gundermann is comparing black with white; the sad fact is that in England even the entrepreneurs lacked the motivation to think too hard about Whittle, but the basic argument is indisputable.

In the early days of airplanes entrepreneurs were the only kind of people involved. They had to be chief designer, lead stressman, head of structural testing, shop foreman, manager of the erection department, chief test pilot and probably sales director and leader of the crash crew. The kind of people who gravitated into such an industry tended to be giants in one way or another. Some were big and extravert, others small and quiet, but all had abundant guts; in any case, they were driven inexorably on by the fantastic excitement of what they were doing. Others thought them mad; Edouard Niéport registered his company name as Nieuport to avoid embarrassing his family, and many other pioneers have told of stern gatherings of the clan which sought to show them the error of their ways.

Early airplanes either could only just get daylight under their wheels or failed to rise at all. Once aviators began to fly in earnest it became tragically clear that airplanes could crash fatally. Yet progress was fast. New prototypes were created in days. Even when military aircraft had become quite complicated, in 1916, it was possible for a planemaker, proposing to deliver 5000 aircraft in six months, to write "The drawing office will be busy for ten days. Then the woodworkers and metal fitting shops will be engaged for three weeks on production of parts. Following this, erection and testing will absorb a further three to six weeks, and then the whole factory would be unemployed." At least that enthusiast, who actually did have a busy aircraft works, recognized that the reason for planemaking is to sell products. There

have been times when a company seemed to think the objective was to fly a prototype.

All the planemakers in this book produced aircraft in quantity. Others who did this are absent or accorded only skimpy treatment because their fascinating inside story has never become available. All the stories are of course the proverbial "quart in a pint pot," and I have naturally dealt superficially with most of the aircraft themselves, except where they impinge strongly on the story; there are a thousand books on them already. One of the obvious problems was finding an acceptable structure for an entry such as Aérospatiale of France. This was formed by merging two large groups, but each of these groups itself had been formed by merging other groups, which in turn had stemmed from the abrupt nationalization in 1936–37 of more than two dozen famous companies with stories that generally started at the dawn of heavier-than-air aviation.

To end on a trivial note, students of nomenclature will find planemaking a fruitful area. In the early days there was little need to allocate designations. The Royal Naval Air Service hit on the shortsighted method of calling each type by the serial number of the first example, so that one had to remember that the Short 320 was an exception because this number was the horsepower of its engine! One of the most important types was known as the Sopwith 9700, despite the fact that this number came part-way through the third production batch, while the popular name, if it can be called a name, was 1½-Strutter – whose origin is still a matter for conjecture. Before long most British aircraft had a name, and after 1945 names tended to be perfectly selected to put off export customers. One name was Britannia; another was Viceroy, which after the withdrawal from India was quickly changed to Viscount. This aircraft

was so good it sold widely despite the name, so all over the United States one found cards stuck on office walls saying "pronounced VI-COUNT." Today we realize that aircraft sell on merit and do not need a name. Curious that one of the first British products not to have a name should have been saddled with the designation BAC-111, so that while the maker calls it the One-Eleven most of the rest of humanity speaks of it as the "Back three." As for the DH.125, HS.125, BH-125 and BAe.125, I trust that this particular plane will not have too many more makers in future.

Advanced engineering shops attention for a General Dynamics F-16 single-seat advanced combat fighter.
General Dynamics Corp.

BEECH AIRCRAFT CORPORATION

Wichita lies in Kansas, in the vast flat prairies in the center of the United States. In 1919 a barnstormer – broke, of course, but with a Curtiss Jenny that sometimes still flew – came to Wichita and asked Jake Moellendick to send him to the Chicago airshow to buy a new plane. Jake was a tough but rich oilman who was trying to make Wichita the capital of the Midwest. The gamble of aviation appealed to him, and the upshot was that in 1920 the barnstormer, Billy Burke, brought planemaker Matt Laird from Chicago to Wichita and, with $15,000 from Jake, set up the E M Laird Company. The first Swallow three-seat biplane was finished in April 1920, and Wichita was in the planemaking business.

The little Swallow biplane was perhaps the first successful private-owner airplane in history. Laird grew, gathering on to its payroll men who were to become famous in aviation; namely, Buck Weaver, the Stearman brothers and Walter H Beech. The company ought to have prospered, but Jake was impossible to work for and one by one his fine team quit. Laird went back to his own company in Chicago, which built high-quality private machines up to World War II. In 1924 Lloyd Stearman and Beech joined up with barnstormer Clyde V Cessna to form Travel Air Manufacturing Company. Beech himself had been a barnstormer, and even tried to fly his homemade glider in Pulaski, Tennessee, in 1905, at the age of 14. His experience and piloting skill helped Travel Air become America's No 1 planemaker by 1928, and in 1929 the company merged with the giant, Curtiss Wright. Beech went to New York as vice-president sales and chief pilot.

In 1924 Beech had hired a young secretary, Olive Ann Mellor. Despite her Kansas background, she had run a bank account at seven and, with the help of Travel Air engineers (who explained the technicalities) and the pilots (who never flew her the right way up), she quickly became an aviation expert. She proved brilliantly competent, and in 1930 she married the boss in the best storybook manner. The Beeches thereupon resigned from Travel Air, and on a long honeymoon Walter designed a totally new kind of private aircraft; it was an expensive, high-speed cabin machine, faster than contemporary airliners. Not only that; it was a biplane with back-staggered wings, the lower being ahead of the upper.

In the depth of the depression in April 1932, he registered the Beech Aircraft Company, with his wife as director and secretary/treasurer, and rented part of Cessna's inactive factory. With chief engineer T A Wells they got the first Model 17 five-seater into the air on 4 November 1932. It could fly almost 1000 miles at almost 200mph (322km/h), and in January 1933 it won the Texaco Trophy at the Miami races. The prototype was bought by the Ethyl Corporation, and the money just helped the infant company to keep producing. By 1934 the Model 17, already famous, had begun to sell. By 1935 the total was 18, and by the end of that year 54. Some had the 225hp Jacobs engine; the B-17E (no relation to a later much larger B-17E!) had 285hp and fully retractable gear, the 17R had 420hp, and the A-17F had the 690hp Cyclone and even with fixed gear could reach 225mph (361km/h).

By 1935 the name Beech meant the Rolls-Royce of the sky, with curved windshield, flaps, variable-pitch propeller, and a wide sumptuously furnished and heated cabin.

Olive Ann did not really need to push the women's angle by getting Blanche Noyes and Louise Thadden to win the transcontinental race and also to set a new women's speed record. The company moved into a fine new plant to rival those (also in Wichita) of Stearman and Cessna. The "Staggerwing" continued to sell (up to 781 in 1948, in fact); and its distinctive shape had no rival, although Beech had come to feel Cessna might have been right to pick the monoplane. There was tough competition in monoplanes, but not in the twin-engined types. In early 1937 Beech himself flew the first Model 18, a truly

modern stressed-skin monoplane, with a steel-tube spar bent round to pass ahead of the six-seat cabin, but behind the two-seat cockpit. It was as fast as the fastest Model 17, but instead of being priced at $12,000 to $24,000 it hit the market at $35,000 with two Jacobs engines, or $38,000 with Wrights. Beech asked his wife if they would find customers. She said they would.

Right: Founder of the company, Walter H Beech, and his wife Olive Ann inspect one of the handsome new Bonanzas introduced in 1946. Beech died a few years after this picture was taken and his wife succeeded him.

Below: The Beech Aircraft Company's works at Wichita, Kansas, in the middle 1930s, where the first purely Beech machine, the Model 17 Staggerwing, was born. This aircraft established the company's leading and lasting position in general aircraft design and manufacture.

She was right. Sales were slow at first, but even before the war the Model 18 line was profitable. When the US Army and Navy needed navigation trainers, liaison transports and trainers for bombardiers and gunners, the Wichita plant was soon bursting at the seams. The much-loved Twin-Beech remained in production until 26 November 1969, a 32-year record unequalled by any other aircraft. The total was 7091, all built in the Beech plant (and almost all with neither of the original engines but the 450hp Pratt & Whitney Wasp Junior instead). Hundreds are still in use, and many have been rebuilt by others; some – such as Volpar Turboliners – employ a Beech 18 windshield and twin fins fixed to a new aircraft.

In 1946 Beech again hit the market exactly right, with one of the most beautiful aircraft ever – the vee-tailed Bonanza. [I

flew one in that year, and yearned to own one, and Bonanzas look as modern in 1980 as they did 34 years earlier.] Another staple product arrived in 1948, the T-34 Mentor military trainer. Walter Beech died in 1950, but his successor was never in doubt. Today Olive Ann Beech, nearing 80, drives the company from one annual sales record

to the next. Still the Rolls-Royce of general aviation, Beech today supplies the very best in luxury travel – as well as major parts for fighters, transports, helicopters and many other products including targets, RPVs and systems for the Space Shuttle Orbiter. Well may Mrs Beech's own Super King Air be named *The Free Enterprise*.

Below: A Beech D-17S Staggerwing preserved and maintained in flying condition in England by Customline Limited.

Right: Aircraft production line of the 1930s, at the Beech Wichita plant; assembly of the A-17F, an uprated version of the Staggerwing with 690hp Wright Cyclone engine.

BELL AEROSPACE TEXTRON

By concentrating on difficult projects and true innovation, Bell Aircraft established a list of "firsts" that no other company can equal. Among its pioneering accomplishments are to be found the first American jet, the first jet fighter (defined as the first combat-ready jet in the world), the first supersonic aircraft, the first certificated helicopter, the first swing-wing aircraft, the first jet VTOL and the first aircraft to reach Mach 3. A successor, Bell Helicopter, has far outproduced all other helicopter companies, one of its products being the most-produced military aircraft of any kind since World War II.

Lawrence Dale (Larry) Bell was born at Mentone, Indiana, on 5 April 1894. He was the perfect boy enthusiast for the new era of flying machines. As soon as he left school he spent all his time as unpaid helper to famous aviators, and in 1912 became a paid mechanic to Lincoln Beachey, greatest of all the pre-1914 show pilots. A year later Bell became lead mechanic for Glenn L Martin, where he rose to become superintendent and then vice-president and general manager. In 1928 he moved to Consolidated at Buffalo, NY as sales manager, soon becoming vice-president and general manager there also. Diminutive in stature, Larry Bell was a giant in capability and a very personable man.

In 1935 Consolidated moved to San Diego. Bell stayed in Buffalo and told Consolidated workers they had a job in the same plant if they wished, and was embarrassed at the response; it included the assistant general manager Ray P Whitman, and the chief engineer Robert J Woods. Despite the burden of a big factory and massive weekly payroll, Bell Aircraft Corporation quickly gathered in subcontract business sufficient to pay the bills. On the side, Woods and his team launched into the most difficult business of all – unconventional new fighters of the most advanced kind, with strange configurations and all-metal stressed-skin structure.

The first was the amazing XFM-1 Airacuda, completed in July 1937, with two pusher nacelles housing the new Allison liquid-cooled engines. In the front of each nacelle was a gunner with a 37mm cannon, supplementing a battery of 0.5s in the fuselage. The Army bought a service-test batch of 13, while Bell got on with the Model 400. This was a basically conventional monoplane fighter with the Allison engine installed on the center of gravity above the wing, driving the tractor propeller through a long tubular shaft. Other unusual features were tricycle landing gear and car-type cockpit doors. The claimed advantages included superior maneuverability, better pilot view and heavy nose armament including a 37mm cannon firing through the propeller hub. The Army bought a prototype, the XP-39, in October 1937. It flew in April 1939, and among other things demonstrated the unprecedented speed for a fighter of 390mph (628km/h).

By all rights such an odd machine should have faded away, especially after various changes degraded the performance until it was inferior to traditional machines. But the P-39 Airacobra was tough and an excellent ground-attack platform – the most suspect part – the vital shaft passing between the pilot's legs – never gave the predicted trouble. By July 1944 no fewer than 9584 P-39s of various kinds had been delivered, about 5000 to the Soviet Union and over 2000 to the USAAF in the Pacific, Mediterranean and other theaters. Bell's Niagara Falls plant also delivered 3303 P-63 Kingcobras, which resembled the P-39 but were actually a new design with a laminar-section wing and many other changes. The Soviet Union received 2421, and 300 of them, with 165 P-39s, formed the nucleus of the Free French Air Force.

In April 1941 General Arnold, USAAF Chief of Staff, became excited at Whittle's jet developments. He at once asked General Electric to build Whittle-type turbojets, and looked for a company to build a jet aircraft. The choice was predictable. He called Larry Bell to Washington, briefed him, and signed a contract for three Bell XP-59 Airacomets. The code had previously identified a pusher piston-engined fighter, and when the first XP-59A was assembled at Lake Muroc in California in September 1942 it even had a dummy propeller.

Company pilot Bob Stanley flew the first US jet on 1 October 1942. Eventually, by May 1945, Bell delivered three XPs, 13 service-test YPs, 20 P-59As and 30 P-59Bs, the last-named having more powerful engines, clipped wings and fin and other changes. Poor engine thrust, high fuel consumption and a large airframe made the P-59 a poor performer, but it was gentle to fly and useful as a trainer and test platform; many served as drones or drone directors. The XP-83 was a much more powerful and longer-ranged twin-jet, and the XP-77 a baby wooden piston fighter of 1944.

Final manifestation of the Bell unorthodox engine-in-the-middle series of fighters was the P-63 Kingcobra, which first flew in December 1942. Most of the 3300 or so built went on Lend-Lease to the Russian and Free French Air Forces. After the war numbers of the P-63s were rebuilt and used privately and for racing, as was the one pictured here.

By 1943 the company had expanded outside its Buffalo/Niagara Falls complex. The largest single plant was a gigantic government-owned facility at Marietta, Georgia, where Bell assembled and delivered Boeing B-29s. In 1946 this plant was deactivated, and in 1951 was reopened as the Lockheed-Georgia Company, again to build a Boeing bomber. Another Bell plant

A classic among helicopters is the Bell Model 47, which was in production for more than 25 years and accounted for 6000 of the total of more than 23,000 helicopters produced by Bell. Here, pictured at Bell's Fort Worth, Texas, test-flight facility is a three-seat 47G-4A fitted with optional luggage carrier.

One of two XV-15 tilt-rotor research aircraft, developed by Bell from its experimental Model 301 to meet a NASA/Army VTOL requirement, is about to demonstrate its first hovering flight in May 1977. Wingtip-mounted engines and rotor/propellers are set vertically for take-off and descent and can be swivelled for gradual transition to or from forward flight. The Army requirement calls for a VTOL transport for 15 equipped troops at speeds up to 400mph.

was at Burlington, Vermont, but the most challenging of all its projects was at the original factory at Buffalo. It was the XS-1 (experimental supersonic No 1).

From 1942 the National Advisory Committee for Aeronautics, the Army Air Force and the Navy had collaborated in studying the new phenomenon of compressibility. A special research aircraft was needed, able to fly faster than the speed of sound safely, and from December 1943 Bell was the company involved. Design was well advanced when, on 18 February 1946, Bell received a USAAF/NACA contract for three XS-1s. The first made a free gliding flight on 19 January 1946, and in the hands of USAF Captain "Chuck" Yeager flew to Mach 1.06 on 14 October 1947. Later the same aircraft reached Mach 1.45. A series of improved X-1 aircraft followed, one of them reaching 1650mph (2655km/h), Mach 2.5, in December 1953. Bell's final supersonic design was the X-2, a swept-wing exotic-material research aircraft ordered in July 1947. One X-2 reached a height of 126,200ft (38,466m) and a speed of 2094mph (3370km/h), Mach 3.2.

On 20 June 1951 Bell flew the world's first variable-sweep ("swing-wing") aircraft, the X-5 developed from the German Messerschmitt P.1101 and built for the USAF. In 1954 the company flew a self-funded VTO (vertical take-off) research aircraft with two J44 turbojets on pivots to give lift or thrust, and a Palouste compressor for reaction-jet controls. It was followed on 17 February 1957 by the first flight of the twin-jet X-14 "flat riser," the first vectored-thrust jet VTOL to fly. The single X-14 was flown for no less than 20 years by the USAF and NASA.

Larry Bell sketched his idea for a light helicopter in 1941. His main new feature was a self-stabilizing two-blade rotor with weights carried on the ends of a bar set at 90 degrees to the blades. In almost non-existent spare time the yellow Model 30 was built and flown in mid-1943. Today this pioneer helicopter is being restored by the US National Air and Space Museum. By 1945 a larger two-seat helicopter was flying, from which evolved the classic Model 47, about 6000 of which were made in many countries until 1978. A totally different rotary-wing machine was the Army/USAF XV-3, a tilting-rotor VTOL

of 1955. For the Navy the HSL-1 was put into service as the first anti-submarine helicopter, with a 2000hp Double Wasp radial engine driving rotors at nose and tail. Far more worthwhile commercially was the XH-40 of October 1956. This simple US Army utility prototype led to the vast "Huey" family and its various Cobra gunship derivatives, which by 1979 had reached production totals in excess of 11,000.

In July 1960 Textron Incorporated began operating Bell's defense business under two new companies formed as Bell Aerospace subsidiaries. One was Bell Aerosystems, now called Bell Aerospace Textron, at Buffalo; the other was Bell Helicopter, now Bell Helicopter Textron, at Fort Worth, Texas. The Buffalo plant diversified into liquid rocket engines, space capsules, ICBM post-boost systems, Jet Belt personal VTOL systems, air-cushion vehicles, all-weather landing systems and many other advanced products. The Texas company has now built nearly 24,000 helicopters and as well as the Hueys, Cobras and big 214s is producing various JetRangers, LongRangers and the new twin-engined 222.

BELLANCA

Giuseppe Mario Bellanca built his first aircraft in a Brooklyn, New York, basement soon after arrival in the US from his native Sicily and the company he later founded produced numbers of notable aircraft before it

disappeared in 1959 through mergers. One successful design was the Pacemaker of the 1930s; the one pictured served with Alaska Coastal Ellis Airlines before acquisition for preservation by the Canadian

National Aeronautical Collection. The present Bellanca Aircraft Corporation produces light and light aerobatic aircraft. It has only the most tenuous connections with the original company.

THE BOEING COMPANY

William E "Bill" Boeing was born in Detroit on 1 October 1881. Graduating from Yale in 1904, he naturally entered his father's timber business and within ten years had his own company. Seattle, Washington, is great timber country, and Boeing prospered. He was equally engineer, businessman and perfectionist, and he had an inquiring mind. From July 1914 he occasionally rode as passenger in a primitive Curtiss seaplane from Lake Washington. Seeing a great future for better flying machines, he studied the Curtiss carefully and said to his friend Commander G Conrad Westervelt, a Navy officer attached to a Seattle yard, "I think we could build a better machine."

Boeing bought the best seaplane he could find, a Martin TA, and learned to fly it. With Westervelt he rented a large boathouse (not, as often reported, a specially built factory) on the shore of Lake Union, where he stored the Martin and goaded a team of 21 to design and build the new seaplane, which was called simply the B & W. Early in 1916 Westervelt was transferred back to the East and while there he brought the B & W to the notice of the Navy; the excellent behavior shown by the seaplane on its first flight on 29 June 1916 later resulted in Navy orders. The first of two B & Ws was named *Bluebird* and the second *Mallard*, and in 1918 both were sold to New Zealand where they flew as mail carriers and trainers until 1923. (Pity nobody preserved one.)

Boeing still regarded aviation as a sideline, but was so encouraged he formed Pacific Aero Products Company, registered on 15 July 1916. Better seaplanes followed, including a 1917 batch of 50 for the Navy, and just after the USA entered the war the

A replica of the B & W floatplane, the first aircraft built by William E Boeing in partnership with Conrad Westervelt in Seattle in 1916. The replica was built for the Boeing participation in the nine-day Transpo 72 International Transport Exhibition held at Dulles Airport, Washington.

firm was re-registered as Boeing Airplane Company on 26 April 1917. Next came a big order to build Curtiss HS-2L flying-boats (later cut to 25, but still a big contract for the small team) and Boeing Airplane had to move to bigger sheds at the Heath shipyard on the Duwamish river. A string of seaplanes and flying-boats was leavened by landplanes, such as the EA trainer and three-seat BB-L6, which were tested from various fields, including Camp Lewis about 50 miles to the south.

After the Armistice Boeing Airplane kept its workforce partly by making boats, barges (including a seagoing sled from which landplanes were operated) and even furniture. On 3 March 1919 Boeing opened the first international air-mail service

between the US and Canada (Seattle-Victoria), using a Boeing CL-4S. Not for the last time the company demonstrated its ability to keep going efficiently in a "bathtub," the American term for a period when orders are few. Even in the lean years after the war Boeing was busy and built on an already great reputation; in 1920 Boeing found itself low bidder for the 200 Thomas-Morse MB-3 pursuit aircraft that comprised virtually the whole of the new buying of the Army Air Service at that time. The order not only swelled the company but triggered off a wish to do better (again).

Boeing Airplane was fortunate. It not only broke even on the "two-offs" built for two technically challenging ground-attack designs of 1921–22, which bristled with guns of up to 37mm calibre, but from 1920 it received a succession of contracts for the Army DH-4M and DH-4B and Navy O2B. These improved versions of the de Havilland DH-4, by 1925, reached a total of 298 and provided bread and butter for a

William E Boeing holds the bag of mail carried on the first Canada-US air-mail flight between Victoria and Seattle on 3 March 1919. The machine was a direct derivative of the B & W – the Boeing Model C, a commercial version of a two-seat floatplane trainer produced for the US Navy.

growing company. With this solid under-pinning Boeing could take risks. Its core of skilled designers were eager to produce a dramatically better pursuit plane than the Thomas-Morse (in fact they even put an improved tail on the last 50 MB-3As for the Army).

Boeing gave the go-ahead in December 1922, and the new aircraft flew on 2 June 1923. (Later, in 1925, model numbers were allotted to all Boeing aircraft, and the pursuit prototype became Model 15.) It was possibly the cleanest pursuit in the United States if not in the world, but the chief advances were less obvious. One was that the wartime Wright-Hispano 300hp engine was replaced by the new 435hp Curtiss D-12. The other was that the complex wooden structure, which had metal joints and needed continual re-rigging by tightening wires, was replaced by steel tubes cut precisely, shaped and swiftly welded by the electric-arc method. (Boeing studied Fokker's technique here, and improved on it.)

The Army was starved of funds and said it had no need for new pursuit aircraft anyway; but, again not for the last time, Boeing judged the risk worth taking. By demonstrating courage, of a kind even then (long before the money was measured in millions) rare, Boeing secured its position as the only major rival to Curtiss in the Army and Navy pursuit business. As early as 3 August 1923 the Army was evaluating the new Boeing pursuit at McCook Field (later Wright Field and today the Wright-

Patterson AFB, home of Aeronautical Systems Division). In 1923 there was just a grass field, similar to the Wrights' "test ground" at nearby Huffman Prairie. There was only a rudimentary schedule of tests for a new aircraft; one tried to discover the maximum speed, poled it about to see if it did as it was told, and subjected it to a full-throttle steep dive and pull-out to see if the wings came off. With the Boeing the speed was well over 160mph (258km/h), the fastest then clocked at McCook Field for a combat type, and the wings hardly even creaked.

Barely three months after Frank Tyndall first flew the new pursuit the Army scraped up money and ordered two for service test, with designation XPW-9 (ninth type of

watercooled pursuit, experimental). In 1924 Boeing received an order for 12, soon increased to 30. The National Advisory Committee for Aeronautics bought one as its standard high-speed research platform, probably the first such purchase in history.

By 1925 the Navy was buying the FB-1 version, and there followed a seemingly endless series of PW-9 and FB versions, with various engines and including many seaplanes. They led, in 1928, to the most important single family of American pur-

Four Boeing aircraft production lines spanning about half a century and nearly 28,000 aircraft, counter clockwise from top right: US Army MB-3A fighters in 1922; PW-9 fighters and 40A mailplanes in 1927; B-17 bombers, World War II; and 727 airliners in 1968.

Above: Boeing as a fighter producer stretches memories, but in the late 1920s the Boeing P-12, illustrated here, represented a most important family of interwar fighter aircraft developed and built in quantity for the US Army and Navy (as the F3B/F4B series) as well as for export. The final versions of the P-12/F4B, built in the early 1930s had metal fuselages and with good streamlining had a top speed of nearly 190mph.

Left: After the 1934 Air Mail Act forced the break-up of the huge United Aircraft and Transport Corporation, Boeing went free again with the Stearman Wichita plant as a wholly owned subsidiary. This picture shows Boeing's Stearman Aircraft Division's final assembly at the height of production of the PT-13 trainer; over 10,000 Kaydets were built by the end of World War II.

suits (fighters) of the interwar era. The F3B/F4B/P-12 family, nearly all of which were powered by Pratt & Whitney Wasp engines, sustained a production run of almost 600 examples, finishing with a second batch for Brazil in 1933. It is only the senior citizens of today who remember Boeing as a leading builder of fighters.

Even in its infancy Boeing did much work "on the side"; for example it supplied the twin-float landing gear for the Douglas World Cruisers in 1924 and three years later rebuilt the most famous of all Fokker transports into *Southern Cross* for Sir Charles Kingsford Smith. But a more significant event was Boeing's design of the Model 40 (the first to have a type number from the start) as a replacement for the DH-4 as standard US Mailplane. The Post Office stipulated use of the heavy and un-reliable watercooled Liberty engine, and Boeing was not impressed by the result, though the open-cockpit biplane was good.

In 1926 he found the answer in the new Wasp radial engine fitted to an FB-4 Navy fighter. Quickly he redesigned the mailplane to use the aircooled engine. Shorter and lighter, it allowed the fuel tank to be moved ahead of the wings to make room for a cramped two-passenger cabin, allowing $400 extra revenue to be earned on a single trip along the Chicago–San Francisco mail route. Learning that mail was to be assigned to private operators on 1 July 1927, Boeing applied for this route and won. He formed Boeing Air Transport, and set about building 25 of the new Boeing 40A transports. By 1 June only one had been completed, but by midnight on the 30th all 25 were waiting at their assigned locations along the route. Almost every observer, including the experts, predicted Bill Boeing would lose his shirt; by 1934 BAT was being cited in the Senate as a

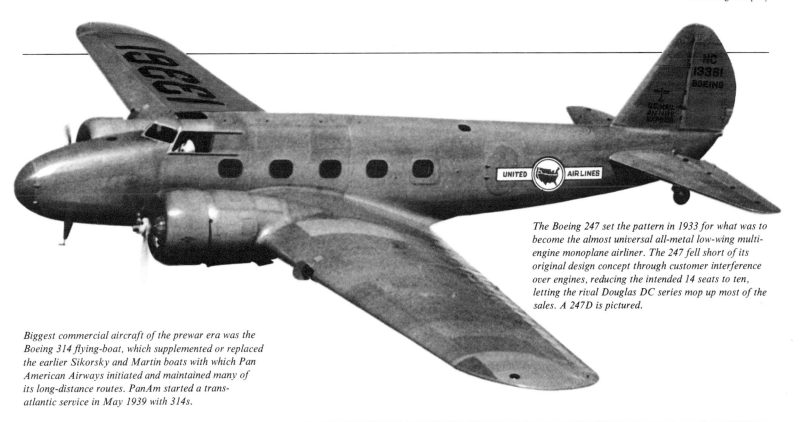

The Boeing 247 set the pattern in 1933 for what was to become the almost universal all-metal low-wing multi-engine monoplane airliner. The 247 fell short of its original design concept through customer interference over engines, reducing the intended 14 seats to ten, letting the rival Douglas DC series mop up most of the sales. A 247D is pictured.

Biggest commercial aircraft of the prewar era was the Boeing 314 flying-boat, which supplemented or replaced the earlier Sikorsky and Martin boats with which Pan American Airways initiated and maintained many of its long-distance routes. PanAm started a trans-atlantic service in May 1939 with 314s.

flagrant example of "exorbitant profits" made flying the mail!

Altogether Boeing made 81 of the 40A and 40B (with Hornet engine), and they were the workhorses of the mail route for many years. They pioneered the routes and also the concept of passenger air travel in the United States, and encouraged Boeing to build a much larger all-passenger carrier. This materialized as the Model 80, flown in August 1928. It was the first true airliner in the United States. Powered by three Wasps, it had an open cockpit for side-by-side pilots and a comfortable cabin

The B-17 Flying Fortress strategic bomber developed from the Boeing Model 299 was the best-known of World War II bombers and nearly 13,000 of them were built during the war by Boeing, Lockheed and Douglas. The one pictured is a B-17G Fortress preserved in flying condition in England by Euroworld Limited.

with 12 leather seats, hot/cold water, electric lights (including reading lights) and a seat for a registered nurse, the world's first stewardess. BAT used 16 successively improved models until 1934.

By 1928 the company had grown to 800 employees, the largest in the United States. Instead of towing each new machine behind a truck ten miles to Sands Point it opened a new and much larger factory at Boeing Field, only two miles from Seattle at the former King County airfield. Boeing Field also became the HQ of BAT, which swallowed Pacific Air Transport and also, at Oakland, opened the Boeing School of Aeronautics, one of the nation's largest and

most famous aviation schools. The following year, 1929, was just as momentous with the acquisition of Hamilton Metalplane, the establishment of Boeing Canada at Vancouver and then the formation of the gigantic United Aircraft and Transport Corporation in which Boeing joined with Pratt & Whitney, Vought and Hamilton. Soon UATC swallowed Sikorsky, Stearman, Standard Steel Propeller and three more airlines. In 1930 the airlines, including BAT, were merged into United Airlines. Later, in 1934, the Air Mail Act prohibited one management both building and operating airliners. United was hived off, and UATC became United Aircraft (Pratt &

Whitney, Sikorsky, Chance Vought and the merged propeller firm Hamilton Standard) while Boeing went free again with Wichita-based Stearman as a wholly owned sub-

Below: Boeing's own production of Fortresses was prodigious and reached one complete aircraft every two hours. Here, pictured outside the Boeing flight test hangar in Seattle, are four B-17Cs which, with a fifth were delivered to the US Army one day in 1940.

Bottom: The B-17 was followed into production in 1943 by the mighty B-29 Superfortress, but at a new Boeing plant at Renton, on Lake Washington, designed specifically for the assembly of the new giants. The B-29 pioneered the assembly of major sections made in other States or even other countries.

sidiary which was to build 10,346 of its tough PT-13 Kaydet biplane primary trainers by the end of World War II. In 1939 it became the Boeing Wichita Division, so that nearly all the Kaydets had Boeing nameplates though universally called Stearmans.

By this time Boeing himself had retired. He had always meant to go at 50, and he considered it ironic that he should, in 1934, receive the Guggenheim Medal "for air manufacture and air transportation" and at the same time be told by the government to stop it! He sold his stock, returned to breeding horses and cattle and, after a ride in the first 707, died aboard his yacht in 1956. His successor was Clairmont L Egtvedt, the company's first employee and one-time chief engineer.

Egtvedt enjoyed a big hand in pushing the company into the new era of cantilever monoplanes of all-metal stressed-skin construction. The first was the dramatic Monomail (Model 200), which also had partly retracting landing gear. First flown on 6 May 1930, it carried a much heavier load than the 40B and was 10mph faster, on the same power. Next followed a splendid bomber along the same modern lines, the B-9, which just happened to be eclipsed by an even better one from Martin. But Boeing really set its sights on building a modern airliner, combining all the advances of the Monomail with a larger fuselage, twin engines in Townend-ring cowls and driving variable-pitch propellers, rubber de-icer boots and many other new features.

Boeing rightly judged it could produce the standard new mainliner of the next generation, but when United's pilots saw the specification of the 16,000lb (7258kg) twin-Hornet Model 247 they refused to accept it. They insisted on two Wasps and 12,000lb (5443kg) maximum. Accordingly the 247 was scaled down, flying on 8 February 1933 as a ten-seater. Eventually United bought 59, by far the largest and most costly fleet in any world airline at that time, and they were later rebuilt as the faster 247D version, of which United bought another 13 direct. But the short-sighted objection of the airline crews robbed both United and Boeing of pre-eminence, and by 1935 the DC-2 had taken over the rest of the market.

On 28 July 1935 Boeing flew the Model 299, later known as the forerunner of the B-17 Fortress strategic bomber. Much bigger and more powerful than most aircraft of its day, it had four engines, not to carry more bombs but to carry them faster and higher. By 1939 many were in service with turbocharged engines for use at

heights exceeding 30,000ft (9144m) and the B-17E, F and G became the most famous US bomber of World War II, particularly in the England-based 8th Air Force; a total of 12,731 was delivered by Boeing, Vega (Lockheed) and Douglas. In 1938 Boeing flew the first 307 Stratoliner, the world's first large pressurized airliner, and the Model 314 flying-boat, the largest commercial machine of the prewar era. The Navy funded Plant 2 at nearby Renton, on Lake Washington, and there the heaviest, most powerful and most complex aircraft of the wartime era, the B-29 Superfortress, went into production in 1943 to set a totally new standard in aviation technology; the factory built 2756 by May 1946, and Bell and Martin added a further 668 and 536. From this outstanding bomber were derived the more powerful B-50, the C-97 series of military transports (with the Boeing-patented Flying Boom refuelling system) and civil Stratocruiser.

In the immediate postwar years Boeing shrank from over 60,000 employees (44,800 at Seattle) to below 10,000, but it produced the futuristic XB-47 Stratojet six-jet swept-

wing bomber, flown in 1947, and got into surface-to-air missiles (the future Bomarc program and small gas-turbine engines. Between 1948 and 1952 it developed its greatest product yet, the monster B-52 bomber, which – utterly contrary to prediction – is likely to have no successor and remain in service until the year 2000. Then, in 1952 Boeing took its greatest single decision. Under its dynamic leader, lawyer Bill Allen, the board voted to commit over $20,000,000 – almost the net worth of the company – to build a long-range jetliner. This led to the KC-135 tanker, of which 732 were built, and the civil 707 of which sales by 1979 were over 950. It also led to the related 720, the more grossly redesigned 727, the small 737 and, in 1966, to risk more than the company's net worth – well over $1,000,000,000 – on the 747. This was the first of the new generation of "wide-body"

Two Boeing occasions and a ten-year span are represented in these pictures showing roll-out of the 5000th Boeing-built B-17 in 1944 and roll-out of the prototype 707 jet airliner in 1954. The Fortress, nicknamed "Five Grand," was covered with thousands of signatures of Boeing workers.

Below: Following in the tradition of the B-17 and B-29, and the interim six-jet B-47 Stratojet, Boeing started development of the eight-jet B-52 Stratofortress bomber in 1945. The first operational result was the B-52B which entered service from June 1955. Around 350 B-52s were still in the USAF Strategic Air Command in 1980, most of them B-52Gs and Hs, of which the latest, with turbofan engines, like the 52H pictured, are unique in the world as being scheduled to remain in frontline service for 40 years after their manufacture.

Above: The 707's advent on the world's air routes, starting with the North Atlantic in October 1958, founded the family of Boeing jet airliners from the "baby" 737 to the Jumbo 747, which took a thousand-million-dollar investment and a new monstrous production facility at Everett to launch. Here, an early 747 of Trans World Airlines, in the carrier's earlier livery, is seen approaching London Airport.

transports, and despite sharing costs with partners such as Northrop (fuselage sections) and Fairchild Republic (wing movables) the risk was awesome. One of the minor tasks was clearing 780 acres of forest and creating the world's largest-volume building and a major airfield at Everett, Washington to handle the program. In 1968 employment peaked at over 105,000.

In the 1970s Wichita concentrated on military aircraft; Boeing Aerospace (Kent, Washington) handled the Minuteman ICBM, Saturn (Apollo) rocket, Lunar Orbiter and many other space and missile programs; Boeing Vertol (acquired in 1961) built large helicopters; and what in May 1961 was renamed The Boeing Company relied for about half its business on the Boeing Commercial Airplane Company. Despite prolonged success of all the latter's programs, a dearth of orders in the 1968–75 period brought a staggering reduction in the workforce: over 60,000 were laid off. How to make money at production rates of one or two jetliners per month, instead of perhaps 20, was an exceptional test of the management, now under Tom Wilson. Exceeding care goes into everything Boeing does and when it cut back on unnecessary expenditure it did so in a quantified way. It knew just how long to leave the many square miles of lawns uncut, and just how long to avoid oiling the hangar doors. When, one day, one door refused to open, it judged the time had come to return gradually to normal. And this it has been doing throughout the second half of the past decade. Thanks to massive orders for the 727, 737, 747 and the launch of the 757 and 767, employment has increased over 30,000 and production has soared to 26.5 per month. In monetary terms, this is more than any other two planemakers combined.

Right: The Boeing Vertol company was established in 1960 after acquisition of the Vertol tandem-rotor helicopter design. It has various new projects under development but its main output is the tandem-rotor CH-47 Chinook (illustrated) which can take payloads of up to about 25,000lb and has a cruising speed of up to 160mph. About 3000 of the tandem-rotor helicopters have been produced, mostly for the US military services.

CESSNA AIRCRAFT COMPANY

Clyde V Cessna was one of the original barnstorming pioneers, and like the majority grew up in midwest farming country, in his case it was Oklahoma. During a slack time on the farm – 11 February 1911 – he went to Oklahoma City to see an aerial circus. The impact it had was such that he bought a Blériot and spent most of the rest of the year trying to fly it, altering it slightly on each cycle of the sequence take-off/crash/rebuild. This procedure did not prove lethal, and by the fall of 1911 Cessna was able to start displaying his prowess. He spent the next five years giving displays, mainly at county fairs, in the summer and rebuilding the first Cessna (it could no longer be called a Blériot) in the winter.

In 1916 Cessna was offered free space at J J Jones's auto factory at Wichita in return for a reliable airplane for use as a Jones advertising platform. Cessna decided to form the Cessna Aircraft Company, but only a year later the war halted business. Cessna went back to farming until he was hired by oilman Moellendick as outlined in the Beech story. In 1924 he founded Travel Air with Beech and Stearman, still in Wichita, but in 1926 this fine team broke up. By now Cessna had a little capital, and he opened his own factory at Wichita in 1927, incorporating Cessna Aircraft on 7 September 1927 as a public company with a board of directors.

Part of the trouble at Travel Air had been Cessna's lack of interest in biplanes. If anything he was ahead of his time, for he believed the monoplane did not have to be festooned with wires and struts and could be strong and efficient. Except for a helicopter (that did not see production) all Cessna products have been clean monoplanes, most without any external bracing. Even his 1928 Model A, an expensive four-seater, had a cantilever wing, and it won the New York–Los Angeles Air Derby in 1928 and also flew to Siberia and back. Developments followed, but the Depression almost brought business to a stop. Despite a $398 glider and a $975 powered version the new plant at East Pawnee, Wichita, shut in 1931.

Clyde and his son Eldon formed their own Clyde V Cessna Aircraft Company, renting space from Stearman. They produced a series of brilliant midwing midget racers, with retractable landing gear, which worked up speeds far in excess of 200mph (322km/h) on a 145hp Warner radial. (Meanwhile, part of the Pawnee plant was rented by Beech.) Not until January 1934 did the directors agree to restart business. By this time Cessna had a new plant manager. His nephew, Dwane L Wallace, was so determined to get into aviation he worked his way through Wichita University in aero-engineering at the height of the

Left: The second product of the rehabilitated Cessna company in the middle 1930s was the T-50 light twin cabin monoplane, a basically clean and simple design that appeared in timely manner for development into the AT-17 Bobcat (RCAF Crane) advanced trainer and UC-78 light transport, several thousands of which were produced for service in World War II and after.

Below: Justified ceremony in the mid-1970s by the world's most prolific planemaker. Cessna's chairman, Russ Meyer, hands over the 100,000th single-engine aircraft produced by the company – a traditional strut-braced high-wing cabin monoplane. By the end of the 1970s the total of single-engined machines had topped 120,000 and the total of all types of powered aircraft had exceeded 150,000.

Neat and efficient twin-turboprop Cessna 441 Conquest executive or feeder transport, the prototype of which flew in August 1975. The Conquest is pressurized and takes up to 11 passengers at a maximum cruising speed of about 320mph over a range exceeding 1000 miles.

Below: At the top end of the Cessna range is the twin-turbofan executive transport, which first flew in September 1969 and went into production in 1971 as the Citation seven/eight-seater with a cruising speed of about 400mph. The original Citation I (illustrated) was further developed into the eight/ten-passenger 420mph Citation II for delivery from 1978, and a greatly advanced Citation III, with new wing and engines to take up to 15 passengers at 540mph, scheduled for first deliveries in 1980.

Depression, which his friends thought sheer lunacy. His uncle had nothing to offer, and the tall craggy soft-spoken graduate began his career working for Beech. But when Cessna reopened he was given the job of chief engineer and plant manager, with no salary but with the opportunity to design, build, test, sell and even race new Cessnas.

Wallace was an exceptional man among exceptional men, and he soon was judged worth salary as well. His first creation was the C-34, a Warner-powered high-winger of outstanding efficiency. In 1935 Cessna had a lot of ground to make up, and ranked about eleventh among US builders; that year's *Flying* gave many lightplane firms half a page in its annual review issue, but Cessna rated a single photo, with a caption noting that it had flaps. But by 1936 the C-34 had catapulted Cessna into the front rank. Cessna himself retired, naturally being succeeded as president by Wallace – whose brother Dwight was vice-president and treasurer. The Wallace dynasty was to last until 1975. Under Dwane's solidly based direction Cessna increased its number of models in simultaneous production from one to today's 48, and became the world's No 1 planemaker by a clear margin – in terms of numbers sold. Since the reopening in January 1934 the company has never changed its name or headquarters; but it has expanded, opened new factories, started or purchased new subsidiaries, and become a mighty force in aerospace despite the generally low dollar value of its products.

Nobody really needs an introduction to the aircraft products (the others include McCauley propellers, avionics, fluid power systems, and a wealth of military hardware and subassemblies). In 1936 Wallace was strongly developing the C-34 into various Airmaster models, and then boldly produced the T-50 light twin. He flew the T-50 himself on 26 March 1939, and by holding the price below $30,000 hoped to find a market. He need not have worried; war came and the military bought 5401 as the Crane 1 (RCAF), followed by the AT-17/UC-78 Bobcat. Cessna did much more in the war, and also built the C-106 transport but peace came and it did not go into production.

Wallace set course again with the P-780 which led to the radial-engined 190 and LC-126 family, followed by the 120, 140 and 170 lightplanes and the 305, first of the military Bird Dogs. Since then there has been a swelling flood of success, punctuated only by the 620 four-engined transport and CH-1 helicopter of 1957. Modern twins began with the 310, flown on 3 January 1953, and the 318 (flown 12 October 1954) led to the T-37 family of twin-jet trainer and Co-in attack aircraft. The low-wing AG family was announced in 1971, and in 1968 the Fanjet 500 (later renamed Citation) began a family of bizjets. The first turboprop was the highly efficient Conquest announced in 1974.

Wallace retired in 1975, and was succeeded by pilot Russ "Corky" Meyer. By 1979 the Pawnee factory, where singles are made, had topped 120,000, while the total of all Cessnas (not including 750 wartime CG-4 troop-carrying gliders and prototypes) exceeds 150,000.

CURTISS-WRIGHT CORPORATION

Glenn Hammond ("GH") Curtiss, a shy and reserved man who could never put two sentences together in public but made life-long friends, was one of the original pioneers of the airplane. Until World War II the company that bore his name was second to none in the field of fighters, transports, engines and propellers. Then, with staggering swiftness, inept management caused it to wither until it became a mere shadow – and no longer a plane-maker.

Like the Wright brothers, GH was a bicycle maker. By 1902 he graduated to motorcycles, both building and racing them, and his company grew by 1908 to over 100 employees, working round the clock to meet demand. Part of the demand came from "crazy aviators" whom Curtiss charged a premium for his coveted air-cooled engines. The first such customer was "Uncle Tom" Baldwin, whose Curtiss-powered airship was flown by Lincoln Beachey, later No 1 barnstormer. In 1905 the famed Alexander Graham Bell, inventor of the telephone, asked Curtiss for an engine for one of his kites. The wily Scot required Curtiss to deliver it in person to his research laboratory at Baddeck, Nova Scotia, and offered $25 per day to come and talk about flying. This bait just overcame Curtiss's reluctance to quit his thriving

factory on a fool's errand, and once he was at Baddeck, Bell and his team converted the quiet American into an aviation enthusiast.

On 1 October 1907 a formal agreement was ratified setting up the Aerial Experiment Association (AEA) by Bell, Curtiss, F W "Casey" Baldwin, J A Douglas McCurdy and Lieutenant Tom Selfridge of the US Army. Curtiss engines powered Selfridge's *Red Wing*, flown (briefly) from the ice of Lake Keuka, NY, on 12 March 1908, and Baldwin's *White Wing*, flown more successfully in May. It also powered the successful tethered helicopter of typewriter manufacturer J Newton Williams. On 20 June 1908 Curtiss's own *June Bug* flew 1266ft (386m), and on 4 July it won the *Scientific American* prize of a silver trophy for the first officially observed flight in the USA exceeding one kilometer. The AEA was wound up as planned in March 1909, Curtiss receiving its patents. In the same month he teamed up with Augustus Herring to form the Herring-Curtiss company to make airplanes, the first incorporated planemaker in the United States.

From 1908 Curtiss was losing large sums in dispute with the Wrights, who prosecuted him for infringing on their wing-warping patents. Both *White Wing* and *June Bug* had ailerons hinged as extensions of

the upper plane and worked by a pilot shoulder harness. With *Gold Bug* of June 1909 Curtiss placed the ailerons between the wings, the latter now being of constant section with broad square tips. This became a standard Curtiss feature, with tricycle landing gear (or floats), pusher propeller and a circular "steering wheel" for the rudder on the control column that worked the nose elevator.

In August 1909 Curtiss took his 63hp *Golden Flyer*, a more powerful edition of *Gold Bug*, to the great Rheims meeting in France. He walked off with the two major prizes, the Gordon Bennett trophy for the fastest time round two laps of the speed course and the Prix de la Vitesse for the best three-lap time. Then on 29 May 1910 Curtiss won the $10,000 Pulitzer (*New York World*) prize for a flight down the Hudson from Albany to New York. In the same summer Curtiss set up a flying school which soon branched out to Hammondsport, San Diego and Miami and took pupils from the US military services as well as many hundreds of civilians. A US Army officer did the first air-to-ground firing in history from a Curtiss aircraft and McCurdy both sent and received wireless messages in the air. Curtiss himself dropped lead bombs on a raft at Lake Keuka, and gradually made the US military forget the

$50,000 it had wasted on Professor Langley at the turn of the century and renew its interest in aviation.

On 14 November 1910 Eugene B Ely, one of what had become a large team of Curtiss employees who toured the country giving great flying displays, made the first take-off by airplane from a ship, just managing to get airborne from a board runway erected over the bows of USS *Birmingham*, at anchor. Even more remarkable was the same aviator's successful landing on a quarterdeck platform on USS *Pennsylvania* on 18 January 1911, using sandbag-retarded arrester cables. Eight days later Curtiss flew his first true marine aircraft, the first really practical floatplane. He had to convince the US Navy that a flying machine could land on the ocean and be hoisted aboard, and on 17 February he was hoisted aboard *Pennsylvania*, chatted with the captain, was swung back over the side again and took off from the sea. This satisfied the Navy, which promptly set up an aviation section and purchased two machines from Curtiss.

In February 1911 Curtiss flew the first amphibian, with retracting landing wheels, and in January 1912 tested the first flying-boat. This soon discarded its front elevator and became a standard Navy patrol aircraft, with almost 150 delivered. The usual engine was the OX, a simple Curtiss V-8 watercooled unit that was manufactured in vast quantities. Two were fitted to the first large flying-boat, *America*, which a retired RN officer, Lieutenant-Commander John C Porte, planned to fly across the Atlantic to win the *Daily Mail* £10,000 prize. War prevented the take-off, but Porte got the Admiralty to buy the two *America* boats so far built and adopt the Curtiss H-4 as the standard patrol flying-boat; Porte also used it as the jumping-off point for his improved Felixstowe boats.

Yet another OX user was the JN, or Jenny, a tandem landplane trainer derived from the J (designed by B D Thomas of Sopwith to Curtiss's specification) and Curtiss's own Model N. The trainer was built to meet a 1914 US Army requirement, and by late 1918 total production of

The World's first practical floatplane was the Curtiss "Hydroplane" pictured here in San Diego Bay after its first flight, with founder Glenn H Curtiss and pioneer naval airman Lieutenant T G Ellyson in control, on 26 January 1911. A further development took the first amphibian, with retractable landing wheels, into the air a month later.

First of the Curtiss landplanes built in any quantity was the JN or "Jenny," a two-seat trainer developed to meet a US Army World War I need. More than 6000 were built during the war and many were used for private flying for years thereafter. Among the score or so examples of the Jenny preserved is the one illustrated, a Canadian-built JN-4 maintained in flying condition in the Canadian National Aeronautical Collection.

several versions exceeded 6000, flown by over 95 percent of all American pilots at that time. Nearly all were built by the Curtiss Aeroplane & Motor Company, whose Hammondsport factory even in 1914 was building ten aircraft a week. In October 1917 the first HS-1L flying-boat took off as the first machine ever to be powered by the Liberty engine. By this time the company plants at Hammondsport and Buffalo were only just able to meet requirements working three shifts every day of the week; thus with capital from the Willys-Overland Car Company, Curtiss set up Curtiss Engineering Corporation at Garden City, Long Island, to build 150 of the H-16 *Large America*-derived boats each with two Liberty or Rolls-Royce Eagle engines. In August 1917 the US Navy bought four of the most powerful aircraft then designed, the NC (Navy Curtiss) boats. NC-1 lifted

Below: An important development in the interwar years was the Conqueror liquid-cooled engine; it powered many of the famous early Hawk series of fighters as well as the 1927 Condor B-2 bomber (illustrated) and its civil counterpart, the 1929 18-seat airliner.

Above: The single pusher and three tractor engines show up well in this picture of the Curtiss NC-4, which in May/June 1919 made the first airplane Atlantic crossing from Newfoundland to England, with stops at the Azores and Portugal.

51 people into the air in November 1918, then a world record, on three Liberty engines. NC-2 had four engines, two tractor and two pusher, and NC-3 and -4 had three tractor and one pusher. In May/June 1919 NC-4 made the first airplane crossing of the Atlantic in separate flights from Newfoundland via the Azores to Portugal and England.

After World War I GH himself virtually ended participation in the Curtiss Aeroplane & Motor Company, which had become one of the largest planemakers in the world. He remained design consultant and a not-very-active chairman of the board, while effective control passed to Canadian financier Clement M Keys (see Rockwell story), who steered the giant through two tough decades so that, far from collapsing in the postwar slump and 1930s depression, it diversified and prospered.

One string to its bow continued to be good watercooled engines. Charlie Kirkham at Garden City had, in January 1918, run a 12-cylinder unit better than the Liberty, the K-12, and this was to develop through the geared C-12 into the D-12,

Above: Co-operation with the Naval Aircraft Factory, Philadelphia, in the NC (Navy Curtiss) series of flying-boats continued and generated several successful designs that won export as well as home orders. The F5L shown under construction in the NAF in 1919 was one of 138 built there; a further 60 of the type were built by Curtiss, and Canadian Aeroplanes Limited built 30 more.

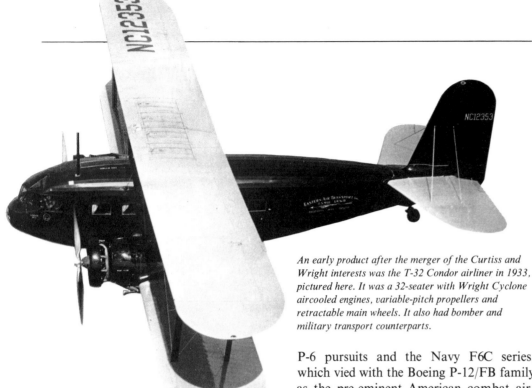

An early product after the merger of the Curtiss and Wright interests was the T-32 Condor airliner in 1933, pictured here. It was a 32-seater with Wright Cyclone aircooled engines, variable-pitch propellers and retractable main wheels. It also had bomber and military transport counterparts.

made in large numbers throughout the 1920s for Curtiss pursuit, observation and bomber aircraft and also made under license in Britain as the Fairey Felix. Special racing D-12s were used in the profusion of Curtiss racers including the Army R-6 and Navy CR-2 which took the first four places in the 1922 Pulitzer Prize, and the R3C-1 (winner of the last Pulitzer) and R3C-2 (winner of the 1925 Schneider Trophy).

The D-12 was developed into the V-1570 Conqueror, used in many of the famous Hawk family of Army PW and

P-6 pursuits and the Navy F6C series, which vied with the Boeing P-12/FB family as the pre-eminent American combat aircraft of the interwar era. At the other end of the size scale Curtiss developed the Condor B-2 bomber in 1927, followed in 1929 with a civil transport version for 18 passengers, then an exceptional capacity. Lead designer George A Page, Junior, followed with the T-32 Condor in 1933, a much more advanced biplane with Cyclone engines, variable-pitch propellers, retractable landing gear and up to 32 seats, which was a mainliner on US air routes and a successful bomber and military transport.

The 15,000th Curtiss-Wright P-40 Warhawk comes off the Buffalo production line on test flight in December 1944. The machine is decorated with the insignia of the 28 Allied Air Forces which had used Curtiss aircraft.

On 9 August 1929, when Curtiss himself was busy developing the State of Florida, the bitter old rivals Curtiss Aeroplane & Motor and Wright Aeronautical merged to form the giant Curtiss-Wright Corporation. Guy Vaughan assumed the presidency, with Burdette S Wright as vice-president in charge of the Airplane Division, where G A Page became director of engineering. Other companies and divisions produced engines, propellers and other aircraft parts. Business fairly hummed, especially for the military, the Army buying Shrike attack bombers, many kinds of pursuits, observation aircraft and transports, and the Navy a long series of Hawk, Goshawk and

Sparrowhawk pursuits, various observation machines and a prolific series of Scouts and dive-bombers culminating in the Helldiver SBC. In 1936 the Model 75 monoplane Hawk introduced stressed-skin construction in the modern style, leading to the P-36 fighter (Hawk 75C to the French and Mohawk to the RAF) and thence to the prolific P-40 series of which 13,738 were delivered by December 1944.

Throughout World War II the plants at Buffalo and Kenmore, NY, Louisville, Kentucky, and St Louis, Missouri, remained in top gear with the P-40, SB2C Helldiver, SOC Seagull, SC Seamew and giant C-46 Commando, biggest twin of its day, and

others. But the attempts to find a top-quality fighter to replace the P-40 all failed. The top management became increasingly weak, and one product-line after another withered. All four of the great wartime plants closed, and Airplane Division activity became concentrated at Columbus, Ohio. The lavish HQ at Rockefeller Center, New York City, closed and was replaced by one at Wood-Ridge, New Jersey. On 15 February 1948 the great black XF-87 Nighthawk four-jet fighter made its maiden flight. It was the last aircraft to bear the Curtiss name, and only one was built. It is a measure of the once proud giant's collapse that in 1950 its only

aircraft project was license-production of the Doman helicopter, a plan which never matured. The vast Wright Aeronautical lacked the vital talent to move into the jet era, despite the license-production of the British Sapphire engine, and has never found a successor to its once world-leading piston engines.

The name Hawk continued in use for later Curtiss-Wright fighters, right up to the mass-produced P-40 series of which more than 15,000 of the various marks were produced as the Tomahawk, Warhawk and Kittyhawk, powered variously by the liquid-cooled Allison or Packard Merlin engines. The picture shows P-40s, the first version of this prolific family, in part of the final assembly shop in the Curtiss-Wright Buffalo, NY, plant.

FAIRCHILD

For 50 years the Fairchild empire was led by one man, Sherman M Fairchild, born in Oneonta, NY, 7 April 1896. After graduating from Harvard his relative wealth and good connections enabled him quickly to form his own company, Fairchild Aviation Corporation, in 1924. Not for him years with oily rags in hangars; as board chairman from the start it was his mission to organize capital and companies, and he did this supremely well. He was very much an advanced-technology man, but he was careful never to attempt too much. A subsidiary, Fairchild Airplane Manufacturing Corporation, concentrated on what were then called two- or three-place ships, only gradually moving into the utility transport field after 1930. Meanwhile Fairchild Aerial Surveys and Fairchild Camera and Instrument showed the founder's other interests.

Actual manufacture of aircraft began in 1925, as it did at Kreider-Reisner Aircraft which Fairchild took over in 1929. Later that year the combined company became part of E L Cord's giant Aviation Corporation of Delaware (Avco) but Fairchild liked to run his own show and re-purchased his interests in 1931. Two years later French-born Armand Thieblot became disenchanted with one of the other giant groupings, General Aviation, and joined Fairchild at his Hagerstown, Maryland, plant. He was called chief structures engineer, but soon became chief engineer. At last the company could really build superior aircraft. To round off the early metamorphoses, in 1935 the parent company's name was changed to Fairchild Aircraft, and a year later the Fairchild Engine & Airplane Corporation was formed to take over relevant subsidiaries. In 1939 this became the parent, with offices in Rockefeller Plaza, New York City; the Hagerstown plant was called Fairchild Aircraft Division.

Most of the late-1920s aircraft were simple tandem-seat highwing or parasol monoplanes of mixed construction with engines of 90–150hp. Production was in ones and twos, but in 1930 the Kreider-Reisner takeover brought the Model C-8 which started a family of strut-braced cabin machines that by November 1944 numbered more than 2000, exceeded by only one other company product. From 1932 called the

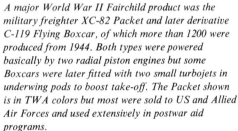

A major World War II Fairchild product was the military freighter XC-82 Packet and later derivative C-119 Flying Boxcar, of which more than 1200 were produced from 1944. Both types were powered basically by two radial piston engines but some Boxcars were later fitted with two small turbojets in underwing pods to boost take-off. The Packet shown is in TWA colors but most were sold to US and Allied Air Forces and used extensively in postwar aid programs.

Model 24, these machines were three- or four-seaters, with typical wooden wings and welded steel-tube fuselage, usually powered by the 145hp Warner Super Scarab (R-500) radial, despite Fairchild's wish to use the company's own 200hp Ranger in-line engine. Called the UC-61 Forwarder by the USAAF, GK by the Navy (K for Kreider-Reisner) and Argus by the RAF, these were among the most important small utility machines of World War II.

In parallel, the company built up a firm line of business with tough transports for the "frozen north" and similar outback areas, such as the embryonic air routes in Latin America. Many of these were built at the Longeuil (Montreal) factory of Fairchild Aircraft Limited of Canada, erected in 1930 and until after World War II a source of traditional "bush" aircraft. These were characterized by Whirlwind, Wasp or even Hornet radial engines, folding wings, wheel/ski/float landing gear and interiors for 5–12 passengers or a ton of mixed cargo. Fairchild Aircraft Limited later shared production of Hampden bombers, developed and

A modern Fairchild Hagerstown, Maryland, production-line scene that harks back to the Fairchild start there in the early 1930s: one of the company's products in both periods was a strut-braced high-wing cabin aircraft. This picture shows final assembly of the Fairchild AU-23 Peacemaker (based on a Swiss Pilatus design), a STOL eight/ten seat utility transport.

Major Alexander P de Seversky, founder of the Republic Aviation Corporation, flies one of his record-breaking SEV-3s over New York City. The machine is the 3L in which he competed in the England–Australia air race in 1934.

built the Bolingbroke derived from the Blenheim and mass-produced the Curtiss Helldiver as the SBF.

In the late 1930s the Hagerstown plant built small numbers of the Model 45, a trim low-wing monoplane with retractable landing gear, and the Model 91 amphibian with a tractor Hornet or Cyclone in a pylon-mounted nacelle. But the staple product was the big Model 62 primary pilot trainer, with tandem cockpits, low wing and either a 175 or 200hp Ranger or a 220hp Continental R-670 radial. Fairchild's main output comprised the PT-19, also built by Aeronca; the radial PT-23 was made by Howard, Aeronca and St Louis, and the enclosed-cockpit PT-26, called Cornell in Canada and Southern Rhodesia, was made by Fleet. Total production was 7260. Another important wartime product was the AT-21 Gunner crew trainer, with two 520hp Ranger V-12 engines, made by the patented Duramold bonded-veneer process bought along with the inventor's Clark Aircraft in 1939.

The company's biggest challenge was the XC-82 project of 1941. The Army Air Force wanted a purpose-designed military freighter, and the XC-82 Packet first flew on 10 September 1944, leading to 220 for the USAAF/USAF followed by 946 redesigned and more powerful C-119 Flying Boxcars plus 141 supplied under aid programs to friendly Air Forces. In 1954 Kaiser-Frazer's inability to deliver the C-123 Provider resulted in the Hagerstown plant taking over the USAF contract for 300, many of which had Fairchild's own J44 turbojets in wingtip pods to boost take-off. The company formed lavish engine and missile divisions at newly built centers on Long Island in the 1950s, but nearly all the programs failed to lead to production. On the other hand the bold decision to obtain a license for the unproved Fokker F27 Friendship in 1956 resulted in a 15-year program for 205 aircraft, including Fairchild's own "stretched" FH-227.

The FH designation reflected the take-over in 1964 of Hiller Helicopters. This had been a father-and-son success story begun in sunny California, in 1942, with patents

Fairchild Republic production line at Farmingdale, Long Island, New York, with some of the first production batch of A-10A close-support aircraft nearing completion. The A-10 was successful in a USAF fly-off competition and is in line for USAF contracts totalling over 700 aircraft.

Close formation flying by two USAF Fairchild A-10s during a North Sea air refuelling exercise in October 1979. The A-10 first flew in May 1972 and won the competition in January 1973. The machine is turbofan powered for a maximum sea-level speed of 449mph and is armed with a new-type multi-barrel 30mm gun in the nose and underwing pylons for 16,000lb of various ordnance.

for new transmission and control systems for a co-axial helicopter. The Hiller-copter was demonstrated in San Francisco in August 1944, but the real winner was a more conventional machine, the 360 of 1948, seating three abreast on 178hp. Hiller's plant at Palo Alto delivered over 1000, most of them UH-12 Ravens for the US Army. It also developed the FH-1100 turbine LOH (light observation helicopter), which sold in modest numbers after the takeover and integration of Hiller assets into the Fairchild Aircraft Division. Another product-line came with the Pilatus license to market and build the Porter STOL aircraft, a few of which were designated AU-23 Peacemakers.

Biggest of all the 1960s takeovers was Republic. This had been formed in February 1931 by Major Alexander P de Seversky, an emigré Russian from Tiflis, Georgia. He was a champion of aviation who not only built aircraft but wrote books and, at the height of World War II, produced a full-length Hollywood epic, *Victory through Air Power*. Also from Tiflis came his chief designer (later vice-president engineering) Alexander Kartveli. Money came from the Moore brothers, Edward and Paul, the latter being an active Sever-

sky director. Boldly, the two Alexes decided to jump straight into the financially challenging business of advanced cantilever monoplanes with stressed-skin construction.

Their new factory at Farmingdale, Long Island, leapt into the spotlight by world speed records gained in 1934 by the SEV-3 amphibian, a two/three-seater with a 420hp Whirlwind. The Air Corps bought 35 basic trainers developed from it, followed in 1935 by the swiftly built SEV-2XP from which stemmed the first production pursuit for the Air Corps with retractable landing gear, the 281mph (452km/h) P-35. This led to 120 EP-1s intended for Sweden, the P-35A, the P-43 Lancer and finally the famed P-47B to P-47M Thunderbolt, which with 15,660 delivered, ranked first among US fighters of all time. A few (354) were P-47Gs made by Curtiss-Wright, and a far greater number were produced by a new plant at Evansville, Indiana, which Republic vacated in 1945. The manager at Evansville was Munday I Peale, who after the war succeeded to the presidency. Under his direction the F-84 Thunderjet/Thunderstreak/Thunderflash jet programs were successfully completed, and the great F-105 Thunderchief launched.

In September 1965 Fairchild Hiller acquired Republic's assets, the vice-president and general manager Don Strait becoming a Fairchild board member and the company later being renamed Fairchild Republic Company. It brought with it major subcontract programs involving airframe sections of such aircraft as the F-4 Phantom and 747, as well as the A-10A Thunderbolt II close-support aircraft for the USAF. Subsequently it won the vertical tail of the Shuttle Orbiter and several other valuable contracts. President today is Dr Norman Grossman, who played a major role in the F-105 and F-15 programs.

Almost a takeover was Fairchild's purchase of 90 percent of Swearingen Aviation of San Antonio, Texas. Ed Swearingen had produced the original Excalibur rebuilds of various Beech twins, and then designed his own Merlin and Metro twinturboprops whose main wing structures had been built at Hagerstown. Today his company is a subsidiary of what in 1966 became Fairchild Industries, under president Edward G Uhl. It has 11 operating companies including Fairchild Aircraft Service in Florida, Fairchild Space and Electronic in Maryland and Fairchild Stratos in California.

Ranked No 1 in numbers produced of US fighters of all time was the Republic P-47 Thunderbolt. For a long time it was also the biggest and heaviest single-seat fighter, with an all-up weight of around eight long tons in its main P-47D production form. Although the P-47 appeared fairly late in the war, making its first operational appearance in April 1943, no fewer than 15,660 were built for the USAF and RAF. The one illustrated is the final production mark P-47N, developed primarily for Pacific-area operations with long range and a sprint speed of 470mph and gross weight of over 21,000lb.

"Thunder" in the name became part of the Republic fighter image, passing through the F-84 Thunderjet/ Thunderstreak/Thunderflash series up to the F-105 Thunderchief Mach 2 long-range tactical fighter/ bomber which first flew in October 1955. Progressive improvement led to the F-105D (illustrated) and two- seat F which played a major part in the Vietnam war.

FORD

An aircraft that revolutionized American air transport in the middle 1920s was the Ford 11-seat 4-AT and larger 14-seat (illustrated) 5-AT Trimotor airliner. The machine was designed by W B Stout and built by the Stout Metal Airplane Company after it came under the control of Henry Ford senior. The Trimotor was unique in its Alclad-covered wing and fuselage and immensely strong, making it particularly long-lived in outback areas remote from maintenance facilities. Perhaps the biggest tribute to the Trimotor is the fact that the manufacture of a modernized version was restarted after 1975, as the Bushmaster 2000 23-seat utility transport, and work continues on its further development in 1980.

GATES

Founded in 1960 by William P Lear senior as the Swiss American Aviation Corporation to build fast business aircraft based on a Swiss fighter aircraft. design, the Lear Jet Corporation was taken over by the Gates Learjet Corporation and continues to produce the earlier and new designs of twin-jet executive transports. Illustrated is a Learjet 35A twin-turbofan eight-passenger machine introduced in 1976. Over 1000 Learjets have been ordered.

GENERAL DYNAMICS CORPORATION

Such names as Fleet, Stinson, Vultee and Consolidated form the chapters of this fine story, but the earliest beginning was the 1897 idea of Edson Gallaudet that an airplane could be controlled laterally by warping the wings. This was five years before the Wrights hit on the idea and prosecuted anyone who tried to infringe on their patents. Gallaudet, however, was too busy as a professor of physics at Yale to do more than make simple tests, culminating in a successful floatplane glider of 1898. Later he founded Gallaudet Engineering Company of Norwich, Connecticut, where he concentrated on marine aircraft. His first design, around 1912, was the amazing fully streamlined A-1 Bullet, with aluminum-tube structure, pusher propeller (a three-blader!) behind the tail and speed of 130mph (209km/h). There followed a big flying-boat with hull engines driving two pusher wing propellers, and a succession of unique US Navy float seaplanes with the patented Gallaudet drive. In this the engine(s) drove a propeller with a large-diameter hub encircling the fuselage aft of the wings. The D-1 of 1916 had tandem seats in a finely streamlined fuselage ahead of twin engines driving a rear four-blader; it was said to be so fast pilots were afraid to fly it.

This 1916 machine typified Gallaudet's flair for innovation. In early 1917 the company was reconstituted as Gallaudet Aircraft Corporation, with a factory at East Greenwich, Rhode Island, where the Liberty-engined D-4 bomber seaplanes were built. Curtiss seaplanes were also built here, but the Armistice cut off these lucrative contracts, and buyers failed to appear

for the postwar designs. The future lay in the capable hands of general manager Major Reuben H Fleet, who, while still in uniform, had organized the first US Air Mail service in nine days in May 1918. He had got Curtiss to deliver six much-modified JN-6H Jennies with mail hoppers and doubled fuel capacity, himself pushed an ordinary cork into an unwanted hole in one of the added "gas tanks" and got the whole system operating both ways on the New York–Philadelphia–Washington route by Wednesday 15 May. He left the Army in 1922 and joined the ailing Gallaudet.

Over in Dayton, Ohio, where the Wright cycle shop still flourished, a much bigger company was feeling the postwar draft even more acutely. Dayton-Wright had been organized in early 1917, with Orville

Wright as consultant, and only three months later won the biggest contract to build an Americanized DH.4. Together with an order for 400 TA-3 trainers of its own design, this triggered expansion into three plants with over 8000 hands, which by the Armistice had delivered all the trainers and 2703 DH.4s, the last thousand in two months. General Motors wanted a foothold in aviation and bought the com-

Below: Final assembly shop of the San Diego plant in 1936 with Consolidated PBY-1 flying-boats under construction.

Bottom: Roll-out at San Diego in 1937 of the prototype four-engine PB2Y Coronado long-range patrol bomber/transport. Over 200 were eventually built at the plant, as well as about 3300 of the earlier and smaller twin-engine PBY Catalina flying-boats.

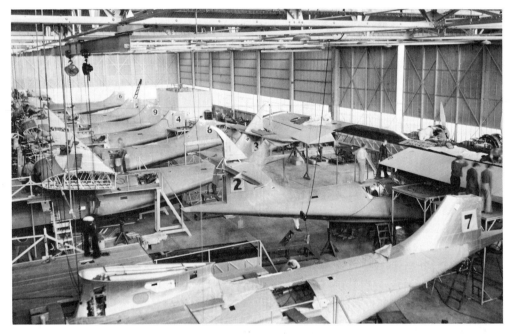

pany in 1919. It was a bad investment. Despite the advanced design of the RB racer of 1921 – it had fully retractable landing gear, variable-camber wing and full-span flaps – and the profusion of conversions and rebuilds of the DH.4, such as the Honeymoon Express in which the two passengers faced each other in a cramped cabin shut off from the pilot, business wound steadily downhill to zero in early 1923.

It was hardly the time to start an aviation company, but Fleet was a man of true vision. He had no difficulty in putting up the money to combine the assets of Gallaudet and Dayton-Wright to form one viable company. GM had had enough and wanted out, despite the last-minute receipt of an order for 20 of the new TW-3 trainers designed for Dayton-Wright by Colonel V E Clark. Edson Gallaudet had already resigned from his own board. Fleet had the stature to lead the two demoralized firms into one unit, formed on 29 May 1923 as Consolidated Aircraft Corporation.

The batch of 20 TW-3s was the key to survival, though this side-by-side biplane was not judged a good idea. Widely called "the first American aircraft built of steel tubing," and nicknamed the "Chummy," it had a 180hp war-surplus Wright Hispano V-8 watercooled engine and was originally ordered by the Army Air Service as a successor to the Jenny. Fleet suggested to Clark that he should design an improved TW-3 with tandem seating. The result was the PT-1, and it put Consolidated firmly on its feet. Fleet had submitted a bid to supply 50 to the Army and it was accepted. Soon the old Gallaudet plant was inadequate and Consolidated moved to the giant wartime plant at Buffalo that had belonged to Curtiss. It leased a part of it and the part kept growing, until in 1931 building extensions were being added, the floor area having multiplied by ten in six years.

The PT-1 entered service in 1925. By the end of 1926 it had trained over 600 students, mainly at Brooks Field, San Antonio, without one serious accident.

Eventually the Army used 221, to train a whole generation of pilots, while the Navy bought the NY-1 float version with Whirlwind radial. In 1928 Consolidated was hard-pressed to meet demand for the PT-3 Husky and Navy NY-2 series, both with the R-790 (J5) Whirlwind; total production exceeded 800. Six foreign Air Forces were customers, and several remained in use until World War II. These popular trainers had wire wheels, four interlinked ailerons and 13 lines of detailed stencilled data on the fabric on the right side of the fuselage.

To show something of Fleet's qualities, the Husky Junior, designed as a smaller PT-3 for the civil market, refused to sell. Consolidated's board wanted to eliminate it. Fleet himself took on the program, renamed it the Fleet, formed his own personal subsidiary to build it, and in mid-1929 had such a busy production line he sold the rights back to Consolidated. Total production was approximately 1000.

In 1927 Consolidated hired Isaac M "Mac" Laddon, reputedly the best structural design engineer of large aircraft in the Air Corps. It wanted to build a large flying-boat, and the result was a masterpiece. The first Consolidated Admiral was also the Navy XPY-1 prototype patrol aircraft, with a 100ft (30.5m) monoplane

Top right: Consolidated's answer to the Army request for a strategic bomber "that would fly the skin off any rivals" appeared in December 1939 as the Model 32 or XB-24 Liberator. It fulfilled its promise by becoming the most numerous American aircraft of all time, with over 19,000 built, and serving on all fronts. This Liberator which served with the Indian Air Force, is preserved in Britain by the RAF Museum.

Right: A successful design of the Vultee element of the Convair amalgamation at its Downey, Los Angeles, factory was the BT-13 Valiant basic trainer, of which over 11,500 were built, mostly for the USAAF as its standard primary trainer during the war years. A version for the US Navy was designated SNV-1. This BT-13 has been preserved.

Below: A product of the original Consolidated factory at Buffalo, New York, in the early 1930s was the 32-passenger Commodore airliner, with which Consolidated founded an airline and later sold it and the 14 flying-boats built to Pan American.

Top: The Stinson takeover by Convair contributed the Vultee-Stinson L-1 Vigilant light liaison/observation aircraft, originally the Stinson O-49, which was built in fair quantity at the Nashville, Tennessee plant.

Above: The Vultee A-31/A35 Vengeance had the distinction of being designed initially for the Royal Air Force in 1940–41 to fill its supposed need for a dive-bomber (a type the RAF had never possessed) after initial successes of the German Ju87 against poorly defended targets. Although little used as a dive-bomber the Vengeance, particularly later marks, was built to a total of nearly 2000 for American, Australian and British forces and used in action in Burma.

wing and three Wasp engines. It flew in January 1929, but in those days anyone could bid for a production contract and Martin undercut the Buffalo company and in June 1929 was awarded the P3M production order. Consolidated promptly turned the Admiral into the 32-passenger Commodore civil transport and then started an airline, NYRBA (New York–Rio–Buenos Aires), to operate it. NYRBA was a success and eventually operated no fewer than 14 of the great boats. NYRBA was then sold to PanAm, leaving Consolidated with a solid foundation of experience of big flying-boats in airline service.

In 1929 Consolidated bought another of the famous names in early US planemaking, Thomas-Morse. William T and Oliver Thomas were English engineers who set up planemaking in upstate New York in 1910. Thomas Brothers Company built excellent aircraft but did not prosper until B Douglas Thomas (unrelated) joined in 1914. BD had been lured away from Sopwith by Curtiss to design his Model J trainer that led to the Jenny. In 1915 the British RNAS bought 12 T-2 trainers (along with 11 Burgess "Gunbuses"), followed by a second 12. This prompted a move to a bigger factory at Ithaca, where the Thomases reputedly set up the first true assembly line in US planemaking. Here the S-4 family of trim single-seaters, which looked like Sopwith Pups (perhaps not surprisingly) but were mostly trainers, was in such demand from the Army and Navy that in 1917 Thomas Brothers let their big neighbor, Morse Chain, take control and reorganize on a bigger scale as Thomas-Morse. Over 600 S-4 versions were followed by the chief American fighter of World War I, the MB-3. This fast Wright-Hispano-engined machine was good but too late, and T-M built only 50. Then it was hit between the eyes by the only big postwar order, for 200 of its own design, going to a company in far-off Seattle called Boeing. T-M never recovered, but kept going with an aviation school as well as a series of prototypes, and even got the outstanding O-19 observation aircraft into production for the Army when Consolidated took over.

It is a measure of the strength of Fleet's company that at its lowest ebb, in 1932,

when wages and salaries were cut 20 percent, it still sold nearly 100 aircraft, mostly quite powerful. One was the Fleetster, almost a copy of the Lockheed Vega but slightly bigger and with a metal stressed-skin fuselage. Most were eight- or nine-passenger transports or mailplanes, but a few served in the Army and the Navy's Cyclone-engined XBY-1 is thought to have been the first aircraft to have integral-tank wings. Meanwhile the company had not taken the loss of the Navy boat order to Martin lying down; Mac Laddon produced the much-improved P2Y in April 1932 and saw it develop into the P2Y-1 (23 built) and P2Y-3 (23 built) which really gave the Navy long range at last. One formation flew nonstop from Norfolk to Coco Solo in the Panama Canal Zone, and the whole of Squadron VP-10 flew 25 hours nonstop from San Francisco to Pearl Harbor, Hawaii, in January 1934.

In 1931 the Detroit-owned Lockheed company failed, leaving unfulfilled contracts for Y1P-24 two-seat fighters, speedy monoplanes with stressed-skin construction and retractable landing gear. Many of the employees found work at Consolidated and in 1932 built the even faster Y1P-25, followed by the P-30/PB-2A, the Army's first modern pursuits with turbocharged V-1570 engine, constant-speed propeller, cantilever wing with flaps, fully retracting landing gear and enclosed heated cockpit. The order was placed in December 1934, but production did not all take place at Buffalo.

On 20 October 1935 Fleet said at the dedication of a great new factory at San Diego that Consolidated's new location provided "year-round flying weather . . .

unhampered by snow and ice." Plant 1 was already in business with 850 workers, 411 of whom had moved to the balmy California city from Buffalo. (Many of the rest joined the new Bell company.) The biggest job facing the new plant was the production of by far the biggest order ever placed at that time for patrol flying-boats – 60 of Mac Laddon's brilliant new PBY, later named Catalina by the British. A second 60 followed, leading to expansion of the plant, and by April 1945 total production had reached 3290 in North America plus many hundreds in the Soviet Union, an all-time record for any water-based aircraft. A further 216 were made of the much larger PB2Y Coronado, first flown in 1937.

In January 1939 the Army asked Consolidated to design a strategic bomber that

Convair's essay into modern civil aircraft was at first very successful with its series of medium-range 240, 340 and 440 twin-engine Convairliners, but eventually ended disastrously with heavy financial loss over the rectification of deficiencies in the company's long-range jet airliners. Pictured is one of the medium-range aircraft after its conversion from its original piston engines to Rolls-Royce Dart turboprops to become the prototype Convair 600. Conversion to Dart or Allison engines gave several score turboprop Convairliners a long new lease of life.

The airplanes that brought Convair commercial aircraft design to an end and the company a record financial loss was the CV-880 and -990 series, the first of which flew in January 1959. Pictured is a CV-990A Coronado, one of 12 of the type operated by the Spanish airline Spantax in the late 1970s.

would "fly the skin off any rivals." Laddon's team were at once under intense pressure, pressure that was to last throughout seven years of warfare and today is the natural environment for advanced planemakers. On 29 December 1939 the Model 32, the XB-24 Liberator, made its maiden flight. It led to the biggest aircraft program the world had then seen, in some ways never again equalled. Despite being the most advanced and complex aircraft in the world at the time of its design, it was built in numbers greater than any other American wartime aircraft, a total allowing for spares of 19,203, in dozens of versions used on all wartime fronts.

What this did to Consolidated was predictable. On the side, the company had to get into the real-estate business, swelling the size of San Diego from 170,000 to nearly half a million, of whom over 45,000 were company employees. At Fort Worth, Texas, work began in April 1941 on a windowless air-conditioned building 320ft (100m) wide and nearly a mile (1.6km) long. Soon this too had 31,000 people building the B-24, while Ford built another giant B-24 plant near Detroit. Consolidated had become the biggest single cog in the so-called Arsenal of Democracy. Fleet recognized that new direction was needed, searched for answers with Washington's help and in December 1941, just after Pearl Harbor, sold his vast company to Avco via its subsidiary Vultee. Tom Girdler, former president of Republic

The first operational aircraft to be fitted with variable-sweep wings was the General Dynamics F-111 two-seat tactical fighter, produced for the US Air Force (and originally the US Navy) after the GD Convair Fort Worth Division's design beat a Boeing submission in competitive evaluation in the 1960s. The design has since been developed also into the FB-111 strategic bomber and both types are in wide USAF service. Here an F-111F with wings fully extended for low-speed flight approaches a KC-135 tanker aircraft to refuel.

An F-111F maneuvers on the ground with wings fully swept, as they would be in high-speed flight.

Steel, took over as chairman, while Harry Woodhead, former Vultee chairman, became president of the new company which was formally constituted in March 1943 as Consolidated Vultee Aircraft, or Convair.

The marriage linked Consolidated with two of the most famous names in plane-making, Vultee and Stinson, but the actual involvement of the two founders had been tragically short. Eddie Stinson was born in 1894 into a truly airminded Michigan family. With his brother Jack he was taught to fly by big sister Katherine, while young Marjorie was sworn in as a US Mail pilot at the age of 17. Eddie barnstormed before and after World War I but also laid a solid foundation of advanced flying experience and engineering design. In 1926 he set up planemaking at Wayne and produced the Detroiter, a biplane with heated four-seat cabin, self-starter and wheel brakes. It soon established an enviable reputation, and the monoplane Detroiter of 1927 was a great success, triggering other types. In 1929 the onset of the Depression caused Stinson to sell control to auto tycoon E L Cord, who in 1933 formed Aviation Corporation (Avco) to combine a vast range of manu-

The assembly at Fort Worth in 1973 of the General Dynamics prototype YF-16 single-seat combat fighter. The type was developed under the USAF's Lightweight Fighter program to explore the capabilities of a comparatively low-cost aircraft as a complement to the complex costly machines into which general-purpose fighters had evolved. The design progressed into production as the F-16 and has been adopted as a tactical fighter by US, Belgian, Danish, Dutch, Israeli and other Air Forces.

facturing and operating activities. The 1934 Air Mail Act prohibited companies from both making and operating aircraft, and Avco hived off its airlines. Stinson hit the big time in 1930 with his trimotor Airliner, expanded into a new plant at Nashville, Tennessee, and designed the first of the famous Reliants. Then in 1932 he was killed trying to make a forced landing in Jackson Park, Chicago. But his name lived on with the Reliant, 105/Voyager and its military offshoot the L-5 Sentinel of which 3590 were made at Wayne from 1941 to 1945.

Jerry (Gerard) Vultee, born in 1900, soon showed himself to be a brilliant design engineer, and was responsible for parts of all the early cantilever-monoplane Lockheeds before founding Airplane Development Corporation in 1932. Again he was assisted by Cord, who put up $50,000 and whose American Airlines asked for an all-metal monoplane that flew in 1933 as the V-1. The sheer performance of this advanced single-engined transport led to the improved V-1A, sold to many customers and responsible for the first roundtrip North Atlantic flight in 1936. The V-11

attack bomber followed, and in a giant new factory at Downey, Los Angeles, Vultee planned a family of stressed-skin aircraft using similar parts but covering the range from primary trainers to fighters. Then, at the same age (38) as Stinson, Vultee was killed with his wife in a Stinson in Arizona. But the company prospered, was incorporated in 1939 as Vultee Aircraft (subsidiary of Avco), and in 1940 took over Stinson. The latter's plant at Nashville was doubled and doubled again, making the Vengeance, the Stinson-designed Vigilant and other types. Downey built Vanguard fighters and 11,537 of the related Valiant trainer series, mostly after it had combined with Consolidated.

Yet another acquisition was Hall Aluminum Aircraft, a Navy flying-boat constructor, in 1940. By late 1943 Convair had 13 operating divisions in ten States, producing over 42,000 combat aircraft. Then came contraction, and in 1947 a mere 10,000-strong company was acquired by Atlas Corporation, Floyd B Odlum becoming chairman. Main products by this time were the Convair 240 at San Diego

and monster B-36 at Fort Worth. Then in 1953, when expansion was dramatic, control was bought by John Jay Hopkins, architect of General Dynamics. As one of the largest GD operating companies, Convair blossomed into missiles and space, creating the pioneer Atlas ICBM, F-102 and F-106 supersonic interceptors, the B-58 supersonic bomber and the CV-880 jetliner. Aviation is risky, and though the 880 and faster 990 were technical successes they lost the company more than $450,000,000, then a record for a single product. In 1961 GD separated Convair, Fort Worth, Astronautics, Pomona and Daingerfield into separate divisions; products were called General Dynamics. In 1969 San Diego and Fort Worth were reunited into Convair Aerospace, but split apart again in June 1974.

Today Convair Division at San Diego makes DC-10 fuselages, Shuttle Orbiter mid-fuselages and the versatile Tomahawk cruise missile. Fort Worth, having finished the F-111 program, is busy with the F-16 and also runs Pomona's many missile programs.

An F-16 prototype in formation with a pair of Aerospace Defense Command Convair F-106 Delta Darts. Both types have a top speed above Mach 2 but the F-16 has an empty weight of only 12,000lb and weapon capacity of 15,000lb compared with the nearly 24,000lb weight and 11,400lb load of the F-106, a pure interceptor.

GRUMMAN AEROSPACE CORPORATION

Few aviation enterprises present such a straightforward story of success as the famous Grumman company. It has always been intimately associated with the US Navy, always been based on Long Island, always had more or less the same name, and never been taken over, merged, or in any other way appreciably altered. With the years the people have changed, but the consistent engineering excellence has not. [And, in passing, it is worth noting that in a book on modern military aircraft I once wrote, Grumman had considerably more entries than any other company, with 17 distinct types in current use.]

The founder, Leroy Randle Grumman, was an extremely well-qualified engineer. Born at Huntington, Long Island, in 1895, he graduated from Cornell, MIT and Columbia. After a short spell with the NY Telephone system he joined the Navy as a pilot and served until 1921 when he was persuaded by Grover C Loening to come and be his general manager and test pilot. Loening Aeronautical Engineering Corporation was founded in 1917 by another good engineer, and during Grumman's time, which lasted until 1929, was noted for its characteristic central-float amphibians. Increasingly Grumman assumed the duties of chief engineer.

In 1928 Loening accepted a thumping cash offer of $3,000,000 for his entire company from a group of investment bankers. Part of the deal was Loening's agreement he would never start up afresh in competition. With the Navy's agreement he backed Grumman in setting up a company to provide service support for the Navy's existing Loenings – something the bankers overlooked – and he put up $30,000, almost half the launch capital. He thought it

best to stay remote, but his elder brother, Albert P Loening, joined as vice-president and treasurer. Leon A "Jake" Swirbul and five others made up Grumman Aircraft Engineering Corporation in 1929, and operations began in an abandoned garage in Baldwin, NY, on 2 January 1930.

Grumman had two important strings to his bow in patented "Sto-wing" foolproof folding wings and a stressed-skin float into which the landing wheels retracted on double-hinged arms. The Navy bought the float for the Vought O3U Corsair. Far more than that, it accepted Grumman's proposal to develop an extremely advanced two-seat fighter, with NACA-cowled Cyclone driving a variable-pitch propeller (ten years before such propellers reached RAF fighters) and with the landing gear taken from the amphibious-float design. The resulting XFF-1, flown in late 1931, set the company's style in having a portly deep-bellied fuselage, sliding canopy and distinctive main gears cranked upwards into recesses ahead of the lower wing. The fuselage was stressed-skin. Despite a rather lumpy appearance the XFF reached 201 mph (323km/h), faster than any aircraft then in the Navy or, so far as I can discover, any Air Force at that time. The company moved to a new plant at Farmingdale.

Though the concept of the two-seat fighter itself was in some degree faulty, the FF-1 (popularly dubbed "Fifi") and its SF-1 scouting partner were major types making up half the force embarked aboard the carrier *Lexington* in the mid-1930s. Their serviceability and toughness earned the

This Grumman J2F-6 Duck general utility and observation amphibian of the middle 1930s illustrates well the classic Loening form of single float into which the landing wheels could be retracted.

company a reputation it has jealously guarded. It also helped, in the depth of the Depression, to land important contracts for F2F and F3F single-seat fighters which were among the most advanced biplanes in history. An even more powerful machine was the Gulfhawk, built for Al Williams and sponsored by Gulf Oil. Contemporary with these fast, maneuverable biplanes was a family of two/three-seat utility and observation amphibians identical in form to the classic Loening and designed as the older type's replacement. The first XJF-1 flew on 4 May 1933, and from it stemmed nearly 600 of six sub-types, mostly powered by a Cyclone, used for transport, rescue, photography, target towing and even (with the Marines) fighting and bombing. The

final 300 were made by Columbia Aircraft a few miles away at Valley Stream.

In 1937 Grumman flew the first G-21 Goose six/seven-passenger amphibian. Its

Right: The remarkable speed and toughness of the Loening-Grumman amphibians led to orders for Navy fighters using a similar patented landing gear; the FF-1 (Fifi) two-seat fighter (illustrated) was the first of a long line of Grumman carrier-based fighters which have retained their pre-eminence for more than 50 years

Below: Grumman amphibian development continued and the twin-engine six/seven-passenger G-21 Goose of 1937 was followed by the three/four-passenger G-44 Widgeon in 1940. Both were built in fair quantities for naval and civilian use and some have remained in small airline service throughout the 1970s. Illustrated is a Widgeon in service on tourist routes in Auckland, New Zealand, in November 1969.

first monoplane, the twin-engined Goose gave the firm a small civil and export market – although by a roundabout route its old Fifi had by then seen action in the Spanish Civil War, being made under license by Canadian Car & Foundry, exported ostensibly to Turkey and diverted through France to Republican Spain. Further FF-1 fighters were used by the RCAF as the Goblin I. But the Goose, powered by two Wasp Juniors, was a product with wide appeal which saw useful sales in both military and civil markets. Even today several are in regular airline service, and many more with private owners. It was partnered from 1940 by the smaller G-44 Widgeon, originally designated J4F by the Navy, which had Ranger in-line engines. Today many Goose and Widgeon airframes have been re-engined with later piston or turboprop power, a comment on their toughness and freedom from corrosion or fatigue after nearly 40 years of use.

In 1935 Grumman began to develop a new Navy biplane fighter, the XF4F-1; but monoplanes were by this time beginning to out-perform the fighter biplane and the contract was changed to the XF4F-2 monoplane, with a large almost rectangular wing in the mid-position on a rotund compact fuselage, still with the patented landing gear. The prototype flew from the growing factory at Bethpage on 2 September 1937. By this time there were two adjacent airfields on Long Island, each home to a major producer of combat aircraft. Farmingdale had become the airfield of Seversky; later, when that company changed its name to Republic, the Long Island Rail Road opened a station called Republic.

Next door at Bethpage is the Grumman complex. Both areas are a few miles down the line from Mineola, a Navy and Marines field since 1916 and once a former airship base.

For various reasons the F4F was delayed during the vital two years before the outbreak of war, but by 1940 production G-36 fighters ordered by France were being received by the British Fleet Air Arm as the Martlet 1. They were among the earliest combat aircraft from the US to get into action, and on Christmas Day 1940 one shot down a Ju88. Subsequently the F4F became the chief, and virtually only, American carrier-based fighter until autumn 1943. Named Wildcat, and powered variously by the Twin Wasp or Cyclone, it achieved an impressive record throughout the war. A total of 7898 was built, all but 1978 by a General Motors subsidiary called Eastern Aircraft, which in March 1942 was brought in to utilize automotive productive capacity for the war effort and leave Grumman free to concentrate on new designs. Eastern had its HQ at Linden, New Jersey, and plants there and at Bloomfield and Trenton in the same state, as well as at Baltimore and at Tarrytown, NY. Its whole output was devoted to Grumman products.

An even more important task assigned to Eastern was production of the Avenger. Grumman was awarded a contract for the TBF-1 Avenger on 8 April 1940, this three-seat torpedo bomber being urgently needed to replace the ageing TBD. Grumman accepted a great responsibility with the TBF, which predictably was a large and tough bird with the R-2600 double-row Cyclone,

an electrically driven dorsal turret, enclosed weapons bay and outward-retracting landing gear. Like the Wildcat its wings pivoted on skewed hinges to lie alongside the rear fuselage, upper surfaces outward. By 1945 Grumman had built 2290 TBF-1s, and Eastern delivered 2882 of this version and 4664 of the heavier and more powerful TBM-3 version.

With the much-needed F6F Hellcat Grumman established a truly outstanding production record. The original development contract for this pugnacious carrier fighter was signed in June 1941. The prototype flew on 26 June 1942 with an R-2600 Cyclone; then it was re-engined with the more powerful R-2800 Double Wasp and made a second "first" flight 34 days later! Equally impressive was Grumman's flight of a production F6F-3 on 4 October 1942, by which time the production line was already humming inside an unfinished factory that doubled the total floor area at Bethpage. In the following two years this one line delivered 12,274 Hellcats, which – far more than any other aircraft – achieved complete air supremacy throughout the Pacific. This is believed to be a record output from one assembly line.

Other important Navy/Marines combat aircraft followed: the F7F Tigercat, F8F Bearcat, F9F (later F-9) Panther and Cougar, F11F (F-11) Tiger, AF Guardian, SA-16/UF (later U-16) Albatross amphibian, S-2 Tracker, E-1 Tracer and C-1 Trader, OV-1 Mohawk family (for the Army), A-6 Intruder and EA-6B Prowler family, E-2 Hawkeye, C-2 Greyhound, F-14 Tomcat and the EF-111A for the Air Force. Though there have been occasional

Left: First of the Grumman monoplane Navy fighters appeared at the Bethpage plant as the XF4F-2, still with the patent landing gear, in September 1937 and went into production as the F4F Wildcat two years later. First operational use occurred with the RAF as the Martlet and with both the Fleet Air Arm and the US Navy the F4F established a high reputation. Well over 7000 were produced, nearly 2000 by Grumman and approaching 6000, as FM-1 and -2, by General Motors. The FM-2 (illustrated) was the final version built by Eastern Aircraft Division.

Top right: The Grumman TBF Avenger first appeared in 1941 and entered service with the US Navy in spring 1942. After a disappointing start it developed into an extremely successful carrier-based torpedo bomber and, with the Royal Navy (initially named Tarpon), it became a general-purpose light bomber, minelayer and strike aircraft. Nearly 10,000 Avengers of various marks were produced, including about 7000 as TBM-1 and -3, by General Motors.

Right: The current US Navy's standard carrier-borne fighter is the Grumman F-14 Tomcat, a two-seat air-superiority and general-purpose machine with variable-sweep wings that can carry a devastating gun/missile armament at speeds approaching Mach 2.5.

technical or financial problems, every one of these programs has been fully successful and in nearly all cases sustained manufacturing workloads at Grumman and, often, at foreign licensees, for many years. The biggest program financially is the Tomcat, initiated in 1968 to replace the F-111B on which Grumman was General Dynamics' associate contractor. Design and development under program director Mike Pelehach was a model of swift and thorough competence. A dramatically advanced aircraft, the F-14A inherited the extremely long-range Hughes AWG-9 radar and AIM-54 Phoenix missile from the YF-12 and F-111B. The first flew on 21 December 1970 but crashed on the second flight through total hydraulic failure. This caused only a brief hiccup, and deliveries to VF-1 and -2 at Miramar began in late 1972.

However, by this time Grumman was in deep financial trouble. On 11 December 1972 it refused to build the 48 aircraft in Lot 5 and called for renegotiation of the contract. It had lost $135 million on the previous 86 aircraft, even at what many thought a high unit price of $16.5 million; after prolonged court disputation the Company and the Navy reached agreement, with a new price structure allowing for inflation, but Grumman accepted a further loss of $105 million on Lot 5. Such things are seldom understood by the general public, and were not even mentioned in a book on the F-14, but they made a profound difference to Grumman.

Grumman himself had retired in 1946. His successor was Jake Swirbul, whose advanced ideas on employee relations had helped the company from the start in its splendid productivity. Sadly, Swirbul died in June 1960 and his successor was another of the "original six" ex-Loening men, E Clinton Towl. Chairman of the executive committee was W T "Bill" Schwendler, another of the originals and the man chiefly responsible for the design of the famous wartime machines. In 1966 former lawyer and much-decorated bomber crewman Llewellyn J Evans moved up to the presidency. Then, in 1969, the company was restructured into a holding company, Grumman Corporation, with five operating subsidiaries, one of them Grumman Aerospace. Today the management looks quite different; chairman of the parent is John C Bierwith and president is former Army Aviation General Joe Gavin. Top man at Grumman Aerospace is George M Skurla, whose "empire" includes a plant at Milledgeville working on Thunderbolt II wings, CH-53 airframes and other subcontract programs.

At one time Grumman had a major involvement with general aviation. This is discussed in the next entry, under Gulfstream.

Illustrated is still another Grumman carrier-based type, an E-2C Hawkeye, symbolically in formation with a pair of Tomcats. The Hawkeye (which has a top speed of 375mph compared with the 1600mph or so of the Tomcat) provides airborne early warning for the fleet and acts as forward air controller for the fighters, with a mass of electronics served by the large rotating radome automatically integrated with the overall Navy control and information communications system.

Another current Grumman carrier aircraft, the A-6 is a versatile design employed by the USN as the A-6E Intruder long-range all-weather attack bomber (illustrated), which can carry tactical nuclear weapons, as the EA-6B Prowler four-seat electronic counter-measures aircraft, and as the KA-6D shipboard inflight refueller.

GULFSTREAM AMERICAN

In the mid-1950s Grumman and his president, Leon Swirbul, sought civil products to back up their diversified and prosperous military business. The last civil amphibian, the Mallard, had sold in small numbers and appeared to be the last of the line. After much market research the choice of new product fell on an agricultural biplane, the Ag-Cat, which was flown in May 1957. It easily out-performed the wartime Stearmans and other rivals and established itself as a market leader. By 1979 it had sold over 2500 units with various piston and turboprop engines, made under subcontract by a pre-eminent sailplane manufacturer, Schweizer Aircraft, of Elmira, NY.

In parallel Grumman took a far bigger gamble. The G-159 Gulfstream, first flown on 14 August 1958, was a new species, a large purpose-designed executive machine. Powered by two Rolls-Royce Dart turboprops, it had a slim body seating from nine to 24 passengers in great comfort. It far out-performed rivals such as the DC-3 or converted bombers, but it was many times more costly. Steadily the Gulfstream sold, and 200 were produced by February 1969. In early 1965 the decision was taken to build a jet successor, and the Gulfstream II (GII) went straight into production, the first flying as early as 2 October 1966. Powered by Rolls-Royce Spey turbofans, the totally new GII proved even more successful than its predecessor, and by early 1980 production was completed at 258.

In 1976 the considerably modified Gulfstream III was announced. This was shelved for financial reasons revolving

around the difficulty of recovering the very large investment, but in 1978 it was decided to go ahead with a less-ambitious GIII, the first of which flew in mid-1979. This is referred to again later.

A major move towards further diversification came in late 1972 when it was decided by mutual agreement to acquire an existing builder of small general-aviation machines, American Aviation, of Cleveland. AA had been formed in 1964 by Russell W "Corky" Meyer to build the AA-1 Yankee, previously called the Bede BD-1 of Jim Bede, who continued to develop his own company. AA grew and produced new designs and, with capital from the takeover, centered on a large new factory at Savannah, Georgia, under the name Grumman American Aviation Corporation ("Aviation" was soon dropped). Grumman American (GAC), a subsidiary of Grumman Corporation, took over all civil programs including the Gulfstreams and Ag-Cat, and by September 1978 had delivered well over 4000 aircraft including the Lynx, Tiger, Cheetah and twin-engined Cougar.

In that month it was announced that AJI had purchased Grumman's 80-percent holding in GAC and made a cash offer to the holders of the remainder. AJI, American Jet Industries, was formed in Los Angeles in 1951 to repair and convert aircraft. Under Allen E Paulson's dynamic leadership it prospered, took over the Temco Pinto small jet trainer, moved into big-time rebuilding and conversion of turboprops and jets, and after moves to

Santa Monica and Van Nuys (in the same area) announced plans in 1975 to build a radically different general-aviation aircraft of its own design. Under Robert W Lilibridge the Hustler 500 was designed as a pressurized vehicle for up to nine people, with a PT6 turboprop at the front and JT15D turbofan at the back.

Takeover of GAC was beneficial to both. AJI today continues at Van Nuys, which has become the West Coast service center for Gulfstreams. Aircraft development and new-build production is centered at what has become Gulfstream American Corporation, with Paulson as president. Under a contractual agreement Grumman is completing development and certification to guaranteed performance of the GIII, which is going into production at Savannah at 24 units a year. Altogether the new GAC has 2400 people, and its 1978 sales were $220 million, a sizeable force in general aviation.

Successor to the Dart turboprop-powered Grumman Gulfstream big executive aircraft of the 1958–60 period is the Gulfstream II powered by Rolls-Royce Spey turbofans, now produced by Gulfstream American Corporation. As a small airliner the Gulfstream II can take up to 19 passengers at cruising speeds up to 560mph over ranges up to about 3500 miles.

LOCKHEED

In 1903, before the Wrights flew under power, a monoplane glider was under construction in California, built by Professor James Montgomery at the University of Santa Clara. In February 1904 the finished machine made towed flights along the beach and then appeared in the university exhibition hall. Nobody studied it more intently than 15-year-old Allan Haynes Loughead. Speed-mad, he was expected by the good folk of Alma, a township south of San Jose, to come to an early death, probably in his homebuilt racing car. But from 1904 his dream was a powered flying machine.

For the next five years he avidly studied aviation, while avoiding death as a race driver and hot-rodder. Then in 1910 he found that his half-brother Victor had two books published in Chicago – *Aeroplane Designing* and *Vehicles of the Air* (they became best-sellers). He worked his way from one race meeting to another until he reached Chicago, where by luck he landed the job of mechanic to Jim Plew whose Curtiss pusher was kept at the Hawthorne Race Track. It was still winter, and Loughead watched as two pilots spluttered through the snow, failing to get airborne. Then he yelled, "Help me turn it around, I know I can fly it." He tinkered with the carburetor, climbed in, opened up and roared across the field. To everyone's amazement – probably including Loughead's – the lumbering Curtiss staggered into the air, made a complete circuit of the track and then came in for a rather bumpy landing!

Allan saved money, had some airplane parts built and sent to San Francisco, and then persuaded his full brother Malcolm to join him in a construction project. Together they found $1800, and even talked a local taxi company into putting up another $1200. They called their creation the Loughead Model G, to give the impression they had built machines before. It was a remarkably sound design, a big biplane with six-cylinder Kirkham engine, ailerons *à la* Curtiss between the wings, seats for a pilot and two passengers and, because water seemed a likely landing surface, central-float alighting gear. On 15 June 1913 Allan climbed aboard, and the G was pushed down a ramp on to San Francisco Bay; the crowd was almost unanimous – it would never fly. They were wrong. The first Loughead made a serene 15-minute flight over the entire city.

After a few more flights the brothers left aviation while they prospected (successfully) for gold. Then, suddenly, the 1915 Panama-Pacific Exposition opened in San Francisco. They bid for the flying conces-

sion, lost to famed barnstormer Bob Fowler, then saw Fowler crash on his first flight. Out came the Model G and, what was truly remarkable, it flew 600 passengers in more than 300 successful flights (more than 300 because the total payload had to be under 320lb (145kg) and some passengers weighed almost that by themselves), netting $4000! This was almost certainly record earnings for any flying machine at that time and for several years afterwards.

Model G had been built in a small garage at the corner of Pacific and Polk, but now the brothers decided to go for the big time. In the summer of 1916 they planned a giant flying-boat, the F-1, to be powered by two 160hp Hall-Scott engines and carry a payload of 3100lb (1410kg), ten times that of the G. In a small workshop behind a garage on State Street, Santa Barbara, they set up Loughead Aircraft Manufacturing Company, with Berton R Rodman, owner of a local machine shop and major investor, as president. Allan was vice-president and Malcolm secretary and treasurer. Then a 21-year-old mechanic appeared and said he wanted "any job just to get into aviation?" He said he could draw and undertake stress analysis. Thus John K Northrop was given the job of laying out the F-1 hull and stressing the wings.

On 28 March 1918 Allan was at the controls on a most successful first flight. True to form the F-1 was a winner, often carrying as many as 12 passengers at a time, and, late in 1918, making a world record flight nonstop to San Diego. This impressed the Navy, which set the infant company on its feet with a $90,000 order for two Curtiss HS-2L flying-boats – but cancelled a follow-up deal for 50 at the Armistice. Loughead rebuilt the F-1 as the F-1A landplane and then back to a boat again, where it gave many years of service as a vehicle for

The first Lockheed aircraft, the Model G of 1913, about to be launched down the ramp on to San Francisco Bay by the Loughead brothers, at the same time launching the famous Lockheed Aircraft Corporation. The Model G made more than 300 flights and carried 600 passengers on trips at the 1915 Panama-Pacific Exposition.

cinema cameramen and as a movie star itself. The company took full-page advertisements proclaiming "LOUGHEAD (pronounced Lock-heed), builders of aircraft since 1912, every one a success." It built the trim S-1 side-by-side two-place sporting biplane, with company-designed 25hp engine and monocoque fuselage molded from plywood in concrete forms. Not one customer appeared, and in 1920 the brothers suspended operations.

Malcolm devised a superior hydraulic brake for road vehicles and founded Lockheed Hydraulics, from which sprang the vast Bendix, Automotive Products and other industrial giants. Meanwhile Allan changed his name to the way it was pronounced and, in December 1926, at last managed to restart by forming Lockheed Aircraft Company in a small shop at Sycamore and Romaine in Hollywood. President this time, again because he put up the cash, was Fred S Keeler. They enticed Northrop back from Douglas and set him to work on a kind of super S-1. The unbraced high wing was not a new idea though Allan considered adding struts to placate worried pilots or customers. But when it was mounted on a beautifully streamlined wooden monocoque fuselage the result was what Allan had always sought – a truly efficient high-speed airplane. On 4 July 1927 the first Vega was rolled out, painted bright orange with red trim, and with the Lockheed star on its fin. Hired test pilot Eddie Bellande took off at 4pm from a hayfield that today is LA International Airport. When he returned he announced, "She's a dandy. You'll sell this airplane like hotcakes."

In fact the Vega is one of the immortals of aviation. It did sell like hotcakes, and most of them achieved fame with trail-blazing epic flights. The first was snapped up by Hearst Newspapers. The second was the choice of Sir Hubert Wilkins and pilot Ben Eielson for a ski-equipped flight 2200 miles (3540km) across the North Pole from Alaska to Spitzbergen. At the first US National Air Races in Cleveland in 1928 the more-powerful Wasp-engined Vega won all the speed trophies. Colonel Roscoe Turner commented "All you have to do is buy a Vega, point it at a distant destination and there's another record." Altogether 144 Vegas were built, nearly all in a big new plant at Burbank a mile or two from the Hollywood site, and they set 34 world records. Art Goebel's white *Yankee Doodle* set an eastbound coast-to-coast record in 24 hours 20 minutes, with only one stop at Phoenix. Then he returned nonstop in 18 hours 58 minutes. Lockheed chief test pilot Herb Fahy kept one aloft 36 hours 56 minutes. Amelia Earhart won a race at 175mph (282km/h), much faster than anything in the Air Corps, and then flew to Europe in only 15 hours 48 minutes. But the most famous Vega of all was *Winnie Mae* (today in the NASM) flown round the world in eight days in 1931 by Wiley Post, the one-eyed pilot, and Harold Gatty, and then two years later round the world again in seven days 18 hours $49\frac{1}{2}$ minutes by Post *solo*.

In July 1929 Lockheed was one of 11 companies purchased by financiers seeking quick profits from large groupings; this one was called Detroit Aircraft Corporation. Lockheed prospered, with the parasol-winged Air Express and low-wing Sirius, the latter used by Lindbergh variously with wheels or floats to survey routes for PanAm, and the even faster Altair for Kingsford Smith and others which had a neat inwards-retracting landing gear partly engineered by Vultee. In April 1931 came the brightest of all the early Lockheed stars, the Orion. This was really a modernized Vega, with low wing, retractable gear and cruising speed with six passengers exceeding 200mph (322km/h). Varney Speed Lanes had an 86-minute schedule between Los Angeles and San Francisco, and in Europe Swissair halved the times of their competitors and triggered off the He 70 for Lufthansa (but no answer from Britain).

Despite the market crash in 1929, Lockheed continued to prosper under Allan Lockheed and Detroit's man, former Army

pilot and co-founder of Stinson, Carl B Squier. But Squier's bosses milked all the money, prohibiting any investment in new designs or research. Lockheed needed to progress beyond wooden monocoques, but with nothing to offer and customers going broke the decline was swift, bankruptcy following in late 1931. Squier struggled on, mortgaging his own possessions to pay the workers at Christmas 1931. By April 1932 the staff was down to four, and a Federal receiver offered the assets for sale at $42,456.

All this had been watched by a native of Boston, Robert E Gross. A Harvard man, Bob Gross had invested in Stearman and, with his brother Courtlandt, had formed the successful Viking Flying Boat Company. He helped Varney operate his fast airline, and on 6 June 1932 he stepped aboard an Orion for Los Angeles. Just before

Passengers boarding the first service on 29 June 1934 of a Northwest Airlines Lockheed Electra 10, a neat ten-passenger stressed-skin twin-engine monoplane, first product of a once-more re-formed company, that founded a line of outstanding passenger aircraft which in turn formed the basis of a successful patrol bomber. The picture is of the very first Electra, identified by the raked windscreen.

11am he met Squier and Stearman and they took their places in the US District Court. Judge Hollzer offered the assets of Lockheed for sale and picked up the only bid before him, for $40,000. He looked at Gross and asked "Do you have the money?" Gross did. Though Allan Lockheed had been trying to raise funds and was in the room, there was no other bid. The judge rapped his gavel and approved the sale; then, because the three men were clearly insane, he leaned over and said to all three "I hope you know what you're doing."

Gross became chairman and treasurer,

Stearman president, Cyril Chappellet secretary and Squier vice-president sales. Gross hired a bright young MIT engineer, Hall L Hibbard, to help Stearman work out what to build. But they had no spare cash; it had taken every cent, and generous aid from Varney, to buy the assets. So Gross spent half his time tearing round California in a battered Chevy coupé selling stock to any investor who would listen. One day he found himself in the coffee shop at Burbank's Union Air Terminal. On the ramp was a sleek Orion (only one engine), a Ford (noisy and slow) and one of the new Boeing 247s. Gross raced back to Hibbard. "Forget the single-engine ship," he said. "Passengers are going to want a twin." The result was the trim stressed-skin Model 10 Electra, first product of the reformed independent Lockheed Aircraft Corporation. It first flew on 23 February 1934, with a twin-finned tail added by the young engineer who did the tunnel testing for Lockheed at the University of Michigan. Soon he joined the company and for the next 40 years spearheaded the drive of the winged star to Mach 1, Mach 2 and Mach 3. He was Clarence L Johnson, actually of Swedish extraction but dubbed Kelly because as a kid he always seemed to be fighting.

Priced at only $36,000 at first, the Electra sold faster even than the Vega, and it enabled Lockheed to build the Model 12, the Model 14 Super Electra (fastest transport of the 1930s) and the turbocharged XC-35, the first pressurized aircraft. The latter set a few flight records at speeds and heights typical of the airlines of 15 years later, while the 14 not only took British Prime Minister Chamberlain to Munich but Howard Hughes round the world in the amazing time of three days 19 hours. Then in April 1938, as war clouds loomed in Europe, Britain sent a purchasing commission to the United States. Just five days before the team visited Burbank Lockheed got wind of the foreigners and got a military version of the 14 studied. When the British arrived, they were impressed to be greeted by name by people who seemed to anticipate their every thought. In the plant was a mock-up of the Model 214 reconnaissance bomber. The British studied it with great care, and finally presented a list of major and minor changes the RAF would want. Lockheed advised that these would be ready for inspection next day.

On 23 June 1938 the British signed a contract for 200, naming the aircraft the Hudson. It catapulted Lockheed into the front rank, and the order was many times repeated until 2941 had been built. By 1940

Top: This busy wartime scene at the Lockheed Burbank plant shows a section of the assembly area turning out Hudsons for the RAF; the RAF received over 2000 through purchase and Lend-Lease.

Above: A group of Lockheed employees gathers for a ceremonial farewell as the last of the Hudsons leaves the Burbank final assembly building in August 1943 after 4½ years in production. The Hudson's place on the production line was taken by the Constellation and its military role in both USAAF and Navy and the RAF was taken over by the bigger and faster PV-1 Ventura built by the Lockheed subsidiary Vega Aircraft Corporation's new plant, also at Burbank.

Left: The military derivative of the L-14 in 1938 was the Hudson maritime patrol bomber developed originally and produced in quantity for the Royal Air Force. The Lockheed Hudson IV (illustrated) is preserved in flying condition by the Strathallan Aircraft Collection in Scotland; it saw action with the Royal Australian Air Force in 1942 and was flown to Scotland from Australia in 1973 for preservation in RAAF markings.

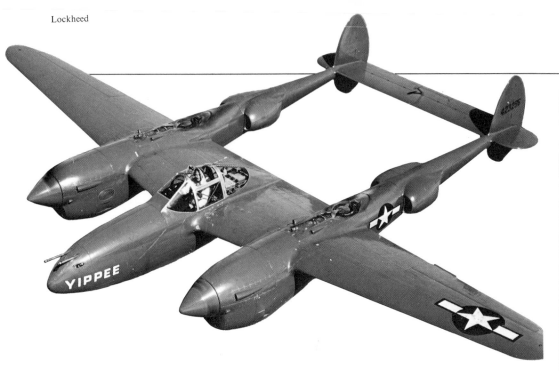

over 100 commercial 14s and 600 Hudsons had been delivered, the bigger 18 was in production in civil and military transport versions and the bomber version, the Ventura, was in production at a completely new Burbank plant run by Vega Airplane Corporation, a wholly owned subsidiary. A year after Pearl Harbor the main plant was in massive production of the amazing P-38 Lightning, a typical Johnson creation which used turbocharged Allison engines and combined pleasant qualities with great range and an almost eerie silence – whole squadrons could beat up an airfield at 400mph (644km/h) with only a gently rustling whoosh. Vega was turning out the B-17. Employment peaked at 94,000 in 1943, and by VJ-day Lockheed had delivered 9942 P-38s, 2750 B-17s and over 5600 twin-engined patrol bombers.

Peace saw Lockheed firmly ahead with the biggest and fastest wartime transport, the Constellation, the P2V Neptune Navy patrol aircraft that set the nonstop world record by flying from Perth in Western Australia to Columbus, Ohio, and the best available jet fighter, the P-80 Shooting Star. The company made errors in trying to build a lightplane (Little Dipper and Big Dipper) and feederline transport (Saturn), as well as the giant R6O Constitution for the Navy, but the P-80 was redesignated F-80 and led to the mass-produced T-33 jet trainer and a succession of F-94 Starfire night fighters. The P2V Neptune remained in production in various forms until the last sub-type came off a Japanese assembly line 34 years after the prototype. Kelly Johnson went to Korea, found the pilots wanted performance at all costs and designed "the missile with a man in it," the F-104 Starfighter. He discovered the CIA wanted a covert spy aircraft that could fly across hostile territory and, in his famous

Above: The unorthodox Lockheed solution to the USAAC's 1938 requirement for a long-range fighter/ bomber is well shown in this picture of the P-38 Lightning. The one pictured is a P-38L, most numerous (nearly 4000) model of a total of about 10,000 Lightnings built. It was armed with a 20mm cannon and four .50 machine-guns and could carry up to 4000lb of bombs or rockets at more than 400mph over a range of about 2200 miles. The Lightning had the distinction of shooting down more Japanese aircraft than any other Army fighter.

Right: Lockheed's Constellation was one of the most graceful of the various series of big four-engine airliners. Its development began in 1939 to meet a TWA requirement but war intervened and the first aircraft to appear in early 1943 were modified to serve as the C-69 military transport. After the war the first Model 049 civil Constellations appeared on TWA's New York–Los Angeles service in February 1946 and were soon in service with other airlines. The picture shows some of BOAC's second batch of 17 Constellations, 749As, supplied between 1948 and 1955.

secret Skunk Works, created the extraordinary U-2, a kind of jet-propelled sailplane.

Thanks to the Berlin Airlift of 1948–49 the USAF asked for a really capable modern logistic transport. Lockheed won the job and Johnson, Willis Hawkins and E C Frost created the C-130 Hercules. The prototype flew on 23 August 1954. Burbank was bursting at the seams, but out at Marietta, Georgia, Lockheed-Georgia Company had been formed to take over the vast wartime plant where Bell had built the B-29. Under the previous manager James V Carmichael, Lockheed reactivated the factory to build the B-47 and delivered 294. In 1954 this work was complete, and the C-130 took its place. Since then the giant Lockheed-Georgia plant has delivered over 1600, and production continues. The factory also designed and built 284 C-141 StarLifters and 81 of the monster C-5A Galaxy. Both the latter types are being recycled back through the plant for major

NO
SMOKING

B·O·A·C

structural refurbishment and, in the case of the C-141, lengthening of the fuselage to match cubic capacity to available payload.

With Lockheed-Georgia (Gelac) formed, the original plant was christened Lockheed-California Company (Calac). On 6 December 1957 the latter flew the attractive Model 188 Electra, of which 161 (fewer than expected) were built. In 1959–60 Electras suffered several catastrophic accidents. The cure was as hard to find as that of Britain's Comet 1 fatigue weakness, but instead of giving up their customers, as in the British program, Lockheed quickly rebuilt every Electra and helped their customers market them as Electra IIs. Out of this program emerged the P-3 Orion submarine hunter, by far the most widely used long-range ocean patrol aircraft, of which 600 had been built by 1979, with 45 remaining on the production line in Japan. Another of Calac's programs was a series of high-speed and very maneuverable helicopters, while Gelac handled production of the JetStar, the world's first business jet, and the XV-4A Hummingbird jet V/STOL research aircraft.

Top: Massive long-range maritime power is represented in this picture of a Lockheed P-3 Orion anti-submarine reconnaissance aircraft at the USN's Jacksonville, Florida, base. The design, based on the turboprop-powered L-188 Electra airliner, won a development contract in 1958 and thereafter production orders for the US and several other Navies.

Below: The Lockheed F-104 Starfighter, although widely used, is probably the most controversial of all modern military aircraft. The original design, which first flew in February 1954, was sold in only limited quantities for the USAF but a later much redesigned multi-role version has been built in Canada, Germany, Italy, Belgium, Holland and Japan as well as by Lockheed and used by the Air Forces of at least ten nations.

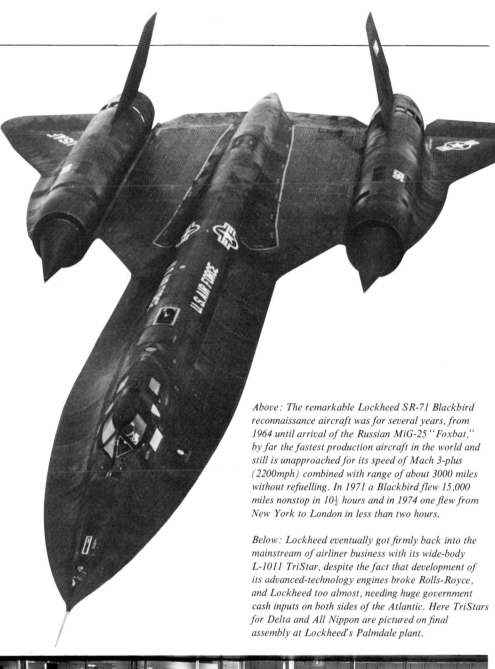

The biggest project at the Skunk Works was the Blackbird series for the CIA and Air Force. Built and flown in secrecy, these fantastic 2000mph (3200km/h) reconnaissance machines were announced by President Johnson in 1964, as the A-11. A few were YF-12 research interceptors, but the majority were bigger longer-ranged SR-71s, used by SAC's 9th Strategic Reconnaissance Wing from Beale AFB on flights planned like space trips. One holds the world speed record, while another flew New York–London in one hour 55 minutes. F-104 production was limited in the United States but swelled in Europe, Canada and Japan, and continued on the F-104S interceptor version in Italy until 1979. Meanwhile Calac's biggest program since 1968 has been the L-1011 TriStar widebody civil transport, augmented until 1976 by the S-3 Viking carrier-based ASW aircraft. TriStar assembly takes place in a big new plant at Palmdale. In 1980 military programs included the TR-1 multisensor reconnaissance platform derived from the enlarged U-2R, and the Skunk Works effort called Project Stealth which might have flown in 1977 but is truly stealthy!

Aircraft represent only a part of the total business of Lockheed Corporation, which ranks 80th among US industrial giants. One of the world's biggest defense contractors is LMSC, Lockheed Missiles and Space Company, responsible for the entire US Navy fleet ballistic missile program and the Polaris, Poseidon and Trident missile systems as well as very large efforts in space. Other giant subsidiaries include Lockheed Electronics, Lockheed Air Terminal and

Above: The remarkable Lockheed SR-71 Blackbird reconnaissance aircraft was for several years, from 1964 until arrival of the Russian MiG-25 "Foxbat," by far the fastest production aircraft in the world and still is unapproached for its speed of Mach 3-plus (2200mph) combined with range of about 3000 miles without refuelling. In 1971 a Blackbird flew 15,000 miles nonstop in $10\frac{1}{2}$ hours and in 1974 one flew from New York to London in less than two hours.

Below: Lockheed eventually got firmly back into the mainstream of airliner business with its wide-body L-1011 TriStar, despite the fact that development of its advanced-technology engines broke Rolls-Royce, and Lockheed too almost, needing huge government cash inputs on both sides of the Atlantic. Here TriStars for Delta and All Nippon are pictured on final assembly at Lockheed's Palmdale plant.

Lockheed Shipbuilding and Construction. Ontario, California, is home to Lockheed Aircraft Service (LAS), a division rather than a subsidiary. Yet it is rather remarkable Lockheed is still in business. After the collapse of Rolls-Royce in February 1971 Lockheed was thrown into turmoil and survived only after prolonged negotiations and massive government loans. Much of the burden fell on the then-chairman, Gelac-raised Dan Haughton, and president A Carl Kotchian. Today these positions are filled by Roy Anderson and I O Kitchen. On the board are old-timers Cyril Chappellet, Hall Hibbard, Kelly Johnson and Willis Hawkins.

After the widely used C-130 Hercules multi-role turboprop military transport, Lockheed won a competition in 1961 for a USAF long-range strategic jet freighter with its C-141 StarLifter design, of which 284 were produced. The picture shows a C-141A being modified by Lockheed-Georgia to C-141B form by building in two fuselage extensions, fore and aft of the wing, providing an extra 23.3ft in length and increasing capacity by 35 percent.

MARTIN

Like Curtiss, Martin was one of the leading names in American aviation from the earliest days of individual pioneers until after World War II. Then the proud name faded, but it was not this time because of bad management. Martin was one of those rare companies that took a conscious decision to move on from aircraft to missiles, space and electronics. Whether it had to give up planemaking is doubtful; 25 years ago it seemed a good idea.

Glenn Luther Martin was a small-town boy from Iowa, born on 17 January 1886. He attended Kansas Wesleyan University but was so busy studying aviation that his business administration course took second place and he never graduated. Instead, in 1905 he set up a car repair business in Santa Ana, California, and two years later was airborne in his own glider from the beach. After a further two years he was ready with a powered machine, a well-conceived pusher with which he taught himself to fly. In 1919 he boldly gave up his garage business, set up an airplane manufacturing shop on the same site and by 1911 was incorporated as the Glenn L Martin Company. Slim bespectacled Martin looked like a young professor; the papers said he was "wild eyed" but that was journalistic nonsense. He received Aviation Certificate No 56 and Expert Aviator's Certificate No 2.

In early 1912 he moved to bigger premises at Griffith Park, Los Angeles, with several employees, and proceeded to build ever-better aircraft. All had tractor engines and enclosed fuselages, the chief types being based on the Model T tandem-seat land- or floatplane. One of the customers for a TA was Boeing. In conformity with Curtiss, Martin used a wheel for the rudder and a shoulder yoke for the ailerons, but by 1916 had adopted the system that became universal. There were many derivatives of the T, including the Army TT trainer, one of which stayed aloft seven hours four minutes with a pilot and two adult passengers.

This is the place to mention the pioneer research of Wilbur and Orville Wright at their bicycle shop in Dayton, Ohio, and on the windswept dunes at Kitty Hawk, North Carolina, which culminated in the first powered airplane flight on 17 December 1903. The brothers were so eager not to go off at half-cock that they told nobody, and did not form a company until the Wright Company was incorporated on 22 November 1909. Even then it came about solely because of the efforts of young Clinton R Peterkin, who a year earlier had been an office boy for the great J Pierpont Morgan. The firm opened impressive offices at

Glenn Luther Martin in 1949, with models of his company's aircraft during his 40 years as its leader. He is holding a model of the XB-48 six-jet bomber.

527 Fifth Avenue, New York City, with a large and growing factory at Dayton; but in 1912 Wilbur died of typhoid and Orville, dispirited by the festering dispute with Curtiss, bought all the stock (except that of a friend who held on for sentimental reasons) in 1914 so that he could sell out. In October 1915 he closed the deal with a group of industrialists.

In September 1916 the Wright companies, which included flying schools, were merged with several others including Martin to form the Wright-Martin Company. But the merger displeased Martin, who in October 1917 severed his connection. (Wright Aeronautical went on and finally merged with, of all people, Curtiss.) Martin moved to a bigger factory in Cleveland, operated under his original name, and in January 1918 landed an Army contract for ten GMBs (Glenn Martin Bombers), big twin-Liberty ships used in several versions for many roles including a 114-hour flight around the United States. Officially designated MB-1, these led to the Navy MBT torpedo carriers and the excellent MB-2 used by "Billy" Mitchell to sink the *Ostfriesland* and other captured warships. Martin made 20, but another 110 were made by rivals who underbid.

Unlike many US planemakers, Martin was never an "Army" or "Navy" firm but supplied both. Between the wars it was one of the leading suppliers of bombers and torpedo bombers, beginning with Navy-designed SC-1 scout bombers and continuing

with the excellent T3M and T4M, some of the earliest types to use the Hornet and Cyclone engines. In 1928 Martin decided to move yet again, to an even larger new plant at Middle River, Baltimore, offering year-round facilities for land and marine aircraft. The first production was of the BM-1 torpedo/dive-bomber, the Navy-designed PM-1 and -2 flying-boats and the Consolidated-designed P2M and P3M.

But the Boeing B-9 of November 1931 gave Martin, and others, a shock. In a matter of weeks Martin's outstanding engineering staff designed and built one of the most famous aircraft of the 1930s, the Martin Bomber. That is how it was de-

Outside the new factory in Cleveland in 1918 is the first of the MB-1 Martin bombers, with members of those responsible for it; from left to right, Lawrence Bell (superintendent and later founder of Bell Aircraft Corporation), Eric Springer, Glenn L Martin and Donald W Douglas (chief engineer and later founder of Douglas Aircraft Company).

scribed by the newspapers, though its Model number was 123. A streamlined machine, powered by two NACA-cowled Cyclones and soon fitted with a nose turret, it carried 2200lb (1000kg) of bombs internally at over 200mph (322km/h), much faster than any Army pursuit. Many were bought as the B-10, -12 and -14, and in 1936 the Army at last allowed exports, resulting even at this late date in 189 foreign sales.

From the classic Model 123 stemmed completely different and even faster new bombers, the 167 and 187. The 167 was bought by the Armée de L'Air and saw action in France before the collapse, thereafter serving Vichy and also the RAF and SAAF as the Maryland. The 187 was the Baltimore, chief tactical bomber of many

The Martin Model 179 Marauder enjoyed high performance achieved at the expense of high take-off and landing speeds, which initially brought a high accident rate and much criticism, but it was a very efficient machine and became a leading tactical bomber in World War II. Marauders of the first production batch constructed at one of the two Martin plants at Baltimore in 1941.

Allied Air Forces in the Italian theater. Even more important was the Model 179 Marauder, an extremely advanced aircraft designed for cruising efficiency at the expense of fast take-off and landing. Once called the "Widow-maker," and other unrepeatable names, it was eventually shown to be safe when properly flown and as the B-26 was a leading tactical bomber of the Allies. With a second Martin plant at Omaha, 5157 were delivered, plus over 250 for training, target-towing and other roles. The government plant at Omaha was run by Martin Nebraska Company, which also built 536 B-29s. The Baltimore complex also built thousands of bomber gun turrets.

In 1934 Martin secured a challenging contract from Pan American for a trans-Pacific flying-boat. The Model 130 *China Clipper*, first flown in December 1934 by William K Ebel and L C McCarty – who as well as being test pilots were respectively assistant chief engineer for Martin and the Model 130 project engineer – set a host of new landmarks in aircraft design. Powered by four of the new Twin Wasps, it took off

Another Martin design that set new standards was the Model 130 China Clipper flying-boat. It was the first application of the Pratt & Whitney Twin Wasp engine and was bigger and faster and had greater payload and range than its contemporaries. The China Clipper first flew in 1934 and later went into PanAm service on trans-Pacific routes.

at 2.2 times the empty weight of 23,100lb (10.5 tonnes) and with its sisters opened and maintained the route from California to China and the Philippines. Later Martin built the bigger long-range 156, the famous PBM Mariner used throughout World War II, and a small batch of JRM Mars. Postwar types included the piston-plus-jet P4M Mercator, the AM-1 Mauler (single-engined, but with a weapon load up to

That was that. There was no new aircraft on the drawing board. Martin had retired in 1952 (he died suddenly in 1955) and new president George M Bunker was a tough man with no background in planemaking. When the last B-57 went out of the door he said Martin had "sloughed off its emotional attachment to the airplane." At the time I thought this a courageous and probably right decision. Martin had to build the mighty Titan ICBM at a vast new plant in Denver, and at steamy Orlando was building a big business in smaller missiles. Baltimore did in fact build a few things that might be called aircraft: the wingless lifting body research machines of the X-23, X-24 and SV-5 families. But the conglomerate Martin Marietta Corporation, formed in 1965 by merging aerospace with many other interests, is not one of today's planemakers.

10,689lb, 4850kg), P5M (later styled P-5) large patrol flying-boat, the moderately successful 202 and pressurized 404 civil airliners, and the unsuccessful 600mph (966km/h) P6M SeaMaster flying-boats, XB-48 six-jet bomber and XB-51 three-jet bomber.

Nothing could have seemed more futuristic than the XB-51 of October 1949. In fact it was just what the USAF did not want. Instead it asked Martin to build a relatively old-fashioned but eminently useful bomber of British design, the Canberra. Quickly the Baltimore line turned out 403 B-57 versions, more than half of which served in Southeast Asia and some of which were rebuilt by GD Convair with grotesque long-span wings and fan engines. Eventually, 403 proved to have been too few for these versatile long-lived platforms.

The Martin company's own postwar designs had only limited success and the big Baltimore plant was turned over to licence-production of the English Electric-designed Canberra twin-jet tactical light bomber for the USAF, for which over 400 were built. This picture shows the final assembly of Martin B-57 Canberras in 1954.

McDONNELL DOUGLAS

McDonnell Douglas Corporation (MDC) ranks about 63rd in the list of US companies, exceeded by no planemaker except Boeing. It was formed in 1967 by the merger of two famous names. One, Douglas, was a giant with a long and prosperous history which had suddenly got into a cash-flow problem of crippling proportions. The other, McDonnell, had a shorter and simpler history, but – despite concentrating on the high-risk area of extreme technical challenge – had expanded rapidly and had money in the bank. So the merger was really a takeover, and for this reason I will tell the story of the "tail that wagged the dog" first.

James Smith McDonnell, who combines business acumen appropriate to Scottish ancestry with a merry twinkle in his bespectacled eyes, was born at Denver on 9 April 1899. Graduating from Princeton in 1921, he attended the school of aero engineering at MIT and also learned to fly at the Army school (Brooks) at San Antonio. In 1925, after leaving Brooks, he received a master's degree from MIT. There followed a succession of industrial appointments as designer, test pilot or engineer with many companies, ending as chief project engineer for landplanes for Martin from 1933 to 1938. He wanted the widest experience so that he would be fully equipped when he started his own company.

He never doubted that he would do this, and McDonnell Aircraft's incorporation was dated 6 July 1939. For $100 a month he rented a room on the second floor of a building at Lambert Field, St Louis Municipal Airport. "Mr Mac" brought with him his male secretary from Martin. Garrett C Covington was appointed chief engineer – not an easy situation when the boss could do the job at least as well – and, while income built up from subcontract manufacture, the two of them planned a radical twin-engined fighter, the XP-67. Two of these were built, but like so many other wartime fighters, the conventional ones were better. But McDonnell Aircraft Corporation, at first known as MAC like its founder and today called MCAir, prospered, opening a plant at Memphis for production of the Fairchild AT-21 Gunner and in August 1943 receiving the first Navy contract for a carrier-based jet fighter.

MAC had been studying the unusual problems of such an aircraft since early 1942, at times considering use of six or eight of the baby Westinghouse axial engines, but the XFD-1 Phantom finally flew on 26 January 1945 as a twin (the

One of the successful earlier McDonnell designs was the F-101 Voodoo, which first flew in September 1954, took the world speed record and set high safety and low maintenance standards in service with US and Canadian Air Forces. This was the first production F-101A, July 1955.

widely published tale that it flew on that date as a single-engined aircraft because no second engine was available is untrue). This tractable machine was a complete success, vindicating the Navy's hope that an untried company could probably do as well as an experienced one on so new a project, but because the state of the art was advancing so rapidly only 60 were built. Possible confusion with Douglas was avoided by changing the designation to FH-1.

In March 1944 the Navy tested MAC with an order for the XHJD-1 Whirlaway which in 1946 was the largest helicopter then flown outside Germany. There followed the attractive XH-20 Little Henry personal helicopter with a Marquardt ramjet on the tip of each blade, the Army XV-1 convertiplane with pressure-jet rotor and pusher propeller which in 1954 became the first aircraft to convert from rotor-supported to wing-supported flight, and studies of two advanced Marine helicopters, the Model 78 XHRH-1 for assault and the Model 86 XHCH-1 crane. As a company venture in 1957 MAC built the triple-turbine Model 120 whose ratio of empty to gross weight has never been surpassed by ordinary helicopters.

When the Navy bought production FH-1s in March 1945 it asked the growing team to design a more powerful successor. This became a staple product. First flown on 11 January 1947, the F2H Banshee was powered by the J34, the only one of the many Westinghouse axial turbojets to work acceptably and sustain major programs. By 1953 MAC had delivered 895 of four major variants, with additional sub-types for reconnaissance and night fighting. The F2H was a most valuable attack aircraft in Korea, and the late F-2C

version was the only jet used by the Royal Canadian Navy.

In October 1945 the large St Louis factory took on the unique job of creating a fighter that could drop out of the bomb bay of a B-36. The XF-85 Goblin, flown off a trapeze under a B-29 in August 1948, was grotesque in appearance and part of a faulty and extremely tricky concept, but it was all good experience. Another faulty concept that provided good experience was the notion that the new Strategic Air Command could escort its heavy bombers with jets. There was no way early jet fighters could fly even one-eighth as far as the B-36, but MAC built the impressive XF-88 Voodoo anyway, flying the first on 20 October 1948. This was a glimpse of the future, showing the shapes, structure, systems and flight characteristics that were to become familiar in the 1950s and 1960s. Vice-president engineering was Kendall Perkins, and the XF-88 project engineer was E M "Bud" Flesh, who had led the design of the radical Curtiss XP-55. The second 88 had afterburning engines and was supersonic, while the first was rebuilt for tests with a supersonic nose propeller.

On 7 August 1951 the now world-class MAC advanced-fighter team flew the XF3H-1 Demon. This was a most challenging project for a carrier fighter able to take on land-based machines such as the F-86 or even F-100. It bristled with high-lift systems and advanced structure. It would have been a major new weapon for the Navy and Marines but for an Achilles heel that was nearly fatal. Westinghouse completely failed to clear the big afterburning J40 engine for service. This almost wrecked many aircraft programs, but it hit the Demon hardest. By 1954 MAC had completed 60, and had many more on

first carrier-based jet fighter and a product of an untried design team. Several successful designs later, the present F-4 Phantom made its first flight in May 1958 and went on to set high fighter aircraft standards and to gain more records than any other aircraft. This USAF Phantom is about to receive fuel from a KC-135 tanker over the North Atlantic.

Below: Synonymous with the name McDonnell in aircraft design and production is the name Phantom. It was first applied to the XFD-1 of 1945, the US Navy's

the line, but they could not even be flown. The first 60 were ignominiously piled on barges and sent off down the Mississippi as instructional airframes, and the sight of these costly but flightless birds being towed through the streets of St Louis, while Congress raged about a supposed scandal, was tough on the planemaker whose airframes had been good. Eventually the Navy switched to the Allison J71 and by late 1956 the new family of F3H-2 Demons were setting a fine record and incidentally mating the APG-51 radar and Sparrow missile.

Likewise the termination of the XF-88 escort fighter in 1950 had a happy ending, for SAC kept thinking and in May 1953 ordered the most powerful fighter then contemplated, the F-101, still named Voodoo. Powered by two of Pratt & Whitney's new J57 two-spool engines, with short afterburners, the first flew on 29 September 1954. SAC clumsily cancelled on the same day, but TAC immediately picked up the 101 as a fighter/bomber and eventually several versions of these excellent and popular machines saw long service with the USAF and Canada; indeed as I write the Canadians have yet to select a replacement! Voodoos captured the world speed record, and established low-maintenance and high-safety records, despite the fact that they looked extremely dangerous. MAC did as much as any company to show that technical challenges answered by good engineering can actually improve standards of safety and operational readiness.

In 1959 MAC went for the USAF UCX order (won by the JetStar) with the Model 119/220 business jet, which looked like a baby 707; it was the first bizjet to be provisionally certificated, but customers

failed to appear. This was not the case for a contemporary project that had its genesis back in 1953 when the company lost the first Navy supersonic fighter contract to Chance Vought. Doggedly, it kept plugging away with mock-ups of what it thought the Navy would need and on 27 May 1958 flew the first F4H-1 Phantom II. Over the following months it became apparent that this big but unpretty fighter was a design of extraordinary potential. It gained more records, of more kinds, than any other aircraft before or since, and although built for the Navy and Marines was adopted in 1963 by the Air Force as the F-110. All versions were then given F-4 type designations, and the 5057th and last was delivered in September 1979. Except for 140 assembled in Japan, all were completed at the St Louis plant, though parts were made by Republic and other US companies and in Germany and Britain. Undoubtedly the new Phantom was the standard against which other fighters of the past 20 years have been judged.

Merger with Douglas, described later, had little effect on the work at St Louis, and later in 1967 the project staff urgently began trying to win the FX contract for the USAF, for an advanced fighter to defeat the Russian "Foxbat." Donald Malvern was chosen to lead this challenging assignment. In 1969 MCAir was selected as a finalist in what had become the F-15 program, and a year later it emerged the final choice of the Air Force. Today the

F-15 Eagle has supplanted the Phantom on the assembly line in Plant 1; it is fractionally bigger, quite different in shape and three times the price.

In 1969 MCAir unsuccessfully tried to market the Br 941 STOL, one of which was imported from France and called a Model 188, but quite different involvement with V/STOL came a year later when the company was appointed foster-parent and potential licensee for the Marines' Hawker Siddeley AV-8A Harrier. Subsequently, after studying an AV-16A and prospects for a joint program with Britain (foolishly rejected by the UK Government in 1975) MCAir developed the greatly improved AV-8B, first flown on 9 November 1978 but omitted from the 1980 US Defense Budget. As the Marines want 342 and the Navy is increasingly recognizing a need for a similar number there are grounds for believing the opposition in Congress to a "foreign airplane" will be overcome. Meanwhile St Louis has a parallel string to its bow in the F-18 Hornet. This came about by a unique chain of events. In June 1974 the Navy requested proposals for a VFAX fighter/attack aircraft, one of the responders being MCAir. A month later Congress terminated VFAX, directing the Navy instead to examine derivatives of the YF-16 and -17. The St Louis company decided Northrop's YF-17 most nearly met the requirements, and teamed with Northrop to propose a derived design with MCAir as prime contractor. LTV protested but the full-scale

contract for the F-18 was awarded on 22 January 1976. Northrop was assigned 30 percent of the engineering effort and 40 percent of the production, which involves 1366 for the Navy and Marines.

MCAir's giant role in missiles and space hardly needs repeating. McDonnell Douglas Astronautics Company (MDAC) is the merger between MAC and DAC interests, McDonnell Astronautics and the Douglas Missile and Space Systems Division having been combined but retaining their original facilities, respectively at St Louis and Huntington Beach, California. The chief MDAC missiles are Harpoon and (phasing out) Dragon, with major involvement in Tomahawk and ASALM, while prior to the merger the two companies handled the Mercury and Gemini manned programs, Roc, Honest John, Talos, Nike Ajax, Nike Hercules, Nike Zeus and Spartan, Genie, the Quail decoy, Thor and the derived Delta space launchers. The largest space items are S-IVB and Skylab, and the Space Shuttle upper stages.

Spacecraft provide a natural link with Douglas, founded by one of the most respected men in world aviation, Donald Wills Douglas. Born in Brooklyn on 6 April 1892, he graduated from the US Naval Academy in 1912 but then changed course and went to MIT. Though he did not quite emulate Loening in graduating in aero engineering by writing the syllabus, he was one of the first at MIT to major in that subject (1914). He stayed a further year as a lecturer, worked for struggling

Left: This scene captures the high drama of an F-4J Phantom of the US Navy as it reaches for the safety of the flightdeck arrester wires of the nuclear-powered aircraft carrier USS Enterprise.

Right: Donald Wills Douglas, in rear cockpit, supervises construction of a Cloudster two-seater in the rented loft of the Davis-Douglas Company in Los Angeles in 1920.

Below right: The Wiltshire Boulevard plant at Santa Monica was an abandoned film studio. The re-formed Douglas Company moved there in 1921; a DT-1 torpedo bomber for the US Navy is parked outside.

Connecticut Aircraft in 1915 and then joined Martin as chief engineer, heading the design of the MB-1 and -2 bombers. In 1920, when such a job might have seemed vital in a land over-populated with planemakers, he amicably left Martin and travelled to Los Angeles. He was impelled to test his belief that the airplane's role was to transport people and cargo. It was to be many years before he was to get into the transport business, but he did much more than merely survive.

His capital was meagre, but wealthy sportsman David R Davis put up capital for the Davis-Douglas company, registered on 22 July 1920. (Davis later developed the highly efficient wing used on the B-24.) It had both a head office and a manufacturing plant, but the office was behind a barber shop and the plant was a rented loft. It also had an order book – one sports aircraft, for Mr Davis. The result was the excellent Cloudster, a tandem-seat biplane big enough for a war-surplus 400hp Liberty engine. It carried a useful load exceeding its empty weight, but in 1921 most people who wanted to fly picked a Jenny off a scrap heap. There seemed little prospect of Ship No 2 until in February 1921, just before the Cloudster flew, Douglas heard the Navy wanted a torpedo bomber. In a week he had the specification, which had 18 pages (today it would be nearer 18,000). By March he had sent in his design, with most of the airframe based on the Cloudster but the cooling radiator on the sides instead of in a ventral tunnel. The main difference was a switch from wood to steel-tube fuselage construction, with single cockpit. To Douglas's delight he got the order, for three, the second and third being changed from DT-1 to DT-2 by having a second seat and a bluff front radiator. The Navy was pleased, and bought another 38, plus others made by licensees. These solidly built machines put Douglas on the map and enabled the reformed (5 July 1921) Douglas company to move to a big abandoned film studio on Wilshire Boulevard,

between a cow pasture and a cornfield.

In 1923 Douglas landed the contract for five aircraft to fly around the world with the Army Air Service. The DWC (Douglas World Cruiser) was a near-relative of the DT-2, and in 1924 two of them really did circumnavigate the globe in six months and six days. Ever after, the company logo was based on a globe, usually with the slogan "First around the world." There followed a succession of military machines, including the O-2 observation biplane, the T2D/P2D twin-engined seaplanes, Dolphin (RD) monoplane amphibian and gull-winged Y1B-7 bomber of 1932, the staple line being Army observation machines derived at first from the O-2.

In 1928 (30 November) Douglas was strong enough to set up his own Douglas Aircraft Company, relocated at Clover Field, Santa Monica, with head office at 3000 Ocean Park Boulevard alongside. In 1932 Jack Northrop, who had been a valued company engineer during the early 1920s, set up a separate company 51 percent owned by Douglas and operated as a subsidiary. He ran a new plant a few miles away at El Segundo where he created the

Gamma, Delta 8A (A-17) and other types variously called Northrop or Douglas. Brilliant Ed Heinemann joined him in 1932 creating the BT-1, from which stemmed the SBD Dauntless carrier-based dive-bomber of which 5936 were built by 1944, and the TBD Devastator, until mid-1942 the Navy's only torpedo bomber. More important even than these famed types was the DB-7 high-speed bomber of December 1938, from which stemmed 7385

Left: As with McDonnell, the first Douglas order in 1921 came from the US Navy and founded a line of Douglas carrier-based aircraft, including the notable SBD Dauntless dive-bomber (which became the backbone of the Pacific air war and of which about 6000 were built in 1939–44) and the A-1 Skyraider, an extremely versatile attack bomber (of which over 3000 were built between 1945 and 1957 for Navy and Air Force use). A preserved A-1 Skyraider (AD-4 under original designation) is illustrated.

Bottom left: One of the world's most widely used and successful aircraft was the Douglas DC-3/C-47/C-53/ C-117 developed first as an airliner in the middle 1930s and then by the thousand as the ubiquitous military cargo and troop transport during the war

Bostons, Havocs, A-20s, P-70s and other wartime variants. From this, after Northrop's departure, Heinemann moved on to the superb A-26 Invader, a major type in 1944–45 and still in front-line use in the Vietnam war.

Meanwhile the main plant at Santa Monica at last not merely entered the commercial transport field but came to dominate it. Boeing was so tied up by United's massive orders for the 247 that

years. The DC-3 used by the RAF as a military transport was named Dakota and the US names were Skytrain for the C-47 and Skytrooper for the C-53. The 400 produced before Pearl Harbor had rocketed to more than 10,000 by the end of the war and a further 800-odd were added thereafter. Many of the wartime-built aircraft were later converted for civil use. Illustrated is just one of several C-47 production lines that contributed to the massive total.

Below: A wartime scene outside the Douglas Santa Monica plant showing mainly DB-7 Boston/A-20 Havoc attack bombers/night fighters for the RAF and USAAF in final stages of assembly. The DB-7 and A-20/P-70/F-3 derivatives were also produced in great quantity, eventually totalled over 7000 aircraft.

its rivals came to Douglas. Santa Monica chief engineer Arthur E Raymond flew in a Ford Trimotor "Tin Goose" and carefully noted all the faults. It was not difficult to do better and on 1 July 1933 the DC-1 flew on two fully cowled Cyclones with variable-pitch propellers, with stressed-skin airframe, flaps, retractable mainwheels and many other advanced features. Thanks to Northrop it had a multi-spar wing which was so resistant to fatigue that similar wings are still in daily use. From this stemmed the DC-2, which entered service with TWA coast-to-coast, with intermediate stops, on 18 May 1934. American Airlines then inquired about a DST (Douglas Sleeper Transport) with 16 berths, or 24 seats as the DC-3 "day-plane." The first flew on 17 December 1935 and the DC-3 quickly became the world's leading air transport. By Pearl Harbor 430 had been delivered, and four years later production at several plants terminated at 10,655, with many others made in Japan and the Soviet Union.

In the late 1930s Santa Monica made two giants, the DC-4 of June 1938 and B-19 flown in June 1941. Both were single prototypes, respectively led by chief engineer Ed Burton (Raymond becoming vice-president engineering) and "Sky" Kleinhans, but they served their purpose and in 1940 Burton set course again and produced a far better and smaller DC-4, first flown as an olive-drab C-54 in April 1942. From this stemmed the main postwar DC products, the DC-4, DC-6, DC-6B, DC-7, DC-7B, culminating in the DC-7C Seven Seas. At its wartime peak in August 1943 Douglas had 157,200 employees, producing one-sixth of the US airframe weight and including 1982 B-17s made at a new plant at Long Beach opened in October 1941 to build military DC-3s.

After World War II Douglas concentrated civil transports at Santa Monica, military transports at Long Beach, Navy aircraft at El Segundo and also reopened Tulsa as a modification plant and second source for the B-66, USAF derivative of El Segundo's A-3 Skywarrior. Among the major programs were the company's biggest gamble, the risk of more than its net worth on the DC-8 civil jetliner on 7 June 1955. PanAm was at once offered two models, both the same size, one with JT3 engines and the other with JT4 engines and long-range tanks. Subsequently there were many variants culminating in the greatly stretched and refined Super Sixty series which brought production to 556 by May 1972. El Segundo produced the evergreen A-1 Skyraider, 3180 being built by 1957, the F4D (F-6) Skyray interceptor, F3D (F-10) Skyknight night fighter and

ECM platform, Skystreak, Skyrocket (first aircraft to reach Mach 2), X-3, Skywarrior and A4D (A-4) Skyhawk, production of which was continuous from 1954 to 1979.

Long Beach produced USAF transports, the C-74 and C-124 Globemasters and C-133 Cargomaster. Chief engineer John C Buckwalter was given the seemingly simple task of turning the Skywarrior into the Air Force B-66 Destroyer and found the task at least as big a job as starting with a clean sheet of paper. From the early 1960s Douglas Aircraft Company (DAC) progressively concentrated all its main operations at Long Beach, where the first major new project was the Model 2086

civil twin-jet which became the DC-9 and flew on 25 February 1965. Previously a GE-powered derivative of the Caravelle had been extensively studied, but this could not have had the success of the DC-9. The demand for extremely rapid output of hundreds of these aircraft put a burden on DAC finance that by 1967 became acute, and a further burden was imposed by the Super Sixty series of improved DC-8. Possibly DAC could have survived by massive borrowing but its bankers decided on a merger. There were numerous bidders, and MCAir was chosen on grounds of financial strength, management expertise and other factors.

Top left: Chief competitor to the Lockheed Constellation series after the war was the Douglas DC-4 to DC-7 series of four-engine long-range transports. Representative of them is the DC-6B (illustrated), operated as the Mainliner 300 *by United Air Lines and by many other carriers in the early 1950s and superseded later in that decade by the DC-7, the 7C (Seven Seas) version of which was the first piston-engined airliner to have nonstop tranatlantic capability with a profitable load.*

Above: Douglas started design studies of a small jet transport for short to medium ranges soon after the DC-8 was launched and flew the twin-jet DC-9 prototype in February 1965, two years ahead of the comparable Boeing 737. DC-9 sales have been roughly 300 units ahead of those of the 737. McDonnell Douglas has in hand at Long Beach a major redevelopment to the DC-9 Super 80 specification to provide superior fuel efficiency and noise suppression; the first entered airline service in 1980.

Douglas entered jet transport service with the DC-8 in September 1959, about a year later than the British Comet 4 and Boeing 707, both of which were providing regular transatlantic services from October 1958. But the DC-8 proved to have excellent development potential and the Super Sixty series of the late 1960s, one of which is pictured, provided mainline services until the advent of the wide-body types. Some are now being remanufactured and re-engined for service until the 1990s.

McDonnell Douglas Corporation (MDC) was incorporated on 28 April 1967. It began with 140,000 employees, sank to 57,800 in the 1976 doldrums and today has about 70,000. By far the biggest DAC program since the merger has been the DC-10, first flown on 29 August 1970. Like the DC-9 the risk was reduced by sharing it as far as possible with suppliers, and (again like the DC-9) the wing was taken on by de Havilland Canada. The floorspace at Malton (Toronto) was later purchased by MDC and the name changed to McDonnell Douglas Canada Limited. Convair received the fuselage; the vertical tail went to Aeritalia at Naples. Thanks to being able to offer a long-range version well ahead of the direct rival, Lockheed, the DC-10 became a considerable commercial success, though its image was inevitably dented by a succession of accidents that received wide publicity. In late 1979 MDC judged that this denting was a temporary phase having little effect on the future order-book. Plans then existed for a stretched DC-10-60 series, to be produced in parallel with the biggest and best of the DC-9s, the Super 80 which entered airline service in 1980.

Below: Airline acceptance and later public preference for the wide-body airliner started by the Boeing 747 brought a demand for similar spacious interiors in smaller aircraft for shorter routes. The McDonnell Douglas DC-10 and similar Lockheed TriStar resulted, both making first flights in late 1970. This photograph of the DC-10 aftersection assembly shows insulation mats and interior panelling being fitted.

Bottom: As well as building the F-15 Eagle and the F-18 Hornet derivative of the YF-17, the McDonnell St Louis plant fosters the British-built AV-8A Harrier "jump jets" (illustrated) operated by the US Marines, and has developed and flown an advanced version of the design in the AV-8B Harrier.

NORTHROP CORPORATION

Few engineers have made a greater contribution to aviation than slightly built softspoken John Knudsen (Jack) Northrop. Born in Newark, New Jersey, on 10 November 1895, he had no formal education beyond high school yet acquired a firm grasp of aviation structural design and proved it by the excellence of the wings he stressed for the Loughead F-1, as related in the Lockheed story. In 1917–18 he served with the Signal Corps, but was furloughed back to Loughead to assist the HS-2L project. There he did his best, helping to design the S-1 "Chummy" sports biplane, but there were no buyers and the company suspended operations.

Northrop spent the next three years learning all he could about advanced metal structures, especially the new stressed-skin variety. In 1923 he got a job with the Davis-Douglas company, his first assignment being to design the tankage of the DWC. In 1926 he rejoined Lockheed and masterminded the design of the ultra-clean Vega.

The main production area at Palmdale in the 1970s for the Northrop F-5E Tiger lightweight fighter when aircraft were being turned out at a rate of 20 a month to meet orders from numerous Air Forces.

The first notable design of the re-formed Northrop Company in the early 1940s was the P-61 Black Widow, the world's first purpose-designed radar-equipped night fighter.

He wanted to move into stressed-skin construction and also believed in the superior efficiency of the all-wing aircraft, but Lockheed was not receptive to either. Accordingly in 1928 Northrop set up his own small company, Avion Corporation, and built an all-wing research aircraft. Ed Bellande, the experienced airline pilot hired by Lockheed to test the first Vega, handled the test flying for Northrop, which was one of the first programs to be based at Lake Muroc (today Edwards Air Force Base).

Northrop tried both pusher and tractor versions of his Flying Wing but recognized a lot of work was needed before a saleable product could result. So he accepted Bill Boeing's proposal that Northrop should form a new company within the new and increasingly unwieldy United Aircraft and Transport Corporation. What UAT wanted was Northrop's sure hand with efficient metal structures, and the new subsidiary

called Northrop Aircraft Company appointed Jack Northrop vice-president and chief engineer. In quick succession from 1929 appeared a remarkable series of outstandingly efficient high-speed single-engined monoplanes all characterized by unbraced stressed-skin construction. The first, appropriately called the Northrop Alpha, was, in May 1930, the first stressed-skin aircraft to go into quantity production. Despite a fixed landing gear it carried seven passengers at 180mph (290km/h) on a 550hp Wasp, and spurred the Lockheed Orion and He 70, thus almost doubling the speed of the fastest airliners in two years.

The Beta of 1931 exceeded 200mph (322km/h) on only 300hp, but the Depression made the UAT management look for ways of saving costs and it told Northrop to merge with Stearman at Wichita. Northrop immediately refused. Instead he went into partnership with Donald Douglas, forming yet another company, Northrop Corporation, as a Douglas subsidiary, the parent holding 51 percent of the stock. In 1933 this went into operation at a new plant

at El Segundo, Los Angeles, with Northrop again vice-president and chief engineer. Previously El Segundo had housed Moreland Aircraft, whose designer, Ed Heinemann, joined Northrop and soon became chief engineer. The two made an exceptional team, and together they catapulted Douglas into the forefront of US military design by 1936 with such machines as Gamma, Delta, Model 2 family, the mass-produced A-17 series (also called the Douglas 8A family) for the US Army and many export customers, and the BT-1 series for the Navy from which came the SBD Dauntless. But by 1937 Douglas was putting on pressure for the El Segundo plant to become a fully owned Douglas division. Northrop again felt the time had come for a parting of the ways, and in 1937 resigned his Douglas directorship and amicably helped Heinemann set up El Segundo division and get started on the design that became the DB-7 family.

It took Northrop until early 1939 before his new Northrop Aircraft Incorporated could begin operations at Hawthorne, Los

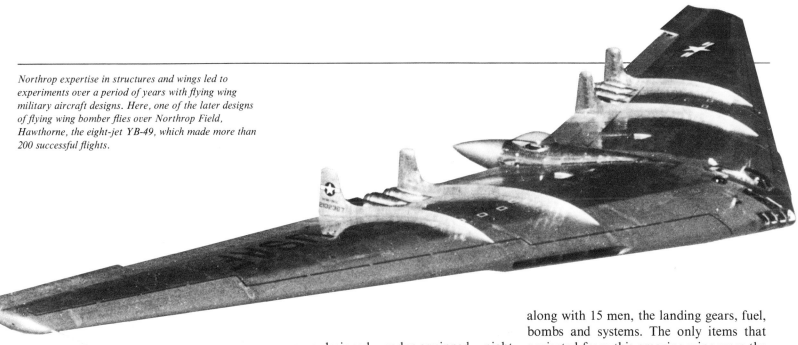

Northrop expertise in structures and wings led to experiments over a period of years with flying wing military aircraft designs. Here, one of the later designs of flying wing bomber flies over Northrop Field, Hawthorne, the eight-jet YB-49, which made more than 200 successful flights.

Angeles. Chairman of the board was La Motte T Cohu; Northrop was appointed president and chief engineer. At first small (40 people), the company grew rapidly in the military aircraft boom. Consolidated assigned Northrop the tail of the PBY Catalina. Norway ordered 24 N-3PB seaplanes. Vultee assigned half the production order for the Vengeance dive-bomber. Boeing needed extra capacity for nacelles for the B-17. Northrop agreed to develop the big axial gas turbine of Joshua Hendy and this led to the Turbodyne project of 1940–50. Most important of all, the Northrop team was entrusted with the world's first

purpose-designed radar-equipped night fighter, the P-61 Black Widow, which kept the company extremely busy until the end of World War II.

In September 1941 the USAF contracted with Northrop for the XB-35, a giant flying-wing bomber to rival the conventional B-36 as a possible vehicle for bombing Nazi-held Europe from North America. First, four N-9 research aircraft were built to get the shape and the control system right. These were among the most aesthetically beautiful aircraft in history. The monster XB-35 took off from Northrop Field, Hawthorne, for Muroc on 25 June 1946. Four 3000hp Wasp Majors were buried inside the wing,

along with 15 men, the landing gears, fuel, bombs and systems. The only items that projected from this amazing wing were the four huge pusher contra-rotating propellers. Subsequently there were numerous developments including the YB-49 with eight jets and the YRB-49A with four buried jets and two in underslung pods. Among many other flying wings were the XP-56 "Black Bullet" fighter, the XP-79 twin-jet prone-pilot fighter and the baby X-4 USAF/NASA research aircraft.

Northrop has never ceased to believe that eventually the world will be able to accept the all-wing aircraft, which remains his proudest achievement. But the business came from the conventional types. The N-23 Pioneer STOL tri-motor led to the C-125 Raider for the USAF. The XF-89 Scorpion, a twin-jet successor to the P-61, flew on 15 August 1948, and led to the production of 1050 Scorpion all-weather interceptors in 1952–57. Radioplane built large numbers of small target aircraft, while the parent company ran a large secret program for a long-range cruise missile, the SM-62 Snark, that after many problems led to operational service with SAC in 1959, with astro-inertial guidance over a range up to 6000 miles (9650km). An even less-known program was the most ad-

Successor to the Black Widow was the twin-jet F-89D Scorpion all-weather interceptor, in its day the most heavily armed of fighters and with automatic aiming and firing control; over 1000 Scorpions were built between 1952 and 1957.

vanced laminar-flow research aircraft, two B-66 bombers completely rebuilt as X-21As.

In 1953 Northrop retired and became a consultant; at 85 he still enjoys a quiet sail or round of golf. Whitley C Collins took his place, and the chief of preliminary design, Welko Gasich, developed a series of small jet proposals from which in 1955 emerged the N-156. This in turn led to the T-38 Talon supersonic trainer, 1189 of which were supplied to the USAF, and to the N-156 Freedom Fighter, first flown on 30 July 1959. The first Freedom Fighter had no US markings because it had not been ordered! Soon it was bought by the US to give to friendly nations, and before long many other customers were paying the full price. The resulting F-5 family, together with the F-5E Tiger II, had by 1980 amounted to almost 2500 aircraft.

In 1959 the company was restructured to reflect its growing diversity. Northrop Corporation set up corporate offices at Beverly Hills, the main aircraft subsidiary being called Norair Division, with plants at Hawthorne, Compton, Torrance, El Segundo, Palmdale and Edwards. Under the dynamic leadership of Tom Jones it won the fuselage of the Boeing 747, built a series of NASA lifting-body aircraft and established many subsidiaries including Northrop Electronics and the former Radio-

plane company renamed Northrop Ventura. From 1965 studies for a new fighter, the P-530 Cobra, eventually led to the YF-17 flown on 9 June 1974. From this in turn McDonnell Douglas and Northrop

derived the F-18 Hornet for the Navy and Marine Corps, and this has served as the basis for the proposed F-18L land-based version which remains a Northrop property.

Above: The Northrop YF-17 on which the new McDonnell Douglas/Northrop F-18 Hornet fighter ordered for the US Navy and Marines is based. Northrop Corporation retains full rights in the proposed F-18L land-based version of the jointly developed design.

Below: Northrop's family of low-cost high-performance aircraft on display at the unveiling ceremony for the YF-17 (right); the others, from the back l to r, are T-38 Talon supersonic trainer, F-5B tactical fighter/trainer, F-5A and F-5E.

PIPER AIRCRAFT CORPORATION

The name that, with Cessna, is known around the world as synonymous with the mass-produced lightplane was not that of an aviation man. William T (Bill) Piper was born on 8 January 1881, and between serving in the Spanish-American War and World War I he became a Harvard graduate and an engineer for US Steel. He was a big name in the oilfields at Bradford, Pennsylvania, where in 1926 the Taylor Brothers Aircraft Company was struggling to sell an indifferent product, the Chummy. Piper offered business assistance, and cash. In 1929, when some people with his assets might have been thinking of retirement, Bill Piper got into the chancy business of aviation. Mainly to keep an eye on the little firm in which he had invested, he agreed to serve as its part-time treasurer.

Despite this, in 1931 the Depression drove it into bankruptcy, and Piper bought the remains for $761. He still judged plane-making ought to be profitable, especially as C Gilbert Taylor had designed a new machine dramatically better than its predecessor. The very epitome of simplicity, the Cub had flown in September 1930. It had a fuselage of welded steel tube, a braced high wing of spruce spars and light-alloy ribs, fabric covering, a tiny engine and seats for two in tandem. At first there were no side windows, brakes, ASI or compass, but at little over $1000 Piper thought the

risk worth taking. It was characteristic of this big quiet kindly man that he named his new company Taylor Aircraft and gave Taylor a half-interest. Piper appointed himself secretary and treasurer, and made it a full-time job.

By 1934 the Taylor Cub was making money, priced at about $1425 no matter whether you chose the 35hp Szekely, 38hp Continental or 40hp Aeromarine engine. Unlike Ford, who offered "any color so long as it's black," Piper even offered customized paint jobs. He became proud of the simple but sturdy Cub, learned to fly it, and was universally called "the old man" in the works. But Taylor was a clashing personality who in 1936 resigned and again set up his own company (which triggered Auster in England but went bankrupt in 1946 and, despite being bought at public auction by C G Taylor himself, again failed to survive). In his place as chief engineer Piper appointed a totally different character, young Walt Jamouneau, whose subsequent improved Cubs were given numbers prefixed by a J.

In 1937, just as business was really picking up, the factory was destroyed by fire. Piper salvaged what he could and kept manufacture going in a warehouse, while he refitted an abandoned factory 100 miles to the southeast on the banks of the Susquehanna at Lock Haven. By the end

of 1937 Taylor Aircraft had been renamed Piper Aircraft Corporation, regularizing the situation that had actually existed since 1931. In 1938 the Lock Haven factory built the last 23 of 1196 J-2 Cubs, 647 of the new J-3 with glazed cabin and 65hp Continental, Franklin or Lycoming engine and not only proper instruments but also a carburetor-air heater, and also the first 31 of a new luxury model, the J-4 Coupe. It was to be the J-3 that was to set production records. In 1941, against official disinterest, Piper managed to persuade the military they could use the J-3. With its own funds it produced a military observation and liaison machine with extended glazing for view above and to the rear, and with military radio, first-aid pack and a rear table for maps which the backseater used by swivelling his seat 180 degrees. A young general named Eisenhower was impressed; so were Mark Clark, Omar Bradley and, eventually, every other US land and air commander in World War II. At first designated O-59A, the military model became the L-4 Grasshopper, and it accom-

Basic but efficient, and a best-seller in every language, is the Piper Cub. From its first flight in September 1930, through widespread wartime service and various improvements and derivations thereafter, the Cub formula provided business for the Piper company up to the 1950s and to a total of more than 40,000 aircraft. Pictured is a J-3 Cub flying over Booker airfield in England.

The single-engine Piper PA-28 Cherokee Arrow is an updated version of the popular Cherokee four-seater (about 15,000 sold); the Arrow improvements include a retractable undercarriage, more-powerful engine and roomier interior, and a 23mph cruising speed increase to 166mph.

plished on 65hp what the German Storch did on 240. Piper built 5673, and they used an estimated 42,000 landing places on any convenient flat area.

In 1945 Piper resumed civil production with 938 J-3s, followed by an impressive 6320 in 1946. This best-seller came to an end in 1947 at number 14,125, but the Cub formula continued with various improved models and today the total of Cubs and successors exceeds 40,000. But in the post-war era some customers were looking for more speed, range and comfort. In 1952 the company produced the "Twin Stinson," soon renamed the PA-23 Apache. While the twins grew in size and power, the singles adopted stressed skin and a low wing with the Comanche family (1956) and Cherokee (1960). Agricultural aviation like-wise moved from the Cub-like PA-18A to the low-wing all-metal Pawnee (1958), which set the pattern for monoplane ag-planes and is still in production in greatly im-proved forms.

From the start there was a big problem with Lock Haven – the river often flooded the plant. In the late 1950s Piper looked for a new site and found one in the warmth of Florida; the Cherokee was designed at the Vero Beach facility, and since then this has been the company's experimental center. The twins grew via the Aztec (1959), Twin Comanche (1962), Navajo (1964), Seneca (1970) and Turboprop Cheyenne (1969), but do not yet include a jet. Singles have blossomed in profusion, a particular star being the new Tomahawk trainer. In 1972 a catastrophic flood smashed the line at Lock Haven and caused almost a year's delay, but today a Piper concern bigger than ever before has many plants in Penn-sylvania and Florida, and also at Santa Maria, California, acquired with the Ted Smith Aerostar Corporation in 1978. Pro-duction averages around 200 per month, and Piper number 100,000 came off the Vero Beach line in April 1976.

The only sad note is struck by Bill Piper's death in 1970. The Pipers – Bill Junior, Howard and Thomas – were ousted in a stock fight. Finally in 1977 Walt Jamouneau – long since relegated from his job of creating the products – decided to retire. But Piper can survive fire, flood and new management.

Increased accommodation compared with earlier Piper twins was made available in the PA-31 Navajo intro-duced in 1964, as well as improved speed and range in some models and the first pressurized Piper in the PA-31P from 1970. Here a Navajo Chieftain fitted for eight passengers is seen in airline service at Eilat with an Israeli domestic operator.......

ROCKWELL INTERNATIONAL CORPORATION

The Rockwell story is one that ends with a name that, although big and respected, is almost unknown to the world's aviation buffs. Today Rockwell International Corporation ranks 37th in the United States, much bigger than any planemaker, but only a fraction of its operations are directly concerned with aviation. These operations rest on two precursor companies, North American and Aero Commander.

North American Aviation Incorporated was not one of the pioneers and built no aircraft until the second half of the 1930s. Then, thanks to brilliant engineering in stressed-skin military types, it overtook all its rivals in terms of sheer numbers, and in 1956 one of its F-100 Super Sabres bore the legend "50 Grand") to mark the company's 50,000th aircraft. At that time it became No 1 US defense contractor, with military sales running at well over $1 billion each year – real money in 1956!

NAA's early history is a microcosm of the US industry before and during the Depression. A root cause of the Wall Street Crash of 1929 had been excessive and uninformed gambling on the stock market, and aviation was a popular target. Like the motor industry the planemakers were numerous, financially weak and a ripe target for takeovers, amalgamations and development. The result was a small number of giant and usually unwieldy groups. The biggest was that organized by supposed financial wizard Clement M Keys, former editor of the *Wall Street Journal*, who figured in the Curtiss story. He founded North American Aviation on 6 December 1928 as a paper holding company to manage his proliferating empire of aviation acquisitions, which even then included Curtiss, Wright, Curtiss-Robertson, Cur-

tiss-Caproni, Travel Air, Moth and Keystone. In 1929 Keys bought Sperry Gyroscope, Ford Instrument, the famed pursuit-aircraft builder Berliner-Joyce and Pitcairn, and extensive air-transport operations were added including Faucett, Cubana, NY Airways, Eastern and half TWA. Two million shares were quickly sold before the bubble burst, and NAA even bought an interest in Douglas.

Aviation did not, and could not, collapse in the Depression, and 1933 found a shaken NAA selling 29 percent of itself to General Motors. The latter had set up a General Aviation Corporation, whose main component was Fokker Aircraft, itself formed by merging Atlantic Aircraft with Dayton-Wright (after the latter's assets had gone into Consolidated). Clearly there were too many companies, and NAA hived off several of its holdings into the Sperry Corporation, another holding company. General Aviation took over Berliner-Joyce, becoming General Aviation Manufacturing Corporation, and actually set itself up as a planemaker in the Dundalk, Maryland, plant originally operated by Curtiss-Caproni. General Motors sent Ernest R Breech to run the operation as NAA president. He imported two of the exceptional team of engineers formed by Douglas, James H "Dutch" Kindelberger and John Leland Atwood, to head the Dundalk engineering and management team.

There was yet a further upheaval, caused by the 1934 Air Mail Act, which required the separation of air-transport interests. TWA and Eastern were hived off, leaving NAA as solely a planemaker. Breech appointed Kindelberger president and Atwood vice-president and chief engineer. Thenceforth new products were known by

the title North American. The plant near Baltimore had 75 employees, and a motley collection of products and responsibilities including service-support for Fokkers, and manufacture of the AF-15 (ex-Fokker) flying-boat as the FLB, later redesignated PJ-1, J being the Navy letter assigned to NAA. General Aviation's own designs included the speedy GA.43 transport and 43J floatplane version, and the advanced Cyclone-powered GA-15 observation aircraft for the Army, which became the North American O-47. Kindelberger and Atwood personally directed the extremely swift design of a low-wing monoplane with tandem seats to meet an Army requirement for a modern basic trainer, the prototype being flown in April 1935. As the last previous military GA number was -15 the new machine was designated NA-16. Within ten days of first flight it was flown to Wright Field and there evaluated by the Army Air Corps. Before April was out NAA had the order.

Kindelberger decided to go for military aircraft, and selected the trainer market as the most immediate because of worldwide Air Force expansion. Dundalk did not appeal; he longed for the sunny weather and open space of California, and in January 1936 NAA set up a production line in a brand-new factory at Inglewood on the edge of Mines Field, now part of LA

Roll-out of the XFV-12 V/STOL fighter/attack aircraft prototype under development for small carrier operations at Rockwell International's Columbus, Ohio, Division in 1977. The vertical lift is obtained in novel fashion by diverting exhaust gas from the single turbofan through jets in wing and canard "tail" surfaces, thus inducing ambient air to flow over the surfaces and provide lift force considerably greater than the engine thrust.

Above: North American came comparatively late to planemaking but two of the company's designs achieved immediate success. One was the NA-16 trainer, from which was evolved the BT-9, AT-6, T-6, SNJ – Harvard, Texan and Yale – equipped variously for instruction in most of the aerial martial arts, and built in several plants to a total exceeding 20,000. Examples are still in service in various parts of the world, as the AT-6 Harvard pictured, are preserved in flying condition.

Below: A preserved example of the North American P-51D Mustang fighter, most numerous of the several marks and powered by a Packard-made R-R Merlin. After a rather muddled start recounted in the text, the Mustang turned out to be an outstanding World War II aircraft; nearly 16,000 were built.

International Airport, with 150,000 square feet (13,935m²) and 150 employees. Far-sighted Dutch – the name betrayed his ancestry, though his father had been a West Virginia steelworker – sited the ultra-modern plant so that it could swiftly be expanded. In his wildest dreams he could not have envisioned how large NAA was soon to become.

Ray Rice, who made his name on the structure of the Martin Bomber, was hired to help design a new twin-engined bomber. Ed Schmued became his assistant. In 1936 NAA had made floats for SOC-1 seaplanes to earn bread, but by 1937 the only problem was how to expand fast enough. The story of the next 30 years can be covered quickly. From the NA-16 trainer came a diverse family called BT-9s, Yales, AT-6s, T-6s, SNJs, Harvards, Texans and many other names. Their propeller snarl and gentle engine rumble were heard around the world [the author spent years sitting behind their reliable Wasp engines] and eventually, taking into account license-production and spares, the total added up to more than 20,950 aircraft. The bomber eventually matured as the B-25 Mitchell, again a familiar part of every theater of World War II and active in several inventories well into the 1950s; production at Inglewood and Kansas City amounted to 9817.

How the NAA Mustang was born is one of the classic tales of aviation. In November 1939 the British Air Purchasing Commission was expanding its efforts to buy warplanes in the United States, very much

A successful between-wars North American design was the F-86 Sabre jet fighter/fighter-bomber, which was of outstanding performance and built in several countries to a total of well over 9000. Although Sabre fighters continued (and continue) in service here and there, North American used the name also for its series of twin-jet passenger aircraft, the first of which appeared as a trainer/utility prototype in 1958. It was developed as the Sabreliner, the largest version of which, the Sabre 75 (illustrated) can take two crew and up to ten passengers.

in competition with the even more desperate French. Arthur Blaikie Purvis asked Dutch Kindelberger whether NAA could take on license-production of the Curtiss P-40 solely for Britain. Dutch telephoned Atwood and in minutes agreed that a better answer would be to build a newer and superior fighter. The British ought to have snapped up this offer, and at once hastened the Rolls-Royce discussions with the US Army and industry about license-production of the Merlin in the USA. Instead they raised all kinds of footling doubts, dragged their feet over the Merlin and made little progress for six vital months. Then, reluctantly, they said that, provided NAA purchased Curtiss P-40 wind-tunnel data (a waste of $15,000) and promised to get into production quickly, they would place an order for 320 of the proposed NAA fighter. The contract was signed on 23 May 1940. The resulting NA-73 was designed and

built in 102 days, the main engineering staff working a 16-hour day throughout. Allison were 20 days late delivering the engine and Vance Breeze finally got into the air on 26 October. Subsequently Inglewood and a new Dallas plant built 15,586 Mustangs, most of them USAAF P-51 models powered by the Packard-built Merlin. They played a greater part than any other aircraft in bomber escort and, especially in defeating the Luftwaffe at the close of World War II.

In 1944 NAA had 91,000 people, and also built 966 B-24s at Kansas City, but VJ-day brought cancellation of large contracts for the C-82 at Dallas and the P-80 at Kansas City. After the war the NAA scene was not bright and an attempt to enter general aviation with the Navion lost over $3 million (though the design itself was fine, and later made at a profit by Ryan). In 1948 General Motors had had enough

and sold its holding. GM's appointed chairman, Henry M Hogan, retired and Kindelberger took his place, Atwood became president and Rice vice-president and chief engineer. From then on NAA was on its own.

In the event, the Berlin Airlift and Korean War put renewed impetus into combat aircraft. While the F-82 Twin Mustang, FJ Fury, B-45 Tornado, AJ-1 Savage and T-28 Trojan provided bread-and-butter income, Rice's splendid team quickly applied German 35-degree swept aerofoil data to produce the prototype XP-86 Sabre, flown on 1 October 1947. As with the P-51, the F-86 Sabre out-performed all its rivals, which in Korea included the unexpected MiG-15, and it helped boost employment from 19,000 in early 1947 to 55,000 in 1954. By 1957 NAA had delivered 6933 Sabres, the most numerous sub-type being 2504 of the extremely complicated and grossly redesigned F-86D Sabre Dog all-weather gunless interceptor. Licensees built a further 2458 of various versions.

Many of the later Sabres were made in the

The second of the original designs was ordered virtually off the drawing-board to become the B-25 Mitchell medium bomber. The picture shows some of the first of the nearly 10,000 Mitchells built at North American's Inglewood and Kansas City plants on delivery to an Army Air Force unit in the Far East.

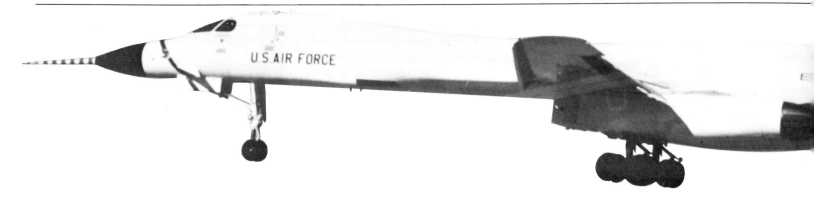

big government plant at Columbus, Ohio, that had been the last home of Curtiss in planemaking. Here was established a first-class engineering team specializing in aircraft for the Navy, including the FJ-2, -3 and -4 Furies, AJ-2 series and remanufactured T-6 variants. The former Vultee plant at Downey, near Inglewood, handled the T-28, AJ-1 and T-6G before becoming the nucleus of the Missile Development and later Space Divisions. In the 1950s it was all technical challenge and expansion. The biggest program in the first half of the decade was the F-100 Super Sabre, first

combat aircraft to reach supersonic speed in level flight, made at Inglewood and Columbus. Then Columbus developed one of the least-known but most technically advanced and successful of all warplanes, the A3J (A-5) Vigilante, which in 1979 still had no successor as the strategic eyes of the US Fleet. Columbus continued with the T-2 Buckeye and OV-10 Bronco, while Inglewood flew the first Sabreliner, built to meet the USAF UTX specification, on 16 September 1958. But the biggest projects did not mature, among them the F-107, F-108 Rapier, XB-70 Valkyrie and, by far

the greatest of all, the B-1 bomber. These events gradually demolished the once-titanic standing of NAA as top combat plane-maker, but from 1953 the lure of new technologies had resulted in the creation of very large and growing subsidiaries. Autonetics was first to fly an inertial navigation system, and became the supplier of guidance equipment for warships and spacecraft. Atomics International operated in nuclear power. Rocketdyne was almost a monopoly supplier of large lox/RP-1 engines for the Atlas, Thor and Jupiter and later for the great engines used by the Apollo Saturn rockets and Space Shuttle Orbiter. Missile Development managed the gigantic $691 million SM-64A Navaho cruise missile, the air-launched Hound Dog and numerous later programs, while Space and Information Systems succeeded it as prime contractor for the entire Apollo spacecraft, under the dynamic leadership of Harrison Storms, who had previously managed the amazing X-15 program at Inglewood from 1954 to 1964.

In 1962 NAA established the impressive Science Center, and undertook the design of many new projects including the NAC-60 SST. But the national mood gradually changed to retrenchment, and in 1967 Kindelberger, the man always regarded as Mr NAA, died in harness just two years before his company took men to the Moon. At once a long-discussed merger with a large and many-faceted automotive and light engineering company, Rockwell-Standard of Pittsburgh, took effect. Willard F Rockwell replaced Kindelberger, but At-

Above left: The North American F-100 Super Sabre, the first combat aircraft to go supersonic in level flight, was a product of the 1950s at Inglewood and Columbus. It was still in service in August 1978 when this photograph of Missouri Air National Guard Super Sabres was taken at St Louis.

Left: One of the most advanced warplanes of the 1960s was the North American A-5 Vigilante, a carrier-based Mach 2 long-range reconnaissance bomber that remains in front-line service with the US Navy into the 1980s. Pictured is an RA-5C Vigilante being hooked to a catapult on USS America for launching on a photographic sortie.

40158

The USAF s advanced manned strategic aircraft (AMSA) project of 1965 resulted in the Rockwell (North American) B-1 Mach 2.2 long-range bomber, here pictured on the prototype's first flight in December 1974. The B-1 has variable-sweep wings and a maximum range of over 6000 miles and was designed to carry a 115,000lb load at subsonic speed to distant targets and make a supersonic dash over the target protected by a mass of electronic devices. B-1 production has been cancelled but development flying continues.

wood remained as president until his retirement in 1969; his successor was Robert Anderson.

Rockwell's previous involvements in aviation included the Aero Commander company. This stemmed from the enterprise of a Californian, Theo "Ted" R Smith. Ted had been project engineer on the A-20 series for Douglas, but in 1946 set up Aero Design and Engineering Corporation at Culver City and designed and built a speedy light twin – with quite a flavor of the A-20 about it – called the Aero Commander. It flew well, matured as a product, and the company moved to Bethany, Oklahoma. Gradually engine powers, weights and capability increased, and in 1958 Aero Commander

was purchased by Rockwell. Smaller single-engined aircraft .were added, both by internal design and by external purchase, and after the merger the new North American Rockwell Corporation continued the general-aviation line as its Commercial Products Group. To avoid Anti-Trust Law infringement by having two competing business jets the Jet Commander was sold as a complete program to Israel Aircraft Industries.

Subsequently there was a succession of reorganizations. The arrangement in mid-1979 was for the parent, Rockwell International, to control North American Aircraft Group, with offices at El Segundo at 2230 East Imperial Highway, formerly the

front door of the plant called Douglas El Segundo Division, and North American Space Operations at the same address. The Aircraft Group has five operating divisions. Los Angeles Division, at 5701 West Imperial Highway, on the same Los Angeles street, at what was called the Inglewood plant, handles the B-1 and derived projects and makes tooling and parts for the DC-9, 727, 737 and 747 and many other aircraft. Columbus handles the OV-10, T-2 and XFV-12 programs. Tulsa is another big producer of tooling and parts, mainly under subcontract. Sabreliner, with executive offices in St Louis, has an expanded range of models of its proven bizjet. General Aviation at Bethany produces a wide range of singles and twins, the latest being the Commander 700 and 710 developed in partnership with Fuji of Japan though Rockwell looks like pulling out of this new light twin project.

Rockwell International OV-101 Enterprise Space Shuttle Orbiter, the first produced for NASA, takes off atop an adapted Boeing 747 during a series of unpowered approach and landing tests completed in 1977.

RYAN

Ryan's most prestigious products were a series of
primary trainers for the Services. The company was
reconstituted in 1931. PT-21 Army and NR-1 Navy
trainers await delivery at Lindbergh Field, San Diego.

Standing in front of his most famous product is
T Claude Ryan, founder in 1922 of Ryan Airlines
Incorporated, the company which designed and built
the monoplane Spirit of St Louis in which Charles
Lindbergh made the first nonstop flight from New York
to Paris in May 1927. To reach the starting point
Lindbergh tested both his own and the plane's mettle
by flying from San Diego to New York City with a
single stop.

SIKORSKY AIRCRAFT

To a unique degree this is the story of one man. A man who, although quiet, unassuming, modest to a degree ("If I had not done this, someone else would have") and the very personification of what we mean by the adjective "good," had yet the unshakeable tenacity to persist in the face of seemingly insuperable obstacles. As a result his life was described as "almost too rich in achievement for one man." In effect he had three careers. The first resulted in the large multiengined airplane. The second resulted in the long-range transport flying-boat. The third resulted in the practical helicopter.

Igor Ivanovich Sikorsky was born in Kiev, capital of the Russian Ukraine, on 25 May 1889. He chose his father well; Dr Ivan Sikorsky was, among many other things, professor of mental and nervous disorders at the University of Kiev and was said to "work a 36-hour day." His second son, young Igor, entered the Naval Academy at St Petersburg in 1903 and the Kiev Polytechnic Institute in 1907; in 1908 he decided his immediate objective was to build a helicopter. With his family's blessing – though brother Sergei, at least, tried to prove the objective nonsensical – he went to Paris in January 1909 and returned to Kiev four months later with an Anzani engine, plenty of advice and a few scraps of hard fact. Working day and night he built a co-axial helicopter, started it up in July – just

as Blériot was crossing the Channel on the preceding engine off the Anzani line – and measured its lift at 350lb (159kg). He then returned to Paris, watched airplanes in flight, bought two more Anzanis and built a second helicopter that very nearly lifted completely off the ground.

Had it actually flown Igor would have clung to helicopters, would have failed to find success and would probably have been injured or killed. Instead he decided he ought to shelve this kind of aircraft for a while and build airplanes. He also roared round Kiev in a high-speed four-seat sleigh driven by one of the Anzanis with which he gained not only notoriety but also much knowledge of propeller design and construction. In early 1910 he began testing his S-1 biplane, but the 15hp Anzani simply could not quite get it off the ground. By June he had built S-2, with a 25hp Anzani arranged to drive a tractor propeller; he had seen too many of his friends killed by being crushed by rear-mounted pusher engines. On 3 June 1910 S-2 took off and flew for 12 seconds. On many subsequent flights Igor learned a bit more, but take-off, cruising and landing speed were all about the same, and the S-2 always settled back on the ground of its own accord after a short distance.

It was not until April 1911, after agonizing financial support from his family and a conscious decision to abandon any "pro-

per" career and give all to aviation, that Sikorsky took off in S-5, a superior 50hp machine in which he at last made sustained flights. By the end of summer 1911, he was flying an hour at a time at 1500ft (460m). In 1912 the 100hp S-6 disappointed, but Igor worked at it until, in the S-6A, he had a machine that could fly at 70mph (113km/h) with three adults aboard. Sikorsky's fame spread, and in April 1912 he was appointed chief engineer and designer of the new aircraft division of the Russo-Baltic Wagon Works. He won an important military aircraft competition, repaying most of the debt he owed his family. Most important, Shidlovskii, the chairman, enthusiastically agreed with his young designer's suggestion that they build a large four-engined machine. On 13 May 1913 the resulting *Le Grand* made a perfect first flight.

From this stemmed the even larger *Ilya Mourometz* of January 1914, which five months later made a truly remarkable cross-country flight to Kiev from St Petersburg and back, with one stop in each direction. During the flight there was fire in the air, turbulence, a forced landing, a downwind take-off over a cliff, over 20 hours of blind cloud flying and a few marvellous periods when Igor walked on the catwalk above the fuselage enthralled at the scene above the turbulent clouds. There followed orders for a military bomber version, the formation of the EVK, the Squadron of Flying Ships, and production of more than 75 great IM-type bombers, which made over 400 missions against targets in German-held territory. Only one was shot down, and that after destroying three German fighters.

Then came the Revolution, chaos, summary shooting of the EVK officers and what Igor considered elimination of moral values. In March 1918 he sailed alone from Murmansk with nothing but a suitcase and a few hundred English pounds; he left behind the equivalent of about $500,000. For some weeks he worked on a big bomber for France but it was cancelled at the Armistice. Again he set sail, on 24 March 1919, for New York. There followed years of heartbreak, for it was the worst possible time to arrive on the US aviation scene; but on 5 March 1923 the Sikorsky Aero Engineering Corporation was registered in New York, and proceeded to build the S-29A on a chicken farm on Long Island. It suffered engine failure and was wrecked on its first take-off. Somehow Sikorsky raised $2500, rebuilt it with 400hp Liberty engines and made a splendid flight on 25 September 1924. It subsequently flew on every kind of mission all over the US, often piloted by Colonel Roscoe Turner,

Igor Sikorsky holds a model of his heavy-lift CH-54 Tarhe helicopter for the US Army; it was developed out of the S-64 Skycrane prototype first flown in May 1962.

and finally "died" in a staged crash as a "German bomber" in Howard Hughes epic film *Hell's Angels*.

Always tottering on the edge of bankruptcy, Sikorsky and his brilliant co-designer Mike Gluhareff achieved a production total of ten aircraft with their first nine US designs. In November 1926 the surprisingly growing company moved into a fine rented factory at College Point near the future site of New York's La Guardia airport. Here was designed the S-38 ten-seat amphibian. The Navy tested it, ordered two, followed by PanAm and a host of other customers, until 114 had been built. In 1928 the company was reorganized as the Sikorsky Aircraft Corporation, growing fast, and in the spring of 1929 SAC became a subsidiary of the great United Aircraft and Transport Corporation. Eugene Wilson, appointed the Sikorsky president, was told to cut costs, but Igor explained that, to Russians who had lived through a revolution, a stock crash was a mere tremor!

The next ten years were spent building bigger and better boats for PanAm's growing long-distance routes. Charles Lindbergh, PanAm consultant on new routes, recalled the long all-night meetings with PanAm chairman Juan Trippe, chief engineer Andre Priester and Igor all arguing in their extremely contrasting accents. But out of it came such great aircraft as the S-40 and S-42, the former with its walnut-panelled corridor which Igor vividly "saw" in every detail – in flight – in a dream in the year 1900.

While the Stratford plant produced the even more efficient S-43 amphibian and the giant XPBS-1, United Aircraft moved Vought out of Hartford and into Stratford, calling the combined division Vought-Sikorsky. The production civil XPBS-1 thus became the VS-44, not just S-44. The merger lasted from 1 April 1939 until 31 December 1942. And in that period Igor developed a practical helicopter. His temporary shelving of the concept had lasted over 30 years. And it matured just in time to save the division from being closed down, because flying-boats were no longer wanted.

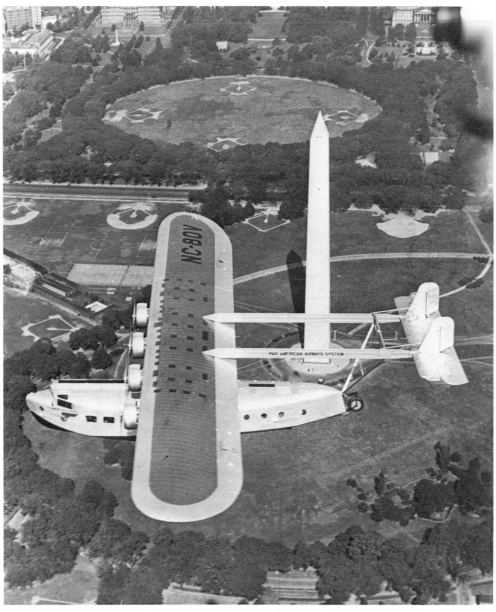

Above right: Sikorsky's first commercial designs, for the Russo-Baltic Wagon Works, were the huge four-engined Le Grand *(pictured) and* Ilya Mouroumetz, *of 1913–14, on which were based the successful Russian bombers of World War I.*

Right: Sikorsky's first success after emigrating and setting up in the US occurred with amphibians and flying-boats for early long-distance airline services. The machine pictured here flying over Washington, an S-40 amphibian American Clipper *built for Pan American, was vividly "seen" by Sikorsky in a dream in 1940.*

Igor had never stopped thinking about the helicopter, and in 1926 and again in 1930 drew machines very much like the one he actually built. But not until the late 1930s could he devote all his energies to it in the way he knew the difficult rotary-winged craft would demand. After prolonged research and test he climbed into the first-built of what was to be a much-rebuilt VS-300 and, on 14 September 1939, lifted the wheels off the ground. The craft vibrated, pitched, bucked and seemed hard to control, but disaster was avoided by four ropes underneath on which hung a tray so heavy it could not be lifted off the ground. Gradually, with several false starts, the VS-300 became the 300A, while the by-then-small Sikorsky company moved to a renovated factory at Bridgeport (the Vought division stayed at Stratford building Corsairs).

In spring 1941 the US Army ordered a two-seat observation and training helicopter, the XR-4. On the day after Pearl Harbor the VS-300A flew in its final simplified configuration and the XR-4 followed on 13 January 1942. From this two-seater came all subsequent Sikorsky helicopters, whose success caused the division of what on 1 May 1975 was renamed United Technologies Corporation to rise once more from being a loss-making dwarf into a profitable giant. Igor retired as engineering manager in July 1957, and died in October 1972. Today, under a predictably outstanding president, Gerald J Tobias, Sikorsky Aircraft is bursting at the seams with business and has licensees in countries around the world.

Above: Sikorsky's return to his original interest in aviation resulted in the world's first practical helicopter, the VS-300, which first flew in September 1939. Here Sikorsky flies the VS-300A in 1941.

Below: One current example from the remarkably versatile range of helicopters that have been developed out of the VS-300's basic principles, is the pair of Sikorsky RH-53 mine-countermeasures Sea Stallions in service aboard the nuclear-powered carrier USS Nimitz.

VOUGHT CORPORATION

Chance Milton Vought was another of those fortunate men born in the right place (in this case New York City) at the right time (26 February 1890) to make his mark in aviation. At the same time it was not possible to do this without having exceptional qualities. Vought had several, despite the modest means of his parents – his father was an immigrant boatbuilder. Vought was one of those who died young, but the company he founded, after many changes, mergers and takeovers, still proudly bears his name.

Young Chance struggled through school and the University of Pennsylvania and in 1910 travelled to Cicero, Chicago, to learn to fly at the Wright-founded Lillie School of Aviation. But he was no wild barnstormer. By this time he was already a mature engineer, and soon became an above-average pilot. Modest in stature, and neat and dapper in appearance, he was instant in his responses and engagingly profane. He personified the slick fast-talking guys in the early Hollywood movies, but behind it was a deep knowledge and sound judgment.

From 1912 he consulted for the Aero Club of Illinois, taught at the Lillie School, rebuilt a Wright pusher as a tractor (it went faster), edited the weekly *Aero and Hydro,* designed a trainer for the Mayo

The Vought F-8 Crusader was the winner of a 1953 competition for a supersonic fighter capable of landing on a carrier's flightdeck and deliveries began to the US Navy in March 1957. The French Navy bought a batch of a later developed version, the F-8E (FN) of 1961, one of which is pictured here.

Brothers, joined the Wrights in Dayton as structural engineer, became the chief designer at Wright-Martin, and then, in early 1917, went into partnership with his father-in-law, Birdseye B Lewis, to build military aircraft. The Lewis & Vought Corporation set up shop in Long Island City on the third floor of a small factory already humming with war contracts.

Vought's first production design, the VE-7, was a classic that was to influence both his own and others' aircraft for 20 years. A mere trainer, it out-performed many pursuits, and the Navy bought 128 in the post-Armistice doldrums, some made by the Naval Aircraft Factory. That Vought could actually deliver any at all is remarkable, because the parts of each machine were lowered by pulley-block out of a window and final assembly took place on the ground outside. When each machine was complete it was tethered by the tail to a nearby telephone pole for the engine test.

In 1922 Lewis retired, and the company was renamed the Chance Vought Corporation. Its first product was the UO-1 observation aircraft, and the derived FU-1 pursuit. The factory was improved so that it had a proper assembly hall, and it was here that in January 1925 Frederick B Rentschler came to see his old friend. Rentschler had lately resigned as chief executive at Wright and wanted to start up a new company to build a better engine. But times could hardly have been more adverse, and he wanted Vought's opinion. According to the history of Pratt & Whit-

Jimmy (later Major General) Doolittle, one of the giants of flying, and the Pratt & Whitney Wasp-engined Vought O2U-1 Corsair biplane which became the standard Navy observation aircraft. The Corsair in this picture was the research aircraft of the Guggenheim Flight Laboratory with which Doolittle conducted practical research into the problems of flight in poor visibility.

ney Aircraft – which Rentschler soon founded – Vought's immediate reaction was "You're blasted right; things are in a hell of a shape, and getting no better fast." He then asked Rentschler "When are you coming back into the rat-race anyhow? A man can't develop ulcers and high blood-pressure half as fast anywhere else as in aviation,

and you damn well know it." So Rentschler told Vought about his plans for the Wasp engine, and Vought broke a firm rule and told Rentschler about his plans for the Corsair. Thus in 1927 the Wasp reached the Navy in the first of a long family of mass-produced Corsairs (and in many other aircraft), and the company was hard-pressed to meet demand.

Predictably the company was snapped up by the investors and in 1929 became a division of the giant United Aircraft and Transport Corporation. In fact, the three prime instigators of the vast enterprise were Vought, Rentschler and Boeing. The first two built large new plants in East Hartford, Connecticut, into which they moved in 1930. Both plants were planned for future expansion, despite the depression. Expand they would, but Vought was ill, brought on by overwork, and when he contracted blood-poisoning in the pre-penicillin era his body had no defense and he died on 26 July 1930.

Rex Beisel headed the engineering team in the new plant, and under his direction Vought produced newer Corsairs, the SBU scout bomber, and numerous prototypes. In October 1934 the Navy ordered the first SB2U monoplane, later named Vindicator and a valued scout and dive-bomber until 1943, used by the French Aéronavale as the V-156F and by the British Fleet Air Arm as the Chesapeake. In March 1937 came the first order for an even bigger series, the OS2U Kingfisher, the most important shipboard scout of the wartime Navy of which

1006 were delivered from Stratford in 1941–42. Stratford had been the home of Sikorsky, but on 1 April 1939 the merged Vought-Sikorsky Division went into action to allow Pratt & Whitney to expand into the previous Vought plant. While merged, the Sikorsky XPBS-1 was developed into the Vought-Sikorsky VS-44A boats, and the wartime products were known by the name Vought-Sikorsky despite the fact that the rather strained union only lasted until the end of 1942.

On 1 January 1943 Chance Vought Division became sole occupier of the growing Stratford works. By far its most important product was the great F4U Corsair, bearing no resemblance to any of the Corsair biplanes. When Beisel designed this fighter in 1938 it had the biggest engine, biggest propeller and probably largest wing of any fighter in history. The first XF4U flew from Stratford on 29 May 1940. On the fifth flight bad weather and near-zero fuel resulted in a forced landing on the Norwich golf-course which, because of the wet

grass, was almost fatal. The great Corsair ended upside-down among trees but was so strong it was flying again in the autumn and on 1 October 1940 reached 405mph (652-km/h) in level flight. This world record for a fighter was a key factor in the termination of Pratt & Whitney's liquid-cooled engines and concentration on the R-2800 Double Wasp. Eventually the Corsair reached the Navy in October 1942, though it was Britain's Fleet Air Arm that first used it from carriers. Production was augmented by Goodyear and, to a smaller degree, by Brewster, and Corsairs continued to be built until December 1952, the last piston-engined combat aircraft in production. The

The Corsair name and the Wasp engine link were retained for the Vought F4U Corsair, mightiest fighter of its day, which first flew in May 1940 and went on to serve with the British and New Zealand forces as well as the US Navy and Marines and end up as the last piston-engined warplane to be built, with a total production of over 12,500. Pictured is an F4U-4 aboard the escort carrier USS Sicily being armed for a strike on Korea in 1950.

The continuing Vought and Pratt & Whitney co-operation brought the Twin-Wasp Junior-powered Vought-Sikorsky XSB2U monoplane in 1936, which entered service with the US Navy as the Vindicator in 1937 and served until 1943 as a fleet scout and dive-bomber. An SB2U-3 is illustrated.

final total of F4Us built was 12,571.

The F6U Pirate suffered from the low-thrust J34 jet and only 30 production examples were built in 1949. A year previously the division had been asked by the Navy to move to the Naval Industrial Reserve plant at Dallas, Texas, and the move took most of 1949. By this time the general manager was Frederick O Detweiler, who had previously worked for Pratt & Whitney and Sikorsky and was thought to be a strong United Aircraft man. Yet under him the company ceased to be a division, and in 1954 was incorporated with Detweiler as president. Almost at once it won the extremely important F8U Crusader contract for a supersonic carrier-based fighter, while producing the radical and often troublesome F7U Cutlass. (The even stranger circular-wing V-173 and XF5U remained prototypes.)

Vought built 290 of the final F7U-3 version of the Cutlass, as well as 514 Regulus 1 cruise missiles and numerous supersonic Regulus 2 missiles and KD2U targets. The first F8U went supersonic on its first flight on 25 March 1955, and by 1965 the production total had reached 1259, over 450 of which have been remanufactured for further service. On 31 December 1960 the company was renamed Chance Vought Corporation, reflecting its diversity, but on 31 August 1961 it merged with Ling-Temco Electronics to form Ling-Temco-Vought (LTV). The Dallas plant became LTV Aerospace Division. Work continued on the LTV/Hiller/Ryan XC-142 tilt-wing V/STOL transport, and in February 1964 the company won the very important VAX attack competition that led to the A-7 Corsair II, of which 1500 had been delivered by 1979. In 1972 LTV Aerospace became a subsidiary of LTV Corporation, but after further changes the name was changed on 1 January 1976 to Vought Corporation with employment stable at 11,400. Vought made most of the airframe and landing gear of the Lockheed S-3A Viking, as well as tails for 747s and DC-10s, parts for C-130s and P-3s and many other items as well as, in Vought's Michigan Division, the Lance missile.

Above: An LTV A-7 Corsair II light attack aircraft with its hook just about to pick up an arrester wire as it touches down on USS Nimitz. The A-7 is an Allison (Rolls-Royce) Spey-engined development of the LTV F-8 Crusader and as well as a multi-barrel 20mm cannon it can carry a massive 15,000lb load of various weapons.

Below: Like many of the big aerospace concerns, LTV has a stake in general aviation through its Vought Aircraft Services Division, but specializing in modifying and/or finishing other makes of, rather than building, business and private aircraft. Here Aerostar twins are seen at VASC's Fort Worth hangar ready for individual customers.

This company, originally called Boulton & Paul, had been long established in Norwich as structural engineers specializing in frames for buildings in wood and later in steel. By 1915 it was caught up in the war effort, receiving a contract for 25 FE.2bs that was soon and often increased. The Aircraft Department of Boulton & Paul had the good fortune to be managed by Geoffrey Ffiske, a man who actively sought work and did not hesitate to innovate and to improve existing machines, which later included FE.2ds, Camels and Snipes. By 1917 the company had decided to set up a design office, and again struck it lucky in securing the services of John Dudley North.

North was one of the teenagers who got in on the "ground floor" of aviation by solid capability backed up by enthusiasm. In 1911, when he was 18, he became a member of Horatio Barber's Aeronautical Syndicate, and a year later he was appointed chief engineer of the Grahame-White Company. In 1915 he became superintendent of the aviation department at Austin Motors where he handled the design of several machines including the promising Austin-Ball scout, which might have become a major type but for the death in action of Major Albert Ball VC. In 1917 he joined the Norwich firm as chief engineer and director.

His first Norwich design was a biplane fighter, at first called the P.3 Hawk but later given the odd name of Bobolink. It had a better performance than the rival Sopwith Snipe, and some observers were puzzled at the latter's selection as the

replacement for the Camel. Next came the P.6, the first pure aerodynamic-research aircraft. (As the parent company's sales manager used it on his business trips, it was probably also the first company executive aircraft.) Then came the P.7 Bourges, a substantial twin-engined bomber which, had it appeared earlier in the war, would have inflicted severe damage on the opposition. In the hands of Frank Courtney it was publicly looped, rolled, spun, and held its own in combat with two of the contemporary Nighthawk fighters.

In the lean early 1920s North devised and perfected a way of making tubing from stainless steel by wrapping rolled strip around onto itself through grooved rollers and pinching the edge over a bead formed on the opposite edge. Allied to neat standardized attachment fittings this gave light, strong and maintenance-free construction and was first put to use in the Sidestrand bomber of 1926. A descendant of the Bourges, this twin-Jupiter machine not only outflew RAF fighters but set new standards of bombing accuracy. It equipped 101 Squadron for seven years, being replaced in 1934 by the Overstrand. The P.64 and 71A were fast civil transports contemporary with the Overstrand.

In 1934 a new company, Boulton Paul Aircraft, took over the B & P aircraft business, and two years later left its Mousehold airfield near Norwich in favor of a large new works and airfield near Wolverhampton. There North led the design of the Defiant, to specification F.9/35 calling for a fighter armed with a turret with four

machine guns. Flown on 11 August 1937, it proved to be pleasant to handle, and in its first actions with 264 Squadron in May 1940 seemed to be hacking down Luftwaffe fighters with ease. By the end of May the Messerschmitts had learned how to cope, and showed that the Defiant concept was a great mistake. Despite this, production continued until 1064 had been built, some later being used as night fighters, target tugs and in air/sea rescue duties. BPA also produced many thousands of gun turrets used in Halifaxes, Liberators, Albemarles and many other types, and also produced Fairey Barracuda carrier-based attack aircraft.

The main postwar type was the P.108 Balliol, a side-by-side Merlin-powered advanced trainer of which 132 were made by Boulton Paul plus a further 30 made by Blackburn. They were popular, and much used in weapon training, night attack and fighter control research. North became BPA managing director in 1948 and chairman in 1951, and designed a series of Mach 0.95 research deltas, the P.111, 111A and 120 which were enterprisingly flown by chief test pilot "Ben" Gunn throughout the early 1950s. By this time the company was a leader in powered flight controls, providing such systems for the Vulcan, Buccaneer, VC10, One-Eleven, Belfast and Concorde. It also moved strongly into aircraft armament systems, electronics and automatic controls, and pioneered fly-by-wire technology from 1950 to the present. In 1969 it was acquired by the Dowty Group and is now called Dowty Boulton Paul.

Left: After Boulton & Paul's entry into the aircraft industry building FE.2s and Sopwith Camels and Snipes, the company embarked on its own designs, specializing in multi-engine fast and remarkably maneuverable reconnaissance day bombers of which the best-known was the Sidestrand of the late 1920s. Among the several designs that preceded the Sidestrand were the Bourges, the Bolton, the Bugle and the Bodmin. The last-named (illustrated) was of steel construction and featured a pair of nosewheels (as did the Bolton) to prevent noseovers and two fuselage-mounted engines each driving tractor and pusher propellers by bevel gears and shafts.

Above: The 1930s and threat of World War II brought Boulton Paul back to the single-engine fighter concept from which the Defiant two-seater stemmed. Oddly, it had no fixed forward-firing guns but a powered turret mounting four .303 Brownings, which occasionally took the enemy by surprise. More generally, however, the Defiant came off badly in day fighting but it proved much more successful as a night fighter. A wartime Defiant production line is pictured.

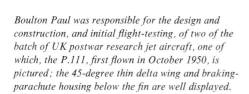

Boulton Paul was responsible for the design and construction, and initial flight-testing, of two of the batch of UK postwar research jet aircraft, one of which, the P.111, first flown in October 1950, is pictured; the 45-degree thin delta wing and braking-parachute housing below the fin are well displayed.

BRITISH AEROSPACE

For many years Britain's Labour Party adopted nationalization of major industries as a basic political creed, and it was especially eager to take over aerospace manufacturing because of the high proportion of government funding and general government involvement in major programs. It became a subject fraught with emotion and acrimony, especially after the wholesale cancellations of almost all the British military aircraft programs between 1955 and 1965. The violence of the arguments for and against can be imagined, while the general consensus view was probably that it was a lot of steam generated to little purpose, as nationalization was at best irrelevant and at worst diverted money to shareholders (as compensation) that might have been used to fund programs. After a most stormy passage the Aircraft and Shipbuilding Industries Act 1977 was passed by a hairsbreadth majority, as a result of which on 20 April 1977 ownership of BAC, HSA, HSD and Scottish Aviation was vested in a new government-owned corporation called British Aerospace.

Who was included caused as much argument as the basic idea. BAC and the aviation parts of Hawker Siddeley could not escape, but while Scottish Aviation was said to be strongly pro-nationalization (even if its owner, the Cammell Laird Group

was not) the workers at Westland took the contrary view, whereupon the government stated that making helicopters was not planemaking. The Act aroused further controversy by giving whoever might be the appropriate Minister the power to take over any other company he saw fit to add; in particular such major accessory companies as Lucas and Dowty were named, but not at that time nationalized.

British Aerospace was restructured on 1 January 1978 into an Aircraft Group and a Dynamics Group, the latter being responsible for missiles, RPVs and space. While corporate headquarters is at the former Vickers works at Brooklands Road, Weybridge, the Aircraft Group headquarters is at the former HSA factory at Richmond Road, Kingston. Within the Aircraft Group are six operating divisions. Kingston-Brough Division administers Kingston-upon-Thames (3350 employees, Harrier and Hawk), Dunsfold (800, Harrier, Hawk), Brough and Holme-on-Spalding Moor (4700, BAe 146, Harrier, Hawk and parts of six other programs), Hamble (1750, Harrier, Hawk, A300/310) and Bitteswell (1100, Hawk assembly and major work on Buccaneer and Vulcan). Hatfield-Chester Division administers Hatfield (3600, BAe 146 and parts of A300/310 and 125) and Chester (3700, A300/310 and 125). Weybridge-

Bristol administers Weybridge (4000, 146, One-Eleven, VC10 tanker, Tornado and parts of six other programs), Bristol (4600, 146, VC10 tanker, One-Eleven and parts of four others) and Hurn (2050, One-Eleven and parts of nine others). Manchester administers Chadderton (3600, Nimrod 2 and 3, 748, 146 and parts of A300/310), Woodford (2700 Nimrods and 748) and Bracebridge Heath (200, divisional repair and overhaul). Warton comprises Warton itself (6000, Tornado, Jaguar and Strikemaster), Preston (5550, same products) and Samlesbury (2700, same, plus Canberra). Scottish Division has 1400 at Prestwick on Jetstream, Bulldog, 146 and Tornado.

The BAe predecessor groups were British Aircraft Corporation (BAC), Hawker Siddeley Aviation (HSA), Hawker Siddeley Dynamics (HSD) and Scottish Aviation. HSD is not included in this book because it was not a planemaker. The stories of the other groups are outlined on the following pages, beginning with BAC whose constituent parts were Bristol, English Electric, Hunting and Vickers. HSA and its predecessors then follow, starting with AWA on page 113. Scottish Aviation and predecessors begins on page 133. Other (non-BAe) companies continue from page 141.

A new shape appeared in the sky and new levels of speed, with journey times between North America and Europe and the UK and Middle East virtually halved, followed introduction of Concorde into airline service in 1974.

G-BOAC

BRISTOL AEROPLANE CO.

Unlike almost all other planemakers, the great Bristol company was formed by wealthy businessmen having no connection with aviation, who in 1909 took the almost unbelievable step of sinking a personal fortune in an industry that scarcely existed. Sir George White (Baronet), his brother Samuel and son George Stanley White had been the proud family that had formed the Imperial Tramways Company, which in the era of the horse-bus had provided many British cities with electric tramways (street-cars); in Bristol it also added a city-wide taxicab network. Unlike almost all their associates, they had the vision to see a future in which airplanes would carry people and goods commercially; after visiting French pilots and constructors they decided in September 1909 to start a major aircraft company in Bristol.

They announced their intention at the annual meeting of the Bristol Tramways in the Grand Hotel, Bristol, on 16 February 1910, taking care to emphasize that every penny was coming out of their own pockets and not from the Tramways stockholders. Sir George registered four new companies three days later, choosing the third name – the British and Colonial Aeroplane Company – as the trading company, with £25,000 capital. As well as Sir George, Samuel and G Stanley, the officers included Henry White Smith as secretary and Sydney E Smith as manager. License-manufacture of the French Zodiac biplane, itself a Voisin design, began in Tramways sheds at the northern terminus of the line at Filton, but in May 1910 the first failed to fly at Brooklands and eventually the license was cancelled. George Challenger at once produced drawings of a biplane copied from the Henry Farman but with improved details. Dubbed the Boxkite, it was a great success, and 76 were built. The last six came from the Tramways works at Brislington, which swelled production to meet demand, while "Bristol" flying schools were soon thriving at Brooklands and Larkhill. At the latter field pupils were sometimes grateful for a gap in the line of hangars, which was actually left to allow the rising Sun to be seen on midsummer day at Stonehenge.

Production in World War I included 371 of the nimble Scout C and D series, a 100mph design flown in February 1914; hundreds of B.E.s; 125 beautiful M.1C monoplanes, another potential war-winner unappreciated by the authorities, but snapped up as their personal hacks by senior officers; and the superb F.2B Fighter, total output of which, by numerous manufacturers, was 5252.

On 31 December 1919 the name was switched to the Bristol Aeroplane Company, with capital of £1 million, and a year later Roy Fedden's engine team from the defunct Cosmos company started the Bristol Engine Department, which swiftly overtook the original business in sales and

Bottom left: Aircraft erection in progress at the Filton works of the British & Colonial Aeroplane Company in February 1911. Under construction are Boxkites (background) and one of the monoplanes designed by George Challenger and Archibald Low, later of Vickers (British & Colonial Nos 35 and 36).

Left: The Bristol Bulldog was the standard RAF home defense fighter from 1929 until the middle 1930s; it represented a significant advance over its predecessors with a top speed of more than 170mph and a time to 20,000ft of about 17 minutes. Pictured here is a Mk IIA after its restoration to flying condition. It crashed and was destroyed shortly after the photograph was taken.

Below: Chief engineer of Bristol Aeroplane Company between the wars, Captain Frank Barnwell, takes a close look at the 490hp Jupiter engine of a Bulldog. (created by his opposite number for engines, Roy Fedden).

On display at the RAF Pageant at Hendon in 1936 is the Bristol 143, an intended passenger version of the Type 142 Britain First *that became the Blenheim medium bomber. It was fitted with Bristol Aquila sleeve-valve engines in place of the Blenheim's poppet-valve Mercury engines.*

profitability. While the Jupiter, Mercury, Pegasus and the new range of sleeve-valve engines sold all over the world, there were only two real production aircraft between the wars, the Bulldog fighter of 1927 and the Blenheim bomber derived as a private venture from a high-speed transport in 1936. In 1935 Bristol became a public limited company, and began a process of expansion that took it in 1942 to a payroll of over 52,000. Output during World War II included 3672 Blenheims (preceded by 2540 prewar), 1317 Beauforts and 5557 Beaufighters; a further 700 Beauforts and 364 Beaufighters were made in Australia.

Most of the Beaufighters were made at a government Shadow Factory (a duplicate of the original design authority's facilities) at Old Mixon, Weston-super-Mare, and design and manufacture went on in over 340 separate locations, mainly in the Bristol area. On 1 July 1944 the overdue establishment of separate Aircraft and Engine divisions took place, and in January 1956 these were renamed Bristol Aircraft and Bristol Aero-Engines. From 1944, while Leslie Frise and Archibald Russell directed fixed-wing design, Raoul Hafner developed helicopters, the first of which was the Type 171 Sycamore. After building 94, production was transferred to the Weston-super-Mare factory where the tandem-rotor Type 173 gradually evolved via the 191 into the RAF Belvedere. Fixed-wing products included

the giant one-off Type 167 Brabazon, the successful Type 170 Freighter of which 214 were sold, and the Type 175 Britannia, an outstanding long-range turboprop liner which, had it matured more swiftly, would have sold in hundreds instead of only 79. Britannia developments included the Canadair CL-28 Argus and CL-44 and various more powerful or thin-winged versions studied in partnership with Convair.

In the late 1950s the environment was one of government pressure towards "shotgun weddings," typified by the failure of the outstanding Bristol 200 in the face of the

so-called Airco consortium to build the DH.121. When Vickers and English Electric teamed up to get the TSR.2 contract, the Bristol board decided this was their best bet in a bleak future and formed 20 percent of British Aircraft Corporation in February 1960, Bristol Helicopter Division being taken over by Westland after pressure from Duncan Sandys. In April 1959, again with TSR.2 business in view, Bristol Aero-Engines amalgamated with Armstrong Siddeley Motors to form Bristol Siddeley Engines. Sadly for former Bristol shareholders this company sold out to Rolls-Royce in 1966, which went bankrupt less than five years later.

Above light: The Bristol 167 Brabazon was one of the series of postwar civil projects set up as a result of the Brabazon Committee's report, which gave rise also to the Vickers Viscount and de Havilland Comet developments. The Brabazon itself was designed as a piston-engined 100-passenger machine with transatlantic range. However, development of it, and a turboprop Mk 2 version, was dropped in 1953 in favor of the later Britannia design. Here the sole Brabazon to fly is seen on landing approach above Cody's tree at Farnborough.

Right: The Britannia assembly hall at Filton in the early 1950s shows some of the first 100-series machines under construction. The great hall was built as a hangar for the Brabazon and could hardly be more unsuitable as floorspace for production. (Later it was used for British-assembled Concordes.) Troubles with the Proteus turboprop engines delayed full entry into BOAC service until 1957 and in December the same year the developed 300-series Britannia inaugurated the first turbine-powered nonstop transatlantic service.

ENGLISH ELECTRIC

When the Canberra jet bomber burst on the scene in 1949 many observers were startled to see the name of its maker, and some (this is true) had to be reassured that it was not electrically driven. Had they been planemaking buffs they would have known of the English Electric Company's long involvement in aviation.

It began when the Coventry Ordnance Works (COW) started making aircraft to subcontract in 1911, following in 1914 with major orders for aircraft in the prolific BE.2 series. A year later the Phoenix Dynamo Manufacturing Company of Bradford was in production with the Short 184, followed by other Short seaplanes, and in 1917 the big Felixstowe F.3 flying-boat was in production by both Phoenix and Dick, Kerr & Company of Preston. In 1917 the Admiralty was anxious to try the rounded monocoque Linton Hope type of hull and the result was the Phoenix P.5 Cork, flown in the summer of 1918; one of the two Corks was still in RAF use six years later.

In 1918 COW, Dick Kerr, Phoenix and two other large companies amalgamated to form the powerful English Electric Company. It kept the Phoenix aviation team at Bradford as a viable entity, and designed and built a succession of impressive flying-boats including three marks of Kingston and the Ayr. It also built three Wren ultra-

An English Electric Wren ultra-light airplane of 1923, one of the two owned and still regularly flown by the Shuttleworth Trust, flies past the first P.1, prototype (first flight 1954), of the Mach 2 Lightning, the first and only entirely British supersonic fighter.

lights, one of which demonstrated 87 miles per gallon in 1923 and was until the 1970s the lowest-powered airplane, with only $3\frac{1}{2}$hp. Sadly, lack of orders forced closure of the EECo aircraft department in 1926.

In 1938 the need for rapid expansion of aircraft production resulted in the former Dick Kerr works at Strand Road and other locations being entrusted with mass-production of the Handley Page Hampden. The orders multiplied, and by 1942 850 Hampdens had been delivered. The three Preston works then tooled up to build the much larger and more complex Halifax and made more than any other company, a total of 2145. In parallel, the company gradually acquired design and development capability, and would have developed and built the 2500hp Folland F.19/43 fighter had it not been cancelled. In 1944 de Havilland was quite unable to handle production of the DH.100 Vampire, and the entire responsibility for production – which involved a lot of final development and customer liaison with this pioneer jet fighter – was entrusted to the by-then-enormous Preston works. Work began in April 1944 and the first Vampire F.1 flew at Samlesbury, the assembly shops east of Preston, on 20 April 1945. English Electric completed over 1000 Vampires despite the fact that after the end of the war de Havilland was able to handle Vampire contracts itself.

Towards the end of the war Sir George Nelson and his board had decided to remain in aircraft production and build up its design staff. W E W "Teddy" Petter came from Westland as chief designer, and in the

postwar environment of extreme austerity had to struggle to get things started. His project office was for a time housed in the former bus garage of Barton Motors in Corporation Street, Preston, and research and test facilities at Samlesbury and the former military base at Warton were created from scratch. But the team that grew, and the facilities that built up, were to become the strongest in Western Europe. Their first product was the A.1 jet bomber, flown by Wing Commander "Bee" Beamont on 13 May 1949. Named Canberra, it went into urgent production not only at Preston but also at Avro, Handley Page and Shorts, and the Australian Government Aircraft Factories; in 1951 it was adopted as the B-57 by the US Air Force and put into production by Martin. Today Canberras and B-57s are still in service, and Preston is recycling them for use until the end of the 1980s.

Next came Britain's first supersonic aircraft, and the only all-British supersonic aircraft of any type to enter regular service – the P.1, later developed into the Lightning interceptor, an aircraft of extremely advanced design and endowed with most pleasant yet exciting qualities. Third was the mighty TSR.2 program, again a beautiful performer but one which for strange political reasons was thrown away in favor of a bug-ridden American aircraft (the F-111, which eventually was not bought either!). In 1965, five years after EECo had merged its aviation company into BAC, the project team at Warton began work with Breguet on the Jaguar; and today as part of BAe it is a major member of Panavia.

Right: Before the P.1 appeared, English Electric had cut its military jet teeth on the Canberra light tactical bomber, whose original production team is pictured here in May 1949 after the Canberra's maiden flight. Left to right, F D Crowe, chief structure designer; D I Ellis, chief aerodynamicist; S C Harrison, chief draftsman; A E Ellison, chief designer; W E W Petter, chief engineer; R P Beamont, chief test pilot; D B Smith, assistant chief engineer; F W Page (today Sir Frederick Page, chairman and chief executive of BAC Aircraft Group), chief stressman; H S Howat, resident technical officer.

Below: The Canberra has been sold to 15 countries to a total of about 1400 aircraft; more than 400 were built under license in the US as the Martin B-57. More than that, the design brought a second round of work to BAC in rebuilding many of the original aircraft for export and a new guaranteed ten-year period of service. This picture shows the Canberra rebuild line at Samlesbury in the early 1970s.

VICKERS-ARMSTRONGS

In 1908 Vickers Sons & Maxim Limited contracted to build a rigid airship for the Admiralty; on 24 September 1911 the completed *Mayfly* emerged from its shed at Barrow, was hit by a sudden gust and broke in two. Undeterred, Vickers continued to build not only airships but also as many advanced types of aircraft as any other company.

In 1910 Captain (later Major) Herbert F Wood, one of the first graduates of the Bristol school at Brooklands, recommended that Vickers should take a license for French REP aircraft and engines. On 28 March 1911 he was appointed manager of the Vickers Aviation Department, with a drawing office at Vickers House, workshops in the Vickers factories at Erith and Crayford and an airfield nearby at Joyce Green, where Monoplane No 1 flew in July 1911. No 1 was by no means a copy of the French original. The redesigning was done by A R Low, G H Challenger, pilot F Macdonald and the famous aviator-designer, Howard Flanders. It was followed by a series of excellent monoplanes used at the Vickers Flying School at Brooklands which trained 77 pilots in 1912–13 and 36 in the first seven months of 1914, a record for Britain.

While Erith, Crayford and, from 1915, a growing new aviation works at Weybridge built large numbers of Factory-designed machines, as well as 1½-Strutters, the Low/ Challenger team created improved Farman Boxkites, a large biplane called the Hydravion and, after studying impressive twin-engined machines with a 37mm gun in the nose, the EFB.1 (Experimental Fighting Biplane) displayed at Olympia in February 1913. From this eventually stemmed the FB.5 Gunbus, a Gnome-Mono pusher with a Lewis gunner in front of the pilot, which can fairly be called Britain's first combat aircraft. The first reached the Western Front in February 1915 (though one took off from Joyce Green on Christmas Day 1914 and, according to local evidence, shot down a Taube); 119 were built, plus 99 more in France. It was followed by the more rounded FB.9, of which 95 were built.

In August 1914 the design office moved from Vickers House to Crayford, and a former apprentice, R K Pierson, was put in charge. Rex Pierson was also a qualified pilot, and was destined to become one of the leaders of British aircraft design for 30 years. New prototypes appeared seemingly every week or two until the Armistice, but the most important was the FB.27A which became the Vimy bomber, a standard postwar RAF type, the conqueror of the North Atlantic, the first to fly to Australia and South Africa and, in Vimy Commercial form, one of the first true airliners. From it stemmed such famous and enduring machines as the RAF's Vernon, Victoria and Valentia bomber/transports (which did more than any other aircraft to pioneer air routes within the Empire), the Virginia heavy bomber and various civil derivatives.

Immediately after the war Pierson started a new product line with the Viking pusher amphibian – built in a Weybridge dancehall and towed to Brooklands in 1919 – using the Consuta copper-sewn mahogany hull technique of Saunders, then a Vickers subsidiary. This led to competition with Supermarine, which became a subsidiary in 1928 though retaining its identity. During the 1920s an airship team under B N (later Sir Barnes) Wallis and N S Norway (later Nevil Shute, the novelist) created the R.100 at an *ad hoc* factory at Howden, Yorkshire; after the crash of the rival government-built R.101 the R.100 was arbitrarily broken up and Vickers was not even fully paid for it, despite the fact it handsomely exceeded all requirements, because it appeared to show up nationalized industry in a bad light! Wallis then applied his geodetic form of construction to the RAF's first production monoplane, the Wellesley bomber (which in 1938 gained the world long-distance record) and twin-engined Wellington. The latter was the only British bomber in production throughout World War II, a total of 11,461 being built by Weybridge and the giant wartime plants of Chester and Blackpool.

In July 1928 the Vickers Aviation Depart-

Vickers Limited Aircraft Division was established at the Brooklands (Weybridge) motor racing circuit in 1911. This picture shows the company's flying school in action there in 1912.

Above: Pictured at Hendon is a replica of a Vickers FB.5 "Gunbus" built for the RAF Museum. The replica represents No 2345, one of a batch of eight Gunbuses delivered to the RNAS in 1915 and taken over by the RFC in February 1916 when the latter assumed responsibility for UK air defense from the former.

Left: The Vickers Vildebeest shore-based torpedo bomber was a successful between-the-wars Vickers design; nearly 200 were built for the RAF and RNZAF from 1929. Illustrated is a Vildebeest IV fitted with the Bristol Perseus engine, the first sleeve-valve engine used by the RAF.

Right: A famous Vickers aircraft was the World War I Vimy heavy bomber, immortalized by two pioneering flights in 1919 – the first nonstop flight between North America and Europe by Alcock and Brown in June, and the staged England–Australia flight by the brothers Ross and Keith Smith in November and December. The Smiths' Vimy IV is illustrated.

First flown in 1936, the Wellington was the most numerous British bomber, with a total production of over 11,000. It was a mainstay of the RAF in World War II in a wide variety of roles from straightforward medium bomber that first carried 4000lb 'block-busters', through minelayer and 'minebuster' to troop transport. It was additionally noteworthy for the fantastic amount of punishment it could take, mainly through the geodetic construction system devised by Dr (later Sir) Barnes Wallis. This system is well shown in this picture of Wellington IA production.

ment was elevated to the status of a company, Vickers (Aviation), and in October 1938 both this and Supermarine Aviation Works were taken over by Vickers-Armstrongs, the parent formed by a heavy-engineering merger with the Armstrongs group in 1928. In turn the vastly expanded postwar facilities were taken over by a new aviation company, Vickers-Armstrongs (Aircraft) Limited.

While immediate postwar income was provided by the Viking, an uninspired airline derivative of the Wellington with a stressed-skin fuselage (and, from No 20, a stressed-skin wing), work went ahead on two much more advanced aircraft that were to go into high-rate production side-by-side and make a major difference to British aviation. Both stemmed from the forceful direction of G R (later Sir George) Edwards, who had joined the design staff in 1935. His brilliance, eloquence, cool head and long-range vision were to prove desperately needed in postwar British aviation, and he rose to become managing director in 1953 and architect of most of the things that subsequently mattered. His two great designs of the 1950s were the Viscount turbo-prop airliner, which entered service in 1953 and sold 445, and the Valiant bomber which was built to an extremely tight schedule to give the RAF 104 modern bombers that should have been ordered earlier. Vickers also built a specially strengthened Valiant B.2 for low-level operations, but though an obvious need for this capability had existed

Above: Viscounts in production at Weybridge. A great postwar achievement of the Vickers-Armstrongs Weybridge team was the development of the world's first production gas turbine-powered airliner, the Viscount, powered by Rolls-Royce Dart turboprops. The V.630 prototype first flew in July 1948 and obtained full passenger clearance to start a month's scheduled service with BEA in July 1950 before returning to development flying. The larger production Viscount 700 entered full BEA scheduled service in April 1953 to usher in a new era of faster, smoother, quieter and more comfortable air travel.

Right: The world's airlines soon got the message and orders came in from around the world, including the US. Here Continental Airlines President Robert F Six is discussing a Viscount purchase at Weybridge with Vickers-Armstrongs (Aircraft) managing director George (later Sir George) Edwards.

since 1950 it was cancelled. Accordingly, when the Valiants were forced on to low-level operation in 1964 they soon suffered the fatigue cracking which Vickers had predicted in 1953.

Further government myopia was shown by the cancellation of the V.1000 long-range jetliner in November 1955, when the first of an RAF order was well advanced in construction. BOAC refused to show any interest in this 707-size swept-wing jet with fan engines, saying the aircraft it had on order would "fully meet requirements well into the 1960s." As the prototype 707 was then already flying the mind boggles at trying to comprehend this assessment. Within a year BOAC had bought 15 Boeing 707s and was trying to buy a non-existent V.1000-type jet called the DH.118. In May 1957 it signed for 35 quite different aircraft, to be built at Weybridge, called the VC10. This was a 707-size aircraft specifically tailored to a tight specification by BOAC

demanding the ability to operate from very short hot-and-high runways. By the time the VC10 was in service the runways had, without exception, been lengthened to handle the 707 and DC-8. BOAC thereupon publicly criticized the VC10 as "grossly uneconomic" and demanded a government subsidy for using it; it did not read its own annual Report and Accounts which showed it to be more profitable than the 707.

Thus BOAC managed to outdo even the military procurement machine in utter idiocy, and like de Havilland with the Trident, Vickers were to lose heavily on the program. The company also lost on the Vanguard, a second-generation turboprop that followed the Viscount. In this case, however, there was little wrong with the BEA specification, which simply failed to appreciate that, for a time, airlines would prefer jets to quieter and more fuel-efficient turboprops. Today the Vanguard would be better appreciated.

In February 1960 Vickers bought 40 percent of British Aircraft Corporation, transferred to it all its aviation assets in-

cluding the Weybridge and Hurn factories, and collaborated with English Electric Aviation on the TSR.2. One of Sir George Edwards's appointments was as chairman of Hunting Aircraft, a BAC subsidiary, where he organized the project design of the One-Eleven. He also masterminded the British side of Concorde, though that had its center of gravity at Bristol.

Below: Successor to the Viscount and with much greater passenger and underfloor cargo capacity to match the growing traffic was the Vickers Vanguard, the first of which flew in January 1959. It entered BEA service in March 1961, a month after TCA (now Air Canada) had opened its Vanguard service. One of the 23 TCA Vanguards is illustrated.

Bottom: The final passenger aircraft to come out of Weybridge was the VC10 and Super VC10 (illustrated), developed as a second-generation jet airliner for BOAC. It was also sold to the RAF and to a few small airlines to a total of just over 50 aircraft. Though publicly criticized by BOAC, for whom it was designed, it proved cheaper to operate than the Boeing 707, and its outstanding quietness and comfort consistently attracted higher passenger loads than other types.

PERCIVAL/HUNTING

To Basil B "Hendy" Henderson goes credit for demonstrating the potential of the efficient cantilever monoplane in an era when, in Britain, the biplane was almost universal. In 1928 he designed the Hendy 281 Hobo at Shoreham, and built it the following year. In 1930 his Hendy 302, a tandem-seat cabin machine, was built by George Parnall and Company of Yate. In 1934 the superb 3308 Heck was built by Westland; later various Hecks were built by Parnall, and "Hendy" himself joined the Parnall/Nash & Thompson group to design bomber gun turrets.

One of the many impressed by the Hobo was a mercurial Australian who had flown gliders in 1912, served with the Australian Light Horse and been a founder of 111 Squadron RFC/RAF. Captain Edgar W Percival had designed a trimotor "able to carry 1000lb for 1000 miles," built by Saro. He asked Henderson to build him a cabin two-seater, the 302. Predictably the men quarreled, and Henderson was replaced by R H Bound (who later achieved greater fame as chief designer of Dowty undercarriages). Bound created a real winner, the three-seat Gull, made by Parnall using Henderson's wing design. The first flew in March 1932. Percival Aircraft Limited was set up with an office in London and service shops at Gravesend Airport, and Parnall made 23 more Gulls sold by the new company at the high figure of £1250 each. By 1934 Percival Aircraft was in production itself at Gravesend. Bound produced the powerful Gull Six, added flaps and then, after the inevitable row, left, being replaced by A A Bage. The firm flourished, and in 1936–37 moved to a large new factory at Luton, about 35 miles north of London.

At Luton the Q-Six and military Proctor were staple products, and in 1946 the Prentice – an indifferent design to a poor RAF specification – provided mass-production of all-metal structures. It led to the Provost and Jet Provost, while the twin-Gipsy Merganser led to the Alvis-engined Princes, Pembrokes and Sea Princes. Major customers for survey and geophysical Princes were various companies in the Hunting Group, and following the latter's financial control the Percival company became Hunting Percival Aircraft on 26 April 1954 and plain Hunting Aircraft Limited on 5 December 1957. Work on Napier tip-drive helicopters was unsuccessful, but the Jet Provost proved capable of much development. When BAC was formed in February 1960 it bought a controlling interest in Hunting Aircraft, and on 1 January 1964 BAC bought the remaining shares and the Hunting name vanished. Hunting's greatest legacy was the H.107 short-haul twin-jet, which was developed by BAC into the H.111, finally produced as the BAC One-Eleven.

In 1955 Edgar Percival left Luton to Hunting, set up shop at Stapleford Tawney and, helped by a handful of bright engineers, quickly produced a tough utility aircraft, the EP.9. The first of these high-wing cabin machines flew on 21 December 1955. It was clearly promising, with ability to carry bulky cargo as well as a long ton (2240lb, 1016kg) of chemicals. It sold quite well, considering its shaky base; but in 1957 Edgar Percival Aircraft was taken over by Samlesbury Engineering and re-named Lancashire Aircraft. A few Lancashire EP.9 Prospectors emerged from Samlesbury until 1961.

Above: The Provost was one of a series of Percival training aircraft produced for several air forces, which ended with the Jet Provost/Strikemaster trainer/strike aircraft still in service. Illustrated is one of nearly 40 preserved Provosts. It is maintained in flying condition by the Shuttleworth Trust.

Below: Hunting Percival product, popular with the Services as a light transport and twin-engine trainer was the Prince, with accommodation for up to 12 passengers. Developed versions were the Sea Prince, Pembroke and President. Illustrated is a standard P.50 civil Prince fitted as an eight-passenger feederliner of 1948.

SUPERMARINE

In its embryonic period heavier-than-air aviation tended to throw up characters who were "larger than life." Not all were large in stature; they were just possessed of immense personality, drive, energy and plain nerve, and none had more of these things than "PB" Noel Pemberton-Billing. He decided one day he would be a barrister, learned Latin in four months and proceeded to "eat his dinner" in chambers in the decreed manner. In 1903 he was airborne in his man-lifting kite. He designed a series of truly incredible monoplanes. He waged a one-man election campaign and became Member of Parliament for East Hertfordshire. He joined the RNAS and singlehandedly planned the entire pioneer bombing raid by Avros from Belfort to the Zeppelin works. Perhaps his most staggering achievement was his one-man defense in a libel action (hardly surprising in view of his outspokenness) before Lord Justice Avory in the course of which he repeatedly bested that most famous judge on matters of law!

In September 1913 one of his sidelines was to take over a small works on the water's edge at Woolston, Southampton, and start building the Supermarine PB.1 flying-boat. He used "Supermarine" as a trade mark and telegraphic address. The completed boat was at the Aero Show at Olympia in March 1914, and in June he formed a limited company, Pemberton-Billing Limited. He intended to test the PB.1 himself (it is not known if he did so), having the previous September taken £500 off Frederick Handley Page in what must have been the only losing wager HP ever made that nobody could learn to fly from scratch and "take his ticket" between dawn and dusk of one day.

PB did things fast. When war broke out he decided the nation needed lots of nimble single-seat scouts. He told his staff they could go home when the prototype was flying. In hours he had drawn the outlines on the walls, carried out preliminary stressing and begun detailed lofting of parts. The resulting PB.9 flew within a week, being popularly called "the Seven-day Bus," and then everyone took the afternoon off. (What is more, it was a first-class machine and was used by the Royal Naval Air Service as a trainer at Hendon. A few

thousand might have been an excellent idea.)

Next came the PB.23 Push-Proj (pusher projectile) and 20 of the PB.25 production model for the RNAS. Then followed the big PB.29 anti-Zeppelin night fighter, which PB explained in a best-selling book, *Air War: How to Wage it*. The idea was to cruise very slowly lying in wait for the airships and then blast them with a Lewis gun from a position on top of the four wings, the airship being lit up by a searchlight in the bow cockpit. For some reason the design and construction took seven weeks – the staff must have been allowed to go home at nights – and it was then taken to Chingford where it was flown by Commander J W Seddon early in 1916. It was followed by the even more extraordinary PB.31E, which was so low-powered it could hardly catch the airships but bristled with a 1½-pounder Davis gun and two Lewises, as well as a remotely pointed searchlight fed from a 2.25kW generating plant which also

provided the crew with electric heating.

When PB was elected to Parliament on 10 March 1916 he sold his holding in his aircraft company to avoid any suggestion he was a war profiteer. His co-directors, led by Hubert Scott-Paine, renamed the company the Supermarine Aviation Works. The chief designer was Reginald Mitchell who helped Harold Bolas of the Admiralty Air Department produce the AD Navy-plane and then later in the war designed the excellent N.1B Baby fighter flying-boat. Mitchell had no hand in the AD Flying Boat of 1916, at least 27 of which were built at Woolston, but after the Armistice he modified this type into the civil Channel which saw service all over the world. In 1920 his Amphibian Mk I came second in an Air Ministry competition and led to a great family of biplane amphibians, mainly single-engine pushers, which led to the mass-produced Walrus of World War II and the later Sea Otter and Seagull.

After fairly desultory aircraft activity on further Pemberton-Billing designs during World War I, including some PB.25 Scouts for the RNAS, Supermarine settled down after the war to production of flying-boats and amphibians, at first with wooden hulls, as this Channel naval trainer for the Peruvian Navy in 1920, and the early twin-engine Southamptons for the RAF which by the late 1920s had metal hulls.

Left: In 1915 the RNAS ordered two of these monstrous PB.31E (Supermarine Nighthawk) quadruplanes designed by Pemberton-Billing for trials on anti-airship patrol work. Results are not on record but perhaps not surprisingly no more were ordered.

Above: Fame came to Supermarine with R. J. Mitchell's series of superb seaplanes with which the RAF High-Speed Flight achieved world records and won the Schneider Trophy outright in 1931. Here the S.6B is brought ashore from the Solent at Calshot after the "race" in which there were no other contestants.

In 1925 Mitchell designed the beautiful S.4, a bold monoplane, for the Schneider Trophy seaplane contest. It suffered from aileron reversal and crashed, so Mitchell used stiff wire-braced wings on the S.5, S.6 and S.6B which won three races in a row thus bringing the contests to an end in 1931. Mitchell had no illusions about the need to progress beyond the biplane, but a short-sighted Air Ministry eventually cancelled his splendid six-engined monoplane boat ordered for comparison with the biplane Short Sarafand (which was not cancelled), and when he wanted to build a fighter to F.7/30 specification it was a struggle to adopt stressed-skin construction and a poor machine resulted.

Mitchell himself continued work to develop the Type 224 into a really good fighter, and, in the course of this company-funded effort, adopted the eight-gun armament recommended by Squadron Leader Sorley, the Rolls-Royce PV.12 engine,

modern stressed-skin construction and retractable landing gear. It is unfashionable to criticize this classic design, upon which so much was to depend, but Mitchell adopted a curving semi-elliptic wing shape with the strength in a strong D-nose ahead of the tubular multi-layer spar at 25-percent chord. The Air Ministry soon saw the Type 300 was far better than anything else in sight, wrote specification F.37/34 around it, and it went into production both at an expanded Woolston and at a giant Shadow works at Castle Bromwich as the Spitfire. Mitchell then designed a high-speed four-engined bomber, the prototypes of which were destroyed at Woolston by bombing, and died of TB in June 1937 after having totally spurned the insistence of his doctors that he should ease off a bit and stop working such long hours.

Subsequently a splendid team led by Joe Smith doubled the weight and power of the Spitfire and transformed it in other ways,

while a growing subcontract organization helped the production total grow to 20,334, plus 2556 Seafires. After 1945 a series of jet fighters culminated in the big Scimitar carrier-based attack aircraft, assembled at South Marston, Swindon, the design team having, since the war, been centered at Hursley Park near Winchester southwest of London.

Though it made little difference at shop-floor level, the company had been taken over in November 1928 by Vickers, becoming Supermarine Aviation Works (Vickers) Limited. In October 1938 it ceased to exist, becoming a division of Vickers-Armstrongs, though it retained its identity on its note-paper, factory and aircraft names. In 1959, a year before the last Scimitar was delivered, even the division ceased to exist. The design team, in final years led by George Henson and Alan Clifton, was dispersed; a few, after producing the first studies for TSR.2, went to Weybridge.

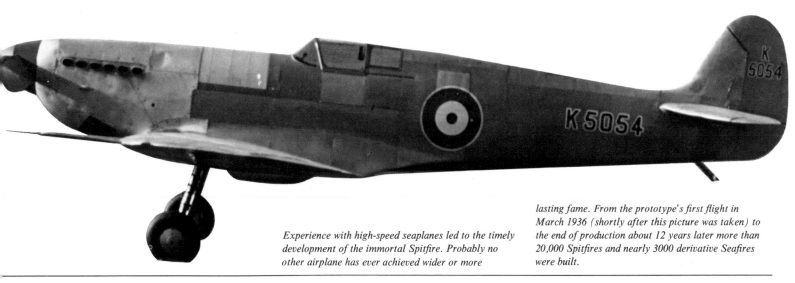

Experience with high-speed seaplanes led to the timely development of the immortal Spitfire. Probably no other airplane has ever achieved wider or more

lasting fame. From the prototype's first flight in March 1936 (shortly after this picture was taken) to the end of production about 12 years later more than 20,000 Spitfires and nearly 3000 derivative Seafires were built.

BRITISH AIRCRAFT CORPORATION (BAC)

The first official intimation that the British government intended to enforce mergers in the aerospace industry was given at a meeting at the headquarters of what was then the Ministry of Supply, Shell-Mex House, London, on 16 September 1957. The carrot of a new military aircraft was dangled before the heads of the 12 great companies, who were asked to submit proposals for a new strike/reconnaissance aircraft by 31 January 1958, together with their proposed industrial grouping. English Electric teamed up with Shorts, but the government wanted to combine the best features of the EE design with that from Vickers, and invented a revised specification to exclude the Belfast submission! On 1 January 1959 a joint contract was awarded for the TSR.2 aircraft to Vickers-Armstrongs, called main contractor, and English Electric Aviation.

Originally the Vickers team had been the former Supermarine engineers at Hursley Park, but before long they moved to Weybridge where air commuting to Lancashire was more practical. Subsequently TSR.2, though an outstanding aircraft, was cancelled and replaced by American aircraft (also later cancelled); but the pathetic performance by the customer could not alter the fact that the shotgun marriage had forced Vickers-Armstrongs (Aircraft) and English Electric Aviation to amalgamate. Bristol had joined of its own accord, the respective percentage shareholdings in what was named British Aircraft Corporation being 40, 40 and 20. At the same time a controlling shareholding was purchased in Hunting Aircraft.

For a time all BAC companies continued trading as subsidiaries, together with BAC (Guided Weapons) in which were merged the missile and space interests of the three principals. But on 1 January 1964 the old names vanished into BAC divisions: Weybridge Division, Preston Division, Filton Division and Luton Division. The Luton works was now wholly owned, and in July 1966 it was closed, despite the fact that the Hunting team had originated the first true BAC product, the One-Eleven airliner. Luton's One-Eleven work was transferred to the Weybridge and Hurn factories, and the Strikemaster/Jet Provost went to Preston.

Largest BAC engineering effort was devoted to the Concorde supersonic airliner, launched by an Anglo-French intergovernmental agreement of 29 November 1962 which promised 50/50 collaboration. No company was formed to run this program, in which BAC was teamed with Sud-Aviation and then Aérospatiale. Though Weybridge's Sir George Edwards was the chief architect and missionary for Concorde it was primarily a Filton Division program, concluded in 1978. A second major Anglo-French project was the Jaguar, for which BAC teamed with Dassault-Breguet and formed a joint company called SEPECAT. This was centered squarely at Preston Division from May 1966. Largest of the BAC military programs was MRCA, later named Tornado, awarded in March 1969 to a tri-national company called Panavia whose shares are held $42\frac{1}{2}/42\frac{1}{2}/15$ by BAC, MBB and Aeritalia.

On 1 June 1971 BAC was reorganized into a Commercial Aircraft Division, based at Filton, Weybridge and Hurn, and a Military Aircraft Division centered at the Preston factories. A Guided Weapons Division was split between Filton and Stevenage. BAC was taken over by the nationalized British Aerospace on 29 April 1977.

Bottom left: A prominent feature of later BAC activity is international co-operative projects, which have included the Anglo-French Concorde SST and Jaguar tactical fighter and the Anglo-German-Italian Tornado. This picture shows Jaguars on final erection by British Aerospace Warton Division.

Below: The 1976 BAC Concorde assembly line with, from the left, Concordes 212 (12th), 214 (14th) and 210 (10th) in various stages of production, with 210 virtually completed and almost due to make its maiden flight. Simultaneous production of Nos 211, 213 and 215 was taking place at the Toulouse plant of BAC's French partner in the project, Aérospatiale.

Bottom: Production of the BAC One-Eleven short-haul medium-capacity airliner continues at the Hurn (Bournemouth) assembly hall, with aircraft for a Middle East corporation and British Airways on view. The One-Eleven was evolved by BAC from a Hunting Aircraft project and first flew in August 1963.

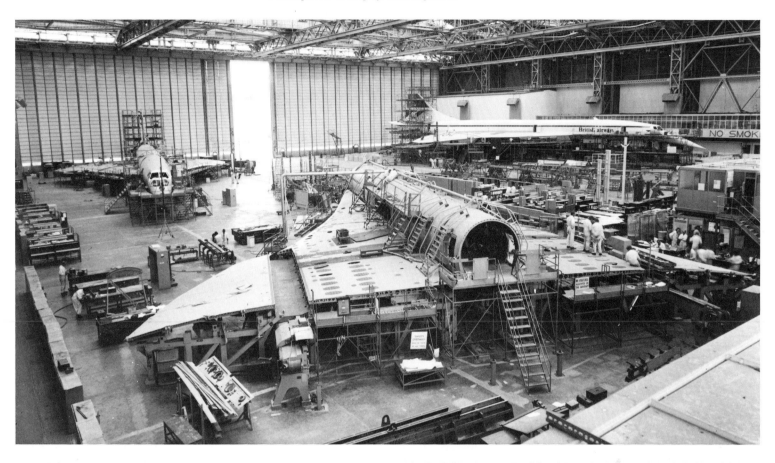

Below: Most cost/effective answer to Britain's extremely severe interception problems is the Panavia Tornado F.2, the first of which flew in 1979. Derived from the three-nation attack aircraft, it has sensors and weapons tailored to the rest of the century.

Bottom: Two stages in the production of a modern airliner. Left: Assembling a main electrical control and distribution panel with its thousands of yards of cables is a highly skilled technical operation and Right: Preparation of the halves of One-Eleven main fuselage shells prior to joining.

ARMSTRONG WHITWORTH

The story of Sir W G Armstrong Whitworth Aircraft will never fully be told because it is complex and most of the records have been lost. There never was a Sir W G Armstrong Whitworth; the famous engineering firm was formed in 1897 by the union of two bitter rivals, Armstrong and Whitworth, at Newcastle-upon-Tyne. In 1912 A V Roe's brother asked if the firm would consider making Avro airplanes, but it declined; and it failed to reach agreement on a request from Sir George White that it should make Bristols ordered by Italy, with assembly at AW's Italian subsidiary. It did, however, make ABC aero-engines and also Leitner's patented hollow-steel propellers (a design just 30 years too early). In March 1913 the Admiralty invited AW to tender for airships, and in 1915 construction began in a new factory at Barlow, near Selby, whence came the SS (Submarine Scout), Coastal non-rigids and the R.25, 29 and 33; the R.33 was a first-class airship (copied from a late-war Zeppelin) which between 1919 and 1928 flew 735 hours, far more than any other British airship.

In June 1913 the board had decided also to build airplanes, and appointed Captain I F Fairbairn-Crawford manager of its Aerial Department. Fairbairn-Crawford was a former Royal Engineers officer, a famous athlete and an official at the 1910 aviation meetings at Doncaster and Bournemouth; he "took his ticket" as a pilot in

1915. The board appointed as his assistant a Dutchman of generous proportions and bonhomie, Frederick "Cully" Koolhoven. Cully was a brilliant and hardworking designer who had been chief engineer and manager at the British Deperdussin Syndicate at Highgate, north London. The great AW works at Elswick proved unsuitable to airplanes, and the first aircraft built by the famous engineering company were two BE.2as assembled in another AW plant at Scotswood. In April 1914 Farnborough complimented the company on its workmanship. However a proper factory was needed, and – like Blackburn and Sopwith – the choice fell on a disused skating rink, in this instance at Gosforth (all these places are on Tyneside).

There AW built the BE.2a, 2b and, in large numbers, 2c. Flying was done from a miniscule (150 by 600 yards) area of Newcastle's Town Moor, moving in mid-1916 to a slightly larger part of the moor and in 1918 to the RAF station at Cramlington farther north. In September 1914 Koolhoven took off from the original "Duke's Moor" field in the FK.1, a baby biplane. His next design is not known, but the FK.3 was his very sensible attempt to produce a machine like the BE.2c but much simpler to build. Work began in August 1915 and the FK.3 was so vastly superior to the Factory machine that over 500 were ordered (though it was not allowed to challenge the official

type in a serious way); production was shared with Hewlett & Blondeau of Luton. The RFC was tickled at the great letters AW deeply embossed in heavy-engineering style on the metal engine cowling, and called this popular multi-role machine the "Ack-W" (A being Ack in the contemporary phonetic alphabet). But in early 1917 the FK.3 changed to "Little Ack" to distinguish it from "Big Ack," the FK.8 reconnaissance aircraft. This even more popular machine, usually with a 160hp Beardmore engine, was the company's main product with at least 1652 delivered by the time of the Armistice. It had a fine record; its crews gained two VCs, and in 1922 two civil examples flew the first mail and passenger services in Australia in the genesis of QANTAS.

Koolhoven produced many prototypes including various FK.10 quadruplanes and the FK.12 triplane with gunner's nacelles on each side of the tractor propeller! However in 1917 he left and after delivering 250 Arab-engined Bristol Fighters, AW's future looked bleak. But a month after the Armistice, talks opened with the Siddeley Deasy Motor Car Company of Parkside, Coventry,

First of a pair of similar Armstrong Whitworth AW.52 research aircraft designed to study a project for a six-jet tailless airliner. This one, with Nene engines, first flew in November 1947 and was damaged in an accident in May 1949 and not flown again. The Derwent-powered second prototype flew in September 1948 and completed the research program with the Royal Aircraft Establishment.

which AW purchased in February 1919. SD had been a major aero-engine firm during the war, and in 1917 had, like others, grabbed good designers from Farnborough. Notable among the acquisitions was John Lloyd, who produced the RT.1, an improved RE.8, followed by the SR.2 Siskin, a first-rate fighter flown at Radford (Coventry) airfield in about May or June 1919. Powered by the unreliable Dragonfly it still outflew almost everything else in the sky, and Siddeley Deasy had a far better engine, Major Green's RAF.8 14-cylinder radial, which matured in the 1920s as the Armstrong Siddeley Jaguar. The set-up now was a parent called Armstrong Whitworth Development Company, with offices at Parkside, and two subsidiaries – Sir W G Armstrong Whitworth Aircraft and Armstrong Siddeley Motors. The old AW empire on Tyneside withered, and in 1928 was taken over by Vickers to form Vickers-Armstrongs.

For 40 years from 1920 Armstrong Whitworth's design team was led by Lloyd and specialized in metal aircraft of vast diversity. Until 1930 technical effort centered at Parkside, but from 1923 the factory was growing at Whitley Abbey airfield two miles south of the city. Its staple products were the Jaguar-powered Siskin fighter (Siskin IIIA with Jaguar IV in 1925 was the world's first production machine with a supercharged engine), of which 485 were built; the Atlas military biplane, of which 446 went to the RAF (1927–33), plus exports; the Argosy biplane airliner (three Jaguars); the AW.XV high-wing monoplane airliner (four Serval) often called Atalanta after the first of the Imperial Airways fleet; the monster AW.27 Ensign (four Tiger, later Wright Cyclone), Europe's largest prewar airliner, 14 of which served mainly in World War II; and the AW.38 Whitley (two Tiger, later Merlin) heavy bomber and ocean reconnaissance aircraft, of which 1814 were built (1936–43). The company's main wartime effort included production of 1328 Lancasters, followed by 281 Lincolns, and management of factories making Stirlings and Barracudas. A "nobody's baby," with which the author was familiar, was one of Britain's first tricycle-gear machines, the AW.41 Albemarle. This had been designed as the Bristol 155 bomber, passed to AW, redesigned by Lloyd to use steel and wood in place of light alloys, and built in shops all over Britain for assembly at Gloster's No 2 Shadow Factory at Brockworth by an invented company called A W Hawksley.

After 1945 AW handled (a) production of the Sea Hawk for Hawker Aircraft, followed by the Sapphire-powered Hunters, (b) design and production of the night-fighter Meteors for Gloster and (c) production of 133 Gloster Javelins. AW's own flying wings, Apollo transport and other projects were unsuccessful, but the Argosy freighter did see limited production. The vastly expanded complex of plants in the Coventry area embraced supersonic tunnels and a beryllium processing facility but, despite success with the Seaslug naval missile, lack of a major aircraft program proved lethal. In 1961 the company merged with Gloster to form Whitworth Gloster Aircraft, two years later merging with Avro to form Avro Whitworth Division of HSA. Cancellation of the HS.681 V/STOL transport for the RAF, which had been an AW design, resulted in closure of all plants save the overhaul factory at Bitteswell, now part of BAe Kingston/Brough Division and the location of the Hawk assembly line.

The AW.650 Argosy, evolved from a project founded by the Hawker Siddeley Group for Armstrong Whitworth, first flew in January 1959; it was the first specialized turboprop freighter designed for easy cargo handling and could have full-width doors at both ends of its box-like fuselage. The Argosy looked a natural winner but orders were disappointing; only 16 were built for civil use, seven going to US operators and nine to BEA; the bulk of production went to the RAF.

Alliott Verdon Roe, who like Handley Page took his middle name from his mother's family, was born in Manchester in April 1877. He was thus older than most of the pioneer aviators, and before becoming incurably bitten by the bug in 1906 had been an engineer in Canada, apprentice at the Lancashire & Yorkshire Railway under Sir John Aspinall, prizewinning racing cyclist, engineer at Portsmouth Dockyard, 4th Engineer on the Royal Mail Line and designer in the infant car industry. In 1906 he was Secretary of the Royal Aero Club, designer of a large helicopter in Denver (Colorado) and winner of the top prize of £75 in a *Daily Mail* competition for a flying model airplane. This capital enabled Roe to build a full-size canard biplane, which made seven short flights at Brooklands in June 1908, the first on 8 June. Roe, a small low-voiced self-effacing man, called them mere hops. It is strange that, 20 years later, a Royal Aero Club committee formed to decide who was the first Briton to fly in Britain should, often by showing clearly partisan disregard for the evidence, have solemnly decided it was Lord Brabazon in his French Voisin in the spring of 1909. At least Roe's flights are now recorded on the memorial plaque at Brooklands.

In late 1908 "AV" began to build a completely different machine, a spidery little triplane with rear tail. He chose a 9hp JAP motorcycle engine, and one of the Prestwich (JAP) brothers even gave financial help. Before the end of the year a young businessman, George Friswell, ordered a machine just like it, probably the first airplane sold in Britain. The Brooklands racetrack authorities hated aviators and Roe, like the rest, had to get out (by 1910 there was a new Brooklands management and a new respect for aviation, and a proper airfield opened at Brooklands). Roe eventually took over two arches under the Great Eastern Railway at Lea Marshes in east London and thence emerged the tiny triplane, weighing well under 220lb (100kg), in April 1909. By May it was making short hops, to the intense displeasure of Hackney Borough Council. Finding there was no law against it, it summoned Roe for causing a public nuisance for daring to fly 330yd (300m) on 23 July 1909. Two days later Blériot flew the Channel; the stalwart councillors suddenly realized what a story their prosecution of Roe would make in the newspapers – which were already saying "wake up England" – and quickly discontinued proceedings.

On 1 January 1910 A V Roe & Company began building airplanes in a basement shop of Everards, elastic-webbing makers of Manchester. One of their chief products was the "Bullseye" range of trouser braces, which explains why the little triplane was named *Bullseye* – what had become known as Avro aircraft were held up by braces. AV delivered Friswell's machine, and work then built up rapidly at Manchester with capital from AV's brother HV (Humphrey Verdon). By the end of 1911 Avros had been involved in at least 27 major or minor crashes without anyone being seriously hurt, and the various biplane and triplane land- and water-planes were augmented in 1912 by a remarkable monoplane (the Type F) whose pilot sat wholly inside the Celluloid-skinned fuselage. Another cabin machine, the two-seat Type G biplane, completed all tests in the 1912 Military Aeroplane Trials; like several others of the modern entrants, the Avro was a staggering contrast to the winner, Cody's ancient concept which, apart from having 120hp, differed little from the 1903 Wright Flyer.

A V Roe provided naval and military aircraft from the earliest days and one of the first practical machines was the Roe IV Triplane. The original machine is in the Science Museum, South Kensington. The one pictured is a replica built for the film Those Magnificent Men in Their Flying Machines *and is now maintained and flown by the Shuttleworth Trust.*

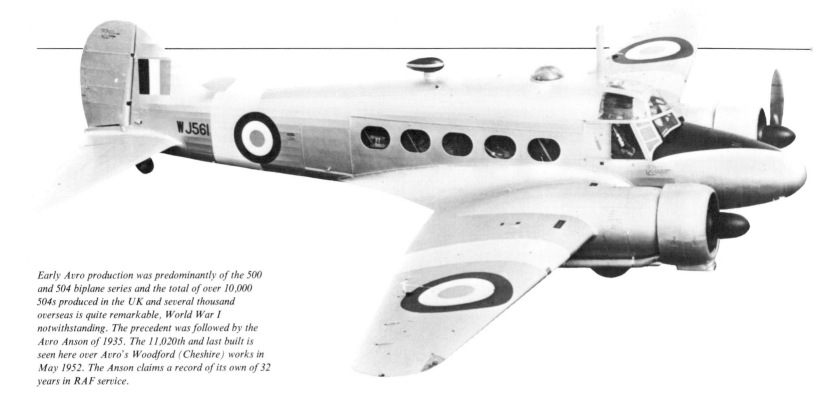

Early Avro production was predominantly of the 500 and 504 biplane series and the total of over 10,000 504s produced in the UK and several thousand overseas is quite remarkable, World War I notwithstanding. The precedent was followed by the Avro Anson of 1935. The 11,020th and last built is seen here over Avro's Woodford (Cheshire) works in May 1952. The Anson claims a record of its own of 32 years in RAF service.

By 1912 Avro aircraft were being designed by two qualified draftsmen, R J Parrott and young Roy Chadwick. (The latter was responsible for most subsequent designs until he was tragically killed in 1947 in a Tudor airliner in which the aileron controls had been connected in reverse.) The company had a busy flying school at Shoreham, whence it had moved because traffic at Brooklands was getting dangerous. AV himself had a dream of a great aviation works on the south coast with a specially built garden-city for employees. He chose Hamble, but war broke out and it was soon impossible to keep building because of material shortages and restrictions. The main works remained in Manchester. A V Roe and Company Limited was registered as a public company on 1 January 1913 and, after intense planemaking at Clifton Street, Miles Platting, the company leased a large extension of the Newton Heath factory of Mather & Platt, a famous engineering firm, and bought the adjacent land for a new Avro-owned plant.

In April 1912 AV had realized what a fine machine would result from fitting a Type E tandem biplane trainer with a Gnome engine. The result led to the most successful British aircraft of the pre-1939 era. It was so good Roe called it by a type number, and he began at 500. In July 1913 the refined 504 was in the air. This made history on 21 November 1914 when three which had been bought by the RNAS and hastily fitted with bomb racks made a daring raid on the Zeppelin works at Friedrichshafen. But it was mainly as a trainer that the 504 was used by the Allies, and by many other countries up to the start of World War II. Avro alone delivered

3696 of various sub-types by the Armistice, and total production up to 1933 was 8970 in Britain and about 1300 elsewhere. But the 1920s were lean years and the big Newton Heath works was half empty despite incredible diversification.

In 1925 a large farm was bought at Woodford, Cheshire, southeast of Manchester, and turned into the main company airfield. In 1929 AV sold his shareholding in order to make flying-boats at Saunders-Roe, and Avro came under the control of John Siddeley, later Lord Kenilworth, who quickly concentrated planemaking at Manchester (and, with Armstrong Whitworth, at Coventry) and turned Hamble into Air Service Training, a large school with facilities that in World War II were to produce many aircraft. In 1935 Avro's parent, Armstrong Siddeley Development Corporation, merged with Hawker to form the nucleus of the vast Hawker Siddeley Group.

This group was well placed to take a full part in the RAF expansion of 1936–39, masterminded by Sir Frank Spriggs but with Roy Dobson firmly in charge at Manchester as managing director. "Dobbie" had impressed AV outside the factory gates in 1914 and been hired on the spot. Dobbie's courage was not only of the boardroom kind; in 1916 he had climbed out of the rear gunner's cockpit of the Avro Pike (type 523) and clambered forward against the slipstream until he reached the bow position, thus enabling F P Raynham to maintain control and land safely. In World War II Avro was to be a giant, and Dobbie was the calibre of man needed.

From 1936 Newton Heath was packed with Blenheims, and the same type occupied the giant new Shadow factory built at

Chadderton, northeast Manchester, in 1937–38. The Anson, the faithful coastal-reconnaissance bomber that found it could do almost everything else, moved out to another new Shadow works at Yeadon, today Leeds-Bradford Airport, and as the load built up further immense facilities grew at Ringway (now Manchester Airport), Bracebridge Heath, Langar and elsewhere, with company employment topping 40,000. By far the greatest load was the Lancaster, the fine bomber that grew Phoenix-like out of the unacceptable Manchester. Out of 7366 built, Avro delivered 3050 at Manchester, with assembly at Ringway or Woodford, and 620 at Yeadon, the Avro plants alone reaching a monthly output of 155 plus as many again repaired or rebuilt at Langar. Even this total was dwarfed by the figure of 11,020 Ansons, but they were a bit easier.

From the beloved Lancaster stemmed the Lincoln, York, Lancastrian, Tudor, Shackleton (still in front-line service in 1980), Ashton jet and (if one counts the same basic wing) Argosy. But the Model 698 was something quite new. This was the mighty Vulcan delta-winged bomber, conceived by Chadwick, designed by Stu Davies (with the radical aerodynamics in the hands of John Ewans, and proved by the multi-

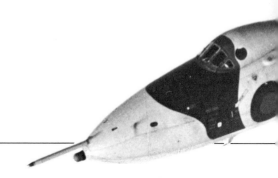

colored 707 research fleet) and brilliantly flown by Roly Falk. Like Britain's industry, Avro peaked in the early 1950s. Then its startling Model 730 supersonic bomber and practically everything else except the Blue Steel stand-off missile was cancelled. But Dobbie never gave up without a fight, and in June 1960 the first 748 twin-turboprop flew in the hands of Jimmy Harrison. It owed something to Aviation Traders' Accountant, which had failed to sell, and it came third into the marketplace behind the F27 and Herald. Yet today, after 21 years, sales approach 400 and output is increasing.

In July 1963 Avro became the main part of Hawker Siddeley's Avro Whitworth Division. In 1978 this in turn became the British Aerospace Manchester Division.

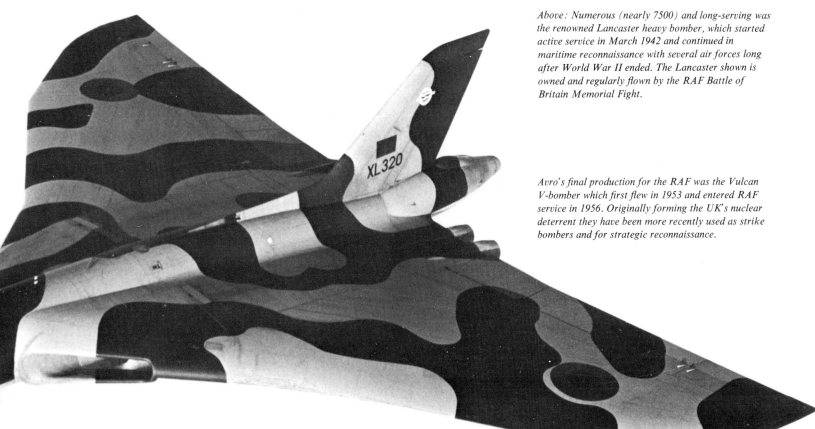

Above: Numerous (nearly 7500) and long-serving was the renowned Lancaster heavy bomber, which started active service in March 1942 and continued in maritime reconnaissance with several air forces long after World War II ended. The Lancaster shown is owned and regularly flown by the RAF Battle of Britain Memorial Fight.

Avro's final production for the RAF was the Vulcan V-bomber which first flew in 1953 and entered RAF service in 1956. Originally forming the UK's nuclear deterrent they have been more recently used as strike bombers and for strategic reconnaissance.

BLACKBURN

Like several other pioneer planemakers, Robert Blackburn became bitten by the bug of flying when he saw Wilbur Wright fly in France in 1908. He boldly threw up his job as a civil engineer in Rouen to sit in a garret in Paris designing a monoplane. Though he had spent little time discussing flying machines, his first effort was remarkably sound, with propeller at the front, tail at the back (with slab tailplane) and wing-warping; the only odd feature to modern eyes was that he put the seat on a separate three-wheel platform under the fuselage. His father, works manager at the famed Leeds factory of Thomas Green and Sons, makers of road rollers and mowers, took a poor view of his son's abandonment of his career, and refused to let him build the aircraft in the works. But when he saw the tenacity with which "RB," then (late 1909) aged 24, set about the constructional task he lent him money and an assistant, Harry Goodyear. The machine was built behind a garment factory in Benson Street. As soon as the winter was over it was taken to the sandy shore at Marske, where in April 1910 young Blackburn managed to get the wheels off the ground several times before crashing on 24 May.

Although No 1 had been unwieldy, the root cause was inadequate power. With remarkable speed RB built a second and superior machine, strongly resembling an Antoinette, helped by R J Isaacson of the big Hunslet engine works who was already testing an outstandingly advanced aero-engine. This gave a lot of trouble, and with his father's help RB bought a Gnome engine, though the Isaacson and other engines were also later tried. On 8 March

1911, eight months after starting taxiing on the beach at Filey, Blackburn No 2 made a most successful flight – in the hands of B C Hucks, who was experienced in every part of aviation *except* piloting! From then on RB did not try to fly but went into business as a constructor, first with an office at 18 Spencer Place, then in converted stables off Balm Road and finally setting up the Blackburn Aeroplane & Motor Company at Olympia, a derelict Leeds skating rink. The company was formed in June 1914 with public capital of £200,000, and by this time RB had sold a substantial number of excellent single- and two-seat monoplanes, most with a 50hp Gnome engine, with wooden structure and distinctive triangular-section fuselage.

There followed production of BE.2cs, Sopwith Babies and torpedo-carrying Cuckoos, and various Blackburn machines, notably Blackburds (carrying the formidable Mk VIII torpedo) and twin-engined Kangaroos which crippled a U-boat and after the war served as civil transports and multi-engine trainers until at least 1929. The company was regarded by the RAF-run Fleet Air Arm as leader in the field of carrier attack and torpedo aircraft, though the results in the 1920s – Swift, Dart, Blackburn, Velos – were lumpy and ugly, and only gradually improved through the Ripon, Baffin and Shark of the 1930s. In 1916 a new factory had been started on the Humber, at Brough, west of Hull, and this soon became the headquarters with not only purpose-designed facilities but also a good airfield and marine ramp. There the company diversified into lightplanes with the neat side-by-side Bluebird, later de-

Above: Blackburn's first order from the Royal Navy in 1914 started an association that lasted throughout the company's existence and evolved a long line of naval and carrier aircraft. Pictured is the first Blackburn aircraft designed specifically for torpedo dropping – the Blackburd of 1918.

veloped into the B-2 trainer, and into large all-metal flying-boats with the Iris, designed by Major Rennie who had worked with Porte on the wartime Felixstowe boats. The Iris, with three Condor engines, was a giant for its day, and led to the Perth of 1933.

In general the company tended to make prototypes rather than money, but it ferreted around for many kinds of business and in 1936 drew all its activities together into a new public company, Blackburn Aircraft Limited, which in 1940 took over

Robert Blackburn and one of his first practical machines, a Mercury monoplane, in its hangar at the flying school operated by Blackburn at Filey, Yorkshire. A very similar 1912 Blackburn monoplane has the distinction of being the oldest British airplane still flying, with the Shuttleworth Trust.

Above right: Busy Blackburn production lines in February 1938 in readiness for the war already regarded as inevitable. In the foreground are Skua fighter/dive-bombers, notable as being the Navy's first operational monoplane and the type that claimed the first British air-combat victory of World War II (against a Do18 flying-boat); beyond are the last Blackburn biplanes – Sharks – by then relegated to communications and torpedo training.

Right: Final Blackburn design before amalgamation was the Buccaneer low-level strike aircraft for operation from carriers or land. Here a RN Buccaneer rests on a catapult of HMS Victorious during the carrier's last commission.

the Cirrus engine business. Stressed-skin monoplanes included the indifferent Skua, Roc and Botha, but the main effort in World War II was production of the Barracuda (635 at Brough), Swordfish (1699, far more than Fairey, at Sherburn) and Sunderland (250 at Dumbarton). The Firebrand naval torpedo-carrying fighter took a disgraceful ten years to develop, and the company lost the anti-submarine contract to Fairey's Gannet, but survived by building Prentice and Balliol trainers and, in January 1949, by acquiring General Aircraft, which resulted in the GAL.60 becoming the Blackburn Beverley. But by far the most important of all Blackburn aircraft was the Buccaneer, designed to a far-seeing naval requirement by a team under Barry Laight and flown at Holme on Spalding Moor on 30 April 1958. So myopic were many air marshals, officials and journalists that this outstanding attack aircraft was derided by the RAF until in 1968, 16 years after the Royal Navy specification and ten years after first flight, it was at last ordered by the RAF, which it has served admirably ever since.

RB died in 1955, happy in hearing of the Buccaneer win against nine rival designs. In 1960 Blackburn Aircraft was bought by Hawker Siddeley, while Blackburn Engines, a licensee of Turboméca, went to Bristol Siddeley and thus ultimately Rolls-Royce. In May 1963 Brough and Holme became part of HSA Hawker Blackburn Division, and today they are important parts of BAe Kingston-Brough Division.

GENERAL AIRCRAFT

General Aircraft stemmed from young H J Stieger, a Swiss engineer who in 1927 injected some modern structural knowledge into the attempt by William Beardmore and Company to build the giant Inflexible. This monster monoplane had a wing constructed on Rohrbach lines, and the whole design was built under the German company's license. Stieger devised a lighter single-spar wing using built-up light-alloy structure based on a Warren-girder spar. His objective was a lighter cantilever monoplane wing, and he patented it in 1929 as the Monospar. Leaving Beardmore, he went into business with F F Crocombe – a fellow-student at Imperial College – as The Monospar Wing Company, of Broad Street, London. The Air Ministry placed a contract for a test wing, designated ST.1, and then a big wing made by Gloster Aircraft and flown on a Fokker F.VII/3m.

The infant company itself got Gloster to build its first aircraft, the ST.3 three-seater, with two 45hp Salmsons. Then it set up its own shops at Croydon, and began a very successful series of Monospar light twins, nearly all powered by two 85 or 90hp Pobjoy engines. Even the very first, the ST.4, sold 30, and by 1935 the ST.25

Jubilee sold ten as four/five-seaters, four as freighters, six as ambulances and no fewer than 40 in Universal form with twin fins. This was a year after the firm had been re-formed as a public company, General Aircraft Limited (GAL), at Feltham, Middlesex. Stieger left in 1935 and Crocombe continued as chief designer of a veritable spate of lightplanes (and the big ST.18 Croydon, with Wasp Juniors, unfortunately stranded on a coral reef in the Timor Sea). D L Hollis-Williams was the chief engineer, and the managing director was E C Gordon England, one of the most famous British pilots of the pre-1914 era. Flight Lieutenant H M Schofield was test and demonstration pilot.

The business prospered. Dropping Stieger's ST in favor of GAL it produced the remarkable unbroken run of projects from GAL.26 to GAL.47 while showing a trading profit! Notable designs included the GAL.33 Cagnet light pusher, GAL.38 STOL Fleet Shadower (a four-Pobjoy three-seater to Specification S.23/37, also tendered for by Airspeed but made obsolete by radar), GAL.41 pressure-cabin research aircraft, GAL.42 Cygnet lightplane designed by C W Aircraft and rebuilt with tricycle

Monospar was the name applied to the light and strong single girder spar used in a wing designed by H J Stieger in the late 1920s. He founded General Aircraft to exploit the technique. Picture is one of a range of GAL Monospar designs that appeared up to the time of the merger with Blackburn in 1949, the ST-25 Jubilee light twin, named for King George V's Silver Jubilee.

landing gear (pioneered in Britain by an experimental Monospar), GAL.45 Owlet tricycle trainer and GAL.47 STOL observation aircraft. While busy on wings, tailplanes and other parts for Spitfires, GAL designed the GAL.48 Hotspur eight-seat glider in late 1940 and built 22; then, as the clipped-wing Mk II glider-pilot trainer, over 1000 were built by woodworking firms. Then came the giant GAL.49 tank-carrying glider; again Feltham built 22 while a team led by Birmingham Railway Carriage and Wagon Company built 390. At the end came the GAL.56 tailless glider (a truly ghastly flying machine), the GAL.59 Mosquito TT.39 naval tug/plotter and, the crowning achievement, the GAL.60 Universal, intended as a 90-seater with four Hercules engines but actually built after the 1948 merger with Blackburn as a freighter with four Centaurus engines.

DE HAVILLAND

Although Hawker stemmed from the Sopwith company, an even more important root-stock was the interest in pioneer aviation by a man who was neither a designer nor a pilot, but who did have money. George Holt Thomas was son of the founder of the *Daily Graphic* newspaper. Seeking good stories he got to know almost every aviator in Europe, and by 1911 he had gone into business with British licenses for the Farman aircraft and Gnome engine. In 1912 he formed the Aircraft Manufacturing Company, with main works at The Hyde, near the important airfield at Hendon. Another plant was set up at Walthamstow, east London, to make Gnomes, and a third at Merton, southwest London, for blimps and balloons.

In March 1914 Holt Thomas managed to wean Hugh Burroughes away from Farnborough to serve as Airco's manager. Three months later came an even greater capture; Geoffrey de Havilland arrived from Farnborough as chief designer.

He was already a national figure. Son of the vicar of Crux Eaton, near Highclere, he built his own motorcycle just after the turn of the century to commute to the Crystal Palace Engineering School. In 1908 he was living in Walthamstow designing buses, when a remarkable grandfather lent him £500 and changed history. Geoffrey teamed up with Frank T Hearle, a Cornish marine engineer, married Hearle's sister, and rented a small workshop off Bothwell Street, Fulham Palace Road. There they built a biplane, spending half the loan on a 45hp engine built by Iris Motors whose chief designer was elder brother Ivon de Havilland. Mrs de Havilland stitched all the fabric and in late 1909 they took the completed machine to a shed on the North Downs at Seven Barrows near Newbury. In December DH tried to take off, but the left wings broke.

Fortunately the engine was little damaged, and on 10 September 1910 DH made a successful flight in a new machine made of better materials. He was obviously a good intuitive pilot, for he was soon doing figure

Sir Geoffrey de Havilland (right) in 1948, talking to test pilot John Cunningham (facing), and F T Hearle (left).

eights, and giving rides to his wife and eight-month-old Geoffrey Junior. He then took the machine to Farnborough, demonstrated it for an hour on 14 January 1911 and sold it for £400. He was taken on as designer and test pilot (Hearle became official mechanic) and directed the design and construction of the FE.2, SE.1 and, with Folland, the BE series. In 1913 he was injured testing the BS.1 (SE.2) but had recovered before leaving to join Airco. In his spare time he exercised as a second lieutanant with the new RFC and served as HM inspector of aircraft.

Two months after he joined Holt Thomas war broke out. DH had already begun the design of a fighting scout, with pusher 120hp Beardmore engine and an observer ahead of the pilot with a Lewis gun covering an extremely wide arc. Farnborough, by then called the Royal Aircraft Factory, wanted all Beardmores, and offered the 70hp Renault instead. DH argued, but was promptly removed from the scene by being posted to RFC No 2 Squadron. He continued to argue, and by 1915 was back at Hendon, as a captain, working on the DH.2. Savage of Kings Lynn had built 70 of the DH.1s and Airco was overwhelmed by an order for 250 of the single-seat DH.2s, an agile machine which – provided the pilot had at least three arms – mastered the Fokker monoplanes and equipped No 24 Squadron, often called the world's first fighter squadron, under Lanoe G Hawker (no relation to Harry).

Everyone knows the DH.4 – the day bomber that outpaced all the fighters, and which underpinned the foundation of US

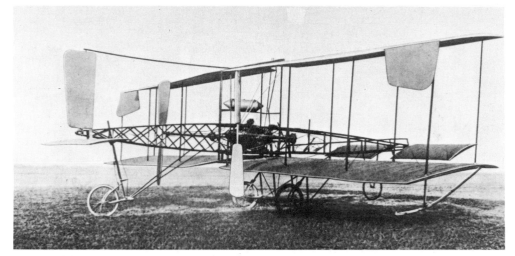

Above left: The first de Havilland airplane of 1909, which failed to fly when the wings broke at the first attempt. A stronger machine made a successful first flight in the following year.

Left: DH.9A, the famed "Ninack," of World War I vintage and mainstay of the RAF overseas for many years thereafter, flies over Kohat, then India now Pakistan, with 60 Squadron in the late 1920s.

air power – and the DH.9 and 9A which remained in service until 1931. Less familiar are the backstaggered DH.5 scout (550-plus) and angular DH.6 trainer (2200), while the outstanding DH.10 Amiens twin-engined bomber would have been a major type had the war continued into 1919 (about 220 were built). In December 1918 the name Airco came into general use (it was spelled Air-Co on aircraft serial plates), and a subsidiary, Aircraft Transport & Travel, flew the first sustained civil international air service between London and Paris, initially using the DH.4A. But times were hard. There was little traffic, and hardly any sale for new aircraft. Holt Thomas sold Airco to the big BSA company, which on strict business grounds closed down the aviation enterprise.

DH had seen it coming, and on 25 September 1920 formed the de Havilland Aircraft Company with about 50 Airco colleagues among whom were Hearle (general manager), C C Walker (chief engineer), W E Nixon (secretary) and F E N St Barbe (sales); Arthur E Hagg soon came as DH's assistant designer. They set up the works in two sheds in a field off Stag Lane, then

open country in Edgware, northwest of London. While carrying on with the Airco (de Havilland) DH.18 biplane airliner, DH boldly designed an efficient cantilever monoplane, the DH.29. Sadly, it exhibited imperfect stability, and this quirk of fate kept the company generally off the monoplane (and stressed-skin all-metal construction) until 1939. But within the context of

traditional wooden biplanes the enterprise prospered, especially after DH saw the shortcomings of the underpowered lightplanes built for Air Ministry Trials and, in 1924, asked Frank Halford to build a 60hp engine. The result, using cheap parts from wartime Renault engines, was the ADC (Aircraft Disposal Company) Cirrus. This, in turn, was the basis of the DH.60 Moth,

De Havilland's greatest success was the Moth lightplane and its various derivatives. Introduced in the mid-1920s as the DH.60, and developed into the DH.82 Tiger Moth, it gave to many their first taste of flying, became the basic trainer of numerous air forces, was the means of many pioneering flights, and has survived by the hundreds in private fliers' hands to the present. Illustrated is a restored RAF Tiger Moth, of which well over 4000 were produced in the UK and almost as many in other Commonwealth countries.

Top left: One of a long line of piston-engined small-to-medium-capacity airliners, the DH.89 first flew as the Dragon Six in April 1934 and was later renamed Dragon Rapide, soon clipped unofficially but permanently to Rapide. Well over 700 Rapides were built to serve airlines faithfully all over the world for many years. Illustrated is the Island-class Rapide RMA Lord Shaftesbury of BEA in 1956.

which DH flew on 22 February 1925.

From this stemmed the most important family of lightplanes in the world in the 1925–35 decade. A crucial factor was Halford's decision to join DH, form an engine division and create a new and better engine which he named the Gipsy. The first prototypes were 135hp racing engines for the DH.71 Tiger Moth monoplane; then came the production Gipsy I derated to 85hp. Even this was enough for DH (in his own Gipsy Moth G-AAAA) to break the world altitude class record, for Hubert Broad to fly over Stag Lane for 24 hours non-stop and for Alan S Butler (the wealthy sportsman who put £7500 into the company and became chairman) to break the 100km closed-circuit record. In 1928–29 G-EBTD flew 600 hours with a sealed engine, the subsequent repair bill totalling a mere £7 2s 11d. The result was orders by the hundred, with Moths coming off the line by 1930 at three a day.

By this time Stag Lane had been swallowed by a spreading London. Need for another site, farther out, was met by a site at Hatfield. Testing moved there in 1930, followed by the DH School of Flying and London Aeroplane Club. By 1932 the production of the Moth Major, Tiger Moth, Fox Moth and Dragon had moved to the new factory. All that was left at Stag Lane was the engine works, while the airfield was covered by a suburban estate that included Mollison Way and de Havilland Road. In 1944 this factory, along with the new turbojet facility at Stonegrove and a rocket and test site at Hatfield, became the de Havilland Engine Company. The license for the Hamilton propeller in 1935, following use of Hamiltons on the DH.88 Comet racer, led in 1946 to de Havilland Propellers Limited which later pioneered air-to-air missiles, the Blue Streak LRBM and a wide range of aircraft equipment.

In 1927 Major Hereward de Havilland shipped a Moth to Perth, Australia, flew it to Melbourne and set up de Havilland Aircraft Pty in a tumbledown shed on Whiteman Street. He gathered a few helpers and began assembling Moths – the first went to the *Sydney Sun* and distributed pictures taken of the opening of the new capital of Canberra – and later made 1085 Tigers, 87 Dragons, over 200 Mosquitos and the locally designed Drover. In January 1928 Moth assembly started in a derelict warehouse at Mount Dennis, Toronto; de Havilland Aircraft of Canada moved to nearby Downsview in 1929 at a site which later delivered 1520 Tigers, 1032 "Mozzies," 375 Ansons, 100 Grumman Trackers and thousands of locally designed Chipmunks, Beavers, Otters, Twin Otters, Turbos, Caribous, Buffalos and Dash 7s. India followed in 1929, South Africa in 1930 and New Zealand in 1939, forming the world's greatest-ever global network of plane-making under one private enterprise.

In the late 1930s Hatfield expanded violently, built 1440 Oxfords designed by Airspeed, the 1934 company based at Portsmouth (backed by the shipbuilder Swan Hunter, whose shareholding was purchased by DH in 1940), and got into stressed skin with the Flamingo airliner. The brilliant Mosquito was made at Hatfield, by a new No 2 Factory at Leavesden, Airspeed, Percival (Luton), Standard Motors (Canley) and a gigantic wartime factory at Chester (Hawarden) which DH

Top right: Experience with the short-lived but handsome Albatross airliner undoubtedly benefited that most remarkable of World War II aircraft – the fighter/reconnaissance communications/bomber maid-of-all-work the DH.98 Mosquito, which was built of wood and out-performed all its contemporaries. This May 1943 picture shows one of several Mosquito production lines that contributed to a total completed of nearly 8000.

took over from Vickers in 1948 for peacetime production. Total Mosquito output was 7781. At the outbreak of war, when work on this project was at last able to start, the design team was evacuated to Salisbury Hall, about five miles west of Hatfield. The first Mosquito was dismantled and trucked to Hatfield but the second, a fighter prototype, was brilliantly flown out from the rough 450yd (410m) field adjoining the Hall by Geoffrey de Havilland Jr, saving at least a month in May 1941.

Airspeed built 4462 Oxfords and 695 of the 3655 Horsa gliders. Brush Coachworks at Loughborough took over the Rapide/

Dominie in 1943, but the company was still overloaded and production of the DH.100 Vampire jet fighter began at English Electric at Preston. In 1948 Chester began Vampire production, followed by Venoms, Doves, Herons, Comets, 125s and Airbus wings; Tridents were built at Hatfield, which, following absorption into the Hawker Siddeley Group in 1960, became the center for all HSA civil programs other than Manchester's 748. Odd man out was the Vixen program, originally a Hatfield project but "navalized" by what had been the Airspeed company and produced by them with assembly at Christchurch.

Below left: In July 1949 de Havilland flew the world's first jet airliner and in May 1952 the first of the airliner Comets entered scheduled service with BOAC. The venture brought early disaster and an epoch-making investigation, but the knowledge thus tragically bought was given to the world to the betterment of aviation. The Comet 3 (illustrated) virtually was the prototype of the Comet 4 with which BOAC just beat PanAm's Boeing 707 transatlantic service by a few days in October 1958.

Below: The DH.112 Venom, which first flew in September 1949, was the natural successor to the Vampire and was supplied in fair quantity as a fighter/ bomber and night fighter to the RAF and FAA and to many other air forces; it was also built in France as the Sud Aquilon. This Venom FB.4 has been preserved at Kai Tak Airport, Hong Kong.

AIRSPEED

Right: The Airspeed Oxford, a military development of the Envoy feederliner, became the RAF's first twin-engine monoplane trainer; from the 400 delivered by the outbreak of war, production in several plants – pictured is a Percival-built example – expanded the final total built to nearly 9000.

Below: The last Airspeed design, the AS.57 Ambassador, was an elegant medium-stage airliner which provided a very comfortable and pleasant ride for up to about 50 passengers. It was worthy of a better fate than the single order for 20 from BEA, after which de Havilland dropped it.

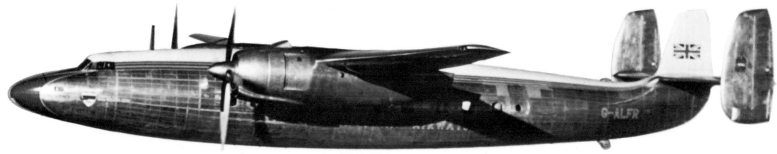

FOLLAND

In February 1936 a group of businessmen headed by A P Good set up British Marine Aircraft, a subsidiary of the British Aircraft Manufacturing Company (which did not actually make aircraft), chiefly in order to build the Sikorsky S-42 flying-boat under license. At that time Imperial Airways had yet to place its big 28-boat contract with Short Brothers, and the S-42 was markedly superior to anything in Britain (the BMA-1, sometimes called BM-1, would have had Perseus sleeve-valve engines, and registration G-AEGZ was reserved). The company acquired a factory at Hamble and spent a large sum on the production tooling.

Emergence of the Short S.23 dealt a death-blow to the BM-1, but the company was loath to give up. In May 1937 it managed to secure the services of Harry Folland as managing director, and was renamed Folland Aircraft. No niche could be found for a new design before the war, but the urgent need for combat aircraft meant the Hamble works was fully occupied on subcontract work. On the side it produced an original design specifically as an engine test-bed, known only by its specification number, 43/37; 12 were built in

1938–40 and they tested every high-power engine of that era except the Prince, Deerhound and Exe. The E.28/40 torpedo bomber and F.19/43 fighter were both cancelled at an advanced stage.

After the war Folland prospered working mainly for major de Havilland and Bristol programs, until in 1950 history repeated itself. From outside the company a powerful engineer arrived to take over as managing director. This time it was W E W "Teddy" Petter, previously designer of the P.1 and Canberra at English Electric and before that of the Westland Whirlwind and Lysander. He had got to know Folland Aircraft on the jet/prop F.19/43, in which English Electric participated. His launch of the P.1 eventually was to give Britain its only supersonic fighter (the Lightning), but Petter was alarmed at the prospect of soaring costs and, as a byproduct, of extreme complexity, unserviceability.

He wanted to build a jet fighter that was much smaller and simpler. Folland gave him a free hand. After prolonged false starts and changes in direction, not helped by the Ministry cancelling any engine that appeared suitable, he eventually created the

After joining Folland, "Teddy" Petter's answer to the great complexity of contemporary fighters was the Folland Midge, the lowest-powered aircraft ever to go supersonic. From it stemmed the Gnat light interceptor and later jet trainer which, as standard equipment until 1979 of the RAF Red Arrows aerobatic team, has thrilled millions around the world with brilliant flying displays.

Fo.141 Gnat, preceded by the low-powered Midge flown on 11 August 1954. With an engine of 1640lb thrust the Midge easily dived faster than sound, and captivated all who saw or flew it. It was contrary to Ministry policy, but eventually various Gnats were exported, the Indian government founded its fighter force on it (and found it an outstanding combat aircraft) and the RAF adopted a much modified trainer version which, after the Hawker Siddeley Group takeover in March 1960, was produced at Dunsfold as well as Hamble. Between 1963 and 1965 the Hamble works became part of HSA Hawker Blackburn Division, and subsequently became a unit in BAe Aircraft Group Kingston/Brough Division.

GLOSTER

The outbreak of World War I had naturally caused an urgent search for ways to expand Britain's tiny aircraft industry. Holt Thomas at Airco asked his chief supplier of spruce and ash, William Mallinson & Son of Hackney Road, to be told that there was good woodworking expertise at Waring & Gillow and H H Martyn. The former was a high-class furniture maker at Cambridge Road, Hammersmith. It was one of the powerful team that made the DH.9, and it is also thought to have assembled American-made Handley Pages. By chance, Samuel (later Lord) Waring had founded British Nieuport. The other company, Martyn's, was at Sunningend Works, Cheltenham. Hugh Burroughes visited them in April 1915 and was impressed. Soon Martyn was working on Longhorn and Shorthorn spares, parts for the DH.2 and BE.2c and fuselages for the DH.4 and 6, as well as complete Bristol Fighters and Nieuport scouts.

In 1917 Airco and Martyn discussed forming a 50/50-owned aircraft company to rent the Sunningend factory and take over Airco's large subcontract business. On 5 June 1917 the Gloucestershire Aircraft Company was registered, and it soon became a major contender. GAC drew employees from throughout the Gloucester/Cheltenham area, and its products, at first Bristol Fighters, Nighthawks and FE.2bs, were trundled seven miles to the Air Board acceptance park at Hucclecote, on the other side of Gloucester. In 1918 GAC was making about 45 aircraft a week; then came the Armistice and there was no more work. GAC did not even have a design staff.

One or two Bristol Fighters and Nieuports continued to be built, though the Nighthawk's Dragonfly engine had been found a totally unacceptable design. Hugh Burroughes left and Holt Thomas, a sick man, sold out Airco to the BSA/Daimler Group. But GAC was one of the dogged band that decided to stay on. A W Martyn was named chairman and David Longden managing director, and as part of its postwar contractual settlement GAC agreed to accept large quantities of Nighthawk parts. British Nieuport had officially been called the Nieuport and General Aircraft Company, and its works at Cricklewood in north London had produced several hundred Sopwith Camels and other types. It had managed to build up a design staff, led by the brilliant Harry (HP) Folland, from Farnborough, who came from the govern-

ment establishment with Major S Heckstall-Smith. Folland designed several first-class "British Nieuports," but the company, part of the Waring Group, could see no postwar future and in November 1920 decided to close.

Folland agreed to help GAC improve the Nighthawk, which was soon flying with some of the very first Jaguar and Jupiter engines, and he also designed an ultra-fast Lion-powered derivative called Mars I. This tiny racer had a half-bear half-camel insignia and was often called the Bamel. It won races and set speed records, ending its days as an RAF seaplane with the RAF High Speed Flight at Felixstowe. Folland also designed a further "Mars" series of Nighthawk derivatives, some being re-named Sparrowhawks and used as fighters and trainers by the Imperial Japanese Navy on the recommendation of the 1921 British Air Mission.

By 1921 Folland had formally been appointed chief engineer of GAC. The Bamel had put the infant company on the map as a top high-speed planemaker, and thanks to the mass of war-surplus Nighthawk parts that had been stored in Cheltenham's Winter Gardens in Imperial Square, GAC was able for a while to produce modern fighters and derived machines at a good profit. By far the most important of

the early products were the Jaguar-engined Grebe and Jupiter-engined Gamecock, standard RAF fighters made in large numbers. In 1926 the company changed its name to Gloster, and also switched to metal structures. One of the last Nighthawk-derived fighters was the Gambet, 150 of which were made for Japan's Navy as the Nakajima AIN. Schneider racers and numerous prototypes were flown; bread-and-butter products included the 229 Gauntlet Mercury-engined fighters built from 1929 to 1937. A refined version, the Gladiator, with a more powerful Mercury and four machine-guns, was the final winner of the protracted F.7/30 fighter competition. It did not reach the RAF until 1937, by which time it was obsolescent, but it was far better than nothing. Highly maneuverable, though gravely deficient in performance and fire-power, 747 were built, 98 being naval Sea Gladiators (three of the latter were Malta's so-called *Faith, Hope* and *Charity*). Gloster exported Gladiators to Latvia, Lithuania, Norway, Sweden, Finland, Belgium, Ireland, Greece, Portugal, Egypt, Iraq and South Africa.

In May 1934 Hawker Aircraft made a takeover proposal which GAC accepted. The latter did not lose its identity, though Folland feared he would play second fiddle to Sydney Camm and so left to set up his

Gloster workers assemble Jupiter-powered Mars VI fighters from surplus Nighthawk parts (note serials) in 1922. They were probably destined for the Japanese Navy as there were no UK orders in hand at that time.

own company at Hamble. GAC received large contracts for Hawker production, starting with the Hardy, Hart and Audax and moving on to the 200 Henley two-seat dive-bombers (wasted as target tugs by the RAF) and 2750 Hurricanes. GAC also handled Typhoon production between 1941 and 1945, a total of 3330. But the company's chief claim to fame was that it was chosen in 1939 to design and build the two E.28/39 jet research fighters (they had provision for four Browning guns), the first of which flew on Whittle's W.1 engine at Cranwell in May 1941.

By this time GAC had three major factories and a good airfield at Hucclecote/Brockworth, a secret prototype shop at Bentham and, from 1943, a flight-test base at Moreton Valence, all in the Gloucester neighborhood. The "A W Hawksley" organization, set up to make the Albemarle, was virtually part of GAC and used the latter's No 2 factory. Folland's successor, W G Carter, worked with Whittle on the trim E.28/39 and then on the F.9/40 Meteor, Britain's first jet fighter. Prototypes were built with all available types of turbojet and it was DG206/G, with Halford H.1 (DH Goblin) engines, that made the first flight on 5 March 1943. The pilot was hefty Michael Daunt, who a little later was badly shaken by being sucked into a

Meteor engine inlet. Subsequently 3545 Meteors were built, the last 575 being night fighters built by Armstrong Whitworth; another 330 were made by Benelux companies led by Fokker.

The last Gloster product was the subsonic Javelin all-weather fighter, produced in nine different marks between 1951 and 1959, 302 made by GAC and 133 by Armstrong Whitworth. In 1956 a thin-winged transonic successor was cancelled, and despite prolonged efforts to find new markets and products GAC was merged into Whitworth Gloster Aircraft in October, 1961.

One of the fastest aircraft of its day was the Mars I "Bamel" built in 1921. Among many advanced performance achievements it established a new world speed record of over 212mph (341km/h) in October 1922. A center-section fairing and wheelspats with which the machine was designed were later deleted as unnecessary.

Below: Having earned a reputation for building high-performance aircraft, Gloster was entrusted with the development of the first British jet airplane, the E28/39, and the first British, and only Allied, jet fighter to see service in World War II. Here a Meteor NF.14 flies in company with a Gloster Javelin FAW.4 and the only remaining flying example of the last Gloster piston-engined fighter, the Shuttleworth Collection's Gladiator.

Perhaps the name in the heading ought to have been Sopwith. After all, Sopwith began it, and the company must later have regretted the change of name in 1920. It is just by chance that later generations never looked on the Sopwith Siddeley Group as the most powerful force in British aviation.

Thomas Octave Murdoch Sopwith was born in 1888 with an overwhelming desire to fly. He joined the Aero Club, visited Wilbur Wright in France and was one of the first customers for Howard Wright's completely original all-steel streamlined machines in late 1909. He was a naturally gifted pilot, and soon took Aviator's Certificate No 31. On 18 December 1910 he set out from Eastchurch and won the £4000 Baron de Forest prize for the longest flight to the Continent by landing 169 miles (272km) away in Belgium. In 1911 he went to the USA to race and stayed over a year, despite being told by the Wrights that his machine infringed their patents (so he bought one of theirs).

Wealthy Sopwith had already made a name for himself in car-racing, ballooning, yachting and other exciting activities in the course of which he had come to rely on Fred Sigrist, an extravert Australian who, always accompanied by his pet bear, could fix any mechanical problem. Gradually Sigrist matured as an able designer and manager, and by 1910 was employed full-time running Sopwith's flying school – one of many at Brooklands – which was the one picked by that most selective of customers, "Boom" Trenchard, the "father of the RAF." Tom Sopwith could have continued living for kicks, but underlying the "jet-set" life was something much deeper. In 1912 he founded the Sopwith Aviation Company, perhaps partly because he had more assets than other planemakers. He had riches, talent, brilliant piloting skill, Sigrist, and two additional Australians, solid draftsmen Ashfield and H G Hawker. Harry Hawker arrived at Brooklands with little save a toothbrush and his own acumen, but Sopwith very soon found that was more than most men possess in a lifetime. He gladly gave Hawker flying lessons, while Hawker worked from dawn to dusk in return.

With such a team Sopwith could hardly fail. He bought a disused skating rink at Canbury Park Road, Kingston on Thames, and built up a total capability in plane-making. After building and flying two nondescript Wright-derived machines Sop-with built the Bat Boat, the first successful British flying-boat. It comprised a Saunders Consuta hull, with two seats side-by-side, attached to a simple Sopwith-designed wing, tail and pusher engine installation. It had a long and active career, being several times modified and eventually serving with the RNAS at Calshot and Scapa Flow. Other aircraft followed, notably the small Tabloid, a single-bay biplane (possibly the first in history) which had the unprecedented range of 55mph (88km/h) between minimum and maximum speed. Hawker flew it on 29 November 1913, hopped over from Brook-lands to Farnborough for official tests and then dropped in late in the afternoon on the regular Saturday show at Hendon. Nobody in the world had seen such a neat, speedy flying machine, and it created a sensation. In 1914, when Hawker was in his own

Above: The small and nimble Sopwith Pup, the aircraft that was used to pioneer carrier deck-landing techniques and precursor of the Camel that finally won ascendancy over the German fighters in World War I. This Pup has been restored to flying condition by the Shuttleworth Trust.

Below: T O M Sopwith (left), who founded his company in 1912, and Harry Hawker, whose name was used for the reconstituted company in 1920, with the neat Tabloid two-seater which caused a sensation when it appeared unannounced at a 1913 airshow at Hendon.

country, Howard Pixton flew a seaplane Tabloid to victory in the second Schneider Trophy race. Subsequently many Tabloids, Schneiders and Babies were built for the RNAS by various makers, along with other seaplanes and a few landplanes.

In December 1915 Hawker, just back from Australia, tested the first 1½-Strutter. This was perhaps the first properly conceived warplane in history, with neat tractor layout, fixed and movable guns (the former controlled by an interrupter gear devised by Harry Kauper, yet another "Aussie") fired from tandem cockpits, and a bomb load. More than 1500 machines were built by Sopwith and other makers in Britain, plus possible exports, while between 4200 and 4500 were made in France. Despite its excellence the airframe cost only £842.30, less than almost any other wartime aircraft. It was followed by the small and nimble Pup, possibly the most perfect aerobatic mount of its day and a pioneer of deck-landing techniques; the Triplane which threw the Germans into a panic; and at Christmas 1916 the Camel, the greatest air-combat fighter of the war.

Though tricky in the hands of a novice, the Camel was deadly when skilfully flown and more than any other aircraft it erased any remaining ascendancy of German scouts on the Western Front in 1917–18. Until 1976 it was confidently reported that its total score was 1294 victories, more than any other type; then a British author, Chaz Bowyer, checked original records and showed the true figure to have been in excess of 2800 for RFC and RNAS Camel squadrons alone. Numerous other types emerged from Canbury Park Road by the Armistice, notably including the heavily armed Dolphin and the Camel's successor, the Snipe.

In 1919 the frantic effort faded, and the Kingston shops nearly emptied. With hindsight Sopwith could have weathered the bleak years, but he liquidated the company on 3 September 1920. Almost at once it was replaced by H G Hawker Engineering, registered on 15 November 1920 to take over the factory and assets of Sopwith; Sopwith never saw anything strange in this, but some have suggested the new company was motivated by Hawker himself, hence the name, a belief quashed by Sopwith who blandly explained that he had started both the Sopwith and Hawker companies and could hardly use the original name a second time. In any event Hawker was killed in a Nieuport in June 1921.

His place as test pilot was taken by F P Raynham, while Sopwith and Sigrist agreed to be joint managing directors. Norman Thompson was appointed chief designer but fairly soon was replaced by W G Carter (later of Gloster fame); a few weeks later there arrived in Carter's team young Sydney Camm, previously with Martinsyde and main designer of Raynham's 1922 glider. His first job for Hawker was the Cygnet ultra-light, a brilliant exercise in the simplicity which was Camm's philosophy ("I have to design things simple, otherwise I can't understand them"). This was to keep

Above: Successor to the Camel in the long line of renowned Sopwith fighters was the Snipe. Here the Ham (Kingston) works is seen as the full flood of Snipe and Salamander production was about to end in December 1918.

Below: Mpst significant recruit to the Kingston company after its re-formation was Sydney (later Sir Sydney) Camm, a major architect of the series of designs that led from the biplanes, through the World War II Hurricane to the Harrier of today.

Left: An important interwar design that introduced a series of aircraft that kept many companies going was the Hart day bomber, first flown in June 1928. This Hart preserved by the RAF Museum at Hendon.

the company in the front rank of military aviation for 40 years.

In early 1925 the one-off Heron fighter proved a method of construction that, though only a poor intermediate stage between wood and stressed skin, was to appeal to a technically backward British industry until World War II. Devised by Sigrist and Camm, it was an economical way of translating traditional structures into steel or light alloy, and features included tubes with square-section ends for simple bolted joints to flat finger plates, and two wing-spars each formed from upper and lower rolled tubes riveted to a sheet web. It was not the most efficient way of using metal, and in the long term significantly delayed the introduction of modern stressed-skin construction at Kingston.

By far the most important Hawker aircraft of the 1920s was the Hart "day bomber" flown in June 1928. From it stemmed more than 2200 tandem-seat biplanes of many species which provided an important base-load of production at a time of depression. Without it, it is doubtful whether Sopwith would have laid the foundations for the modern British aerospace industry. In February 1934 he went public, renaming the firm Hawker Aircraft Limited. Three months later he bought Gloster, and the following year added the Armstrong Siddeley Development Corporation, thus bringing Avro and Armstrong Whitworth under Hawker control. In 1935 the four aircraft companies, plus Armstrong Siddeley Motors and Air Service Training, formed the Hawker Siddeley Group, a new phenomenon in Britain, with headquarters in Pall Mall. Production of Hart variants kept all member-companies busy.

In the early 1930s the Fury was one of the RAF's interceptors, and from it Camm developed various improved biplane fighter designs and also a monoplane. Gradually this changed into a much more formidable machine, with a more powerful engine (the PV.12 which became the Merlin) and eight rifle-calibre guns, all in the wings. For the first time Camm accepted retractable landing gear and flaps, but there was no chance of either stressed-skin construction or a variable-pitch propeller. The result was the Hurricane, first flown at Brooklands on 6 November 1935. Sopwith called a meeting of the Hawker board in early 1936 at which the momentous decision was taken to spend company money on building a completely new factory (at Langley, near Slough) and tool up for 1000 of the new fighters. The program was delayed by having to switch to a significantly different Merlin, but the private-enterprise decision made it possible to have Hurricanes with 18 RAF squadrons by the start of World War II. Subsequently British companies built 12,780 Hurricanes and Sea Hurricanes, and a further 1451 were completed in Canada.

Eventually Camm made an almost complete transition to stressed-skin construction with the Typhoon, production of which was handled by Gloster, followed by the Tempest and Fury which at last recognized the superiority of the aircooled radial when properly installed. The Nene-powered Sea Hawk was subcontracted to Armstrong Whitworth, but the swept-wing Hunter was so important it was built by Hawker, Armstrong Whitworth and the former Wellington factory at Squire's Gate, Blackpool. The Hunter would have been a perfect basis for prolonged development, but this was not recognized at the time. Amazingly, in 1955 the Hawker Siddeley board sanctioned construction of a prototype Hawker P.1121, a large Mach 2 multi-role aircraft, as a private venture. It would have been a powerful and extremely important aircraft, but it matured exactly at the time the Minister of Defence announced that the RAF was "unlikely to require" any more fighters at all. The board chickened out – and who could blame them? – and the only British aircraft to compete with the Mirage, Phantom and other rivals was broken up for scrap.

Its place in Camm's thinking was taken by vectored-thrust V/STOL, leading to the P.1127 – in the absence of any official interest, this again was a private venture at first – from which stemmed today's family

of Harrier-type aircraft. Sadly, Camm died in 1966 after a prolonged battle against official ineptitude and partisan Service customers which led to the cancellation of first the Royal Navy P.1154 and then the RAF version and their replacement by the Phantom.

Camm would have liked today's Hawk, which began life as the Hawker P.1182; it is a simple worldbeater in his tradition. Hawker Aircraft became part of HSA's Hawker Blackburn Division in July 1963 and in 1977 vanished into the Kingston-Brough Division of British Aerospace.

Above left: Contemporary with Camm's Hart/Hind series of clean and simple two-seat biplanes was the Fury single-seat fighter and it led gradually to the timely evolution of the Hurricane, first flown in November 1935 in time to be accepted and to equip 18 RAF squadrons by the start of World War II. This August 1944 photograph shows the last of the more than 14,000 (including 1451 in Canada) Hurricanes newly rolled out from the Langley works, established specifically to build it.

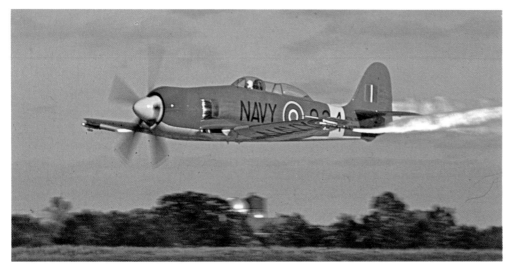

Left: Rather late swings to stressed-skin construction came with the Hawker Typhoon, and to the aircooled radial engine with the Tempest II and Fury/Sea Fury, the last-named being the last Hawker piston-engined design. This particular Sea Fury is maintained in flying condition in the United States.

Below: The evergreen Hawker Hunter made its first flight as the P.1067 in July 1951, followed by the Avon-powered prototype F.1 in May 1953, and entered RAF service in mid-1954. Despite its vintage, the Hunter was still in demand in the 1970s and has provided the manufacturer with a second round of work in refurbishment. The photograph shows an assembly of still-flying Hunters at Greenham Common in the late 1970s with the prototype and one-time world speed record holder, owned by the RAF Museum, nearest the camera.

HAWKER SIDDELEY

Formed in 1935 by Hawker's aquisition of Gloster, Avro, Armstrong Whitworth and other companies, the Hawker Siddeley Group never ceased to grow but let its member-companies operate under their own names and to some degree independently. Though the original founder had been Sopwith (he was knighted in 1953, about 30 years later than one might have expected) the man who was catapulted into the chair in most of the boardrooms was Frank Spencer Spriggs (he became Sir Frank in 1941) who had been taken on by Sopwith in 1913.

In 1945, by which time several other companies including High Duty Alloys had joined the group, Sir Roy Dobson of Avro got his Group board to buy Victory Aircraft at Toronto. It became A V Roe Canada, a major force in world aviation, responsible for the C-102 Jetliner, the CF-100 all-weather interceptor and CF-105 Arrow. The Group also set up Orenda Engines nearby to build advanced turbojets for these all-Canadian aircraft. On 20 February 1959, a black day for Canada, the Canadian

Top: Export V/STOL Harriers on the production line for the US Marine Corps which has taken delivery of well over 100 of these unique aircraft as the AV-8A since the first were delivered to the Americans in January 1971.

Above: Not all the hard-won experience gained in pioneering jet transport was lost when Comet airliner production ended, as the basic design of the Comet 4C was used to develop the world's first jet-powered long-range anti-submarine aircraft, the Nimrod. Here Nimrods are produced at HSA's Woodford, Cheshire, plant.

Prime Minister cancelled the Arrow program; the whole 13,800-strong Avro Canada and Orenda workforce were sent home and in Avro's case hardly any ever came back (Hawker Siddeley Canada picked up a few crumbs diversifying into other activities). Later in that fateful year intense pressure by the British government led to a rash of inter-company horsetrading and, eventually, to mergers that resulted in the Hawker Siddeley Group taking over de Havilland, Folland, Blackburn and General Aircraft and various other companies. Its Armstrong Siddeley Motors joined with Bristol Aero-Engines to form Bristol Siddeley Engines.

On 1 July 1963 the entire group was reorganized into seven major subsidiaries, one of which was Hawker Siddeley Aviation (HSA). This in turn was organized into three divisions – Avro Whitworth, Hawker Blackburn and de Havilland. On that date the active aircraft programs were restyled Hawker Siddeley products, major examples having previously been the Avro 748 and Vulcan, Armstrong Whitworth Argosy, Hawker Harrier, de Havilland Trident and DH.125, Folland Gnat and Blackburn Buccaneer. On 1 April 1965 central strategic control from the large headquarters at Richmond Road, Kingston, replaced three-division working. The first true Hawker Siddeley aircraft was the Nimrod, flown in 1967. Subsequently HSA rebuilt Victor B.2 bombers as K.2 tankers, developed the Hawk and designed the BAe 146 which will fly in spring 1981.

Below: The RAF's latest basic trainer to replace the Gnat, the Hunter and eventually the Jet Provost is the Hawk, the first of which entered service in 1976. Over 150 had been delivered by late 1979. This picture shows a pair of Hawks belonging to the RAF Tactical Weapons Unit.

SCOTTISH AVIATION

Though the first free heavier-than-air flights in the United Kingdom took place in Scotland (Dunne's 1907 glider at Blair Atholl), and Scottish contractors were involved in World War I production, no aircraft industry as such existed in Scotland before 1935. Even then Scottish Aviation was created to run airfields, schools and a repair and overhaul shop rather than manufacture aircraft. The moving spirit behind it was David F McIntyre, who had joined the Glasgow (602) Squadron of the AAF in 1926 and been a pilot on the Mount Everest Flight in 1933. One of the leaders of that mission had been the Duke of Hamilton, who provided much of the capital, and became chairman; McIntyre became managing director.

One of many bright moves was to build an airfield on the Ayrshire coast (now part of Strathclyde) at Prestwick. In World War II this was chosen as the eastern terminal of the Atlantic Ferry service, and was turned into a great modern airport. Scottish Aviation found itself hiring hundreds of workers to modify and overhaul American aircraft; it became a design authority for Boeing, Consolidated, Douglas, Lockheed and others, establishing a reputation which has grown with the years and resulted in the Prestwick apron being crowded with F-86s, F-104s and C-130s (part of whose fuselage is Prestwick-built). Other products include TriStar parts and engine spares.

In 1942 Robert McIntyre (no relation) arrived from Hawker as chief engineer, and under his direction the company produced a three-seat STOL machine to specification A.4/45. From this stemmed the more powerful five-seat Prestwick Pioneer of 1950, 40 of which gave faithful RAF service. In 1955 the first Twin Pioneer was expected to lead to a 200-plus program, but barely 100 were built. On 30 May 1970 Scottish Aviation announced its decision to take over the Bulldog military trainer program from defunct Beagle Aircraft, and advanced versions (not, at present, including the Scottish-developed Series 200/Bullfinch) remain in production. The company was the low bidder for the wing of the Handley Page Jetstream, and after prolonged market study it decided to complete new Jetstreams – initially from HP parts –

and achieved certification of the Jetstream 200 in November 1972. The first batch of 26 were military; eight were delivered as T.1 trainers to the RAF and 16 as T.2 observer trainers to the Royal Navy. On 1 January 1978 the company became the BAe Scottish Division, which in 1979 received the go-ahead on the new Jetstream 31.

Above right: The two original STOL designs of Scottish Aviation are well illustrated in this 1958 picture of a Twin Pioneer flying with two Pioneers, just before handover of the aircraft to the Malayan (now Malaysian) Air Force.

Right: Jetstream 201 twin-engine trainers in final assembly at the Prestwick works in 1973, after Scottish Aviation had taken over Jetstream Aircraft Limited formed when the Handley Page company ceased operation.

AUSTER BEAGLE

Beagle's chief ancestor was Auster, which in turn stemmed from Taylorcraft Aeroplanes (England) Limited, formed with £15,000 capital – ample in those days – on 21 November 1938. Founded to build American Taylorcraft lightplanes, it had an agreement with that company and with Fairchild, but apart from a few jigs nothing was supplied from the US and from the start the British machines were backed by a small design staff who introduced improvements in the very first example built (so it was called the Taylorcraft Plus). Managing director F Bates and colleagues P Wykes, A L Wykes, chief designer (who went to America in 1938), A L Pickering and K Sharp set up the Britannia Works at Thurmaston, outside Leicester near Ratcliffe airfield. Work began at the end of February 1939, the first Plus C (side-by-side, 55hp Lycoming) was completed and sold for £600 on 24 April, and by July the output was three a week. When war began the company moved to Rearsby, a few miles northeast, and for five years took over every factory and shed it could find to cope with demand. The Plus D, with 90hp Cirrus Minor, was the basis for the first military AOP (air observation post), the Auster I. Taylorcraft built 100, followed by 470 Mk III, 254 Mk IV (Lycoming O–290) and 790 Mk V aircraft.

Taylorcraft's wartime effort included tremendous numbers of major parts for Spitfires, Albemarles, Tiger Moths and Hurricanes, and major rebuilds of hundreds of Hurricanes and Typhoons. On 8 March 1946 the complete lack of connection with the US company was reflected in a change of

Among the prolific range of Auster lightplanes, the Aiglet trainer was the first fully aerobatic Auster and first flew in 1951. The Aiglet illustrated was the first of a batch for the Arab Legion Air Force.

name to Auster Aircraft Limited. Chief designer Wykes had died in 1944 and was succeeded first by S E Bostock and then by R E Bird who supervised the amazingly prolific and successful range of postwar lightplanes. In 1955 deliveries began of the Auster AOP.9 (strictly it should have been given a new name, as Auster had become the name of the maker), the last and best of the military observation models. Gradually the welded-steel-tube fabric-covered Austers lost market appeal, and in 1960 the company was taken over by the new Beagle group as Beagle-Auster Aircraft. For a time

a design and manufacturing capability was retained at Rearsby, producing the Airedale and other types, but in November 1968 – long after work in Leicestershire had ceased and Beagle itself had gone bankrupt – the state-owned Beagle sold its Auster interests to Hants & Sussex Aviation, which supported existing Auster owners.

The last design to be built by Beagle-Auster was the Pup, a fully aerobatic lightplane which first flew as the Pup-100 two-seater in 1967 and was developed with four seats. The military trainer version, the Bulldog, survives at BAe Scottish Division.

HANDLEY PAGE

The media would like this company because it precisely fits their usually fictitious mold – a planemaker begun by a pioneer of aviation who to the end of his days loomed, larger than life, over his colleagues, his adversities and, especially, the "little men" at the Ministry. HP was a giant in all meanings of the word. He was rather like a Roman emperor, cruel and kind, generous and mean, brilliant and yet often immersed in pettifogging detail such as accounting procedures that one would expect to leave to a subordinate. All who knew him revelled in his wit, his profound knowledge of the Bible and a million other things – except, perhaps, his faultless memory for one's personal performance.

He was born Frederick Handley Page, Handley being his mother's surname, in Cheltenham in November 1885. Like his parents he was a strict member of the Plymouth Brethren, his abhorrence of opulence and waste sometimes being misinterpreted. He became chief engineer at the electrical firm of Johnson & Phillips, but after meeting José Weiss, the Hungarian aviator, in

1907 he filled his time so completely with study of the Zanonia seed and wings based on it, that J&P fired him (and engaged A R Low, later RFC major, professor and great pioneer of aeronautics). In 1909 we find HP trying to fly a Weiss-type glider at Pemberton-Billing's field at Fambridge. Unimpressed by the field, HP moved to Creekmouth (Barking) where he set up Handley Page Limited and an impressive set of sheds, apparently funding the operation by his consummate skill at poker.

His first airplane, *Blue Bird* (later called Type A) was on show at Olympia in 1910 but crashed on its first flight on 26 May that year. HP decided lateral control was worth having and added wing warping. In between running a pioneer course of aero-lectures at London's Northampton Polytechnic (where, long before it was renamed the City University, the author heard stories from HP of a very different kind) HP built the Type D, dubbed *Yellow Peril* from the anti-corrosion lanolin on metal fittings, and then made a fine profit buying up Horatio Barber's stock of Valkyrie parts and en-

gines and selling much of it to Holt Thomas to assist the formation of Airco. One of the Gnome engines was bolted to the Type G, assembled in the course of a move to converted stables at Cricklewood, northwest London, in September 1912. The Type G flew well, but tragically Wilfred Parke and a passenger were killed in it near Wembley on 15 December. Parke had lost control in extreme turbulence, but as he had been the first pilot to recover from a spin, the previous August, officialdom decided monoplanes were unsafe (a Bristol-Coanda crash contributed to that view) and this blighted the species until the mid-1930s, to the detriment of British military and commercial aviation.

That there was nothing wrong with the aircraft designed by HP, and by young George Volkert who had joined from Northampton Polytechnic as chief designer

Frederick Handley Page in his first airplane, the Blue Bird *or Type A, in 1910. The machine crashed on its first flight, convincing HP that lateral control was necessary.*

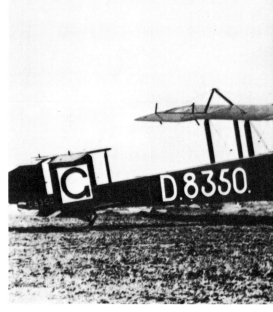

at 15 shillings a week, was shown by the fact that, when someone doubted the inherent stability of the Zanonia form of wing, HP showed that his excellent Type G would fly happily with neither fin nor tailplane. But in August 1914 HP was given a real challenge by war. His proposal for the Type 11 heavy bomber excited Murray Sueter at the Admiralty, who said he wanted something even more powerful – "a bloody paralyzer." The result was the O/100, powered by the second and third Eagle engines made at Derby, designed in nine weeks by a staff of 12, assembled at the Lamson-Paragon (cash register) works opposite Colindale Avenue, towed to Hendon and flown there on 18 December 1915.

It was the start of a series of bombers and civil transports so famous that the company name appeared in the Oxford English Dictionary as "a type of large aeroplane."

The ex-stables were augmented by a skating rink at Cricklewood Broadway and the Rolls-Royce car depot, and then by a gigantic new factory at Claremont Road, Cricklewood, with a large airfield. In 1917 HP began to learn the amazing facility of the official mind for taking decisions and reversing them. Heavy bombers were "on," then "off," then "on" again, and by the Armistice hundreds of O/400s had been built by companies in Britain and the USA, and the Berlin-bound V/1500 had flown with 57 people on board.

In 1919 HP patented the automatic leading-edge slat, which added substantially to company income. In 1929 it also added Dr Gustav Lachmann who had patented the same idea a year earlier but who had the misfortune (at that time) to be German! Subsequently Lachmann masterminded a host of advanced developments in

A selection of Handley Page aircraft, from top left, 1911 Yellow Peril, 1915 0/100- 0/400, 1929 Gugnunc, 1930 HP42/45, 1939 Halifax and 1952 Victor.

Below: The last of a series of Handley Page research aircraft was the HP.115 built for the Ministry of Aviation and first flown in August 1961. Its main purpose was aerodynamic research and the wing had detachable leading edges so that the performance of a variety of shapes could be studied.

aerodynamic fields. A year before Lachmann joined, Jim Cordes had been testing à slatted Avian when the engine failed. He made an emergency landing north of Radlett between Watling Street and the LMS railway. Like de Havilland, HP had seen his works engulfed by a sea of houses as London flowed outwards, and by June 1929 the field at Radlett had become a new airfield and assembly plant.

RAF expansion in the 1930s brought a new works at the north end of the field at Colney Street and further major expansion. The Hampden program was big, but the Halifax was enormous, and the aircraft itself set a level of complexity unprecedented in Britain. The first "Halibag" flew in Jim Cordes's hands – from Bicester, for the official reason that it might have been bombed at Radlett – on 25 October 1939. There followed five years of 15-hour days, seven days a week (the final Halifax design conference was held on Boxing Day 1941, though the preceding day was actually a holiday). In four years 6176 Halifaxes were produced by a nationwide organization. Handley Page took over the MGM studios at Boreham Wood, the Car Mart at Neasden and other floorspace, and combined with London Transport, Park Royal Coachbuilders and Duple Bodies in the London Aircraft Production Group. Altogether the Halifax organization delivered one aircraft

per working hour in 1943 and 1944.

Postwar products included the Hastings military transport, Hermes airliner and an outstanding Mach 0.9 bomber, the Victor, whose structure was as modern as its aerodynamics. By this time the design leadership had passed to Reg Stafford and Charles Joy, who also kept an eye on Handley Page (Reading), the former Miles works, where the Herald local-service transport was developed. At the end of his life HP was told how the STOL military freight version of the Herald would be rejected. The winner, Avro, was put in the position of having to claim it had won on merit, and not – as others believed – because HP had failed to merge into one of the big groups. HP did receive an offer, but the Ministry clumsily cancelled the last batch of Victors – since greatly needed as tankers – and the negotiations fell through. Writing in the Royal Aeronautical Society's *Centenary Journal* G C D Russell, who on Sir Frederick's death on 21 April 1962 took over as chairman and managing director, suspected that "with the old lion's strength gone, those whom he had cuffed and curbed and cowed in the corridors of power were at last feeling brave enough to snap at his heels.... He called his nurse to bring gin and poured me a great helping. 'Drink it, old friend,' he said, 'you look as though you can do with it.... The misguided little men think

The last Handley Page design was the HP.137 Jetstream, a versatile pressurized small transport which first flew in August 1967. Despite a good reception and orders approaching 200, steeply rising development costs brought about the company's voluntary liquidation. The picture shows a Scottish Aviation-built Jetstream T.I, the type chosen by the RAF to replace the Varsity multi-engine trainer.

they are having their revenge.' "

For various reasons, partly connected with overweight early Jetstream aircraft and a totally unhelpful political environment, production of certificated Jetstream corporate and multi-role military twin-turboprop transports was late starting, and after excruciating problems the firm went into liquidation on 8 August 1969, two months after its Diamond Jubilee. K R Cravens Corporation of St Louis soon provided backing, but withdrew in February 1970. Tragically, the whole works at Cricklewood, Radlett, and a new numerically controlled machine shop at Cumnock, Ayrshire, were sold, along with what had become a fine modern airfield at Radlett. Conversion of Victor 2 bombers to tankers was undertaken by Hawker Siddeley, but the sheer merit of the Jetstream caused it to rise again like a Phoenix, and it is now in production in refined forms by BAe Scottish Division (which made the original wings as Scottish Aviation under subcontract).

MILES

In two brief decades a tiny handful of exceptional people not only made the Miles name world-famous but produced so many good aircraft from a trivial floorspace that one feels today's planemaking must be grossly deficient. Leader of the team was Frederick George Miles; C G Grey wrote of him "A man who can design, construct, fly, read and drive as he does must have a future, if he does not break his neck first." Born with the airplane in 1903, "FG" teamed up with famed pioneer pilot and instructor Cecil Pashley in 1925 to form the Southern Aero Club and Southern Aircraft on the inadequate field that is today rather grandly called Shoreham Airport, on the Sussex coast. The club had a clubhouse in which 12 members could gather, if they stood up, while FG maintained an amazing library in the control tower he built at one end of the hut. The aircraft company rebuilt many old aircraft including a Grahame-White of 1911, and in 1928 the staff of 10 designed and built a trim single-seat aerobatic biplane, the Southern Martlet, in their spare time from working on the surrounding Boxkites and SE.5s. The team included younger brother George Herbert ("GH"), Don L Brown and Harry Hull, and they were startled when, on opening the hangar doors in August 1929, FG simply took off.

The tiny Martlet was amazingly maneuverable, and five more, each with a different type of engine, were built for customers. A single Metal Martlet was followed by the pocket-sized Satyr, designed largely by the redoubtable new Mrs Miles. Maxine "Blossom" Miles, wife of FG, was not only the daughter of a famed actor-manager and actress but a most accomplished pilot, structural engineer and draftswoman. She was henceforth a tower of strength to the company and became Commissioner of the Civil Air Guard from 1939.

The tiny Satyr was built by Parnall's at Yate, and on its completion in August 1932 it was flown by FG to Shoreham to show his parents. He stopped on the way for lunch at the new airfield at Woodley, Reading, which had been opened by Charles Powis, of the local car and cycle firm, Phillips & Powis. By the time he finished lunch he and Powis had reached agreement on a new factory to build Miles aircraft, and the formation of Phillips & Powis Aircraft (Reading) Limited. FG knew exactly what aircraft he wanted to build – a modern monoplane successor to the DH Moth. In October 1932 the growing Miles family arrived at Woodley in a caravan (trailer) and began designing the Hawk.

The prototype, G-ACGH, was built by Harry Hull and a 14-year-old helper, while FG managed to buy a quantity of Cirrus IIIA engines at a knock-down price. On the evening of 29 March 1933 he climbed into the new monoplane and, predictably, took off. Within a week it had been flown by everyone in sight – at least 53 pilots, mostly with little experience – and the M.2 Hawk was advertized at the extremely competitive price of £395. Of wooden construction, the M.2 had Dowty sprung legs and folding wings, and was the forerunner of a long line of splendid Miles lightplanes. In the first year over 50 were sold, and the company got into the habit of finishing every aircraft to the specification of its customer. Miles organized a racing team which carried the company's Falcon badge to victory in many King's Cups and other contests, while famous pilots broke numerous records with Miles aircraft over global distances.

In 1936 the Phillips & Powis interest was bought by Rolls-Royce. Impressed by the Miles flair for fast and efficient monoplanes, then almost unheard-of in Britain, the Derby company proposed a high-speed military trainer built around the Kestrel engine of 745hp. The M.9 Kestrel Trainer flew in May 1937 and not only reached almost 300mph (483km/h) but handled beautifully. The Air Ministry ignored the

The Magister was one of a wide range of training and observation aircraft designed and built by Miles Aircraft. It was the RAF's first monoplane basic trainer when it started operation in October 1937, to serve throughout the war. Of over 1200 Magisters built, many transferred to civil flying and private ownership, like the Shuttleworth Trust's M.14A illustrated.

chorus of praise from the pilots and instead ordered a rival from another company which proved to be a complete flop. Reluctantly a much-altered M.9A was ordered as the Master, and this swiftly became the standard British advanced trainer during the vital years 1938–42, production ceasing in 1942 at the 3450th aircraft (with Kestrel, Mercury and Twin Wasp Junior power) to make room for the Mercury-powered Martinet target tug. The initial Master order, placed on 11 June 1938, triggered a vast expansion at Woodley. Over the next three years further plants were built at South Marston (Swindon), Doncaster and Sheffield. In 1941 the Miles family bought out Rolls-Royce and in October 1943 found the odd few moments to rename the company Miles Aircraft.

By this time Miles was a small but intensely busy company, with the M.38 Messenger, the 38th design, in the air. Predictably the M.38, like its predecessors, was extremely advanced, with high-lift flaps derived from those FG had made in 1935 from old gasoline drums. The company's style of fast-moving experiment offended many of the established firms and officials, and this was especially the case when GH designed the radical M.35 and M.39 tandem-wing machines and FG tried to get the Air Ministry interested in the M.26 "Miles X" long-range transport.

The officials were forever mean to companies that lacked political muscle, but were glad to give the Woodley team the challenging task of making the M.52, a supersonic aircraft to specification E.24/43. For this gigantic task, which should have been a great national effort, to be given to the tiny but enthusiastic Miles team betrayed the fact that the official view was that supersonic flight was crazy, and thus well-fitted to the science-fiction Miles company. In fact the Miles team accomplished immense advances in an area where Britain was a complete desert. It worked out the best shape for the 1000mph M.52, completed the engineering design, tested the razor-edge wing on an aircraft dubbed the Gillette Falcon, worked with Whittle's Power Jets to perfect the afterburning engine and completed the preliminary tunnel program and systems design.

Then, in February 1946 the whole project was cancelled. The first flight was only about six months off. The Director-General of Scientific Research, Sir Ben Lockspeiser, actually took the decision partly because he disbelieved in supersonic flight and also because – though it is hard to believe – the top scientists in the ministry were so ignorant of high-speed aerodynamics they believed swept-back wings were essential, not appreciating that this eases transonic drag problems but not supersonic ones. As an excuse Lockspeiser was eventually forced by the Press – when the dreadful affair leaked out eight months later – to give as an excuse that supersonic flight was too dangerous. Even then the Press did not unearth the fact that, on cancellation, the Miles team had been forced to hand over all its M.52 calculations and test data to the United States, where the Bell XS-1, with unswept wings (like the M.52), flew faster than sound in October 1947.

This immense blow to British aviation and to British morale came in parallel with increasing Miles cash-flow problems. The enthusiasm of the company was such that in a few months it tried to design and tool-up to build the M.57 Aerovan, M.60 Marathon, M.65 Gemini, M.68 Boxcar and M.71 Merchantman, as well as launching the original ballpoint pen invented by the Biro brothers. The big M.60 was the straw that broke the back of the struggling firm. In November 1947 dope-maker Titanine presented a petition for winding up the company, and in June 1948 the assets were taken over by Handley Page (Reading), formed for the purpose with the intention of building the M.60 and supporting existing Miles owners and running the flying school at Woodley.

In 1949 FG and his wife formed F G Miles Limited at Redhill, with increasingly diversified interests which began with the rebuilding of Geminis into Aries and the Sparrowhawk into the Sparrowjet. GH became chief designer of Airspeed, where among other things he saw the Ambassador into production and developed the Vampire Trainer, as well as technical director of his brother's firm. He also formed a parent company, Miles Aviation and Transport (R & D) at Shoreham, which, with Maurice Hurel, built the slender-wing HDM.105 and then in 1956 created the trim M.100 Student jet trainer. In October 1960 the Beagle group was formed and both brothers linked in the Beagle-Miles subsidiary at Shoreham, producing the B.206 prototypes and M.218. The Student was chosen for license-production in South Africa, but again the officials stepped in, with an export embargo, losing that market to Italy with the MB.326. GH, however, prospered by forming several new companies, including Miles-Dufon to build flight simulators, today the great Link-Miles organization; while FG, likewise returned to his home field at Shoreham, formed companies in the electronics, marine and plastics fields. It is strange that Britain, cradle of light aviation, should have failed since 1945 to provide an environment in which either small companies or large conglomerate groupings can survive in the great world boom of general aviation.

Brilliant designer George Miles holds a model of Libellula, *one of his radical double-wing canard or tail-first airplanes which he flew during World War II; this one is jet-powered and optimistically carrying the Royal Mail insignia.*

PILATUS BRITTEN-NORMAN

Above: A successful comparatively recent entry into planemaking was made by the Britten-Norman partnership in the middle 1960s with the BN-2 Islander twin-engine light transport for up to nine passengers. With production lines in Belgium and Rumania as well as the UK, sales have totalled around 1000 in over 100 countries; development led to the Defender military version, and in 1970, by the addition of a third engine in the tailfin and extension of the fuselage, to the 17-passenger Trislander. A Trislander, in service with a Jamaican airline, is illustrated. Britten-Norman went broke in 1972, became Fairey Britten-Norman, went broke again in 1977 and a year later was acquired by Pilatus of Switzerland.

Below: First flown in June 1977, the Dowty-Rotol ducted propulsor gives the Islander sprightly performance, better economy and dramatically reduced noise, the engines being unchanged. Test flying is in the hands of Neville Duke. By 1990 such propulsors (ducted fans) will probably have supplanted most propellers.

ROYAL AIRCRAFT FACTORY

Most aircraft have an identity that spells out their origin, usually the name of a planemaker. But more than half Britain's machines in World War I were cryptically called BEs, FEs, REs and SEs, unprefaced by any name at all. This was the result of a lurking idea in the mind of British officialdom that military planemaking should be the monopoly of a government organization. It was a strange idea because Britain had always prospered under private enterprise, and in Navy and Army contracting was actually moving strongly away from Royal Dockyards and Royal Ordnance Factories towards private industry for the increasingly complex warships and weapons.

To some degree the government monopoly idea stemmed from the disinterest shown in aviation by Britain's established industrial companies. Although a few businessmen had the vision to see that the flying machine would become important as a product, none had the nerve to invest much capital (except for a family at Bristol). But it must not be thought the government was forced to set up its own monopoly industry as a last resort. From 1910 the nation was sprinkled with embryonic planemaking companies, all eager for government business that was extremely slow in coming. And in the crucial formative years when the government's chosen instrument might have built up a formidable output it was actually banned from constructing airplanes at all! Truly, the early impact of aviation on British officialdom led to wrong decisions, changed decisions, ambiguous decisions and, whenever the problem looked difficult, to an absence of any decision at all. This disastrous relationship not only continued but actually reached a peak of nightmarish nonsense between 1955 and 1965 which almost eliminated British planemaking entirely.

It all began during the US Civil War when the British Army, in the form of a handful of Royal Engineers, began making balloons and hydrogen. The rather desultory work was given a spurt by the Franco-Prussian War in 1870, and in 1878 Captain

RAF SE.5as in 1917, in the Birmingham production shops of Wolseley Motors, which was one of several companies that contributed to the total of about 5200 of the successful scout fighters built from 1916 on.

James Templer of the Militia was appointed to head the work full-time. He was an impressive man, a skilled and dedicated aeronaut (he became a full colonel, while his nephew became a field marshal) who by sheer force of character and political skill not only survived but built up Her Majesty's Balloon Factory, often at his own expense, demonstrated the value of balloons in the Boer War, and after being inadequately housed at Woolwich, Chatham and Aldershot, finally arrived at Farnborough in 1904. Two years later he was rather unfairly retired, but his successor, Lieutenant-colonel Capper, was of equal stature.

In 1906 an American, Samuel F Cody – a flamboyant crack shot, trick rider, strong man, lasso expert, actor and showman – was appointed professional kite instructor to the British Army. A year later Capper's team helped him design a powered aircraft which on 16 October 1908 made the first airplane flight in Britain (if one discounts Roe's "hops"). Just over a year later the War Minister was advised that one man should not run the Balloon Factory and also be a professional soldier. While Capper continued as CO of the Balloon School, Mervyn O'Gorman, a famous car engineer, was brought in as head of the Balloon Factory.

Among other things he instituted a list of airplane categories, known by initial letters, some of the more important ones being: BE., Blériot experimental (tractor propeller); FE., Farman experimental (pusher); RE., reconnaissance experimental; and SE., originally Santos (ie, tail-first), but later and much more importantly, Scout experimental (essentially a scout was an air-combat fighter). The first factory airplane was the tail-first SE.1, created by rebuilding a crashed Blériot and flown in January 1911. At about the same time the Air Battalion, Royal Engineers, was playing with its first aircraft, a Voisin given to the War Office by the Duke of Westminster. In April this arrived at the Factory – which that month became the Army Aircraft Factory – to be repaired. Again the "boffins" (the World War II term for back-room researchers) seized the opportunity to create an airplane. When they had finished there was not much Voisin left except the 60hp Wolseley engine. The BE.1 was a trim tractor biplane designed by Chief Engineer F M Green (really an engine man) and Geoffrey de Havilland. It was an outstanding machine, far better than Cody's official trials winner of the following year, which amazingly survived hundreds of special trials and about as many pilots until January 1915.

It led to the BE.2 of early 1912, from

Mainstay of British forces on the Western Front in World War I was the BE.2, designed by de Havilland and built by the Factory and other manufacturers. Here a BE.2's engine – usually a 90hp RAF.1 aircooled V-8 – is about to be started.

which stemmed the most important series of aircraft in the world in the period up to the outbreak of war. E T Busk, lately down from Cambridge, learned to fly under de Havilland and then courageously took a BE.2a beyond the limits of controllability in an intensive program to find a truly stable machine that could be left to itself while pilot and observer were busy with notepads and cameras. The result was the BE.2c, but its stability was a death-trap when the sky later filled with Hun scouts. The real fault in the procurement system was its inability to process customer-feedback, so that while thousands of gallant men were being killed in France, thousands of BEs were being ordered in England. Total production of BE.2-series aircraft certainly greatly exceeded 3535.

There were many other BEs, as well as large numbers of FEs which were pure de Havilland designs. On 11 April 1912 the Factory was again renamed, becoming Royal Aircraft Factory, and it did have a quite substantial budget for aircraft construction, though never the facilities for mass production. For example, the Factory built 47 of the 1939 FE.2bs, 45 of the 4077 RE.8s and 238 of the 5205 SE.5s and 5as, which were among the best fighting scouts of the war. Why then the outcry against the Factory? To some degree it was sourgrapes jealousy from various groups who envied the Factory its staff of 4500, including most of the best brains from universities, railway works, shipyards and car factories. In part it was due to the severe RFC casualties stemming largely from mistaken procurement policies, which were formulated

not at Farnborough but in Whitehall, Kingsway, the Strand and other parts of central London by officials who either were unaware of what was going on in France or thought they knew better than the fighting troops. Most of all, it was whipped up by one man, C G Grey, cantankerous editor of *The Aeroplane,* who never ceased to vituperate against Farnborough and its aircraft. In 1915–16 the dreadful statistics of aircombat casualties added immense weight to Grey's superficial and mainly misguided campaign, until on 21 March 1916 Pemberton-Billing, previously a planemaker and now an MP, launched a blistering attack in the House of Commons in the course of which he said "I would suggest that quite a number of our gallant officers in the Royal Flying Corps have been rather murdered than killed." Said in such a place, this charge could not be ignored. Predictably, although neither of the ponderous official inquiry committees could actually pinpoint any malpractice, virtually all the senior staff at Farnborough were fired and O'Gorman was relegated to consultancy.

Farnborough was renamed the Royal Aircraft Establishment. Anyone who researches almost any facet of aviation technology soon discovers that Farnborough probably did it first. And the widespread firings at the height of World War I had the long-term effect of strengthening the rest of British planemakers. It was not so when the government tore the industry to shreds between 1957 and 1965; then there was nowhere to go but across the Atlantic, in what was called the Brain Drain, and the public hardly noticed.

SHORTS

Among existing planemakers none has a heritage going back as far as the Short company which, if only the brothers had looked ahead a bit, could have been registered in 1898, thus comfortably ante-dating the lot. The Shorts were a Derbyshire family, but by the late 19th century the three devoted brothers Horace, Oswald and Eustace Short had moved to the Sussex coast where in 1898 they began flying balloons. In April 1901 Oswald and Eustace set up a small works at Hove for the manufacture of balloon envelopes. They attracted customers, including several from the Indian Army, and in 1903 moved to a leased mews off Tottenham Court Road, London. In 1906 this had to give way to a more roomy works under the arches of the LB&SC railway at Battersea Bridge.

In 1908 Horace rejoined, and Colonel Moore-Brabazon sparked off the idea of heavier-than air construction. He eventually placed an order with Voisin, but later in the year Frank (later Sir Francis) McClean, the greatest patron of early British aviation, asked the brothers to build him a flyer. There was no room in the works, and Horace started the design in his mother's flat nearby, scheming a machine generally similar to a 1908 Wright with absolutely nothing to go on. Eventually this was built, but its car engine was too heavy for successful flights. However, it prompted the formation of Short Brothers Limited in November 1908, by which time another wealthy young patron, the Honourable Charles S Rolls, had commissioned a Wright-type glider. This flew in August 1909, teaching Rolls to fly so that he came back to the company and asked for a powered Wright Flyer.

In fact the Shorts had started a list of aircraft customers even before they registered the company, and they put Rolls's name at the top of the list. McClean ordered two flyers, and made it clear he was thinking of equipping a school. In late November 1908 Eustace visited Wilbur Wright at Pau, who had already entertained most of the top British enthusiasts. Several members of the Aero Club had placed firm orders with Wilbur, who had told them he had no production facilities. Shortly the Astra works in France was to be licensed by him, as was Bariquand et Marre for the engine, but Eustace soon convinced him the Short company could handle the UK market. Eustace prepared rough freehand drawings of the Flyer, but with every dimension marked. Back under the railway arches he and P M Jones drew the first complete set of engineering drawings of a Wright Flyer, and sent one set to the Wrights.

Short Brothers was not licensed but in

Planemaker pioneers pictured in 1909 at Mussel Mano Manor, Isle of Sheppey, where one of the first Short factories was established. Standing, third, fourth and fifth from left, are the Short brothers Horace, Oswald and Eustace; seated, left to right are JTC Moore-Brabazon (later Lord Brabazon), the famous Wright brothers Wilbur and Orville and the Honourable C S Rolls of Rolls-Royce.

March 1909 received a contract direct from Wilbur for six Flyers, to be built to Eustace's drawings. This is believed to be the first airplane production contract. There was no room at Battersea, and in any case Moore-Brabazon had ordered a Short Flyer of slightly different type, to Horace's design. Without losing too much manufacturing time, the whole works was progressively transferred by the end of 1909 to a large marshy area at Leysdown on the Isle of Sheppey which had been bought for aviation by McClean. The main house, Mussel Manor at Shellbeach, was taken over by the Aero Club and became the only British aviation center of the day to rival Brook-

lands. The Shorts put up a substantial wooden factory, and when both Wrights visited them in May 1909 they congratulated the brothers on all they saw. Rolls's Flyer was airborne in October 1909, and the last of the batch in mid-1910.

By this time Short Brothers were in production with additional machines of various Boxkite types based on Farman and Sommer principles and in each case sold before the start. These ran on their own wheels and prompted a move of about two miles to a firmer airfield at Eastchurch, where a larger works was erected in corrugated iron by mid-1910. Here emerged the production S.27 and S.34, some of which were bought by McClean and freely lent to the Admiralty. One of the pioneer RN pupils was Lieutenant (later Air Chief Marshal) Longmore, who recalled (in the RAeS *Centenary Journal*) "Horace was a most interesting character; he had been in all parts of the world in engineering ventures of one sort or another. In the tin shanty that served as our Officers'

A Short Shirl experimental torpedo-carrying seaplane of 1918, one of three built with differing undercarriages for deck landing. N112 is shown carrying a mail container in place of the 18in torpedo for which it was designed but not produced in quantity.

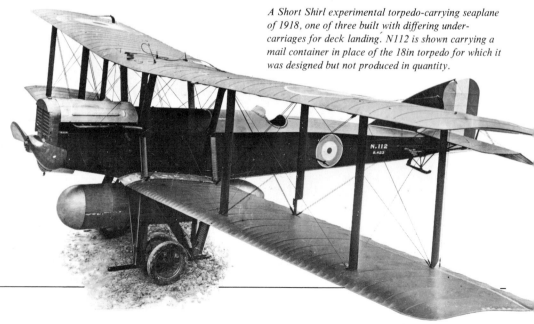

Mess he would sit till the small hours sipping his neat whisky and regaling us with stories . . . Oswald was also of great help to us; with him I worked out how to fit torpedo-shaped air bags to the undercarriage for water landings.''

The stage was set for pioneering growth, now underwritten by the newly formed RNAS, which led to well over 1000 Short seaplanes, plus a few landplanes, that saw service in World War I. A week before war broke out one of the Short Folders (with folding wings) had dropped a full-size 14in (356mm) torpedo, and many of the slow but useful seaplanes were torpedo-capable (especially the mass-produced Type 184, often dubbed the 225 from the power of its original engine, which was sinking Turkish ships as early as August 1915). By this time the

Below: A Singapore I flying-boat in the Short Brothers shops at Rochester in 1926, with a Mussel I seaplane in front of it.

Bottom: Successor to the epoch-making Empire flying-boats for Imperial Airways was the famous Sunderland of World War II service. Illustrated is a Mk V, the final production version with Twin Wasp engines and advanced ASV radar under the outer wings.

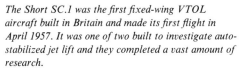
The Short SC.1 was the first fixed-wing VTOL aircraft built in Britain and made its first flight in April 1957. It was one of two built to investigate auto-stabilized jet lift and they completed a vast amount of research.

company had completed its move to a much larger works beside the Medway at Rochester, the Eastchurch site being taken over by the RNAS. In January 1916 the Admiralty tried to improve Britain's poor airship performance and invited Short to build two rigids based on the Vickers R.9. After much vacillation the firm got contracts for the R.31 and 32, whose wooden structures owed much to the German Schütte-Lanz. The government lent money towards a giant shed at Cardington, near Bedford, and the company was re-registered Short Brothers (Rochester & Bedford) Limited. The name stuck, even though in 1919 Cardington had been taken over by the Air Ministry

and the third ship, the R.38, had to be sold to the Americans to avoid cancellation.

During the war Oswald, who had become the surviving brother in charge, had devoted great attention to the new German alloy Duralumin, and to stressed-skin construction. The Silver Streak of 1920 did not generate the interest its advanced structure merited, though the company did build the occasional aircraft among the postwar barges and bus bodies on which it subsisted until in 1924 the Singapore gradually led to a trickle of RAF and Imperial Airways boats. But in 1935 it hit the jackpot with an order for £1.75 million for new Empire flying-boats for Imperial Airways – 28 dramatically modern boats, by far the largest order then placed for commercial aircraft. These led to much longer-ranged developments, mostly with Perseus sleeve-valve engines, to the much bigger G-class and to the wartime Sunderland of which 739 were built, followed by civil Sunderlands, Sandringhams and Solents. In June 1936 the company had gone into partnership with Harland & Wolff, the Belfast shipbuilders, forming Short & Harland to build aircraft at Queen's Island, Belfast. This completely new local industry cut its teeth by building all production Bombays and Herefords, 133 Sunderlands launched straight into Belfast Lough, and 1213 of the 2375 Stirlings, the great heavy bomber that in 1937 was thought likely to be the one that would win a future war and in 1942 was recognized as costly to build, limited in warload variety and deficient in performance (but still a great aircraft).

Rochester was heavily bombed in 1940, and the government decided first, to nationalize the company in 1942 and, second, to move the whole operation to Belfast. The move began in 1943 – the year Oswald retired – but was not complete until July 1948 by which time 12 new prototypes had

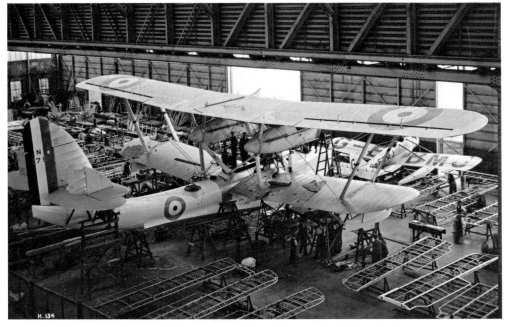

flown. In the past 32 years a further 12 prototypes have flown, the most significant ones
being the SC.1 autostabilized jet-lift machine
and the SC.7 Skyvan, flown with piston
engines (and called "a flying shed") in January 1963 and since produced in several
civil and military forms. From it derived
today's outstanding 330 commuter airliner,
which again has a military version.

In 1977 the company name reverted to
Short Brothers, but for a reason best known
to itself it likes to be called by the plural
"Shorts" – or maybe it is a form of the
possessive, and ought to be Short's. Today
Short Brothers, owned 98 percent by HM
Government but not part of BAe, is an
outstandingly prosperous outfit, 6400
strong, making the Skyvan, the 330, wings
for the F28, many parts for L-1011 TriStars,
pods for many 747s and 757s, various parts
of the 146 and a wide range of missiles and
RPVs.

*Above right: Successful outcome of numerous
prototypes produced after the complete move to
Belfast is the current Shorts 330 commuter airliner,
here seen taking off at the Farnborough Air Show in
1978. The twin-turboprop 330, developed from the
earlier Skyvan design, can carry up to 30 passengers
on short commuter routes.*

*Right: The Short Belfast heavy strategic transport, of
which only ten were built for the RAF and have since
been sold out of service, was remarkable for the sheer
bulk rather than the weight (78,000lb) of load it
could lift over ranges up to more than 5000 miles, and
for being the world's first military transport cleared
for "hands-off" automatic landing under operational
conditions.*

*Below: The present Queens Island, Belfast, works of
Short Brothers (Shorts) with 330 commuter airliners
in production.*

WESTLAND

Somerset found itself spearheading technology when in 1895 Ernest and Percival Petter built one of Britain's earliest cars. Their father's farm-implement works also built oil engines which today are found all over the world, and in April 1915 the two brothers sent telegrams to the War Office and Admiralty placing the resources of Petters Limited at the government's disposal. Immediately the Admiralty replied that it needed seaplanes, and work began on creating a large new Westland Aircraft Works on a new site to the west of Yeovil. A year earlier Percival had interviewed a Mr R A Bruce, and recalled that he had extensive aviation experience – which was lacking in every citizen of Yeovil. He was found to have become Commander Bruce RN, overseer at the Sopwith factory at Kingston. The Admiralty let him go to Yeovil not only to run the factory but also to undertake original design.

The first Yeovil aircraft was a Short 184, sent by rail to the Hamble River and tested there by Ronald Kemp in the first week of 1916. The log of the seaplane carrier HMS *Engadine* mentions how Westland-built 184 No 8359 was chosen for a vital reconnaissance at the Battle of Jutland "because of its greater efficiency." Subsequently the Westland works built Short Canton-Unnés, Sopwith 1½-Strutters and DH.4s, and in April 1917 B C Hucks climbed into one of the DH.4s and took off from a new airfield next to the factory (next day the same bomber departed by air for the Western Front). Bruce designed the neat N.16 and N.17 seaplane scouts, but the factory's biggest job was converting the DH.9 to the Liberty-powered 9A and producing nearly 400 of these long-serving machines. Bruce designed the Wagtail and Weasel, and in late 1918 a large new erecting shop began turning out 25 Vickers Vimys.

Then came something of a desert; from 808 aircraft in three years the Westland Aircraft Works existed mainly on prototypes until in 1926 the Air Ministry invited tenders for a replacement for the DH.9A, using 9A parts wherever possible. The winner was the Westland Wapiti, with Jupiter engine, which beat six rival machines. The works built 517 for the RAF and Commonwealth, and 32 for export; 50 were converted to Wallaces, and 112 Wallaces followed in 1933–36. Other types included the Wessex six or eight-seat trimotor and the radical series of Pterodactyls designed under the direction of Captain (later Professor) G T R Hill. Prophetically, the works also built attractive autogiros in collaboration with Cierva.

In July 1935 Westland Aircraft Limited was formed rather belatedly to run the Petters factory, and in July 1938 most of the share capital was acquired by the John Brown shipbuilding group, which took over the company but with no change in executives. Later AEI bought the remaining shares.

Two RAF Westland Wapitis fly over the Indian northwest frontier in 1930, where they were just replacing DH.9As. The Wapiti had in fact won the Air Ministry competition for a Nineack replacement and Westland went on to build about 550.

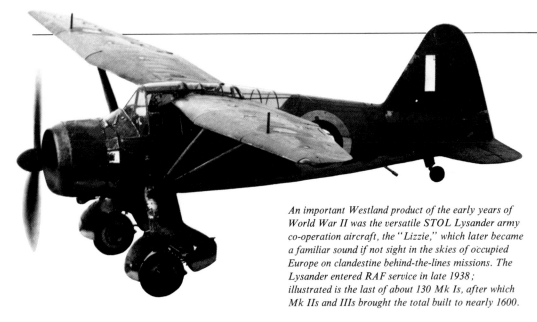

An important Westland product of the early years of World War II was the versatile STOL Lysander army co-operation aircraft, the "Lizzie," which later became a familiar sound if not sight in the skies of occupied Europe on clandestine behind-the-lines missions. The Lysander entered RAF service in late 1938; illustrated is the last of about 130 Mk Is, after which Mk IIs and IIIs brought the total built to nearly 1600.

In World War II the initial products were the STOL Lysander, a versatile aircraft designed for army co-operation but used for everything from dive-bombing Calais to landing secret agents in Nazi territory, and the Whirlwind twin-engined fighter which with Merlins instead of Peregrines would have been a real winner. With Cunliffe-Owen and others, Westland designed and built Seafires. Most of an order for 100 Welkins were also built, though this extreme-altitude fighter was no longer needed.

In 1947 the Eagle-engined Wyvern strike fighter opened the company's final fixed-wing chapter, eventually maturing, after countless severe and sometimes fatal difficulties, as the Wyvern S.4 with 4100hp Python turboprop. This small batch of aircraft, which served on RN carriers from 1953 to 1957, was the end-product not only of devoted airframe and systems effort at Yeovil but also of axial gas-turbine development that began at Farnborough in 1926. Politicians often fail to appreciate that aviation is not a business offering quick returns.

Another long development was that of the helicopter, and in 1947 the Westland board wisely purchased a license from the United Aircraft Corporation to make the Sikorsky S-51. The first arrived from Connecticut in a crate which is still in use as a garage in Yeovil, and led to the Alvis-engined Westland Dragonfly and Widgeon. Next came the S-55, which the Yeovil engineers improved into the turbine-engined Whirlwind 10. Likewise the S-58 was transformed into the Wessex, with single Gazelle or Twin Gnome turbine power, and even the advanced S-61 Sea King was completely re-equipped to serve the Royal Navy as a self-contained submarine-hunter without links with a parent vessel, a technique later adopted by the US Navy. From the original Sea King stemmed uprated ASW and rescue versions, and the Commando for tactical warfare.

Right: Work on the twin Rolls-Royce Gnome turbo-shaft engines of Westland Sea King helicopters under construction at Yeovil; the machine in the background is for the Royal Australian Navy, one of numerous customers.

Below: Westland's Yeovil works in 1978, with a flight of Lynx helicopters overhead. The Lynx is a Westland design, with Aérospatiale in France sharing in production, and is counted among the world's leading multi-role helicopters.

In 1967 a major inter-government deal with France resulted in collaborative production of the Gazelle, Puma and Westland-designed Lynx. Today the latter is fast becoming the world's leading multi-role military and naval helicopter, supplemented by the large-capacity WG.30. For the late 1980s the SKR (Sea King replacement) is planned to be the WG.34, around which an international program is being set up involving Agusta (whose AB 47 was built for the British Army as the Westland Sioux) and other partners which have long been expected to include Aérospatiale.

During the Welkin program so many pressurization problems were solved that a subsidiary company, Normalair, was formed, and today as Normalair-Garrett this is a major company not only in aircraft environmental control but also in flight recorders and many other fields. In 1959 Westland took over Saunders-Roe, adding Fairey and the former Bristol Helicopter Division a year later. In 1966 all helicopter operations were grouped under a new subsidiary, Westland Helicopters, which for a time continued to operate a Hayes Division (see Fairey). Also in 1966 Westland Aircraft masterminded the concentration of British air-cushion vehicle expertise into BHC (British Hovercraft Corporation), providing 65 percent of the capital and most of the top management.

FAIREY

Richard Fairey was one of the giants who built up British planemaking. He matured into a large and formidable character who, despite immense difficulties, saw his company mass-produce more dissimilar types in World War II than any other in the world outside Japan. He began as an electrical engineer at Finchley power station but in 1910, when he was 23, he began winning major prizes with model aircraft and not only sold the rights to Gamage's toyshop in London for the substantial sum of £300 but organized the models' production. J W Dunne, pioneer of inherently stable swept-wing tailless aircraft, informed Fairey that his models were infringing patents held by Dunne's Blair Atholl Syndicate. After meeting Fairey Dunne was so impressed he invited the young enthusiast to join him. Fairey gave up his secure career, joined the syndicate at Eastchurch in 1911, was

poached by the Short brothers a year later and soon became the latters' factory manager and chief engineer.

In 1915 the energetic Director of the Admiralty Air Department, Commodore Murray Sueter, asked Fairey about expanding production. It is remarkable that his employers agreed to young Fairey setting up on his own, with an order for 12 Short 827s! On 15 July 1915 the Fairey Aviation Company was formed with private capital and an office at 175 Piccadilly. After a frantic search – because the contract timing was severe – Fairey leased most of a factory at Clayton Road, Hayes, Middlesex, and bought a small flying field south of the Great Western Railway near Hayes station. The seaplanes were delivered on time for testing on the Hamble River. Then followed the F.2 twin-engined fighter, the excellent Campania patrol seaplane, the Hamble

Baby (with patented variable-camber gear which is generally regarded as the first wing flap) and the Fairey III of 1917 which led to the entire III-series culminating in the Gordon and Seal of 1933–35. These substantial single-engined biplanes formed the company's staple products for almost 20 years; well over 1000 were built.

In the spring of 1918 a new factory was built at North Hyde Road adjacent to the Hayes airfield, but it was far from full after the Armistice despite the design efforts of Major Barlow and the Belgian refugees E O Tips and Marcel Lobelle. Between 1923 and 1926 Fairey built the first RAF postwar bomber, the Fawn, but this was so devoid of streamlining, in order to meet the stringent official specification, that Fairey built a private venture, the Fox, as a contrast. To power the Fox he licensed the Curtiss D-12 engine, but the RAF bought only enough

Refuelling the first of two Fairey long-range monoplanes, which first flew in November 1928; they were developed with the intention of flying at least 5000 miles nonstop "in the direction of India"! This one crashed in Tunisia but the second set up several long-distance records.

Foxes for one squadron, so Fairey's outlay of over £30,000 served mainly to inspire the rival Hawker Hart – with a Rolls-Royce engine. Despite this, Fairey managed to go public on 5 March 1929, the new company with the original name having capital of £500,000.

In the same year £15,000 was spent on a much better company airfield at Harmondsworth. Called the Great West Aerodrome, because it was beside the Great West Road, it was an ideal site, christened by the first Jupiter-powered Hendon monoplane bomber prototype in November 1931. By this time an improved Fox and the Firefly fighter had, despite their rejection by the RAF, been accepted by the Belgian Air Force on condition Fairey built them in that country. Fairey SA was established at Gosselies, near Charleroi, next to the associated Avions Tipsy formed by E O

Above: The Swordfish, revered maid-of-all-work "Stringbag" of the Fleet Air Arm. Developed from a Fairey private-venture design to make its first flight in April 1934, the Swordfish became chief participator in various memorable World War II activities and many of the 2400 or so built went on in service to outlast their would-be replacements. This Swordfish is maintained in flying condition as part of the Royal Navy's Historic Aircraft Flight.

Tips which built beautiful lightplanes.

In 1935 the stressed-skin Battle bomber resulted in big expansion at North Hyde Road, but no factory at Great West Road was permitted. Then Austin Motors at Longbridge was brought in as the first Shadow Factory, and after terrible problems began pouring out Battles in 1937. Fairey then took over the Willys-Overland Crossley motor works at Heaton Chapel (Stockport), built an even bigger new factory next door at Errwood Park, set up a large flight development team at nearby Ringway, organized a factory at Hamble, took over a Saro works at Weybridge and managed the gigantic Burtonwood depot and five other factories in the Midlands and north. From this massive complex, assisted by Blackburn and other companies, poured the Battle, Swordfish, Fulmar, Albacore, Barracuda and Firefly (not the biplane but a Griffon-powered monoplane), while engines were developed and metal propellers made by the thousand.

Unfortunately in August 1942 Fairey himself had had to go to the United States to run the British Air Commission, and in his absence the tangled Fairey production got into a terrible log-jam. Fairey suffered heart attacks and required major surgery, but in 1945 once more resumed control. A year earlier, for reasons never made public, the Air Ministry had taken over the Great West Aerodrome and begun a fantastic expansion with immense runways (after the war it was realized this would make a fine civil airport and it was renamed Heathrow). While Fairey started litigation for compensation that was not settled until 1964, it was offered accommodation at Heston and finally, in 1947, took over White Waltham

Above: The unique Fairey Rotodyne, which had gas turbines powering both rotor-tip jets and tractor propellers, pictured after the project was taken over by Westland in 1960. With great promise of becoming a world-beater and US and UK orders for high-capacity VTOL airliners on the books, government support was withdrawn and about ten years' fruitful work was thrown away.

Right: The last Fairey product (also taken over by Westland) for the Fleet Air Arm was the Gannet anti-submarine and airborne early-warning aircraft, powered by the unusual Double Mamba twin-turboprop driving coaxial shafts and contra-rotating propellers. This Gannet AEW.3 is ready to go on one of the Ark Royal's *catapults in the Mediterranean in 1978.*

near Maidenhead as a flight-test center.

Work began on advanced propeller-assisted helicopters that was to culminate in the outstanding Rotodyne of 1957 which ground to a halt through typical British failure to plan properly so that engines and other parts were ready for a production machine. Even today the 80-seat 200mph Rotodyne has not been equalled, and it is a tragedy that this great program – with customers waiting in the USA and other countries – should have been scrapped. As a crowning insult, temporary government support was gained only on condition Fairey gave up planemaking, and confined itself to missiles and accessories such as were the stock-in-trade of the subsidiaries Fairey Engineering, Fairey Hydraulics and Fairey Surveys. Thanks to Minister of Aviation Duncan Sandys, the Fairey Company, only formed in March 1959 to reflect its growing diversification, had to sell out to Westland in May 1960, leaving only such operations as powered flight controls, fuel-system components and small missile and target programs. Just one of many government follies was to order the Fairey FD.2 research air-

craft, which on 10 March 1956 raised the world speed record by 310mph (38 percent, an achievement never even approached elsewhere) and then hand the supersonic delta fighter to Dassault. The Fairey F.155 fighter had been planned in full detail, and

on 1 April 1957 Fairey was told it would get the contract. Three days later Duncan Sandys, then Minister of Supply, announced that the RAF was not going to have any new fighters at all – ever!

Fairey's last brief comeback into plane-making was to take over the assets of Britten-Norman (Bembridge) in 1972. It was partly the high costs of making Islander and Tris-lander aircraft at Gosselies that led to a second collapse in 1977, the assets this time being purchased by Pilatus of Switzerland.

The only Fairey planemaking today is Fairey SA at Gosselies, which produced Meteors, Hunters and F-104Gs, shared in the Breguet Atlantic and Dassault Mirage programs and is now a leading member of the F-16 consortium.

SAUNDERS-ROE

There is a natural affinity between plane-making and high-speed marine craft, and this was especially evident prior to World War II. Anyone who could build a good planing float or hull was of interest to most pioneer aviators, and when Sopwith built his Bat Boat he subcontracted the hull to S E "Slippery Sam" Saunders, whose company was based at East Cowes on the Isle of Wight. In the late 19th century Samuel Saunders had been intrigued by a Canadian-Indian birchbark canoe stitched with sinews. Eventually he patented his Consuta method of building hulls from multiple thin plies of mahogany stitched tightly with copper wire. In World War I S E Saunders Limited made many Avro 504s, Short 184s, F-boats and the company's own T.1 (T for H H Thomas, the designer) two-seat fighters with the Consuta fuselage.

After the Armistice Saunders persisted with marine aircraft, and among various F-boat derivatives delivered three of the fine Valentias with two R-R Condors. In 1920 Percy Beadle's technically interesting Kittiwake just missed the Amphibian Competition but did not miss the only dangerous rock in the entire Cowes area. Henry Knowler then joined and injected firm direction into the design team, producing the impressive three-Condor Valkeyrie (that is how it *was* spelt) and three-Jupiter A7, the latter introducing an Alclad hull with external stringers formed in the skin panels themselves, with stainless-steel bolts throughout.

In 1929 when Siddeley bought Avro, A V Roe and John Lord left and joined Saunders, forming Saunders-Roe Limited, commonly abbreviated to Saro. Avro had built Fokker basic designs under license and Roe used this style of glued-ply wing in the Cutty Sark amphibian, first flown on 4 July 1929; 12 were built, followed by the Windhover and various kinds of Cloud. Saro won the contract for a boat to replace the Southampton, the resulting London still being in service in 1939. But the Sunderland's rival crashed, and the twin-Hercules Lerwick suffered from such instability it was withdrawn in 1941. By this time Knowler's team had progressed well with a giant four-Centaurus boat, but Shorts also had a contract; at this late stage it was decided to ask the firms to collaborate, and the Shetland had a Short hull and Saro wings. This helped in the design of the SR.45 Princess, a gigantic challenge that was foolishly thrown away in typical British style after flight trials had been completed and three boats built (the excuse was that suitable engines, such as the Tyne, were not quite ready).

Below: The prototype Saro Cloud amphibian, first of a series of Clouds for various roles, at Croydon Airport in the early 1930s.

Saro also flew three prototypes of the SR.A1 twin-jet flying-boat fighter, the first in July 1947, but found it hard to meet the 1944 specification and still survive against modern land-based fighters. In 1951 Saro took over Cierva, whose Skeeter helicopter had flown in October 1948; after protracted development this went into production at Eastleigh and Cowes in 1957. The helicopter team also designed the P.531 from which eventually emerged the Army Scout and Navy Wasp, while the world's first air-cushion vehicle, the SR.N1, was built at Cowes in 1959. Saro was bought by Westland in the same year.

Left: Saro's biggest and (almost) smallest at the company's Cowes works. The hull of one of the huge SR.45 Princess flying-boats designed to carry 100 or more passengers on transatlantic routes, dwarfs one of the three SR.A1 twin-jet flying-boat fighters of the late 1940s.

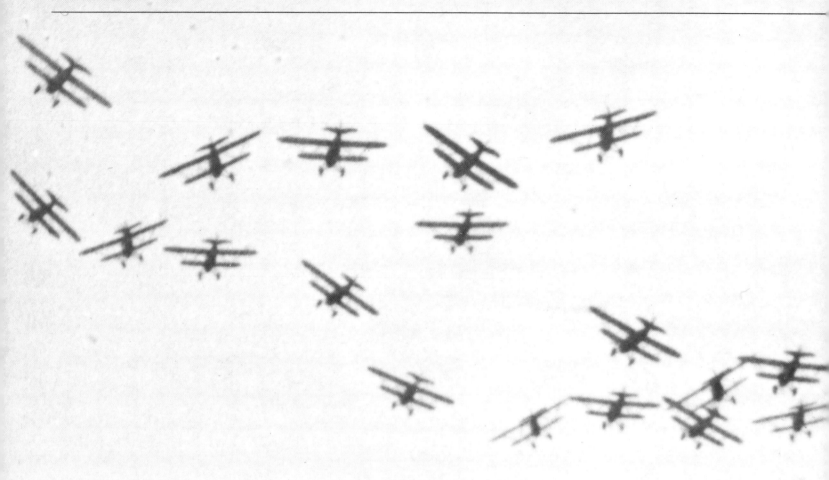

By far the largest Italian planemaker, the Aeritalia group traces its history back to 1915, but in fact the true origin was the formation by the Fiat car company of Società Italiana Aviazione (SIA) in 1908. At first this built only engines, but from 1914 made a number of licensed and original aircraft designs at its own factory in Turin, the most important of which were the SIA.7 and 9 reconnaissance and bomber aircraft. What rescued these from being lumbering and unwieldy were Fiat engines of excep-

tional power, and these engines remained important to the end of the high-power piston era.

At the end of World War I SIA was remerged back into Fiat as an operating department, Fiat Aviazione, directly under the founder Giovanni Agnelli. It acquired the services of the lead designer from Ansaldo, Celestino Rosatelli, who began a famous Fiat career by turning the SIA.9 into the Fiat R.2. A year later his BR (Bombardamento Rosatelli) led to sustained

production, and to a racing version that set a world speed record. From this stemmed the BR.1 of 1924, the first of many Rosatelli biplanes braced by the W-type Warren truss, including the subsequent BR and R biplanes of which 303 had been delivered by 1935.

In March 1926 Fiat Aviazione acquired Ansaldo's Aeronautica d'Italia, which had produced 1295 of the wartime SVA series and 782 of the sturdy and versatile A.300 reconnaissance aircraft since 1919. Fiat

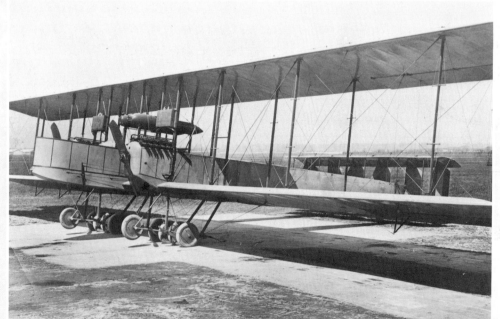

Left: The 1916 SIA.9 bomber was given considerably better performance by its two Fiat 12-cylinder 700hp engines than its looks suggest. The SIA.9 was the basis of Rosatelli's postwar Fiat R.2.

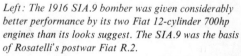

Italian Air Force aerobatics, 1939 style, performed by a "gaggle" of Italy's last biplane fighters, Fiat CR.42 Falcos, which were a delight to fly.

continued Ansaldo's production of the AC fighters of Dewoitine design. Later in 1926 Rosatelli caused a sensation with his CR.20 fighter, 450 of which were produced by 1933. It led to the CR.30, the important CR.32 of which 1212 were made, and to Italy's most numerous aircraft, the CR.42 Falco of which 1781 were delivered between 1939 and 1944 to mark the final swansong of the biplane fighter.

Fiat itself switched to monoplanes with the parasol AS.1 of 1928, a civil tourer of which 243 were built and used for numerous record flights. In 1929 the swelling division took over Marina di Pisa, renaming it CMASA and keeping it chiefly on water-based machines. In 1936 emerged the BR.20 Cicogna bomber, 592 of which were built by 1943, followed in 1937 by the first monoplane fighter, the G.50, production of which reached 791. This led to the German-engined G.55 and 200 Merlin-engined G.59 fighter/trainers. Most of the pre-1939 transports had been prototypes but the three-engined

G.12 of 1940 remained in production until 1950; 110 various versions were built. Fiat also built 223 G.46 trainers, a handful of G.80 and 82 jets, 221 F-86K Sabres under NAA license and, from 1957 to 1977, almost 800 of the sub-types of G.91, including 282 made by Dornier. Fiat was a major member of the European F-104G program, and also developed the F-104S interceptor version of which 245 were delivered.

In November 1969 Fiat Aviazione became the largest element of a new national aero-

The Fiat G.212 for up to 34 passengers first flew in January 1947 and although apparently a considerable advance on its predecessor, the G.12 of 1940 for up to about 20 passengers, only ten G.212s were built compared with over 100 G.12s.

Above: The Aeritalia G.91 which first flew in August 1956, was winner of a NATO design competition for a standard strike fighter. In later developments it served as a light tactical strike/reconnaissance aircraft with Italian, German and Portuguese Air Forces, and as a tandem-seat trainer, like the G.91T3s of the German Air Force (illustrated).

Right: The G.222 medium-range tactical transport is an Aeritalia design, the last of Gabrielli's, with production shared between several Italian planemakers. Here G.222 fuselages are seen under construction at the new Pomigliano d' Arco plant near Naples.

space organization, Aeritalia. Its other two constituents were both owned by the state-controlled IRI-Finmeccanica. One was Salmoiraghi, established in Milan in 1865 and into aviation since 1916, though specializing chiefly in instruments and avionics. The other was Aerfer, the company formed in 1955 by merging the postwar Aerfer (Officine di Pomigliano per le Costruzioni Aeronautiche) which had produced exciting high-speed piston and jet trainers, with IMAM (Industrie Meccaniche e Aeronautiche Meridionali) which had itself stemmed from the Romeo and Meridionali companies and built many of the chief types of Mussolini's Regia Aeronautica.

When Aeritalia was formed the top designer, the renowned Giuseppi Gabrielli (the G in so many aircraft designations), retired, and a new team took over. It joined Panavia with a 15 percent shareholding and complete design and production responsibility for the swing-wings of all Tornados. This work, together with support of all current versions of F-104, is centered at the Combat Aircraft Group at Turin, with offices and factories at Corso Marche and at the Turin airport at Caselle Nord and Caselle Sud. It is here that the design of the Aeritalia tactical attack aircraft, at present designated AMX, is going ahead for a first flight in 1983 and deliveries will begin in 1986.

In conformity with the government's wish to increase employment in southern Italy, the Transport Aircraft Group has its headquarters at Pomigliano d'Arco, Naples, with another plant at the airport at Naples Capodichino; a completely new establishment is being set up at distant Foggia. This group designed the G.222 military transport, the last of Gabrielli's aircraft, and continues to build it. It also builds pod pylons for B.747s, major parts of the B.767 including wing control surfaces, slats, flaps, elevators, fin, rudder and nose radome (after ten years of risk-sharing participation in the so-called 7X7 studies), and makes fuselage panels for the DC-9 and upper panels and complete vertical tails for the DC-10. The southern factories also handle the extensive overhaul and repair business including Br.1150 Atlantics and various jets and helicopters of the US 6th Fleet and other military customers.

Aeritalia also has a third division, Diversified Activities. Turin-based, this handles avionics, systems and equipment, and a wide range of missile and space activities. It is a major participant in Spacelab, ECS, Marecs, Utex and the Ariane launcher. Total employment in Aeritalia is approximately 10,000.

AERMACCHI

In 1911 the Nieuport monoplane was one of the two fastest flying machines in the world. Giulio Macchi, who combined technical skill with financial backing, obtained a Nieuport license in early 1912 and set up the Nieuport-Macchi company at Varese, the largest town in the Italian lake region and a pleasant site for planemaking if one avoids the mountains. Work began on the French design in 1913 (56 in all were built, chiefly for the Corpo Aeronautica Militare), as well as on a parasol derivative. The latter was, if anything, superior, but really effective products had to wait until early 1916 when production began on the two-seat Nie.10. The more famous single-seat Nieuport designs followed, but the company built up its own design strength and, alongside the French fighters, went into production with a useful series of small multi-role flying-boats that firmly linked the company with marine aircraft.

This happened by chance; in May 1915 the Italians captured an undamaged Lohner (L 40) and asked Macchi to make a copy. This two-seat multi-role flying-boat was an exceptionally tough, maneuverable and sound aircraft, and Macchi's design team, led by Buzio and Calzavara, did little except change the engine and gun. They even called the result the L.1 (for Lohner) but eventually, at the L.3, decided it was sufficiently Macchi to be called M.3. Many hundreds of this long and important series were built, post-war examples being military or civil transports and trainers. Another wartime job was mass-production of the Hanriot HD-1 fighter.

Some of the flying-boats were adapted for Schneider Trophy racing, and with such designers as Alessandro Tonini and Mario Castoldi the Macchi company – no longer SA Nieuport-Macchi but Aeronautica Macchi – could hardly fail to spearhead Italy's drive to win the coveted trophy. Castoldi's

first contender was the M.33 of 1925, a trim flying-boat. Behind it came the M.39 (1926 winner), M.52 (great hope of the Italians at the electrifying 1927 race at Venice), M.67 (sadly unreliable in 1929) and the impressive MC.72 (C added in honor of Castoldi) that was too late for the 1931 race but set two world absolute speed records.

Immense effort expended on the tandem-engine propulsion system by Fiat failed to percolate through to military aircraft – indeed it was utterly unworkable for practical aviation – and Castoldi's first fighter, the MC.200 Saetta of December 1937, was underpowered though it met the demand for good pilot view, fast climb and small turn radius. In World War II this obsolescent and undergunned machine was the chief fighter of the Regia Aeronautica – 1151 were delivered by Macchi, Ambrosini and Breda, the last in October 1942. Almost as many were built of the much more formidable MC.202, with DB 601A engine license-built by Alfa-Romeo, but they were late and dogged by problems. Castoldi's final

Mario Castoldi (hatted) congratulates pilot Francesco Agello after one of his record-breaking flights in the Macchi MC.72 seaplane. Note flush radiator under rear fuselage. The MC.72 was the last of a series of high-speed aircraft designed for the interwar-years Schneider contests but it was ready too late for the 1931 event in which it was the only intended competitor for the British.

triumphs were the C.205V and 205N, which were first-class combat aircraft but were too few and too late.

After World War II the company took a long time to rebuild, though the Varese plant suffered less than most in Europe; Paolo Foresio took over as director and Ermanno Bazzocchi arrived to become a tower of strength in engineering design. Modest success was achieved with the MB.308 lightplane and B.320 light twin, while Fokker S.11s were made under license, but the future was assured by the MB.326 jet trainer flown on 10 December 1957. This achieved worldwide success beyond Bazzocchi's wildest dreams, and remains in production (it is also license-built in South Africa and Brazil). Two years after the prototype MB.326 flew, Lockheed bought a substantial interest and one of the results was the production of the AL-60 licensed version of the Lockheed L-60 Conestoga utility transport.

In 1962 the company adopted the trade name Aermacchi, though it officially remains Aeronautica Macchi SA. A fine new factory has been opened at Venegono airfield to supplement the completely rebuilt original works, and while producing the MB.339, a modernized MB.326, the company is also making parts for the L-1011 TriStar and other Lockheed programs. The AM.3C (South African Bosbok) utility machine was produced jointly with Aeritalia, and the same partnership is to handle the AMX tactical attack aircraft program.

Castoldi's first fighter for Macchi was this prototype of the MC.200 Saetta of 1937; although underpowered and weakly armed, the MC.200 was the main Italian fighter of World War II.

AEROSPATIALE

Outlining the story of this nationalized monster is uniquely difficult. Not only was it formed out of at least 25 earlier planemakers, and nearly as many subsidiary and related companies, but the groupings and changes took place over a long period so that when the family tree is constructed – a task the author accomplished (see pages 252–253) – – it looks like a diagram of the hydraulic system of a 747. After much thought the decision was taken to begin with the ancestors and trace their stories through to today's great enterprise.

The world's first planemaker was Voisin, set up by a student architect from Lyons, Gabriel Voisin, who, as early as 1902, had the nerve to fool people into believing that he could fly. After surviving many hops in Wright-inspired Ferber gliders he began making aircraft for sale in 1905; his first customer was Ernest Archdeacon. Voisin himself flew a towed seaplane glider in 1905 and a second built for, and partly designed by, Blériot. With brother Charles he set up a growing factory at Billancourt on the Seine and was the chief European constructor prior to World War I (though rivalled by Blériot after July 1909). Thousands of Voisins were built during World War I but the firm went out of business in 1920.

By 1908 the Voisins basked in the reflected glory of their most famous client, Henry Farman, who lived in Paris and became a French citizen in 1937. In December 1908 Farman ordered an improved Voisin. Secretly Gabriel Voisin sold it to Colonel Moore-Brabazon (later Lord Brabazon). Farman was so incensed he set up his own small aircraft works at Mourmelon, flying his Farman III on 6 April 1909. It was an excellent machine and, unlike the Voisins, had ailerons. By 1913 the Farman Frères (the other

The Farman III of 1909 and its builder Henry Farman as depicted on a contemporary postcard. The ailerons were added by Farman to the basic Voisin design to improve lateral control.

brothers were Maurice and Dick) were in production with the tough and tractable machines popularly known to the RFC and RNAS as the "Shorthorn" and "Longhorn" because of the contrasting forward-projecting skis on the landing gear. They were used to teach British and other Allied pilots, and led to many more advanced machines, notably the big twin-engined Goliath FF.60, flown in September 1918. This was the prototype of the chief bomber of the Aviation Militaire and chief airliner of Air France until the mid-1920s.

Between the wars the gigantic factory at Billancourt was seldom full, but it added high-quality cars and powerful aero-engines

Symbolic of the vigor of the huge French nationalized aerospace enterprise Aérospatiale is the determination with which it has pursued the development and sales campaign of the multinational Airbus Industrie, in which it has a major interest. Here an A300B Airbus is pictured in the early stages of the program.

to its construction programs. By the 1930s a new range of high-wing monoplane bombers were in the works, culminating in the F.221 troop carrier and F.222 heavy bomber. These led to the efficient F.223 but in 1936 a new left-wing government nationalized the aircraft industry causing utter confusion and massive disruption. The three brothers retired, and the works was joined to another famous company, Hanriot, to form the Société Nationale de Construc-

tions Aéronautiques du Centre (SNCAC). The 223 became the NC.223. The ultra-high-altitude NC.150 bomber, flown in May 1939, was the last "Farman" design.

During the war SNCAC built the German Si 204 at both Billancourt and Bourges. The latter was the plant in central France where the last Hanriots, the twin-engined NC.530 tactical reconnaissance series, had been produced in 1938–40. Renamed Aérocentre, the group flew the big NC.211 Cormoran in

1949 and worked on many other designs, but went into liquidation in the same year. Billancourt went to the new SNECMA engine group, Bourges went to SNCAN, and a factory at Chateauroux went to SNCASO.

Possibly the next-oldest French plane-maker was Breguet, founded by the brothers Louis and Jacques of the family that had been clock- and watch-makers to the French court since Louis XIV. In 1907, with Professor Charles Richet, they built and

Above: The passenger version of the twin-engined Farman FF.60 Goliath of late 1918 had seats for four passenger passengers in a nose cabin and eight in a midships cabin and became Air France's principal airliner in the early 1920s.

tested the first helicopter to lift off the ground – though it was to be another 28 years before Breguet flew a really successful helicopter – and the first Breguet airplane followed in June 1909. The Société des Avions Louis Breguet was registered in 1911, and produced many bomber and reconnaissance machines to the outdated pusher design that the French authorities demanded. In early 1917 a far better tractor machine was built, the Bre.XIV, and when the last came off the line in 1926 about 8500 had been built. The successor, the XIX, stayed in production until 1934, the total produced being 3280. Both production figures are fantastic for the lean interwar period. Breguet also built numerous seaplanes and flying-boats, military aircraft and airliners, mostly at Villacoublay.

In 1936 the company tried to remain outside the nationalized groups, but lost all priority in materials and also had its main factories forcibly removed and handed to SNCAN (Nord) and SNCAO (Ouest). The last major program was the outstanding Bre.690 series of twin-engined attack, fighter and bomber aircraft which, had they not been held back for political reasons, would have made an even bigger contribution in 1940. During the war former Breguet factories made Fw 189 wings and assembled Ju 52/3ms, as well as the advanced BV 144

Among postwar products of the Breguet plant before control passed to Dassault was the big and ungainly looking Br.763 Deux Ponts double-deck airliner, the SNECMA-powered prototype (Br.761) of which first flew in February 1949. The Pratt & Whitney-powered Br.763 (illustrated), went into Air France service as the Provence class in 1953 (charging upper-deck passengers a higher fare than lower deck) providing over 100 seats. The basic 761 design was developed into the Br.765 Sahara military freighter.

transport. After the war many new types flew, notably the great Br.763 Deux Ponts (two decks), the Br.1050 Vultur, Br.941 STOL transport and Br.1150 Atlantic, produced by an international consortium called SECBAT. On 14 December 1971 in the midst of the Br.121 Jaguar project with BAC, control of the company passed to Dassault. Breguet had collaborated with Dornier in the design of the Alpha Jet trainer, which eventually went into production under the auspices of AMD/BA, Avions Marcel Dassault/Breguet Aviation.

One Breguet factory had been given to SNCAO in 1937, but the main ones, including Villacoublay, went to SNCAN, which also swallowed up CAMS, Mureaux and part of Potez. ANF Les Mureaux had been established in 1913 but did not produce its own designs until 1930 when, under André

Brunet, a series of tough parasol monoplanes was built for reconnaissance, bombing, night fighting and other duties. Several hundred were delivered to the Armée de l'Air, one becoming the first Allied casualty of World War II (it fell to a Bf 109E). CAMS, under Maurice Hurel, produced a large proportion of the Aéronavale flying-boats from 1923 at its works at Sartrouville. In 1937 it was taken over by Nord, whose first administrator was Henry Potez. He called the great CAMS 141 the Potez-CAMS 141, and followed with the even bigger six-engined Potez-CAMS 161 transatlantic boat that was completed and flown during the German occupation. The last Sartrouville product was the Nord 1400 Noroit series, most of which were Aéronavale amphibians made from 1950 to 1952 with Arsenal 12H (Jumo 213A) engines.

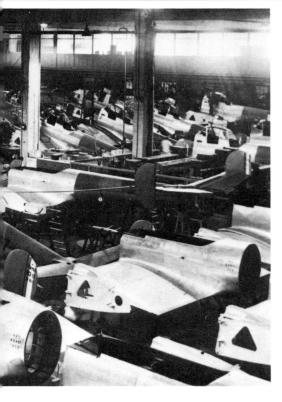

Potez must be included here, though a major part of this long-established company went into the SNCASE group. Henry Potez was born in 1891 at Méaulte on the Somme. Aviation gripped him from boyhood and in 1913 he secured a good job in the Service Technique de l'Aéronautique at Chalais-Meudon. A year later he and Bloch began a joint effort as outlined in the story of Dassault. In August 1919 Aéroplanes (later changed to Avions) Henry Potez was established, with a small factory at Aubervilliers in northern Paris. Although it was a lean time for planemakers, Potez sold increasing numbers, including at least 124 of the Type 8 tandem-seat biplane. There followed a positive avalanche of designs from a much larger plant at Levallois-Perret, the most important being the Potez 25 reconnaissance and bomber biplane of

which possibly 4000 were built by 1934 in 87 sub-types. Important later machines were the 540 series multi-role warplanes and 62 series airliners, both high-wing retractable-gear designs with twin engines carried on the bracing struts. Even more important was the 63 series of high-speed combat aircraft, which were among the first stressed-skin monoplanes in production in France.

Potez was a political animal and warmly embraced nationalization, being rewarded by the top job in the SNCAN (Nord) group. This took over the giant plant at his home town, Méaulte, which produced about 1360 of the various 63 sub-types that saw action with the Armée de l'Air, Vichy forces and Allies, as well as the Axis powers. The large factories at Berre (flying-boats) and Vitrolles (large aircraft) were absorbed by SNCASE. In 1945 Potez, who had been fired in 1940 and played no part in Vichy affairs, began rebuilding from scratch. His Etablissements Potez bought Fouga in 1958 but failed to gain enough new business and was taken over by Sud-Aviation in 1967.

Meanwhile, in 1945 the SNCAN (Nord) began launching diverse new projects. Though today Dornier is trying to launch an updated Do 24, in 1944 Nord closed down the Luftwaffe production line and made only brief studies of new versions. On the other hand the Me 208, mainly designed as well as built at Les Mureaux in 1941–43, was seen as an excellent postwar four-seater and was renamed Nord 1000. From it stemmed hundreds of good lightplanes, chiefly the 1203 Norécrin family. Nord also made Stampe trainers, sailplanes, helicopters and

Above left: One of the earliest French stressed-skin aircraft was the Potez 63 twin-engined multi-role aircraft that first flew in 1936 and of which over 1000 were built before France was overrun. Here Potez 63s are on final assembly at Levallois-Perret in 1940.

Top: This Potez 41BN5 bomber/reconnaissance machine, which demonstrates one way of applying the power of four engines to a big aircraft, was just one of scores of prototypes that appeared in the interwar years, mostly to disappear again almost without notice.

Above: Among the successful Nord designs is the 2501 Noratlas medium-range transport first flown in November 1950, of which over 400 were built in France and Germany. Several of the 2504 variant were used by the French Navy as anti-submarine flying classrooms.

various jets, but the staple product was the Noratlas. This really had its origins in the SECM Amiot, a major warplane builder between the wars whose Colombes factory built such famous types as the 122 biplane bomber (dubbed *La Grosse Julie*), the 143 night bomber (which saw much combat duty in 1939–40) and the beautiful 350 series of high-speed bombers and mailplanes which also saw action in 1940.

Colombes was later taken over by Junkers for Ju 52/3m production. In 1945 the *collaborateur* factories were nationalized, Colombes being styled Ateliers Aéronautiques de Colombes. But another Amiot team at Caudebec-en-Caux joined Nord, built the twin-pusher Nord 2100 Norazur and then the 2501 Noratlas. Powered by SNECMA-built Bristol Hercules, this freighter is still in use; 428 were made, including 161 by a West German grouping. From this stemmed the much larger Transall C.160, made jointly by

Nord (later Aérospatiale) and HFB (later MBB) with VFW-Fokker as program manager.

Yet another thread to the Nord story was added by the Arsenal de l'Aéronautique, a state organization created in 1935. With design or production teams at Le Bourget, Villacoublay, Villeurbanne and the old Brandt works at Châtillon-sous-Bagneux, it was dynamically led by Ing-gén Vernisse, whose VG.30 family of fighters were by a wide margin the best in France in 1940 (though few in number). In 1952 the Arsenal was restyled SFECMAS, producing such advanced things as the first production wire-guided anti-tank missile and the 1402 Gerfaut, the first jet to go supersonic in level flight without an afterburner. From SFECMAS in 1954 Nord inherited the Griffon turbo-ramjet aircraft and a galaxy of missiles and RPVs which have led to Europe's most prolific missile programs.

Last of the major planemakers to be merged into Nord was Avions Max Holste, formed to build lightplanes in 1948. Small touring monoplanes were followed in 1952 by the MH.1521 Broussard STOL utility machine which was just what the Army and Armée de l'Air wanted; 335 were built by 1960. In 1959 the Wasp-powered MH.250 Super Broussard started a family of twin-engined transports, which via the turboprop MH.260 and pressurized 262 led after the merger in 1961, to the Frégate.

The third nationalized grouping was SNCAO (Ouest), formed in December 1936 from a Breguet plant, the Loire-Nieuport company at Issy-les-Moulineaux and the Loire works at St Nazaire. Edouard de Niéport had been a pioneer of flying, but had used the name Nieuport to avoid embarrassing his family. From his growing works at Suresnes in southwest Paris, came thousands of the best fighting scouts of World War I. After the war, designer Gustav Delage joined his name to the company; the ND 29, 42, 52 and 62 were mass-produced fighters of the period 1919–33. In 1933 Nieuport-Delage merged with the Ateliers et Chantiers de la Loire, a major builder of fighters which from 1925 to 1935 had been linked with Gourdou-Leseurre, builder of the fastest aircraft in the world in 1922 and of the LGL 32, a standard French and Rumanian fighter of 1927–31. Loire-Nieuport's main product was the 140 family of naval dive-bombers which saw action in 1940. SNCAO, however, had a short life and in 1941 was merged into SNCASO.

This big grouping, Sud-Ouest, embraced Blériot-SPAD, LeO and a number of Bloch factories. Louis Blériot, a successful maker of large brass motorcar headlamps, tried to fly an ornithopter in 1902, got Voisin (wisely) to fly his glider seaplane of 1905, but from 1907 tried to fly himself with increasingly flightworthy monoplanes. His No VII of 1907 had such modern features as all-moving slab tailerons, used together as elevators and differentially for roll, but he became front-page news all over the world with his excellent re-engined No XI with which he flew from France to England on 25 July 1909. Thereafter he was inundated with orders for his trim monoplanes, which were eclipsed in performance only by the even more streamlined machines designed by

After Nord absorbed Max Holste that company's MH.250 Super Broussard and MH.262 twin-turboprop designs were further developed into the Frégate light transport for up to 29 passengers. Here are two N.262s with a twin-Tyne-powered Transall.

Right: The Sud-Ouest group took in Blériot-SPAD. Blériot is justly famous for his Channel crossing but Deperdussin (originally the D in SPAD) was ahead of Blériot in design with his early monoplanes, which were notable for employing monocoque fuselage structures and for siring the excellent SPAD World War 1 fighters. This 1910 Deperdussin owned by the Shuttleworth Trust enjoys its first flight after restoration at Old Warden in 1976.

Below: The Nieuport element of the SNCAO group was responsible for a line of important fighters. This ND.29C-1 of 1929, one of the earliest of the Delage designs, is preserved at the Musée de l'Air in Paris.

Among Sud-Ouest's production aircraft after the war was this neat SO.95 Corse II small airliner. It was developed from the SO.90, the prototype of which was whisked away to Algeria from the occupying Italians in Cannes on its maiden flight.

Armand Deperdussin who, with Ruchonnet and others, pioneered monocoque structures in which, instead of having a skeleton of girders and bracing wires, loads were carried by the skin, as in a lobster-claw. Deperdussin's company was called Société Pour les Appareils Deperdussin, or SPAD. In 1914 Blériot rescued it from collapse and made the initials read Société Pour Aviation et ses Dérivés. In World War I a succession of SPADs, especially the VII and XIII, were among the best and most numerous of all Allied aircraft, technical direction remaining in the hands of Louis Béchereau who had designed the Deperdussins. In 1921 the Surèsnes factory began putting Blériot-SPAD on the tails of its aircraft, which in-

cluded various fighters and racers including the 61/2 (250 for Poland and 100 for Rumania), 81 (80 for France) and 510 (the last French biplane fighter of which 60 were built in 1936).

During World War II SNCASO built parts of many aircraft including the Fw 189, He 111 and Ju 52/3m. At Châteauroux, in the unoccupied zone, the Bloch 175 high-speed torpedo and multi-role combat aircraft went into production until in November 1942 the Germans marched south and shipped its complete engine packages for the Me 323 program. An especially exciting

episode was the formation of a group of free engineers at Châteauroux in August 1940. All wanted to avoid working for the Germans and in May 1941 they moved to Cannes, forming the Groupe Téchnique de Cannes, where they designed four quite different aircraft and flew the sailplane and mailplane. In November 1942 the big SO.30 airliner was ready, but the occupation of the Riviera by the Italians in that month prevented a test flight. Then the smaller

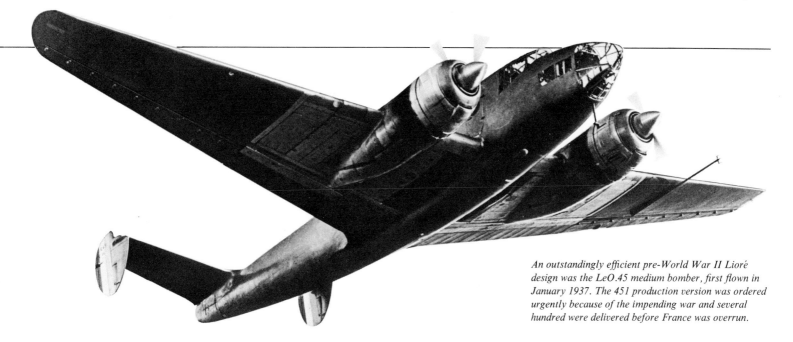

An outstandingly efficient pre-World War II Lioré design was the LeO.45 medium bomber, first flown in January 1937. The 451 production version was ordered urgently because of the impending war and several hundred were delivered before France was overrun.

twin, the SO.90, was completed. Under the noses of the Italian guards the former CAMS chief engineer, M Hurel, took off with eight passengers and flew to Philippeville, Algeria, the maiden flight of the new prototype!

After the war the SO.95, derived from the 90, and SO.30 Bretagne were production transports, followed by the swept-wing Vautour night fighter and attack family. SNCASO also built a wealth of prototypes but lacked staple products and, after being called Ouest-Aviation from 1 September 1956, was merged on 1 March 1957 into Sud-Est Aviation to form Sud-Aviation.

Sud-Est was the 1956 name for SNCASE, the group formed in 1936 by nationalizing LeO, Romano, SPCA, and the remaining plants of Potez-CAMS. LeO, short for the Société Lioré et Olivier, was one of the earliest planemakers, Fernand Lioré and Henri Olivier setting up a large works at Levallois-Perret, Paris, in March 1912. It soon produced one aircraft a day, mainly to the designs of others until the end of World War I when a succession of LeO military types appeared. By far the most important was the Jupiter-engined LeO 20, of which 320 were delivered from a much bigger factory on the next bend of the Seine at Argenteuil in 1926–30. From this stemmed a host of big biplanes including the LeO 25 bomber, H 257 seaplanes built at Rochefort-sur-Mer and LeO 213 *Rayon d'Or* airliners of Air Union. Later in the 1930s M Benoit's team produced the H 43, the French Navy's standard shipboard seaplane, and M Mercier's group designed the LeO 45, by far the best French bomber of its day which combined outstanding speed, range, bomb-load, armament, maneuverability and toughness. First flown on 16 January 1937, the prototype led to the Model 451 which was the subject of a nationwide subcontract program with assembly at Villacoublay and Ambérieu. SNCASE had taken over from LeO five weeks after the first flight, and the giant plant actually managed to deliver 452 of various sub-types by 25 June 1940. Thereafter the program became incredibly complex but at least 159 additional aircraft and 94 rebuilds flew after 1940, mainly from Ambérieu for delivery to North Africa and Syria. The last LeO was the big H 246 flying-boat, examples of which served Air France, the Aéronavale and the Luftwaffe.

Romano was styled Chantiers Aéronavals E Romano, but not all its products were

A major constituent of nationalized SNCASE (Sud-Est) was Lioré et Olivier (LeO), which had developed a long succession of important types even before World War I. Last of the named LeO products were big flying-boats, one of which, the long-range H 246, is seen on roll-out from the Rochefort-sur-Mer works.

Above left: Romano, SPCA and part of Potez-CAMS also went into SNCASE and perhaps that very mixed ancestry was responsible for the extraordinary twin-engined SE.100 fighter. Its cockpit for rear gunner and main wheels housed in the twin fins can be discerned.

Above: Another SNCASE design, mainly stemming from LeO expertise in marine aviation, was the huge SE.200 six-engined flying-boat, which appeared in prototype form only to be destroyed at Friedrichshafen by Allied bombs.

Left: Final Sud-Ouest production design before the merger with Sud-Est to form Sud-Aviation was the SO.4050 Vautour all-weather fighter/bomber. The prototype Vautour first flew in October 1952: a production Vautour II, of which 140 were built, is pictured at the Paris Air Show.

naval; they included fast bombers, a twin-engined fighter and a baby biplane fighter whose length was much greater than its span. Potez-CAMS has already been discussed. SNCASE lost no time in designing its own machines, notable examples being the incredible SE.100 fighter (tandem wings, rear-firing cannon and main gears retracting into the twin fins were just some of its features), the monster SE.200 six-engined flying-boat (the prototype of which was destroyed by Allied bombs at Friedrichshafen) and the SE.400 twin-engined reconnaissance seaplane.

In January 1941 the group was augmented by absorbing the SNCA du Midi, which had gone into liquidation (if that is possible for a nationalized company). Midi had been the famed Dewoitine company, whose origins were in Les Avions Dewoitine set up by Emile Dewoitine in October 1920. Factories et Châtillon-sous-Bagneux and Toulouse built outstanding high-wing or parasol fighters until in 1927 lack of French government orders caused Dewoitine to

move to Switzerland, setting up the EKW works at Thun. In 1927 his famous test pilot Marcel Doret set up a world circuit record in the D.27 fighter, and two years later Dewoitine was told "come home, all is forgiven." He received large orders from many sources, this time including the Armée de l'Air, for the splendid series of fighters that stemmed from his low-wing D.500 prototype of 18 June 1932, while Air France used the D.333, 338 and 620 trimotor airliners. Possibly the best fighter available in quantity in 1940 was the D.520, built by SNCAM at its only major plant, at Toulouse St Martin. After the war Dewoitine emigrated to Argentina where he designed the Pulqui I jet fighter, while the Toulouse works, by now part of SNCASE, built the original Bloch design that had become the SE.161 Languedoc transport.

Predictably, SNCASE prototypes after 1944 were numerous, but to get production going Georges Hereil, the president, went to Hatfield and purchased a license for the

Above: Dewoitine, returned from Switzerland in 1929, produced chiefly fighters and airliners and became SNCA du Midi in the 1936 nationalization. Most numerous of the airliners was the D.338 (illustrated), one of a family of three-engined machines which started with the D.332 Emeraude *which crashed on its inaugural Fast East flight in January 1934. The bigger and faster D.338, of which 31 were built from 1935, could carry up to 22 passengers and served Air France's European, Far East and South American routes.*

Above: The SNCAM D.520, last of a distinguished line of Dewoitine fighters, first flew (prototype illustrated) in October 1938 and was in production in time to be available in reasonable quantity during the short French participation in World War II. Limited production was allowed to continue during the occupation and some went as trainers to Germany and Italy.

Below: After assimilation into the Sud-Est group in 1941, Midi's Toulouse plant took over the prewar Bloch 161 airliner design and developed it into the SE.161 Languedoc, the prototype of which fell into German hands and the service of Lufthansa. Sud-Est dragged its feet with production aircraft to thwart the Germans, but after the war went on to build a total of 100 Languedocs. They served with several airlines and on several research projects. This one served as a launch vehicle for the experimental Leduc ramjets.

Vampire, while Hispano-Suiza did the same for the Nene from Rolls-Royce. SNCASE mated the two, so that the SNCASE Vampire line very soon switched to the FB.51 with "elephant ear" intakes feeding the rear side of the compressor of the much more powerful Nene. By 1951 the completely redesigned Mistral followed, and after this came the Aquilon, derived from the Sea Venom, powered by a Fiat-built Ghost and delivered to French aircraft carriers in four single- and two-seat versions with American Westinghouse radar and Nord 5103 missiles. Meanwhile the giant Marignane, Marseilles, works – built by SNCASE in 1937 – gradually began to take over a new family of helicopters that had originated at an old factory at La Courneuve, Paris. Once a Turboméca gas turbine was put in the Alouette the rotary-wing side never looked back, and it is today the top (at least in terms of numbers) helicopter producer outside the USA and the Soviet Union. The other SNCASE success story was, of course, the SE.210 jetliner, the first short-haul jet and first with rear-mounted engines, which became the Caravelle.

It was mainly the Caravelle that sustained the Toulouse works which in turn became the main fixed-wing factory of Sud-Aviation after its formation on 1 March 1958. On 29 November 1962 a bilateral treaty between the British and French governments launch-

Above: The first Sud-Est (Sud-Aviation from March 1958) major success was the SE.210 Caravelle airliner, the world's first short-haul jet transport, originally designed with three aft-mounted Atar engines but changed to the successful two-Avon concept which first flew in May 1955. Eventual sales to numerous airlines totalled nearly 300. Here the Georges Hereil assembly hall at Toulouse St Martin is seen with Caravelles in full production in the early 1960s.

Above: The first prototype Caravelle, later used as a demonstrator, in the livery of SAS which bought six of the first Mark Is and five IAs.

Sud-Est production relied mainly on foreign licenses in the early postwar years but a domestic development that turned out to be a winner was the turbine-powered SE.313B Alouette helicopter of which over 2000 of various types have been built. Pictured is a Swiss general-purpose Alouette III.

ed the Concorde SST program, whose chief industrial contractors were Sud-Aviation and BAC, with assembly lines at both Toulouse (St Martin du Touch) and Bristol. French officials were sympathetic to the British government policy of putting all one's aviation eggs in not more than two baskets (nobody except the Left talked of nationalizing Dassault). The government basket was to be constructed around Sud-Aviation.

In 1965 the group took over from Potez the management of what had been the proud company of Morane-Saulnier. Léon Morane and Raymond Saulnier (originally with a third partner, Gabriel Borel) had been pioneers of aviation; both were designers and pilots. SA des Aéroplanes Morane-Saulnier, successor to the Morane-Borel-Saulnier company, was formed on 10 October 1911, and its Gnome-engined monoplanes were so speedy and nimble they attracted such famous pilots as Roland Garros (first across the Mediterranean) and Gustav Hamel, a great racing and aerobatic pilot. By 1914 large numbers of several series were in production for military use, and it was in a parasol-winged Type L that Garros was shot down on 18 April 1915 after a startling run of victories over German aircraft. It was found he had fixed steel plates to his propeller – no lash-up but a properly engineered installation – to enable him to fix a forward-firing machine gun ahead of the cockpit. This was because for two years the French authorities had shown no interest in Saulnier's interrupter gear. As soon as the Germans saw the deflectors they asked Fokker to copy them; as the world soon knew, the Dutchman did better and devised his own interrupter, much like

Above: Part of the busy Aérospatiale rotary-wing production facility at Marignane assembling AS.350 Ecureuil helicopters which are now in full production as Alouette replacements.

Below: In 1965 Sud absorbed the still-independent Morane-Saulnier company, notable for its successful World War I fighters with Saulnier interrupter gear and for a long run thereafter of fighters and military trainers; a pair of MS.475 Vanneau tandem trainers is illustrated.

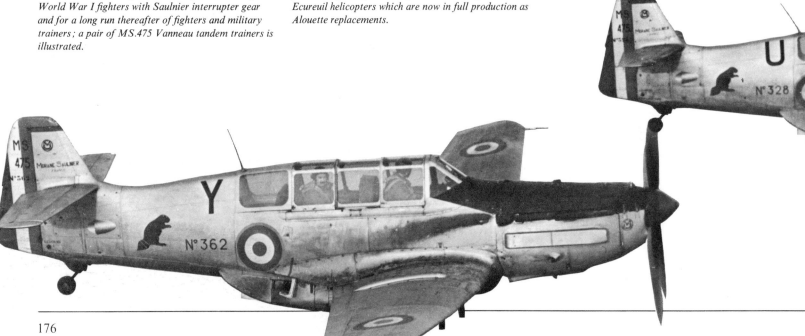

the one ignored in France, and built the first really effective fighter.

Subsequently Morane-Saulnier produced thousands of tough monoplane fighters and trainers, most notably the low-wing MS.406 of 1939 which, although obsolete when it first flew, was the only French fighter in service in significant numbers in May 1940, 1080 being delivered by the 25 June 1940 armistice. After the war the shattered Tarbes-Ossun plant became the main production center for numerous military trainers, notably the MS.472 to 475 Vanneau series and MS.730–733, and the extremely attractive Rallye series of lightplanes. In parallel 163 Paris light twin-jets were built, plus others made in Argentina and Brazil. In 1966 the Tarbes factory came under the Sud-Aviation general-aviation subsidiary Socata, and eventually even the "MS" designations vanished from the various Rallye models.

Last of the groups to be swallowed by Sud-Aviation was the Potez company itself, which had already taken over Fouga. The latter had started in 1936 as Avions Mauboussin, building lightplanes and gliders and, in 1941–43, a freighter biplane looking like a big Dragon Rapide with retractable landing gear. From 1946 to 1950 it built the CM.10 cargo glider, turned it into the powered CM.100 and built a delightful series of jet-propelled sailplanes using the first Turboméca turbojets to fly. On 23 July 1952 the world's first jet basic trainer, the CM.170 Magister, made its maiden flight at Tarbes (CM stood for the design leaders, Castello and Mauboussin). Ultimately 916 were built, including 188 in Germany, 62 in Finland and 26 in Israel. Air Fouga was bought by Potez in 1958, and Potez Air

Fouga in turn relocated at Toulouse and was absorbed by Sud-Aviation in April 1967.

The biggest merger of all took place on 1 January 1970 when Sud-Aviation and Nord-Aviation merged to form Aérospatiale – also called SNIAS, from Société Nationale Industrielle AéroSpatiale – according to a government decree. The merger also took in SEREB, the national ballistic-rocket organization that had already linked the two previous groupings. The result was an organization of 42,000 people in more than 20 major locations, which over its first decade has been slightly streamlined to 40,000 in 18 locations administered in four main divisions.

The Aircraft Division has establishments at Toulouse, Nantes-Bouguenais, St Nazaire and Méaulte. It is a major partner in Airbus Industrie and makes roughly half of Dassault's airframes, but for many years has needed major new projects; only 40 Corvette bizjets were built, the Nord Frégate was not relaunched, and the Fouga 90, an updated Magister, had not found a customer in early 1980. To help provide work, the Transall C.160 was put back into production in 1978. Helicopter Division occupies Marignane and La Courneuve, and is dynamic, busy and prosperous. Tactical Missiles, equally busy, is at Châtillon and Bourges and is linked with MBB of West Germany in Euromissile. Space and Ballistic Systems is at Les Mureaux, Aquitaine and Cannes, and manages many major space programs including the Ariane launcher. Siège sociale (head office) is a Paris mansion at 37 Boulevard Montmorency which exudes a civilized atmosphere but accommodates a tiny fraction of the people needed to run this massive enterprise.

Right: Aérospatiale's fixed-wing production factories at Toulouse St Martin, with A300 Airbus activity in view top left, getting under way in 1975.

AIRBUS INDUSTRIE

By mid-1965 it could be seen that the potential standard vehicle for all except the longest trunk routes would be a wide-body twin, using the technology then being introduced in the 747. Very strangely, this immense market was attacked by the United States only with overlarge trijets with wing and tail design well removed from the optimum, after falling into the previously British trap of designing to meet a specific domestic requirement. Much nearer the mark were such European studies as the Sud Galion and HBN-100 (Hawker/Breguet/Nord). Prolonged and so-called "tough" inter-government negotiations finally led to an announcement by the governments of the UK, France and West Germany on 25 July 1967 that a joint-design "A300 European Airbus" would be produced. The designation reflected the number of seats.

A joint company was to be formed to promote sales, and in return for using a Rolls-Royce engine (to be funded 75 percent by the UK, $12\frac{1}{2}$ percent by France's SNECMA and $12\frac{1}{2}$ percent by MTU of Germany), airframe leadership was assigned to Sud-Aviation ($37\frac{1}{2}$ percent by funding), with Hawker Siddeley of the UK ($37\frac{1}{2}$ percent) and an *ad hoc* group called Arbeitsgemeinschaft Airbus of Germany (25 percent) also participating. It was expected that 300 might be sold by "1985 to 1990," representing £2000 million in sales.

Then several things happened. Rolls-Royce preferred the US market, and sold the RB.211 to Lockheed; in August 1968 it leaked out that this engine effectively precluded timely development of the larger RB.207 for the A300. The Airbus partners, not yet formally linked, decided to reduce the size to about 250 seats, with designation A300B, and to match the aircraft to the JT9D or CF6 as alternative engines. In the event this was wise, because Rolls was unable to offer an engine matched to the requirements. The A300B was launched with the CF6 – with Sud, soon to become Aérospatiale, still holding on to "leadership," though this somewhat childish position gradually faded as Airbus Industrie, the name of the consortium, matured. A further unexpected event was that Britain's relevant Minister, European-minded Stonehouse, was replaced by Wedgwood Benn who immediately withdrew Britain from the consortium for political reasons.

This traumatic shock resulted in AI being formed with the backing of only France, Germany and Spain, with work split 36.1 percent to Aérospatiale, 36.1 percent to Deutsche Airbus (as the team formed by MBB 65 percent and VFW-Fokker 35 percent was called) and 4.2 percent to Spain's CASA. Hawker Siddeley, furious at its government's action, stayed as a non-voting associate and with its own money funded 17 percent of the program, while Fokker-VFW of the Netherlands took on the remaining 6.6 percent. Broadly, Aérospatiale

received the nose, wing center-section (inside the fuselage) and assembly/flight test, DA the fuselage and CASA the horizontal tail and cabin doors; Hawker Siddeley took on the wings, Fokker-VFW the wing movable surfaces and the USA the main responsibility for engines and pods.

Britain's withdrawal did have the immense advantage of eliminating British official influence, so that the A300B4–200 is now selling with a range of over 3000 nautical miles (5560km). But it had the adverse effects, from Britain's viewpoint, of causing its top technical and sales talent to move to Toulouse, the assembly and corporate headquarters, of causing the nation virtually to lose touch with major airlines (previously it had been second only in civil transport expertise to the USA) and of causing the nation to lose nearly all the very large A300B equipment and systems market except in the role of subcontractors or associates.

The A300B program was a tremendous technical success from the start, and even today has the latest and most efficient wing of any airliner, is probably the quietest and undoubtedly has the lowest seat-mile costs over a wide range of sector distances. But the airlines were slow to comprehend all this. Sales crept to 100 by 1979 and then rather firmly moved in that year to 400, including options, the limiting factor being the rate at which production can be increased from three a month to six in 1982 and ten in 1985. In 1978 a smaller version with a new wing, the A310, was launched, while Pratt & Whitney-powered aircraft are now in use and Rolls-Royce belatedly also hopes to get into the program.

In early 1979 Britain rejoined AI, the British shareholding being 20 percent; capital was increased to reduce the French shareholding (which had risen to 48 percent) to 37.9, the same as Germany. CASA remains 4.2, and Fokker of the Netherlands was joined in May 1979 by Belairbus, a Belgian consortium associated chiefly with the A310. Airbus Industrie has not in 1980 succeeded in launching a smaller JET (Joint European Transport), partly because of Fokker's wish not to join AI with its F29 in the same category. The first priority is new versions of the established winners, such as the stretched B9 and long-range B11 with four CFM56 engines.

Below: Airbus final assembly at Toulouse, with the Hawker Siddeley parentage of the super-efficient wing clearly identifiable.

Left: Production of Airbus main components at several plants in different countries entails transport of large structures to the main assembly area at Toulouse; for interplant transport the consortium uses the Aero Spacelines Guppy-201 (modified turboprop Stratocruiser), here seen unloading a rear fuselage section from Deutsche Airbus, and intends to build others.

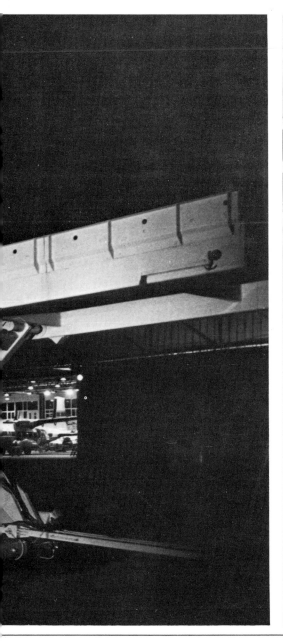

ARADO

Though a famous name, this firm mainly built other companies' aircraft, and it did not re-arise after World War II. At the same time it was responsible for several mass-produced aircraft that played a major role in the wartime Luftwaffe, and also for the world's first jet bomber and reconnaissance aircraft which, in the most difficult circumstances, solved a profusion of challenging problems and restored to the German leaders capabilities they had lost two years earlier – such as the ability to take clear pictures over Allied territory in the West – at a time when it was too late to stave off defeat.

The genesis of the company lay in an offshoot of the Flugzeugbau Friedrichshafen called Werft Warnemünde, established in 1917. In 1921 this Baltic-coast plant was bought by wealthy Hugo Stinnes who, while using it to build pleasure boats and many other products, kept one eye on the possibility of aircraft. In 1924 he managed to obtain Walter Rethel from Fokker; Rethel had earlier been chief engineer of Kondor and was soon to be a pioneer of stressed-skin structures. In 1925 the company was renamed Arado-Handelsgesellschaft. (At the same time Stinnes set up a Yugoslavian subsidiary, Ikarus GmbH, which later became the locally owned Ikarus AD, famous builder of fighters.)

There followed a succession of successful prototypes, but little production until, via the SD.I, SD.II and Ar 64, Rethel produced the Ar 65 in August 1931. This, like its predecessors, was a so-called "sporting biplane," with one seat and a powerful engine;

in 1933 production deliveries began to the three *Reklame-Staffeln* (publicity squadrons) of the clandestine Luftwaffe. It led straight to the Ar 68, an outstanding biplane fighter used in substantial numbers, while the Ar 66 flown in 1932 promised to be an excellent trainer. But in 1933 Stinnes died and the board took the strange decision of bringing in Dipl-Ing Walter Blume as chief engineer over the head of Rethel. Not surprisingly the latter left – to the vast benefit of Messerschmitt – and Blume redesigned the Ar 66, which was to become almost the most numerous biplane in World War II in Europe, serving not only as a trainer but, until the final German defeat, as a night ground attack and close-support aircraft.

On 4 March 1933 the company was reorganized with State funds as Arado Flugzeugwerke GmbH, directly under the control of the RLM (Air Ministry). Subsequently the only place to go was up; new factories were established at Brandenburg-Neuendorf, Babelsberg, Eger, Rathenow,

The Arado Ar 68 fighter was one of the effective aircraft with which the squadrons of the clandestine Luftwaffe were being equipped in the middle-to-late 1930s. Pictured is the third prototype, Ar 68c.

Teutow, Wittenberg, Anklam, Alt-Lönnewitz, Neubrandenburg and, during the war, former Czech and French factories under Arado control. The main aircraft of Arado design were the Ar 96B advanced trainer of which 11,546 were built, the Ar 196 reconnaissance-fighter seaplane, and the Ar 234B twin-jet reconnaissance and bomber aircraft of which well over 200 were flown, though fewer than half reached combat units. The company's bread and butter came from mass-producing the He 111, Bf 109, He 177, Ju 88 and, above all, the Fw 190.

The Arado Ar 234 Blitz (Lightning) was the world's first jet bomber when it entered active service with the Luftwaffe early in 1945; a reconnaissance version had been used for several months previously. This first prototype, seen at Rheine in June 1943, used a jettisonable trolley for take-off.

Formed at the most unpropitious time in 1923 by the famous Cantieri Navali di Monfalcone of Trieste, this company was originally a wholly owned subsidiary called CNT (Cantieri Navali Triestino). Though it made a few small landplanes it concentrated from the start on marine aircraft, the chief customer in the 1920s being the Adriatic airline SISA which bought a succession of the firm's passenger flying-boats. Lead designer Conflenti, previously with "Savoia," gradually made his designs more economic by putting in more seats and refining the structure and aerodynamics, though almost all had watercooled engines by Isotta-Fraschini or Fiat.

Though probably no more than 150 aircraft had been built in all between 1923 and 1931 the company had been profitable, and acquired a good reputation. In 1931 it was reorganized as CRDA Cant (CRDA for Cantieri Riuniti dell' Adriatico), and in place of Conflenti the company appointed Filippo Zappata, who had previously worked for Blériot-SPAD. Over the next decade Zappata produced fewer designs – most with numbers beginning with 500 – but they were outstandingly successful programs. Bread-and-butter work in the 1920s had included a fair amount of license-manufacture for other companies, notably Savoia-Marchetti, but the only known example of such work after 1931 was a batch of SM.81 bombers. The chief trouble was lack of productive capacity. Other companies were brought in to help produce the excellent Zappata designs, but several prototypes never got into production not through any technical failure but because there was nowhere they could be built in quantity.

First of the Zappata designs was the Z.501 Gabbiano (Gull) flying-boat, flown in February 1934. The prototype set distance records in the hands of the company's famous test pilot Mario Stoppani, and at least 250 were built, some serving in the Spanish Civil war and others with the Regia Aeronautica, Rumanian Air Force, Aviazione della RSI and Co-Belligerent AF after the Armistice of October 1943. Even more renowned was the Z.506 Airone (Heron) trimotor seaplane, first flown in August 1935 and produced in quantity as a 16-passenger airliner for Ala Littoria. While various special Airones set new seaplane records, the Z.506B military version proved so successful that about 350 were built. The first batch of 30 was ordered by Poland, and the first was flown by a Polish crew to Gdynia three days before the German invasion, without ammunition in its guns. Another, in Regia Aeronautica service, was probably the victim of the first-ever mid-air hijacking; it was taken over by its unarmed cargo of RAF prisoners (and then got shot at in the circuit at Malta by defending Spitfires!).

The last and most numerous Cant aircraft was the Z.1007 Alcione (Kingfisher), on paper the best of all Italian bombers in March 1937 when the prototype flew. Like all the company's machines it was mainly wooden but was nevertheless tough and fast; 476 were delivered. The stressed-skin Z.1018 barely got into service when Italian planemaking collapsed in October 1943.

Above: The Cant Z.501 Gabbiano (Gull) flying-boat, first flown in 1934, was the first of the Zappata designs; when Italy entered the war in 1940 the Italian Air Force had 15 squadrons equipped with the Gull, totalling about 200 aircraft.

Below: Last and most numerous of the Cant airplanes in the company's 20-year existence was the Z.1007 Alcione (Kingfisher) three-engined bomber, of which over 470 were built. The Alcione had rather light defensive armament and relied on fairly high top speed approaching 300mph to keep out of trouble.

CAPRONI

This entry is one of the exceptions in that it outlines the story of a company that withered away 30 years ago. It also reflects what even today is a problem to Italian planemakers. When you have many companies, all beavering away with unquenchable enthusiasm to satisfy only a very small home market, the result is likely to be a profusion of prototypes and not much else. Italian planemaking has tended to be supported by production runs that could be counted on the fingers, often placed by a benign government just to support the home team. Caproni produced 180 types of aircraft but the total number of all models built only just exceeded 3000. Included in this total, however, were numerous bombers which did much to pioneer the art of strategic attack at a time when some governments still doubted that such mis-

Caproni's claim to fame was based on big bombers during World War I, but none was so monstrous as this Trans Aereo CA 60 "triple hydrotriplane" of 1921. It had a wingspan of 100ft and was powered by eight 400hp Liberty engines, four tractors and four pushers, to carry 100 passengers – about ten times the number of contemporary airliners. The Ca 60 made only two short hops before it crashed. On the left is a Macchi M.5.

sions were possible.

Throughout, both the parent company and a swarm of subsidiaries, several of them connected with aviation, were directed by Gianni Caproni who in 1907 at the age of 21 qualified as an electrical engineer but determined to make flying machines. His first, and the first successful machine of all-Italian design, flew from a field that is today part of Milan-Malpensa airport on 27 May 1910. A year later, in partnership with Agostino di Agostini, he set up a flying school at Vizzola and added a growing factory where on 15 June 1911 a Caproni monoplane flew for 50 minutes with only 28hp (probably a good deal less).

Agostini became disheartened during Caproni's critical illness later that year but his place was taken by Carlo Comitti who helped set up Società Caproni e Comitti in late 1911. Still Caproni had to struggle, and within six months the company was Soc. degli Ingegneri Caproni e Faccanoni. In 1913 the company's test pilot made headlines by (in stages, with long waits for good weather) flying from Milan to Rome. But the government bought only foreign aircraft,

One of the successful series of Caproni twin-engine reconnaissance/light bombers, this Ca 314 has had its dorsal turret removed for service with the Co-Belligerent Air Force after Italy's capitulation in September 1943.

and opened its own flying school, withdrawing students from Caproni's. In the midst of these heartbreaks an Austro-Hungarian colonel was sent to buy Caproni

important from 1924 to 1932, and overlapped the high-wing monoplanes such as the Ca 101, 111 and 133 (all these are selections from prolific families). In 1931 Caproni's empire took in a factory at Bergamo which became Caproni Aeronautica Bergamasca (so-called "Caproni-Bergamaschi") which produced the AP.1 tactical bomber and an extremely successful series of small twins with numbers from Ca 309 to 316, most of them for reconnaissance, bombing or torpedo carrying. In 1935 he bought a company that had license-produced his bombers in 1917, the Officine Mecchaniche "Reggiane" SpA at Reggio (Emilia).

In 1937 Roberto Longhi was appointed chief designer at the works, whose company name did not change, and with Alessio's help very quickly produced two of the first types in Italy to have modern stressed-skin construction (which Longhi had learned in the United States). The Ca 405 Procellaria bomber failed to get the orders it deserved but the Re 2000 Falco, almost a copy of the Seversky P-35, led to a series of fighters for the Regia Aeronautica, Luftwaffe, Aviazione della RSI, Co-Belligerent Air Force and also the Hungarian air arm; had Italy not declared war in 1940 another 300 would have been mistakenly bought for the RAF.

In World War II Caproni's various plants failed to bring forth a new and important design. The only one that achieved notoriety was the singularly uninspired N.1 "jet propelled" machine produced jointly with Secondo Campini. The Ca 135bis bomber was doggedly flown by the Hungarians, and the only lasting memorial to an amazingly prolific company is the world absolute altitude record of 56,046ft (17,083m) set by Mario Pezzi in a Ca 161bis biplane on 22 October 1938, which still stands. The last prototype was the Ca 193 six-seat twin-pusher, tested just before the proud old company went bankrupt in February 1950.

for what was clearly going to be the "enemy side."

One does not know whether the fiercely patriotic Italian was even so much as tempted, but he persevered and eventually achieved success with a 1913 monoplane of such quality that a complete *squadriglia* was soon equipped with it. But the machines which made Caproni famous were the big bombers, and these stemmed from Caproni's own belief in such aircraft, reinforced by the 1913 commander of the Battaglione Aviatori, Colonel Giulio Douhet, a name familiar to every professional student of air power. Caproni's first bomber had three Gnome engines in a close row at the rear of a central nacelle, the rearmost driving a pusher propeller and the others driving tractor screws via bevel shafts leading to the fronts of the tail booms. The latter were of miniature fuselage form instead of the arrangement of open struts common at that time. The weak point was the outboard propeller drives and in the next prototype, completed in September or October 1914, the engines were installed next to the propellers in the usual manner.

In March 1915 the Società per la Sviluppo dell'Aviazione in Italia was formed to mass-produce Caproni bombers at a factory at Milan-Taliedo. By the Armistice more than 1000 large trimotor bombers had been delivered including small numbers made in France and the USA. Their combat exploits on missions sometimes lasting five hours are part of history; many were made by Italian squadrons sent to France (Belfort and Nancy) to help the French bombing effort against German targets.

Apart from the incredible Trans-Aereo Ca 60 of 1921 – the greatest-ever example of a planemaker letting his imagination run away with him – most of Caproni's products were sound but made in trivial numbers. The only commercially successful machines were a unique series of inverted sesquiplanes (biplanes with lower wing much larger than the upper) which were nearly all heavy bombers. These were

Persuaded by the engineer Campini, Caproni took one of the wrong roads to jet propulsion in the CC.1 (officially N.1) here pictured at Milan in 1938. It used a normal piston-engine-powered fan to blow air through a propulsion nozzle in which extra fuel was burned to increase thrust, but it could barely struggle off the ground and was abandoned.

CASA

Although it recently acquired two even older companies – as described later – CASA, Spain's largest aerospace company, dates from 1923 and has remained the same firm with the same name throughout. The founder – who even today remains honorary president – was Don José Ortez Echagüe, who in the most lean period ever experienced by planemakers managed to persuade the government in Madrid that Spain ought to be able to construct aircraft for its Air Force. The decision to do so was taken in early 1922, and Echagüe negotiated manufacturing licenses for the Breguet XIX and Dornier Wal. The company was registered in March 1923 as Construcciones Aeronáuticas SA, or CASA.

Head office and the factory were built at

Bottom: Designed by CASA with German co-operation as a replacement for the license-built Ju 52/3m, the C-212 Aviocar twin-turboprop utility transport first flew in 1971. The Aviocar, which can carry up to 18 fully equipped troops or 12 stretchers, has captured substantial export as well as home orders and is built under license in Indonesia.

Below: Spain's first twin-engined aircraft of indigenous design was the CASA-201 Alcotan light transport, of which 112 were produced from 1949.

Both German and American companies co-operated with CASA in the design of the C-101 Aviojet turbofan tandem-seat military trainer/close-support aircraft, the first prototype of which flew in June 1977. Pictured is one of four prototype Aviojets taking off at the Farmborough Show.

Madrid at Getafe, where between 1926 and 1933 about 103 (some reports claim 400) of the Breguets were completed. The Wal was built at another new factory, with slipway, at Cadiz; the total produced was 40. In 1934 the Getafe plant began making 27 Hispano-engined Vickers Vildebeests, but the Civil War stopped license-production of the Martin Bomber (139W) and various Hawker biplanes before any were completed. In 1937 the Getafe works was bombed, and Cadiz was preoccupied with repair and overhaul. But in 1939 a series of German licenses was negotiated, and Getafe and a new factory opened in 1940 at Seville-Tablada produced 25 Gotha 145s, 25 Bü 133 Jungmeisters, 500 Bü 131 Jungmanns and 200 He 111H-16 bombers, the final 70 of the Heinkels remaining engineless until in 1956 they were completed with Merlins. During World War II a license was obtained

for the Ju 52/3m, and from 1945 to 1952. CASA made 170 as the 352L (Spanish AF designation T-2) with the locally produced ENMA Beta 9C engine.

In 1946 CASA president Anduiza ordered the immediate opening of an *Oficina de Proyectos,* as a result of which in February 1949 a newly appointed test pilot made the first flight of a Spanish twin-engined aircraft, the CASA 201 Alcotan. While 112 of these light transports were being built, CASA also produced 20 of the larger Type 202 Halcon, followed (in 1955–68) by 20 Hercules-engined Type 207 Azors, which are still in use and might even be converted to Dart turboprops. In 1954 the first contract was received for USAF overhauls, and so far the number of aircraft handled for this customer exceeds 6000. In the same year Cadiz flew the prototype Dornier 25, followed by the first Do 27 in June 1955. By this time Dornier was able to re-establish his German company, but CASA nevertheless made 50 Do 27s under license.

It is interesting that CASA has never doubted its need for outside engineering assistance, and it has looked for this to Germany and the United States. In 1961 it began talking to HFB and Northrop, both of which have remained deeply involved. The former resulted in CASA participation in the Hansa Jet design, followed by MBB (HFB's successor) participation in the design of the CASA C-212 Aviocar twin-turboprop utility transport, designed to replace the Ju 52/3m and now not only widely exported but also produced under license by Nurtanio in Indonesia. CASA also studied the BO 105 helicopter at the design stage and now assembles the substantial numbers ordered for the Spanish market. The link with the United States is with Northrop, which resulted in an offer of

technical assistance in return for 24 percent of the Spanish company. In 1965 CASA won its biggest contract in financial terms when the Ejercito del Aire (Air Force) signed for 70 Northrop F-5 fighters license-built by CASA. Today the company's principal new program is the C-101 Aviojet turbofan military trainer, and in designing this both Northrop and MBB participated.

In 1963 discussions extended to Dassault, as a result of which CASA bore 5.8 percent of the loss on the Mercure program but profitably makes the wings for Falcon 10s. CASA also shares in the production of Mirage F1 fighters, though details have not been disclosed. CASA is also a 4.2-percent partner in Airbus Industrie.

In 1972, thinking perhaps that mergers and rationalizations were a good idea, CASA took over Hispano Aviación, followed a year later by ENMASA. Hispano, Spain's first commercial planemaker, had been founded at Guadalajara in 1918, thereafter occupying its plant at Seville mainly with licensed designs such as the Fiat CR.32 and Messerschmitt Bf 109. With the 109, however, considerable effort was applied to developing postwar versions powered by Hispano and Merlin engines. The company was thus emboldened to strike out on its own, with no less a person than Messerschmitt himself in charge of design, producing the HA-100 piston trainer, HA-200 and 220 Saeta twin-jet (of which 96 were made in Spain and at least 70 in Egypt), and the supersonic tailed-delta HA-300 fighter for Egypt which was actually constructed at Helwan near Cairo. ENMASA, founded as a car manufacturer in 1909, produced the majority of Spanish-assembled aero-engines. Incorporating the famous companies virtually doubled the size of CASA, from 4100 to 8050.

DASSAULT-BREGUET

Dassault, both the man and the company, has built up an image of superior skill, superior output, superior planning, superior devotion to duty, and a general air of arrogance which goes well with the French character. It has not been empty talk; for a relatively small team to produce more than 50 advanced military prototypes, all different, in the past 30 years is a unique achievement. Dassault claims to be able to move faster than anyone else in the challenging field of advanced jet aircraft, and the US Air Force was sufficiently impressed in 1973 to ask the Rand Corporation think-tank to investigate the company and advise how to get the same performance from its own contractors. This was a logical exercise in keeping up competitive pressures; Dassault people are not ten feet tall, but they stand as tall as other planemakers, which in Western Europe since 1945 is most unusual.

The man himself was born Marcel Bloch in the naughtiest part of Paris at 47 rue Blanche, and was all set for an electrical career when, in 1909, he looked up in the playground of the Ecole Breguet and saw the Comte de Lambert fly his Wright around the Eiffel Tower. That was enough to make him change course, and in 1913 he and Henry Potez joined the Service Technique de l'Aéronautique at Chalais-Meudon as assistants to Commandant Dorand. When war broke out the Caudron G.3 was selected as a standard reconnaissance machine, but mass-production by Gaston Caudron, even helped by brother René, was inadequate. Dorand asked Captain Etévé (inventor of the first airspeed indicator) to get things moving, and he picked young Bloch to be his man on the spot at the factories at Issy and Lyons. According to Bloch, "He said

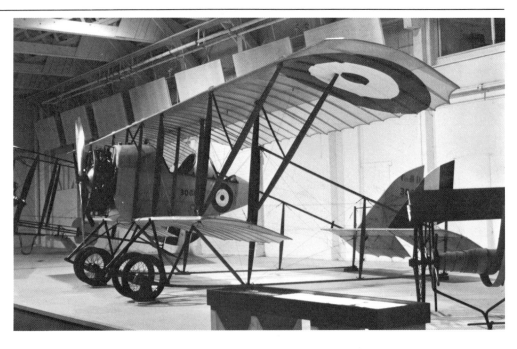

The first Bloch design was the SEA.4 two-seat fighter of 1918. After official tests an order was placed for 1000 SEA.4s but it was cancelled when the Armistice was agreed.

'you will probably be overworked, do you know an engineer to work with you?' I replied 'I would like Potez' . . . to recompense us for our labours Etévé made me a sergeant and Potez a corporal." (Potez tells the story slightly differently; he just wrote "the captain's second assistant was Bloch.")

By 1917 Bloch had developed the improved Eclair propeller, got Potez to help and was one of the four major prop-makers for the Allies. By 1918 he had set up SEA (Société d'Etudes Aéronautiques) in a rented factory at Surèsnes, designed and built the SEA.4 two-seat fighter with 375hp Lorraine, assembled it at Buc in a hangar freely loaned by Blériot and had it officially tested at Plessis-Belleville. The result was an order for 1000—not bad, for the age of 26. Unfortunately for Bloch the order coincided with the Armistice and was immediately cancelled. Bloch went into the furniture business, calling the next 12 years "a desert."

In 1930 came the first glimmerings of a

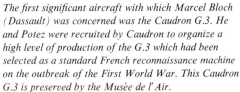

The first significant aircraft with which Marcel Bloch (Dassault) was concerned was the Caudron G.3. He and Potez were recruited by Caudron to organize a high level of production of the G.3 which had been selected as a standard French reconnaissance machine on the outbreak of the First World War. This Caudron G.3 is preserved by the Musée de l'Air.

need for more aircraft. He went to see Albert Caquot, industrial director of the Ministère de l'Air, whom he had known in 1918. He was startled to be at once invited to build a trimotor mailplane for colonial use. Within days, through small advertisements, he had met two men who were henceforth to be his chief lieutenants, Benno-Claude Vallières and Henri Deplante. Soon afterwards followed Paul Deplante, Jean Cabrière and Lucien Servanty, and many other engineers who were to become famous along with the Avions Marcel Bloch company. These men knew their business. Even the prototype *Type Colonial,* tested at Buc by Raymond Delmotte – a renowned pilot lent, like the old hangar, by generous Blériot – was fully satisfactory; 12 saw service on the long Algiers-Brazzaville-Madagascar route.

In time Bloch decided to build an aircraft on his own. Leasing a small works at Boulogne-Billancourt, he set his team designing an all-metal low-wing ambulance aircraft; again the Centre d'Essais en Vol at Villacoublay passed it, and a run of 20 followed, seeing service in Morocco and Syria. Then followed the staggering succession of new types of advanced military and civil aircraft, broken only by World War II, that made this engineering team phenomenal. Bloch moved to a large factory at Courbevoie in 1932 and there produced the Types 130, 131, 200, 210 and 211, 134, 135, 162, 174 and 175 bombers, the 150-157 fighters, and many

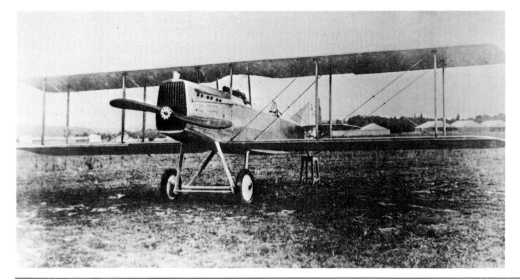

outstanding civil airliners especially including the 220 and the 161 which went into production during and after World War II by nationalized groups.

With this amazing profusion of products, all technically very advanced, it is hard to see how Bloch could later claim to have been one of the *branches mortes* (dead branches) that Pierre Cot did not bother to nationalize in 1936. In fact what happened was that Cot and the radically Leftist government were anathema to Bloch, who simply refused to "play ball." Thus all existing work was taken away; for example, the big 210 bomber was assigned to SNCASE (former Potez-CAMS factory at Vitrolles), SNCAO (former Breguet facility at Bouguenais) and SNCAC (former Hanriot, Bourges). But after Munich in September 1938 the need for warplanes was so urgent that Bloch was suddenly deluged with orders. By the end of October 1939 Bloch aircraft were in production at 14 assembly lines with parts coming from 66 factories, but by then it was a bit late.

Bloch retired to the unoccupied zone, but before long found himself pestered by agents cajoling or threatening him with a view to getting him to go and work in Germany. He steadfastly refused, so in 1943 he was arrested in Lyons and deported to the concentration camp at Buchenwald. There he made the acquaintance of a large chimney whose bricks were often so hot they glowed; it towered over the crematorium and was, he was told, the only available exit for the inmates. After months of nightmarish existence he was among those still alive on 19 April 1945, though temporarily paralyzed from the waist from diphtheria.

He asked about his brother Paul, who as an army general had fallen foul of officials because of his ceaseless campaign for more and better tanks. He became popularly known as "Tank," which in French is *char d'assault.* Joining the Resistance, he took the codename of *d'assault,* and after the war the brothers took Dassault as their proud new surname. After a three-month convalescence Marcel Dassault once more gathered his team of brilliant engineers, including Vallières and Deplante who had managed to escape to Britain and had seen much action as "paras." He set up an office at 46 Avenue Kléber, near the Arc de Triomphe, and gradually built up a factory at Talence in southwest Bordeaux, later adding a fine modern plant a few miles farther west at Mérignac. Until the late 1960s Dassault did all the basic project designs himself, and before he even got his team together he had decided to build a versatile machine powered by two of the SNECMA 12S 580hp aircooled

engines that had been made during the war by Renault (who, incidentally, had been brutally done to death by Communists during his postwar imprisonment when his factories were nationalized). On 10 February 1947 the MD.303 prototype made a successful flight. From it stemmed well over 300 production machines, the best-known of which was the MD.315 Flamant crew trainer, colonial liaison and transport aircraft. SNCASE built the fuselage at Toulouse, SNCASO the wings at Nantes and Morane-Saulnier the tail at Tarbes-Ossun. It was like 1937 again, except that this time the tiny quiet-spoken Marcel Dassault was calling the tune.

On 28 February 1949 the first prototype MD.450 Ouragan flew at Mérignac. It was just one of a shoal of new jet prototypes in

The amazing profusion of Bloch designs between the wars included many successful military and civil types, including the Bloch 220 airliner of the mid-1930s. It was a clean all-metal design built to carry 16 passengers over Air France's main European routes and some survived the war to continue in service with the original Gnome-Rhône engines replaced by Wright Cyclones.

France at that time, but it was the only one to enter service. Dassault delivered 350, and showed not only early competence with advanced jets but a remarkable ability to produce modified versions. (Ever since, it has been company policy always to do new things but never too many new things on the same aircraft.) The swept-wing Mystère II followed. One of this family, the prototype IIC, was the first production aircraft with a French jet engine, the Atar 101D3.

After the war and his change of name, Marcel Dassault got under way with a good production run of twin piston-engined light transports; he then scored a signal success with his MD.450 Ouragan (illustrated) of

1949, the only one of several French first-generation jets to enter service and the foundation on which the company's massive success with military jets was laid.

Top left: A French Mudry CAP 10L aerobatic light aircraft impudently plays tag with the second prototype of Dassault's delta Mirage 2000, an entirely new design which first flew in 1979.

Below: Successive orders for Mystère fighters during the early 1950s, totalling about 600 aircraft, have been followed by production of more than twice as many of the various Mirage fighter and light bomber variants. Illustrated is a French Air Force Mirage IIIB tandem trainer.

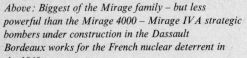

Above: Biggest of the Mirage family – but less powerful than the Mirage 4000 – Mirage IVA strategic bombers under construction in the Dassault Bordeaux works for the French nuclear deterrent in the 1960s.

The Americans were at that time helping the European defense industry by awarding "offshore" contracts for sufficiently good items, and on 28 October 1952 the Mystère IIC was driven into a dive faster than sound by an American evaluation pilot. Dassault was jubilant; his growing plant assembled 150, and soon followed with 421 of the much improved Mystère IVA fighters, 225 of them on an offshore order. Next came the Mystère IVB, with the afterburning Avon, from which stemmed 180 Super Mystère B2s, the first true supersonic fighters (Mach 1.125 on the level) in Western Europe.

There followed the Etendard IV family of naval attack and reconnaissance aircraft, in parallel with which Dassault – inspired by the British FD.2 – built the delta-winged Mirage prototype, flown on 25 June 1955. From this stemmed various larger Mirage IIIs, from which emerged the Mirage IIIC interceptor which entered service with the 2nd Fighter Squadron at Dijon in early 1961. In turn this led to over 1200 Mirage IIIs of various sub-types for 21 countries, plus over 500 of the simplified Mirage 5 day-attack machines. Dassault also built the 62 much larger Mirage IVA bombers of the French nuclear deterrent, a wealth of experimental Mirages including some with swing wings or jet-lift, and over 500 of the high-wing tailed Mirage F1 family. In 1980 the completely new delta-winged Mirage 2000 and 4000 were in test flight, the latter –

Above: Dassault's second attempt to return to the passenger aircraft market with the Mystère 20 business jet in May 1963, received a major boost when PanAm took it up and turned it into the Falcon. A developed long-range version with three aft-mounted turbofans, the Falcon 50, is illustrated.

almost unbelievably – a large twin-engined aircraft developed with Dassault money despite declared disinterest by the French government!

Dassault has plenty of money, and a mighty industrial empire that embraces many things other than aviation. It is the kind of grouping that needs business jets, and after a false start in this field as early as 1955 Dassault flew the first Mystère 20 on 4 May 1963. Soon afterwards the company was visited by Charles Lindbergh, who was looking for a good bizjet for PanAm. After flying the trim French prototype, which had powered controls from the start but at first had GE aft-fan engines, he cabled to the airline "Have found your bird." The Mystère 20 became the Fanjet Falcon, PanAm set up the Falcon Jet Corporation, and today 500 have been sold, nearly half of them by the PanAm subsidiary. From this excellent machine stemmed the smaller Falcon 10 and long-range Falcon 50, with three turbofans of a different type and a supercritical wing.

It was in the civil field that Dassault made a major mistake, though he does not see it in that light. On 28 May 1971 the first Mercure short-haul jetliner made its first flight. It was the first off a production line formed by collaborative agreement between Dassault, the French government and companies in Italy, Belgium, Spain, Switzerland and Canada. Dassault even built a series of major factories on virgin soil to build the Mercure. But, except for an order for 10 from Air Inter, the customers stayed away. Subsequently teams from Dassault, the French transport ministry and even rival Aérospatiale kept hopping across the Atlantic to try to sew up a collaborative deal with a major US planemaker on various Mercure developments.

On 14 December 1971 Dassault acquired the Société Louis Breguet, subsequently trading as Avions Marcel Dassault/Breguet Aviation. Since then AMD/BA has continued the joint program with Britain on the Jaguar (at times causing irritation by showing much greater interest in promoting "Dassault" aircraft, though AMD/BA seldom makes a higher proportion of any of its airframes than the 50 percent on the Jaguar), launched the Alpha Jet in collaboration with Dornier, and developed the ANG (Atlantic Nouvelle Génération) maritime patrol aircraft. It also managed to knock out the already developed naval Jaguar and get it replaced by Dassault's own Super Etendard, though it is easy to show that in purely financial terms this was not good business. But to Dassault outward appearances are very important, and the Super Etendard is all-French. Not even his enemies of the Left, who envy him his incredible achievements and continually call for his nationalization, could call this frail yet indestructible man anything but one of the greatest Frenchmen.

At about the time of the Breguet acquisition, which brought in the collaborative Jaguar and Atlantic programs, Dassault started to build the Alpha Jet light strike/weapons trainer aircraft developed jointly with Dornier; the first prototypes flew in France in October 1973 and in Germany in January 1974. Here the first prototype is pictured on final assembly in the Dassault-Breguet shops at Argenteuil.

DORNIER

Dornier is one of the famous "one-man" companies. Professor Dr Claude (not, as often written, Claudius) Dornier was born in 1884 and from the age of 20 showed exceptional ability in structural engineering as well as intense interest in aviation. In July 1910 he joined the Zeppelin Luftschiffbau and handled increasingly responsible work beginning with the structural design of *Viktoria Luise,* one of the passenger Zeppelins, and moving on through aerodynamic and structural design of ships for Atlantic flights. He impressed Count von Zeppelin sufficiently to be put in charge of a separate research organization set up at Lindau-Reutin in 1914. There most of the work involved airplanes and Dornier liked them to be large monoplanes making extensive use of the new alloy Duralumin. Tragically, the first Reutin-schiffe, Rs I, was wrecked before first flight in mid-1915, but with a span of 43.5m (142ft 9in) it was the largest and heaviest airplane (flying-boat) of its time.

In 1916 Dornier had his own aircraft-

Professor Claude Dornier, master-designer of structures, whose CL I/D I design of 1916 is generally accepted as being the world's first stressed-skin aircraft.

design department at Seemoos, near Friedrichshafen, where the impressive Rs II, III and IV were built with aerofoil-section sponsons and push/pull engine nacelles. Though smaller, the CL I attack aircraft and D I fighter are generally accepted as the world's first stressed-skin aircraft, besides having several other advanced features. After the Armistice Dornier managed to continue Zeppelin-Lindau GmbH at the old Friedrichshafen works at Manzell, where C II reconnaissance biplanes were built for the Swiss. But when Dornier completed the Gs I transport flying-boat and demonstrated it in Holland it caught the attention of the Allied Control Commission who had it sunk off Kiel on 25 April 1920. Subsequently Dornier built small aircraft at Manzell, such as the Delphin and Libelle flying-boats and Komet landplane, which

came within the size permitted by the Allies. For bigger types he set up an Italian subsidiary, CMASA (Costruzioni Meccaniche Aeronautiche SA) at Marina di Pisa, while he renamed Zeppelin-Lindau, Dornier Metallbauten GmbH in 1922.

CMASA rapidly built a development of the Gs II nine-passenger flying-boat, one of the types halted by the Allies, and this flew as the Wal (Whale) on 6 November 1922. It was by far the most successful flying-boat of the interwar era. The prototype had Eagle IX engines, bought new from Derby! The Allied officials fumed, but they would have done better to have negotiated a license, as did Spain, Japan and the Netherlands. Among its other claims to fame were six designs of nose/cockpit, eight designs of tail, nine wingspans, 17 types of engine and gross weight which rose by 202 percent! Dornier carried on with small aircraft, notably including the six-passenger Merkur of which at least 50 were built from 1925, but he was impatient to scale up the Wal to a real monster. CMASA was bursting at the seams trying to build Wals for 21 countries, so Dornier formed another company, this time on the Swiss side of Lake Constance opposite Manzell at Altenrhein. There AG für Dornier-Flugzeug began designing an aircraft much heavier and more powerful than anything previously attempted on wings. The 12-engined Do X

Above left: The giant Rs III flying-boat designed by Dornier at Zeppelin-Lindau in 1917 on the slip at Seemoos, near Friedrichshafen.

Left: Most successful of Dornier's between-the-wars designs, and the world's most successful flying-boat of the era, was the Gs II Wal (Whale) nine-passenger machine first built in Italy in 1922 because of the ban on German-built aircraft above a certain size. It was built in several countries and developed into a wide variety of types for use in over 20 countries. The picture shows military Wals under construction at Marina di Pisa in the early 1920s.

flying-boat rose from the lake in July 1929, piloted by Richard Wagner. Examples were built with Siemens (Bristol) Jupiters, Curtiss Conquerors and Fiat A.22 engines; the first Do X flew from Lake Constance to Rio and back via New York, among many other places, and once flew with 10 crew, 150 passengers and nine stowaways – 103 more passengers than the previous record for any airplane!

In fact the Do X was not a sensible pro-gram, mainly because it was much too large and costly for the world airline industry and had no evident military role. A large secondary reason was that scaling-up on this degree ran into square/cube law prob-lems so severe that the monster boat took 21 minutes to climb to 1000m (3280ft) and never exceeded this height; most of the time it flew "in ground effect." It was re-engined to get more power, but the watercooled engines merely took away 26 percent of the payload. Had not Italy bought two the company would have lost very heavily on the Do X, the sole German example being briefly used for research by DVL and later

Below: The neat and efficient STOL Do 27 light utility/feederliner marked the return to Dornier planemaking in Germany in 1955, though the prototype was built to Dornier design by Spanish CASA. The Do 27 can carry two crew and up to six passengers; over 650 have been sold, followed by several hundred more of the twin-engined Do 28D-1 Skyservant for up to 14 passengers.

being destroyed by bombs in a Berlin museum in 1943.

Subsequently Dornier's love of flying-boats led to the Do 18 (a modern Wal) one of which was the first German aircraft shot down by Britain (a Skua from *Ark Royal*) in World War II; the Do 24 trimotor, produced in France and Holland for the Luftwaffe and the subject of continuing plans in the 1970s for a relaunch in turboprop form; the speedy Do 26; and the gigantic Do 214, larger than any other aircraft of the World War II era, which was never completed. Had it been, this would have been an even bigger "Do X-style" mistake.

By 1930 Dornier was firmly into bombers, beginning with offensive seaplanes for Yugoslavia, large Swiss-built machines for Japan and so-called German "special freight" use, and, in November 1932, the bold decision to start building bombers again in Germany. The Friedrichshafen-built Do 11 was a poor aircraft, and even its successors (notably the Do 23) were not much better, but they put real muscle into Goering's Luftwaffe at a time when the world did not know of its existence.

In 1933 the company was restructured as Dornier-Werke GmbH, opening plants at Löwenthal, Allmansweiler and Wismar, the latter (Dornier-Werke Wismar GmbH)

becoming Norddeutsche Dornier in 1940 and opening factories at Lübeck, Reinickendorf and Sternberg. In 1938 the parent company opened a new establishment at Oberpfaffenhofen near Ingolstadt, and this became the biggest wartime development center for such machines as the Do 317 and push/pull Do 335. Chief wartime types were the Do 17, which only became a bomber by sheer chance, the 17Z/215 and the important but remarkably unprolific (only 1915) Do 217. The company's main output comprised the He 111, Ju 88, Fw 190 and Me 410.

After 1945 Dornier resurrected his company swiftly; he had begun to diversify in 1944, recognizing that aircraft manufacture would soon be forbidden, and created the Technisch-Wissenschaftliche Gesellschaft which took over the wrecked Lindau factory before the war ended. By 1948 the Pfronten works was subcontracting parts for textile machines, and before long Lido (Lindauer-Dornier GmbH) was by far the largest producer of automatic looms in Germany and a world leader. Many other advanced-technology operations followed, today grouped in a subsidiary called Dornier System GmbH, while the parent became Dornier GmbH with offices at a splendid new site at Immenstaad near Friedrichshafen.

Above left: Not so successful was the monster Do X of 1929 which, although a great structural achievement that once left the water with 169 souls aboard, could manage no more than demonstration flights around the world.

Above: Closely packed completed wings and fuselages of Dornier Do 17Z "Flying Pencil" bombers await final assembly as part of the Dornier World War II effort, though the company's main output at that time was of others' designs. The Do 17 became a bomber by chance having been designed as a fast mail carrier for Lufthansa, by which it was rejected.

Planemaking began again in 1955 with the design of the Do 25 at Oficinas Técnicas Dornier in Spain. Over 650 of the STOL Do 27 followed, leading to the Do 28 twin and the bigger Skyservant, which in turn has provided a basis for extremely advanced research aircraft leading to the LTA (light transport aircraft) of the 1980s. The first Alpha Jet trainer, a joint program with Dassault-Breguet, flew on 26 October 1973, 30 years to the day after the first Do 335, and after severe delays entered service in 1978–79. The "grand old man" died in 1969, but the family still owns all the shares and Claudius (correct in this instance) Jr and Silvanus are on the boards of a group of companies which are among world leaders in space, RPVs, V/STOL and many other challenging areas. Still fiercely independent, the Dornier empire employs 7000.

FOKKER

Left: Anthony Fokker at the controls of the Spinne (Spider) II in which he taught himself to fly in 1911, obtaining his pilot's license in May that year.

Below: A famous aircraft of World War I was the Fokker Dr I Dreidecker. Illustrated is one of several recently built Dr I flying replicas which are much in demand for film and demonstration mock dogfights.

The series of World War I fighters built by Fokker was crowned by the D.VII biplane, by all accounts the best single-seater of the war. This aircraft was smuggled out of Germany and sold to the Netherlands Air Force.

Anthony Herman Gerard Fokker was born the son of a coffee planter in a remote settlement in Java in 1890. Until he was six he never wore shoes, and when his father sold up to give him a proper Dutch education he found school boring. After contriving to avoid his year's conscription with the Army, he equally cunningly got on an aviation course at Bingen, Germany. In December 1910 Fokker flew an airplane he had himself built in an empty Zeppelin hangar at Baden-Baden with the help of a rich friend. In May 1911 he obtained his pilot's license at Mainz, and soon made money giving displays at Berlin-Johannisthal. By 1913 Fokker-Aeroplanbau was in business, though not as a registered company. On 1 October 1913 Fokker Flugzeugwerke GmbH was formed, with family backing at first, at Schwerin, Mecklenburg, near the Baltic coast. There

the excellent monoplanes designed chiefly by Fokker himself served the company's own pilot school, and found a thriving export trade.

With the outbreak of war Fokker had to multiply output as fast as he could. He took on new designers, notably Martin Kreutzer and Reinhold Platz. In April 1915 he was shown the bullet-deflector wedges of Garros's Morane and requested to make a copy. Instead he spent two days devising a workable interrupter gear, of purely mechanical cam-and-lever type. Afterwards he claimed to have invented this, though in fact at least five similar proposals antedated him; but the important thing is that he did it and demonstrated it. The next thing that happened was that he found himself in uniform with instructions to prove his proposal by shooting down Allied aircraft! After various

escapades at the Front the job was assigned to a young leutnant, one Oswald Boelcke. The rest is history. So completely did the fixed-gun Fokker E (Eindecker=monoplane) series dominate the sky until well into 1916 that British pilots were called "Fokker fodder."

By 1918 Kreutzer and Platz had created a series of significant combat aircraft, the most famous of which were the Dr Dreidecker=triplane) and D.VII biplane. After the Armistice the D.VII was specifically mentioned in the Allied terms as an item that had to be handed over at once to the occupying power. They had underestimated the wily Dutchman who, under the very noses of both German customs (who were "fixed") and Allied officials (who were not), Fokker sent six trains, each of 60 boxcars, from Schwerin to Amsterdam packed with D.VIIs, engines, spare parts and materials, to say nothing of all the drawings! With them came 150 German skilled men, and on 21 July 1919 NV Nederlandsche Vliegtuigen-fabriek Fokker was registered in Amsterdam. It immediately became as successful as any planemaker in Europe and, despite near-riots and massive skullduggery on all sides, exhibited at the first postwar Paris Salon. In October 1920 the Netherlands Aircraft Manufacturing Company of America opened its office (under Bob Noorduyn, later a planemaker in his own right) on New York City's Fifth Avenue, and in May 1924 Fokker started Atlantic Aircraft Corporation at Hasbrouck Heights (Teterboro, New Jersey). Subsequently large

Roll-out of the first Fokker airliner from the Amsterdam works after the move from Schwerin in 1919; the F.II, which was flown for the first time in October 1919, carried four passengers in the cabin and one more in the cockpit with the pilot. Construction of

an F.I airliner (otherwise V.44) for six passengers in open cockpits had been started but stopped in favor of the F.II.

factories opened at Passaic and near Wheeling, West Virginia, with an output of one large transport every five days.

After 1918 all Fokker aircraft had a form of construction for which Platz was chiefly responsible – precision-welded steel-tube fuselage and tail and a wing or wings of deep section made entirely of wood. The military aircraft, such as the C.V which was produced to the tune of 1085-plus with no fewer than nine types of engine, were usually biplanes; but the civil transports were cantilever high-wing monoplanes which, in general, served as a pattern for many other constructors (and for no fewer than 22 licensees, such as Avro in Britain). Among a profusion of trimotor transports the F.VIIb/3m was the most numerous (147) and most famous, with such pilots as Commander Byrd USN, Amelia Earhart, three young officers – Spaatz, Eaker and Quesada – and Sir Charles Kingsford Smith. William B Stout used the F.VIIa/3m as the basis for his all-metal machine which, in 1926, Henry Ford put into production; to even out the honors Fokker won the Ford Reliability Trial later in 1926. Later Atlantic was renamed Fokker Aircraft Corporation of America, was bought by General Motors in the bout of amalgamations in 1929, became General Aviation Corporation, then North American Aviation and is now part of Rockwell – though no office or factory from Fokker days remains in today's Rockwell empire.

The home plant at Schiphol gradually expanded with sound management, and followed the trimotors with the big F.XXII and XXXVI, and the C.V with the C.X. By 1936 the D.XXI fighter monoplane was in the air, soon followed by the T.VIII/W twin-engined seaplane and T.4 bomber, all traditionally built. With the impressive G.I twin-engined fighter, stressed-skin construction was at last used throughout, but on 10 May

1940 the factory was wrecked by bombs. A few G.Is actually operated during a few hectic days, often engaging the Luftwaffe; two Dutch engineers escaped to Britain in one in 1942. Fokker did not see all this, as he died on 23 December 1939.

After the war the company under Van Tijen picked up the pieces, built such types as the S.11 Instructor, S.13 crew trainer and S.14 Mach Trainer (the first purpose-designed jet trainer), and in 1955 flew the first F27 Friendship. Since then it has never looked back. Friendships, later joined by

the F28 Fellowship, have remained in production into the 1980s, under-pinned by license manufacture of the Meteor, Hunter, F-104G, F-5 and F-16. Under dynamic chairman Frans Swartthout, Fokker, between 1969 and 1979 a 50–50 partner in VFW-Fokker mbH, hopes to launch the much larger F29 in the 150-seat class. Sadly, it has been doing most of its collaborative talking with partners outside Europe; and is emotionally unwilling to accept Airbus Industrie, to which it belongs, as the European partnership for large jetliners.

Top: Most famous of the Fokker airliners, and one that made a major contribution to the early development of air travel, was the F.VII which started in 1924 with a single engine as an eight-passenger machine and eventually became the F.VIIb/3m trimotor to take up to ten passengers.

Above: Recent Fokker activity includes considerable license-production, of such aircraft as the F-104G and the later F-5 and F-16. Here an F-104 Starfighter uses the engine testbed at the Schiphol works.

Below: When the Fokker F28 Fellowship twin-jet short-range airliner first flew in 1967 it broke a 50-year devotion to the high-wing configuration. The basic F28-1000 for up to 65 passengers was joined in 1971 by an F28-2000 development with fuselage extension for up to 79 passengers (illustrated), and by several later variants.

By far the largest aerospace manufacturer in Federal Germany, and one of the most impressive advanced-technology enterprises in Europe, MBB was formed in 1969. It incorporates 14 earlier companies and has many private and corporate shareholders, but among the famous names in its ancestry are Messerschmitt, Junkers, Blohm und Voss, Siebel and Klemm. The best way to tell this story is to outline the history of the first three companies up to the points at which they merged.

Messerschmitt is the chief thread linking it all together, if only for the fact that the man himself died as recently as 1979. He was born 81 years earlier, and to the end of his life could recall every detail of his many aircraft and the way he became "hooked" on aviation by – of all things – reading the newspaper report of the loss of Zeppelin LZ.4 near Echterdingen in August 1908. He at once began drawing improved designs, mainly of heavier-than-air machines, and when his father, a wealthy wine merchant, moved to Bamberg, he was thrilled in 1912 to meet the glider pioneer Friedrich Harth. Harth was impressed by Messerschmitt, who was 14, and let him help make his fourth glider and even fly it from the Ludwager Kulm, a steep eminence near Bamberg. The friends soon lost any master/pupil relationship and jointly designed, built and flew several important gliders before, during and after World War I, in which Harth served in the army and as an aircraft rigging instructor.

After the Armistice Messerschmitt enrolled at the Munich Technischen Hochschule, while Harth joined the BFW (Bayerische Flugzeugwerke), a subsidiary of Albatros-Werke formed in 1916. This company accomplished little, and Harth spent much time gliding with Messerschmitt at the new national center at the Wasserkuppe in the Rhön mountains organized by Oskar Ursinus to keep Germany air-minded without contravening Allied restrictions. Harth-Messerschmitt gliders became famous, but Harth crashed badly in 1921. Two years later Messerschmitt struck out on his own, with a group called Messerschmitt-Flugzeugbau, building ever-better sailplanes, motorized gliders and, in 1925, the M 17 Ello tandem-seat monoplane, his first powered airplane. Roy Fedden came from Bristol with a Cherub engine and found Messerschmitt – tall, dark and handsome – putting the M 17 together in his father's wine cellars. A week later he flew the 32hp machine nonstop across the Alps to Rome, a staggering achievement. Theo Croneiss, famous aviator and director of Sportflug, urged Messerschmitt to build civil transports.

In 1925 Messerschmitt took a giant step forward with the M 18 transport, carrying up to four passengers and wholly of Duralumin construction. Its success prompted him to turn his group into a company, Messerschmitt-Flugzeugbau GmbH, and Croneiss formed the Nordbayerische airline. M 18s sold for only £1250, and Messerschmitt approached the Bavarian legislature to request a subsidy. The reply was that Bavaria was already assisting another company, BFW. This was a second company with this name, formed in 1926 to take over the business and the Augsburg factory of the Udet-Flugzeugbau. It was enjoying some success with the U12 and Sperber but had no creative design engineer. The Bavaria officials hit on the happy solution of a merger, and on 8 September 1927 a formal agreement was signed giving BFW first option on all Messerschmitt designs in exchange for an undertaking by BFW not to manufacture any others.

The little M 19, the first low-wing machine, pleased Croneiss greatly, but the outstanding ten-seat M 20, ordered by Lufthansa, was crashed by pilot Hackmack on its first flight on 26 February 1928. The second M 20 proved the absence of any fault, but in the meantime Lufthansa had cancelled, and the Bavarian State and Reichsverkehrsministerium wished to dispose of their 87.5 percent holding in BFW. Messerschmitt persuaded his wealthy in-laws, the Strohmeyer-Raulino family, to take up the lot, buying the other 12.5 percent himself. All was now set fair for one

of the classic instances of a company run by an engineer to overreach itself. After too many prototypes and an unkind cancellation by Lufthansa of ten M 20b transports that were almost complete (plus a demand for repayment of deposits) BFW went bankrupt in June 1931.

All this time Messerschmitt Flugzeugbau had still existed in name, and Messerschmitt raised 8000 Reichsmark by selling his car and a license for the M 23b two-seater to ICAR of Rumania, and plunged into business. He even got a court order on Lufthansa to take delivery of the M 20bs, and, combined with the success of the brilliant M 29 sports machine, he not only pulled through but repaid most of BFW's creditors and by April 1933 saw BFW fully solvent. By this time the Nazis were sweeping to power, and Messerschmitt was lucky to have sold an M 23 to the party's deputy leader, Rudolf Hess (this connection alone saved his Augsburg works from being taken over as a streetcar depot).

But Hitler appointed Erhard Milch as air minister, and as head of Lufthansa he had become a bitter enemy of the young planemaker. Here was the chance to get even, and though he could not prevent Messerschmitt having any contracts at all he said bluntly he would never buy a Mes-

Professor Willy Messerschmitt in August 1939 congratulates pilot Fritz Wendel in the world speed record-breaking "Bf 109R" which in fact was the Me 209VI and had little in common with the well-known and incredibly prolific Bf 109 German fighter of World War II.

serschmitt design – for reasons which were undoubtedly personal rather than technical. Contracts were received for Do 11 bombers and He 45 reconnaissance-bombers, so that, combined with the increasing popularity of Messerschmitt sportplanes, the employment increased from 82 to 524 between April and December of 1933. Milch scowled, and was joined by Heinkel in the hate-Messerschmitt campaign, mainly because of the way Messerschmitt had refused even to listen when Heinkel had tried to buy his factory. Though sharply contrasting in appearance and personality, they were mercurial men who could quickly have thundering arguments. It is on record that Heinkel refused to allow any BFW employee into his works during the planning for He 45 production!

In October 1933 Messerschmitt's co-manager, Rakan Kokothaki, obtained contracts from ICAR of Bucharest for the M 36 transport and an advanced stressed-skin sportplane with retractable landing gear, the M 37. Milch saw this as an opportunity to issue a public rebuke to Messerschmitt for taking on foreign development activity, but should have realized that this only gave Messerschmitt the chance to broadcast the fact that Germany had failed to offer him a single design contract! While this exacerbated the personal relationships it did bring BFW a contract for a new sportplane for the 1934 Challenge de Tourisme Internationale.

Messerschmitt produced the aircraft extremely quickly, the first Bf 108A (the first of his designs to have the unified RLM numbering) flying on 13 June 1934. Despite politically inspired opposition by the German team manager, Theo Osterkamp, it was such a brilliant success that Messerschmitt's enemies temporarily kept quiet. Later the four-seat Argus-powered Bf 108B followed, and unlike all their contemporaries the survivors still look modern today. Features included a strong single-spar wing with slats and slotted flaps, outward-retracting main legs housed entirely in the wings, and a neat cockpit with hinged canopy. It owed much to Walther Rethel, previously with Arado.

In December 1933 the RLM received a specification from the Luftwaffe for a new fighter, and in April 1934 this was duly issued to constructors – including BFW, to prevent further complaints. Milch doubted that Messerschmitt would even participate, and took it for granted that any BFW prototype would soon be laughed off the scene. He was a poor judge in this, because Messerschmitt, Rethel, project chief Robert Lusser and construction managers Richard

and Hubert Bauer created a masterpiece, the rakish Bf 109, flown by "Bubi" Knötsch at the end of May 1935 (not September, as widely recorded). Owing much to the Bf 108, it suffered every kind of political attack and rumor of vicious handling or structural weakness; but the test pilots – including Oberst Udet, who on first seeing the prototype, and finding it was not an open-cockpit biplane had exclaimed "that thing will never make a fighter" – had no doubt it was dramatically superior to every other fighter in the world. Messerschmitt, who had earlier been assured that the Bf 109 would never receive a production contract, was to see a succession of 109 versions made in larger numbers than any non-Russian type of aircraft in history – an unknown total close to 31,000. From 1937 to 1942 it was virtually the *only* Luftwaffe fighter (and look what it accomplished!) and despite devastating bombing the Messerschmitt empire of 14 major company plants, 21 factories of other companies and countless small dispersed shops delivered a record 14,112 Bf 109s in the year 1944 alone.

It was not all plain sailing. Although the company board were so pleased with their new status that, on 11 June 1938, they voted to change the name of the company to Messerschmitt AG (so that all subsequent designs had an Me prefix), the planned successor to the Bf 110 twin-engine fighter, the Me 210, was an abject failure. With 200 completed and 370 on the production lines at Augsburg and Regensburg the order was given to stop production on 14 April 1942. Milch and his other enemies secured Messerschmitt's resignation, his place being taken by his old friend Theo Croneiss, chairman of the shareholders. Subsequently prolonged effort rectified most of the faults and resulted in the Me 410, but it was an uphill struggle. Far more suc-

cessful in different ways were the Me 163B Komet rocket interceptor, Me 262 twin-jet fighter and Me 321 and 323 Gigant transports. Messerschmitt AG also produced a racer, the nasty little Me 209 which set a piston-engined world speed record unbroken from 1939 until 1969, and the ultra-long-range Me 261 and 264.

In 1948 the original Augsburg factory began to be rebuilt and set to making prefab housing and commercial buildings as the Neue Technik GmbH. Professor Dr-Ing Willy Messerschmitt got his old firm going again in November 1949, at first making automatic sewing machines and a very advanced car with five-cylinder radial engine, and then temporarily left for Spain to carry on planemaking with the Me 100 and 200, built in quantity as the Hispano HA-100 and HA-200 and -220 Saeta. He masterminded the HA-300 supersonic fighter for Egypt, while the German company mass-produced "bubble cars" looking like a fighter cockpit on wheels. By 1956 Messerschmitt AG was rebuilding T-6s for the Luftwaffe, followed by T-33s; in 1958 it began license-production of the Fouga Magister and in 1959 was making fuselages for the German G91 program. By 1961 it was tooling up for fuselages of the F-104G.

In parallel a growing effort on jet V/STOL was being mounted by a group formed by Messerschmitt, Heinkel and Bölkow in June 1958 called Entwicklungsring Süd (Development Group South). Bölkow had been founded only two years earlier as a civil engineering office in Stuttgart, but Dipl-Ing Ludwig Bölkow was clearly going places. In December 1958 he transferred his aero-operation to Ottobrunn near Munich as Bölkow-Entwicklungen, changing this to Bölkow GmbH in 1965 when, with a USAF V/STOL deal in prospect, a minority interest was sold to Boeing. On 31 October

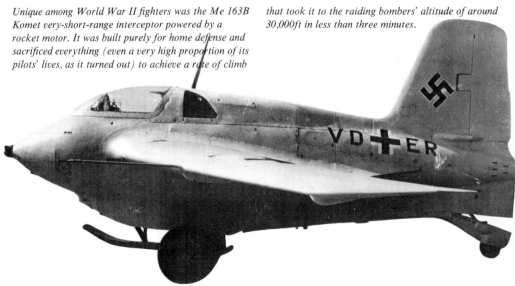

Unique among World War II fighters was the Me 163B Komet very-short-range interceptor powered by a rocket motor. It was built purely for home defense and sacrificed everything (even a very high proportion of its pilots' lives, as it turned out) to achieve a rate of climb *that took it to the raiding bombers' altitude of around 30,000ft in less than three minutes.*

Bottom: A major achievement of Professor Junkers and his company was the development of the use of light alloys in aircraft; it eventually gave rise after World War I to the F 13 passenger plane with which more of the early airline services were founded than any other machine. This picture shows the Duralumin main fuselage center wing structure of the F 13, which weighed only 107kg (235lb).

Below: The Messerschmitt Me 323 Gigant which started life as the Me 321 unpowered glider in March 1941 but was so difficult to tow it was given six engines. It became Germany's most useful military transport, able to carry up to 130 equipped troops or well over 20,000lb of freight, such as this 88mm gun and tractor; about 200 Me 323 Gigants were built.

1968 the giants shook hands and formed Messerschmitt-Bölkow GmbH.

Three years earlier, in 1965, Messerschmitt had acquired the once-gigantic Junkers empire, and thus united the two biggest German planemakers. In fact, from 1935 until 1945 Junkers was (intermittently if not continuously) the world's largest aviation company. It was founded by a highly qualified engineer and gifted visionary, who is generally regarded as the greatest pioneer of the metal airplane; but he was no boyish enthusiast, because Hugo Junkers was born in February 1859. By 1888 he was

assistant chief engineer of the Continental Gas Company, in 1895 he had his own engineering works at Dessau and in 1897 he additionally became professor of heating technics at the famed Technischen Hochschule at Aachen. There he met Professor Reissner, whose spare-time passion was designing flying machines. Junkers was not the type to leap off a high place flapping some wings; instead he thought deeply about aircraft. He decided people and other loads ought to be accommodated internally. He also saw that, as wings are cantilever beams (ignoring external bracing, which he felt

undesirable), the skin ought to carry most of the loads, and in 1910 he obtained a classic patent on a transport aircraft with a thick wing with stressed skins and inside which were the fuel, engines and nearly all the payload. Wisely he made no attempt to build it, though it was sound in concept.

In 1913 Professor Junkers founded Junkers Motorenwerke at Magdeburg, to make oil and diesel engines. A year later he opened an excellent wind tunnel near Aachen, and after intensive research into methods of making aircraft from a framework of welded steel tubing covered with thin spot-

welded sheet-iron skin, he first got his Dessau works to build a wing for static testing and then, after completely failing to secure any official support for such a nonsensical idea as an iron-covered airplane, he got Dipl-Ings Otto Reuter and Otto Mader to oversee construction of the J 1 monoplane. As almost everyone except for the three designers was a disbeliever, the nickname "Blechesel" (tin donkey) is understandable. Junkers towed it to the military airfield at Döberitz where, after much argument, an unfortunate junior officer, Leutnant Von Mallinckrodt, was detailed to be test pilot. After a lengthy run the J 1 took off; the unbraced wing did not fold up and after a prolonged demonstration a much-relieved Von Mallinckrodt pronounced the aircraft nice to fly.

Someone hit on the handy solution of getting Junkers to form a joint company with Fokker, perhaps in case the J 1 maiden flight had been a mirage. Fokker hated collaborating with anyone except licensees, and after a few violent meetings left Junkers alone to get on unhindered. The JFA (Junkers-Fokkerwerke AG) subsequently produced several highly satisfactory warplanes, of which the J 4, J 9 and J 10 (respectively designated J I, D I and CL I by the Aviation Service) saw front-line duty. The J 4 was the first to have Dural light-alloy skin on the wings (it was a large unbraced biplane) and tail, while the J 9 and 10 were neat monoplanes with corrugated Dural skinning throughout. For the next 17 years Junkers was to remain faithful to this distinctive form of construction, which made his aircraft the toughest in the world – though if he had realized that the air hardly ever flowed parallel to the corrugations he would have had a better appreciation of the extra drag.

After the Armistice Junkers turned to civil transports, which were what he preferred anyway. Despite the environment of revolution and anarchy he formed Junkers Flugzeugwerke AG on 24 April 1919, and only two months later, on 25 June, the

Dessau works turned out in force (over 700) to witness the first flight by the J 13. Soon redesignated F 13, this neat aircraft was probably the most important civil aircraft in history apart from the DC-3. Though carrying only four passengers at modest speed it was efficient, reliable and, unlike all competitors, able to stand up to the rough usage it received; over 350 were built, and many were still operating after World War II.

By 1921 Junkers was building his dreamship, the G I with four 260hp engines on a 125ft wing; but the Allies forced it to be scrapped before it flew. Employment dwindled to about 180, but Junkers opened a completely new subsidiary called AB Flygindustri at Limhamn-Malmö which subsequently was a hive of activity in design, development and production, unfettered by Allied restrictions. Junkers even went to the Kremlin and, though private enterprise was not welcome in a Soviet Union still embroiled in bitter civil war, planemakers such as Junkers certainly were. On 23 January 1923 he was awarded a special concession to take over a newly erected factory at Fili, near Moscow, as well as a works making diesels and gasoline engines. For four years the Fili factory not only produced as much as Dessau and Malmö combined but also exerted a great influence on Soviet designers, especially Tupolev. In 1927 the concession was terminated; both sides were happy to end it. Dessau was now becoming, with restrictions lifted and no fewer than eight successful new types having appeared in 1926 alone. Japan and China were among the worldwide market for Junkers aircraft, which since 1923 had been backed up by the Junkers Motorenbau GmbH with aviation engines which included a unique series of opposed-piston two-stroke diesels.

One of the top designers, Karl Plauth, (whose Malmö-built K 47 is regarded as the true ancestor of the Stuka), was killed in a crash in 1927. His successor, Ernst Zindel, was to create most of the most famous

Above: The Junkers F 13, on wheels, floats or skis, brought air transport to the bush. In Brazil the airline Syndicato Condor was formed in December 1927 with the help of Lufthansa and this F 13 named Iguassu.

An outstanding airliner of 1930, the Junkers Ju 52, in its trimotor form won even greater fame. The Ju 52/3m flew in 1932, in time to serve as a bomber in the Spanish civil war and as a military transport in World War II. But the Ju 52/3m was designed as an airliner and was in service with several airlines before the war, including the two featuring in this 1937 Ecuadorian airline photograph.

Below: As well as the demobilized Ju 52s that went into airline service, others found their way into various Air Forces. A few have even survived in military service into the 1980s, like this veteran, one of three used by the Swiss Air Force for transport and paratroop training.

Right: The last great Junkers passenger aircraft was the Ju 90, a big four-engined low-wing 40-seater developed from the Ju 89 bomber. The first Ju 90 flew in June 1937 and broke up in the air during test-flying about eight months later. But production went ahead and ten eventually entered Lufthansa service from 1938 (one of which is illustrated).

Junkers aircraft, including the Ju 52 and its three-engined derivative, the Ju 52/3m, one of the greatest of all transports. By 1933 Junkers and Zindel were at last switching to smooth skins, but not only was the great empire financially shaky but the Nazis regarded Junkers (rightly) as a political opponent with strongly democratic ideas. In 1933 he was told he was being retired with pomp and ceremony (he died 18 months later) and, apart from a plant making housewares, the whole company was taken over by the state. Dr Heinrich Koppenberg, who knew little of aviation but much of business, was appointed director-general. By 1936, by which time Pohlmann's Ju 87 "Stuka" was flying and the first of 14,980 Ju 88s was in the erection shop, Koppenberg welded all branches of the firm into the giant Junkers Flugzeug und Motorenwerke AG, the world's biggest planemaker. Within two years it had 12,000 working at Dessau and major branch factories at Aschersleben, Bernburg, Halberstadt and Köthen, to which were added growing

plants at Arnimswalde, Breslau, Fritzlar, Gandau, Leipzig-Mockau, Leopoldshall, Magdeburg, Merseburg and Schönebeck. By 1945 Junkers had about 140,000 employees, not including Junkers-directed companies in Czechoslovakia and France which brought the total to over 160,000.

The main Junkers centers were in what became East Germany, but the company existed as a legal entity for Messerschmitt to acquire in 1965. In 1968 came the merger with Bölkow, and seven months later, in May 1969, the merger process was almost complete with a link with HFB.

Hamburger Flugzeugbau GmbH was formed on 4 July 1933 as a subsidiary of the great Blohm und Voss shipyard. Walther Blohm ought, according to Nazi guidelines, to have regarded HFB as a mere shadow factory where the designs of experienced

Perhaps fittingly for a shipbuilder, the Blohm und Voss planemaking subsidiary HFB went in for substantial flying-boats; the best known was the BV 138 three-engined long-range reconnaissance anti-shipping machine which first flew in 1937 (picture shows second prototype) and reached a total wartime production of 276, the only BV design to achieve substantial production.

planemakers could be mass-produced. But there is something about planemaking that forever yearns to be creative – countless companies have happily gone broke because of it – and with the backing of the rich Blohm family HFB created one new design after another. One, the BV 138 flying-boat, was actually built in fair numbers, but most were prototypes only. Richard Vogt, ex-Kawasaki, was responsible for nearly all, including such oddballs as the asymmetric BV 141, the gigantic BV 222 Wiking and even bigger BV 238, and the BV 40 which

Blohm und Voss also went in for oddities; the BV 138 was a little off-beat, earning the nickname "Flying Shoe," but the BV 141 was odd in every sense, including the offset tailplane. Only a small batch was built and used experimentally as observation aircraft on both Western and Eastern Fronts.

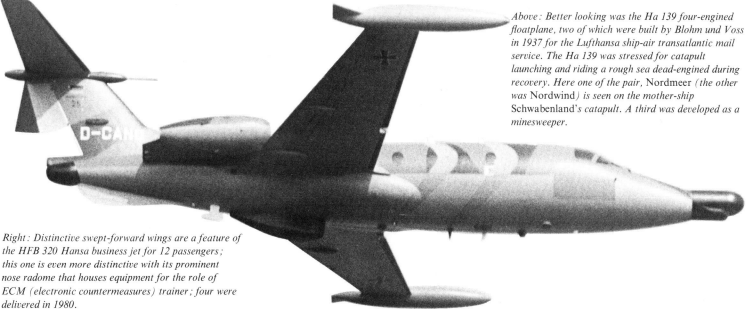

Above: Better looking was the Ha 139 four-engined floatplane, two of which were built by Blohm und Voss in 1937 for the Lufthansa ship-air transatlantic mail service. The Ha 139 was stressed for catapult launching and riding a rough sea dead-engined during recovery. Here one of the pair, Nordmeer *(the other was* Nordwind*) is seen on the mother-ship* Schwabenland's *catapult. A third was developed as a minesweeper.*

Right: Distinctive swept-forward wings are a feature of the HFB 320 Hansa business jet for 12 passengers; this one is even more distinctive with its prominent nose radome that houses equipment for the role of ECM (electronic countermeasures) trainer; four were delivered in 1980.

was probably the world's only interceptor without an engine. The company's real forté was guided missiles, where it was a world leader in air-to-surface weapons.

HFB's first large postwar task was license-manufacture of the Nord 2501 Noratlas, which led to a leading role in Transporter-Allianz creating and building the Transall C.160. The company designed and launched the attractive forward-swept HFB 320 Hansa business jet and linked with VFW-Fokker in Entwicklungsring Nord on the F-104G and third stage of the Europa space launcher, and later in the F28 Fellowship program.

From May 1969 the merged group was named Messerschmitt-Bölkow-Blohm (MBB). It began life with 20,000 employees, a wealth of talent and modern plant, and with the following shareholding: Blohm family 27.1 percent, Professor Willy Messerschmitt 23.3 percent, Dipl-Ing Ludwig Bölkow 14.6 percent, the Boeing Company 9.7 percent, Nord-Aviation 9.7 percent, Sie-

Left: HFB played a leading role in the Franco-German Transporter Allianz which led to the development of the Transall C.160 twin-turboprop medium-range transport, of which about 170 were produced from 1967 including 52 for France and 108 for Germany. A French Air Force C-160F is illustrated.

Right: A major current activity of Messerschmitt-Bölkow-Blohm (MBB) is production of the versatile Bölkow BO 105 twin-turbine helicopter, of which something approaching 1000 have been delivered or ordered since its first flight in 1967. Here BO 105s are seen in the electronic equipment shops at MBB in Hamburg.

Below right: One of several collaborative products (in this case with Britain and Italy) currently occupying MBB's several works is the Panavia Tornado. Pictured is the start of final assembly of the complete GT 010 Tornado trainer, but MBB's main component construction program is well ahead of that number, with 100 wing boxes and 50 fuselage centersections already completed and work started on the 100th centersection and on long-lead items for the second production batch, from No 151 on.

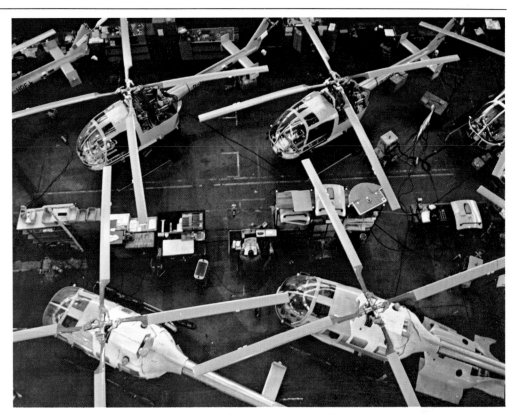

mens AG 9.1 percent and the Bavarian Reconstruction Finance Institute 6.5 percent. Products included the Bölkow-originated BO 105 helicopter, BO 208 Junior (ex-MFI in Sweden) and BO 209 Monsun lightplane, as well as various anti-tank missiles. Prolonged research on the VJ-101C VTOL failed to lead to production, and the joint AVS (Advanced Vertical Strike) program with Fairchild also came to nothing, but the MRCA project that replaced it led to the formation of Panavia, the great three-nation consortium responsible for the Tornado (and, one hopes, follow-on programs), in which MBB has a 42.5 percent holding. MBB is one of the two members of Deutsche Airbus which has a 37.9 percent holding in Airbus Industrie.

Today MBB has over 200 active programs, most of them not directly concerned with aviation, though it is busy with the center fuselage of the Tornado, the main fuselage and fin of the A300B, the rear fuselage and nacelles of the F28, the whole of many versions of the BO 105 and the dynamic parts (including hydraulics, flight-control system and systems integration) of the MBB-Kawasaki BK 117 helicopter. In partnership with Aérospatiale it wants to build a "PAK-2" anti-tank helicopter. Another warlike product is the MW-1 lateral bomblet dispenser now flying on Tornados. Almost the only thing that has gone downhill in MBB is the family shareholdings, the breakdown in 1980 being Fides GmbH 33.78 percent, Bavarian RFI 20.78 percent, City of Hamburg 20.25 percent, the Messerschmitt estate 11.05 percent, Bavarian State 7.8 percent, Ludwig Bölkow 4.14 percent, the Boeing Company 0.99 percent and the Blohm family 0.75 percent (which adds up to 99.54 percent, but is the official listing).

PIAGGIO

As far as can be ascertained the Piaggio company had an unbroken existence without changing its name – Società Anonima Piaggio & Cia – from 1886 until after World War II. The company was founded in Genoa and has always been centered at Liguria in the surrounding district. It built a fine reputation with various engineering products before starting an aircraft department in June 1916 at the Genoa-Sestri factory. Until 1922 it built licensed designs, but then built up a design staff headed by Giovanni Pegna. By this time it had opened a purpose-built factory for aircraft at Finale Ligure, and in 1925 another factory was opened for aero-engines at Pontedera in Tuscany between Pisa and Florence.

Subsequently Piaggio plodded on with many types of aircraft but none was important and most remained prototypes. Notable examples included the P.6 observation seaplane (a small batch of which actually served on warship catapults between 1930 and 1940), the P.7 Schneider racer with hydrofoils instead of floats and marine screws to accelerate to a speed at which the main propeller could be started,

the P.16 trimotor bomber of 1934 with gun barbette under the rudder, and the advanced P.32 bomber of 1936 with large double-slotted flaps but too small a wing. The company kept going with its engines, which were produced by the thousands.

In World War II a handful of P.108B bombers saw operational service; though big and impressive the type was ineffective, and the Luftwaffe only wanted it as a transport. Despite having opened the first private wind tunnel in Italy in 1930 and the first private aircraft water-test tank, Piaggio made little impact on the war except for engines, and it wasted much effort on an extremely challenging P.119 fighter with one of the company's 1650hp engines behind the cockpit but it never got near to production.

Indeed the company only came to life after the war. Restarted in 1946 as Piaggio & Cia Società per Azioni, it began converting C-47s into airliners and then produced various prototypes directed by Giovanni P Casiraghi who had headed design since 1939. One of these was the neat twin-pusher amphibian P.136, flown in 1948. It was

certificated a year later and went into production at Finale Ligure, initially for the reformed Aeronautica Militare. While propellers resumed production at Pontedera, the P.136 was joined at Finale Ligure by the P.148 and 149 trainers, the latter being selected by the new Luftwaffe, and in 1957 the P.166, an enlarged land derivative of the 136, all designed by Faraboschi. The 136 remained in production to 1967, and the 166 is important to this day.

On 29 February 1964 the company was restyled Industrie Aeronautiche e Meccaniche Rinaldo Piaggio SpA; Rinaldo (son of the founder) became chairman and managing director. Casiraghi is still technical consultant, and the company is prospering with 1300 people building the P.166 and parts of the Tornado and G.222 at Sestri, and license-producing the Viper turbojet and various Avco Lycoming engines at Finale Ligure.

The clean-limbed Piaggio P. 148 side-by-side two-seater was selected in 1951 by the Italian Air Force as its standard primary trainer. The prototype flew in February 1951 and 100 were delivered, some of them later going for export.

PILATUS

The Pilatus PC-6 Porter is a versatile light utility transport for up to nine passengers designed especially with STOL performance for efficient operation from Switzerland's Alpine airfields, characteristics which have also brought substantial export orders and license production in the US. There is a wide choice of piston and turboprop engines, the first piston-engined prototype flying in May 1959 and the first turboprop two years later. A Turbo-Porter is illustrated.

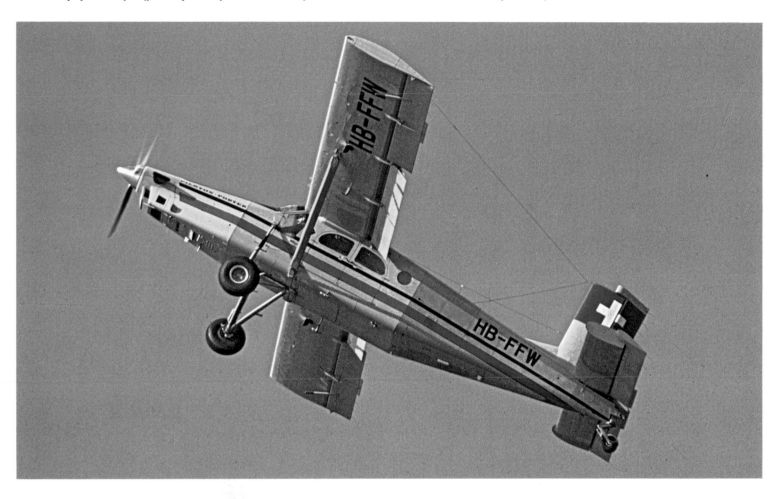

FAF

There was a time long long ago when even small individual concerns could embark on the design of advanced jet aircraft. The Lucerne, Switzerland, Museum of Transport and Communications maintains a memorial to those times in the very handsome FAF N-20 pictured here. The N-20 was the prototype of an intended STOL fighter/bomber developed by the Swiss Federal Aircraft Factory; it was powered by four jet engines for a speed of nearly 700mph but after taxiing trials and some short hops in April 1952 the project died through lack of funds. FAF continues as the Swiss government's aircraft research, development and construction establishment and undertakes license-production and modification of many types for the Swiss Air Force.

SAAB

It is ironic that Sweden, a pioneer of airplane manufacturing as a business and today the world's outstanding example of a country determined to be self-sufficient even in Mach 2 combat aircraft, should have allowed its pre-1918 industry to wither. AB Thulin at Landskrona and Baron Carl Söderström's Södertalge Verkstader both vanished along with several smaller planemakers, and by the late 1920s all that was left was the Air Force workshops at Malmslätt and Västerås and Navy works at Stockholm. The latter built marine types, such as the Heinkel He 5 (S5) while the Air Force built mainly spares and conversions.

A permanent manufacturing industry began in 1921 with the choice of Sweden by several expatriate Germans. The big Junkers operation did not, in the long term, assist Sweden, but in 1921 Carl Clemens Bücker started a company at Lidingö called Svenska Aero AB, Saab for short. By far the best known of its products was the J6 Jaktfalk fighter, but by the time evaluation batches were being delivered in 1930 Bücker was in difficulties. (In 1932 he returned to Germany to set up Bücker Flugzeugbau, with the brilliant Swede, Anders Andersson, as chief designer.) In 1930 AB Svenska Järnvägsverkstädernas (ASJ) had set up an aircraft department ASJA (A for Aeroplanavdelning), and this took over Saab in 1930, putting it on a sound footing and getting into license-production with such foreign types as the Raab Katzenstein, Tiger Moth, Hawker Hart and Fw 44 Stieglitz.

In 1936 the government decided, first, that buying licenses meant being second-best (if for no other reason, at least in timing) and, second, that with increasing political tension it would be prudent to strengthen the home defense industry. Following intense discussions several companies, such

Bottom left: Sweden has for many years maintained self-sufficiency in highly efficient military aircraft but her one postwar essay into the transport aircraft field died out after a quite promising start with the Saab-90 Scandia airliner, of which only 18 were built and the last six of those by Fokker in Holland. The Scandia was a 36-seater and first flew in 1946. Here, completed aircraft await delivery at Linköping in 1950.

Left: Saab has paced the leaders in design and construction of military jets, starting with the Saab-32 Lansen of 1952, one of the earliest two-seat aircraft to exceed Mach 1 (in a dive), and continuing with the double-delta Mach 2 Saab-35 Draken fighter/recce/ trainer in 1955. Here J35A Drakens and 32B all-weather Lansens are seen in production in 1960.

Right: Sweden's current-production military jet, the Saab-37 Viggen of 1967, was designed with comprehensive multi-role capability to take over eventually the wide range of Lansen and Draken duties. The distinctive double-delta layout with separate foreplane and particularly powerful engine are intended to provide STOL capability for operation from roads or short emergency runways. Here a pair of Swedish Air Force Viggens demonstrate take-off in less than 500 yards.

Above: Versatility is evident in all Saab design and particularly in the 105 trainer/light tactical aircraft which first flew in June 1963. As well as its several military roles as a side-by-side two-seater, the 105 can be fitted to carry two more passengers in seats behind the crew.

as Götaverken, were eliminated and the final choice was a completely new company formed in April 1937 with the backing of Bofors, Wenner-Gren, SKF, Frenne and Wingqvist. It was called Svenska Aeroplan AB, and set up a major new factory at Trollhätten. Inevitably it was called Saab, though for a while the suffix -T was added to distinguish it from the previous company, denoting the new location. It competed with ASJA, because the government wanted at least two rival sources, but the two companies set up a joint design and sales office in Stockholm called AFF (AB Förenade Flygverkstäder).

The first major product at Trollhätten was the B3, the licensed Ju 86 bomber. At Linköping grew production lines for the North American NA-16 (T-6) and Northrop (Douglas) 8A-5 attack aircraft. But these were still foreign designs. Engineers were a scarce resource and, after carefully studying alternative sources, ASJA began importing American design staff skilled in advanced aerodynamics (led by M Carl Haddon, later of Lockheed) and stressed-skin structures. They transformed the national plane-making capability, but in September 1939

World War II spurred their recall to the United States. Behind them they left the Saab-17, first flown in May 1940 and produced in several important attack, dive-bomber and reconnaissance versions. While this was being designed the government reluctantly agreed to the merger of ASJA and Saab-T, which took effect on the first day of 1939. Trollhätten became a subsidiary plant which handled the Saab-21 fighter in the late war years and then switched to engines (the Bofors subsidiary Nohab, which became Svenska Flygmotor), and in 1949 began Saab cars. The biggest wartime task at Linköping was the Saab-18 twin-engined bomber, initially planned (with nosewheel) by the Americans before their departure and subsequently produced like the J21 with the most powerful engine the Swedes could get, the German DB 605A.

In the early war years this left a severe fighter gap. The government tried to fill it with 360-plus Republic EP-1s and 2PAs, but this was a wash-out; President Roosevelt banned such exports and all that arrived were 62 near-wrecks carried over terrible roads from Petsamo in embattled Finland. Thus, as a crash program, Nils Söderberg

of the Air Board signed a lease (fantastically well timed, for it expired on 1 July 1945) for an ABA hangar at Stockholm Bromma where the J22 fighter designed by Bo Lindberg was produced by a temporary Air Force organization called FFVS. Saab's own more formidable J21 did not reach squadrons until just after the war. Thus in the crisis year of 1940 the Swedish industry's capacity rose by over 40 percent.

Subsequent Saab products are deservedly famous: the Scandia airliner, Safir light-plane, 29, 32, 35 and 37 major combat-aircraft programs and 105 trainer and light tactical platform. The company became a major missile producer, with design capability, from 1959, and later added military electronics, space equipment and other advanced-technology products. In 1968 Saab, whose car division by this time was a major producer, merged with the Scania-Vabis truck company, and also took over MFI (Malmö Flygindustri) and turned the MFI-17 into the Safari and Supporter as Saab products. Today Saab-Scania AB is an impressive multi-faceted company with 39,000 employees; the Aerospace Division accounts for 6000.

SAVOIA-MARCHETTI

An exception must be made to the rule in this book of using as titles the names of companies – where possible, today's name – because the title above is the familiar "name" even though it was never a company name at all. In general Italian companies had fairly straightforward histories but made up for it either by perpetually changing their name or by using popular titles based on such things as the current chief designer or the geographical location; in this case it was both. And, to ram home the confusion a little farther, the actual name of the company was SIAI. This had two meanings, and was unconnected with another Italian plane-maker called SIA. SIAI called all its aircraft "Savoias," (while the lead designer of the other SIA company was named Savoia!)

The one thing that has never changed was the location – Sesto Calende, in the beautiful country near Lago di Maggiore northwest of Milan. There the original SIAI (Società Idrovolanti Alta Italia) was founded in June 1915 to build *idrovolanti* (seaplanes and flying-boats), receiving a succession of license-contracts for the excellent FBA (Franco-British Aviation) H-series, nearly 1000 of which were built in Italy despite Macchi's products. Technical director Conflenti modestly kept his own name or initial

out of the proceedings, though the outstandingly successful later boats, such as the S.8 and S.16, were entirely his work. By 1917 the company was studying landplanes and changed its name to Società Italiana Aeroplani Idrovolanti, but it continued to rely 99.5 percent on marine aircraft until after 1930.

In 1921 Conflenti went to Cant, and for the next 30 years the company was dominated by Alessandro Marchetti. Although the company designation was painted on the aircraft in the style S55 (for example) it was registered as S.M.55, the M standing for the technical director. This particular design was one of the most renowned of the entire interwar period, despite its unconventional twin-hull configuration, mainly because of the remarkable series of long-range flights made by various military and civil examples (most notably the formation flights led by Italo Balbo with up to 25 SM.55X to the Chicago World's Fair in 1933). The SM.71 of 1933 confirmed a preference for trimotors, leading to the 72 bomber, 73 and 75 airliners, 81 bomber, 82 Canguru (the most capable Axis transport available in numbers in World War II) and 83 high-speed airliner. But the most famous S.M. of all time was the 79, built in 1934 as a civil record-breaker

Right: Best-known and most numerous Savoia-Marchetti aircraft, the SM.79 Sparviero (Hawk) first appeared at the end of 1934 and the prototype set up two world closed-circuit records in 1935. Inevitably, although a civil version was produced in 1937, it was developed as a bomber and, according to many, became the best land-based torpedo bomber of the war. The record-breaking SM.79 (registration indicates pilot Bruno Mussolini) is pictured outside the Savoia works at Sesto Calende, near Milan, in 1935.

and developed into Italy's best wartime bomber and one of the finest torpedo aircraft of its era. Though of prestressed-skin design it was tough and courageously flown, and more than 1330 were produced by the parent company, Macchi and Piaggio. Lesser-known wartime prototypes included the extremely promising SM.91 and 92 twin-engine fighters and the SM.93 dive-bomber, all with Alfa-built DB 605A engines.

The most renowned Savoia-Marchetti aircraft before the company turned to landplanes was the SM.55 twin-hull flying-boat, the instrument chosen by the great showman and air minister General Balbo to stage several mass flights in the 1930s. He led 14 SM.55s across the South Atlantic to Brazil in 1930, leaving the 11 that completed the crossing there, and followed it up in 1933 with a return flight over the North Atlantic to visit a Chicago exhibition with SM.55s. The picture shows the 23 aircraft that completed the double crossing arriving home at Ostia after a round trip of 12,000 miles.

In 1943 work ground to a halt, and revived painfully slowly from 1945. Works existed at Sesto Calende, Vergiate and Borgomanero, but products were mainly trucks and rail rolling stock. Marchetti did manage to sell a few of his wartime SM.95 four-engined transports, but the postwar designs, such as the 101 six-seater and 102 light twin, were non-starters, partly because of their outdated structure.

In 1953, after three years of liquidation, the company again began operations as SIAI-Marchetti Società per Azioni. It participated in other people's aircraft, such as the Nardi FN.333, F-104 and Tornado, built over 500 S.205 lightplanes and large numbers of other small machines, and 100 of the last "S.M." type, the 1019 STOL turboprop for the Italian army aviation. Today Stelio Frati has emerged as Marchetti's successor, responsible for the F.250 of 1964 from which stemmed today's prolific

Current production of SIAI-Marchetti is well represented by this member of the prolific Frati-designed lightplanes, an SF.260 three-seater.

SF.260 family which have proved that piston-engined aircraft are exactly what many of the world's air forces want. Total employment exceeds 2500 at what has grown to become four plants in the original Milan-Varese region, and with eternal optimism SIAI-Marchetti is building a prototype of a small turbofan trainer, to fly in 1980.

Left: The Focke-Wulf company started to mature in 1931, when it took over the Albatros concern, famous for its World War I D.III fighter, and took Kurt Tank onto its staff. Illustrated is the first practical Albatros airplane which flew in 1910.

This major West German group, VFW, incorporated Focke-Wulf, "Weser" and Heinkel, whose stories precede the outline of the modern group.

Heinrich Focke was born on 8 October 1890, son of a Bremen senator. Elder-brother Wilhelm was a pioneer aircraft designer, whose 1909 airplane was built by Rumpler. Heinrich produced what looked like an excellent machine in late 1910, helped by an apprentice, Georg Wulf, but it lacked a sufficiently powerful engine. In 1911 what had become quite a team were given a 50hp Argus; this needed a new airframe and in late 1912 the A5 made a successful flight. Wulf taught himself to fly it, and in World War I both friends flew with the Imperial Army Aviation Service. In 1921, despite Allied restrictions, Focke and Wulf built the A7 Storch, and its award of a government airworthiness certificate in 1922 so impressed the owner of the Kaffee-Hag coffee company that he donated 200,000 marks (at that time a lot of money) enabling Focke-Wulf Flugzeugbau AG to be registered in Bremen on 1 January 1924.

The A16 light transport flew only six months later, and its production success just enabled the firm to totter along to the subsequent successes which included the A17 Möwe, A20 Habicht, and S24 Kiebitz. In 1927 an extraordinary canard, the F19 Ente, killed Wulf and accentuated the shaky financial situation common throughout German aviation. In 1931 F-W took over the famous Albatros Flugzeugwerke of Berlin, some of whose designs it continued to build, but what really made a difference was taking on Kurt Tank in November 1931. Tank, then 33, had formed Akaflieg Berlin at the Technical High School in Berlin in 1924, played a major role in the Rohrbach company whose stress-

ed-skin wings would look modern today, and spent 18 months with BFW Messerschmitt. Like Focke, Tank was to become a professor. He was also a brilliant pilot, and he played the central role in F-W because, after having license-built Cierva autogyros, Focke left in 1937 to form Focke-Achgelis dedicated to helicopter development.

Tank's first winner was a simple biplane trainer, the A44 (Fw 44 in the new RLM scheme) Stieglitz, of which about 2500 were made, plus over 900 by foreign licensees. The Fw 56 Stösser was chosen as the new Luftwaffe's light fighter and advanced trainer; production is usually given as about 1000, though company records indicate this is about double the actual figure. The Fw 58 Weihe light twin was a most useful trainer, transport, ambulance, crop-sprayer and even night fighter; F-W made

1299 and French companies about as many more. Tank used an Fw 58 called *Alex* (D-ALEX) as his personal hack, making many long missions and once returning with 57 bullet-holes from Spitfires.

In June 1936 the company was reorganized as a GmbH (limited-liability company) with enormously increased capital from the vast AEG electrical combine which held control. While Bf 109s and 110s were made for the Luftwaffe, Tank, by then technical director, produced the Fw 200 Condor, the prototype of which flew nonstop to New York and then back. In 1938 came the Fw 189 multi-role front-line machine, of which 853 were built, and in 1939 the Fw 190, a true technical masterpiece. Though this small, strong, nimble and amazingly versatile fighter flew publicly at Bremen during the last three months of peace it was so little known in Britain that, when it burst on a crestfallen RAF in 1941, pilots were told the radial-engined machines must be Curtiss Hawks captured from France! F-W have records of 20,001 completed, but about 19,600 seems more likely, plus fewer than 200 of the final versions which, in Tank's honor, were designated Ta 152. By 1944 there were also numerous jet projects.

After the war Tank went to Argentina, where ironically he was killed in an Avro Lincoln. The vast F-W organization, which in 1944 had embraced 29 major locations

First of the successful Tank designs was the Fw 44 Stieglitz trainer/sportplane. About 3400 were produced including foreign license production.

in eight Nazi-held countries and thousands of small shops hidden in forests or under rubble in the shattered cities, ceased to exist. But in 1951 the same company once more arose at 1–5 Hunefeldstrasse, Bremen, and after making some Kranich gliders went into production with the BL-502, Piaggio P.149D and, as part of ARGE-Nord group, the F-104G. In December 1963 the company merged with "Weser" Flugzeugbau, the Berlin-Tempelhof aviation subsidiary of AG Weser which had once been responsible for the entire Ju 87 "Stuka" production, as well as its own We 271 amphibian. The group was called Vereinigte Flugtechnische Werke GmbH, with major shareholdings by Krupp and the American United Aircraft (now United Technologies). In 1964 VFW took over Heinkel.

Until the late 1930s Ernst Heinkel, short, bespectacled and agitated, had been the leading figure in German planemaking. Born in 1887, he began work at the LVG company in September 1911 under the

famed Swiss, Franz Schneider. Soon he moved to Albatros, and in about January 1914 to the Brandenburgische firm set up by the Taube designer, Etrich. This soon became Hansa und Brandenburgische Flugzeugwerke under Camillo Castiglioni, who appointed Heinkel chief designer. Under his direction the company produced an impressive series of combat aircraft culminating in the W 29 and W 33 monoplane seaplanes which were licensed to Denmark, Norway and Finland.

After the Armistice Heinkel worked outside aviation for two years until in 1921 he joined Karl Caspar's new company at Travemunde. Among other things he produced an improved W 29. At Bücker's suggestion this was demonstrated to the Swedish Navy, and the Swedish S 1 version was soon in production at Bücker's new SAAB works. In May 1922 Heinkel left Caspar and, despite the latter's court action to retain rights to the S 1, set up Ernst Heinkel Flugzeugwerke in a leased hangar at Warnemünde on 1 December 1922. There followed

Top: Another outstanding Tank design was the Fw 200 Condor four-engined long-range airliner for up to 26 passengers. It first flew in July 1937 and performed a number of distance flights in 1938, including Berlin–New York and back, nonstop in both directions. The Condor was bought by several airlines including Lufthansa. Illustrated is one of a pair operated by Syndicato Condor of Brazil. Later came the Fu 200C ocean raider version.

Above: A flight of Heinkel He 8s, derived from the Hansa Brandenburg seaplane fighters of World War I. Those pictured were built by the Royal Danish Navy at Copenhagen (with Armstrong Siddeley Jaguar engines) and some were still flying in April 1940.

a prolific succession of prototypes and short production runs for foreign clients, notably in the Soviet Union and Japan.

Most of these were rather mundane, but on 1 December 1932 the prototype He 70 caused a sensation. Designed by the talented Günter brothers, Siegfried and Walter, it was undoubtedly the most perfectly streamlined transport in the world, and it not only led to various military versions but had a profound effect on other design teams.

For the moment, however, the infant Luftwaffe stuck to fabric biplanes, such as the He 45 reconnaissance bomber, He 51 fighter and He 59 and 60 reconnaissance floatplanes; the He 46, though a parasol monoplane, was cast in the same mold. But on 24 February 1935 the first He 111 changed all that. This modern stressed-skin monoplane was at first as much a Lufthansa transport as a Luftwaffe bomber, but by 1939 it was the chief offensive weapon of a mighty Luftwaffe that laid waste country after country. What Heinkel never expected was that, through failure to provide a successor, the lumbering old He 111 was to stay in production until late 1944, the total output exceeding 7300.

In April 1936, after much argument among his staff, Heinkel took on a young physics graduate, Pabst von Ohain, together with Max Hahn, an outstanding engineer. Together they built the first German turbojet and then assisted a Heinkel team under

Top left: This crowded He 111 wartime production area contributed to the total production of over 7300 of the Luftwaffe's most numerous 1939 bomber. Also visible are He 115 seaplanes for the German Navy. The prototype 115 set up eight world speed records for seaplanes in March 1938 and some were brought prewar by Scandinavian Navies.

Center left: The He 162 Salamander (or Volksjäger), the Luftwaffe's last fighter designed in a frantic last-ditch effort in the winter of 1944–45 and hurriedly put into production at a planned rate of 70 a day without factories.

Below left: Henschel's early contribution to the new Luftwaffe from its big new plant at Schönefeld included some license production of Junkers and Dornier designs and its own Hs 126 reconnaissance/ spotter parasol monoplane, a flight of which is pictured here. After replacement in front-line service it continued to be used for training and glider towing. About 600 were built.

Below: The most important of the many Henschel designs was the Hs 129 anti-tank/close-support aircraft which first flew in 1939. As the 129B-2/RH it greatly augmented the Ju 87 as a tank destroyer. In this latter role the lean clean lines evident in this picture were somewhat blurred by a huge ventral pod housing a gun of up to 75mm calibre.

Dr Christian Hertel to build the He 178, the world's first turbojet aircraft, flown in August 1939 shortly after the start of flight testing the rocket-propelled He 176. Heinkel's company had become Heinkel AG, a private company, in 1935, but despite this it grew rapidly, occupying a vast new plant at Rostock-Marienehe in late 1935 and another new factory, the state-constructed Oranienburg works for the He 111 line, in 1937. In March 1939 the He 100 V8, a prototype of an unsuccessful fighter used by the Goebbels propaganda machine as the nonexistent "He 113," took the world speed record at 464mph (747kmph.)

During World War II the Heinkel empire expanded to 27 main and countless subsidiary works, despite Heinkel's own unpopularity with the Nazi leaders. The He 177 heavy bomber was one of the most troubled military aircraft in history. The He 219 night fighter was outstanding, but held back by Erhardt Milch and problems. The final product, the He 162 – known variously as the Spätz (sparrow), Salamander and Volksjäger (people's fighter) – was brilliant but arrived too late. Designed in six weeks, and to be built underground at the rate of 2000 a month, it was a handful for most fighter pilots and would have been lethal to untrained Hitler Youth.

Ernst Heinkel AG resurfaced in 1953 and, after some success with the brieflypopular bubble cars, got into production with the Magister jet trainer, followed by the F-104G as part of ARGE-Süd. None of its many homegrown projects bore fruit and in 1964 it joined VFW, the Heinkel family itself having a shareholding of 12.09 percent.

VFW bought 65 percent of RFB (Rhein-Flugzeugbau) in 1968 and a year later a 50 percent holding in Henschel Flugzeugwerke AG of Kassel. The latter had been set up in March 1933 after abortive negotiations to rescue the tottering Junkers empire. Initially located at the old Berlin-Johannisthal field, it soon occupied a large new plant at Schönefeld where the Ju 86D, Do 17 and the company's own Hs 123 and 126 were produced for the Luftwaffe. Between 1938 and 1944 the Hs 130 program possibly set a record as the biggest in history never to have turned out a production machine; the factories were also continually thrown into chaos by changes of plan – first the Ju 88, then the 188, then the Me 410, then the Ju 388; it is a wonder that they did manage to deliver 2558 Ju 88s and 859 of their own Hs 129 close-support and anti-tank aircraft.

VFW's Einswarden works was the main production center for the Transall C.160 military freighter, though assembly took place at HFB (MBB) and Nord-Aviation (Aérospatiale). The group participated in the Dornier Do 31E program and, after merging on a 50/50 basis with Fokker on 1 January 1969, in the F28 Fellowship also. The VFW 614 short-haul jetliner, first flown on 14 July 1971, was Germany's only homegrown civil airliner since before World War II; a long development and inflation reduced its economic appeal and though at least 35 might have been sold, the program was terminated at the end of 1977. VFW and Fokker separated once more in 1979, the German company continuing to share in the F28 program (but no longer in the F-16) as well as in the Airbus, Tornado and as prime contractor for Spacelab by ERNO.

Top: A promising VFW design, and the only solely German postwar passenger aircraft design, was the VFW 614 short-range twin-jet airliner for up to 44 passengers, developed in the early 1970s. The unusual overwing position of the engines was intended to cut noise under the flightpath and obviate ingestion of rubble thrown up from rough runways. In addition, for use on such runways the landing gear was stressed.

Above: A novel and pioneering aircraft jointly designed by VFW (Rhein-Flugzeugbau) and Grumman American is the lightweight two-seat Fanliner powered by a Wankel rotary-piston engine driving a Dowty Rotol ducted fan; the second prototype is illustrated. A production version, the Fantrainer powered by an Allison turboshaft engine, has been ordered and is intended to replace the Piaggio P.149D as the Luftwaffe's primary trainer.

Though Australia is a great place for using aircraft, it had no manufacturing capability until well into the 1930s. The seed was sown in May 1934 by the formation of a syndicate. Talks with the government made it clear the latter regarded the primary objective as a national capability in military aircraft, reducing external dependence in time of crisis or war. Meanwhile Wing Commander L J Wackett formed Tugan Aircraft at Sydney Mascot and flew the rather odd Gannet light twin. In October 1935 the government asked the syndicate to form a company, and this was registered as Commonwealth Aircraft Corporation Pty Limited on 17 October 1936. The foundation backers were Broken Hill Pty, Broken Hill Associated Smelters, ICI of Australia and NZ, Electrolytic Zinc of Australia, Orient Steam Navigation (later P&O Orient) and General Motors Holden's Limited. Tugan immediately became a subsidiary.

A license with North American Aviation

Left: The CAC Wackett trainer for the RAAF, the first of their own-design products, was developed as a bridge between the Tiger Moth and the more-advanced Wirraway. The Wackett prototype first flew with a Gipsy engine in 1939 but was produced with a Super Scarab radial.

Below left: The busy assembly lines at Fishermen's Bend, Melbourne, at the height of production – the first CA-1 Wirraway, the license-built North American NA-16, also first flew in 1939 (about six months before the Wackett) and CAC produced over 750 Wirraways over a period of seven years.

for the NA-16 was negotiated and 40 CAC-built versions were ordered in January 1937, while architects drew up plans for a completely new factory at Fishermen's Bend, Melbourne, where ground was broken in February. By September major buildings were occupied and Wackett began to design the Wackett Trainer, an *ab initi* machine which flew with a Gipsy engine in October 1939 but was mass-produced with the Warner Super Scarab imported from the US!

For the NA-16 machine, called the CA-1 Wirraway, the company did try for self-sufficiency and bought a license for the R-1340 Wasp, and later added the R-1830 Twin Wasp, making 680 of the former and 870 of the latter. The first Wirraway flew in March 1939 and the 755th and last in 1946. Engines from the new Lidcombe plant flowed from 1941 and in September of that year the first CA-4 Wackett Bomber (later it became the CA-11 Woomera) flew with two Twin Wasps. The company never produced a production aircraft, but Pearl Harbor threw CAC into turmoil. Fighters were needed, fast. The only engine was the Twin Wasp. In 14 weeks Wackett's team designed the CA-12 Boomerang, first flown on 29 May 1942, and CAC built 249 of these tough birds which played a bigger part in the campaign around New Guinea than their numbers or modest performance might suggest.

Extensions to the NAA license resulted

in CAC building the P-51D Mustang (266 of various sub-types) and, after prolonged study of Hawker fighters and the company's own outstanding supersonic two-seat CA-23, the F-86 Sabre (111 in three sub-types). Redesign of the F-86E to take the Avon (license-produced at Lidcombe) and 30mm Aden gun caused so many problems that when CAC tooled up to make 100 Mirage IIIs in 1963 it ignored the Avon-powered version even though this had been designed, built and flown and was dramatically superior! Instead, CAC license-produced the Atar 9C. Smaller programs included the CA-25 Winjeel trainer (62 delivered by 1957) and agricultural CA-28 Ceres (21). Between 1967 and 1972 CAC assembled, and finally manufactured, the Aermacchi MB.326H and its Viper engine, later turning to assembly of Bell 206B-1 and civil Jet Rangers.

For many years CAC has needed a new aircraft program. The urgent wish to be self-reliant has – it seems – evaporated and even when a much-needed new fighter is selected Australia will be dependent on the United States, though CAC will receive some offset work. To survive, CAC has diversified into mechanical handling for the Ikara and Branik missile systems and the Barra sonobuoy, acting as an agency for Cessna and Hughes, and manufacturing small parts of DC-10s and TriStars, aircraft galleys, buses and, it hopes, high-speed ground transport systems.

AGAF

Australian Government Aircraft Factories is well into the development of civil and military versions of its N2 Nomad twin turboprop light utility, the prototype of which first flew in July 1971. Four versions, two civil and two military, have been announced. An N24A long-fuselage civil Nomad, which can be fitted to carry up to 19 passengers, is illustrated.

CANADAIR

With a few exceptions, such as Airbus Industrie and Boeing, most of the world's planemakers are finding it difficult to keep their people busy and fill the floorspace. Another of the exceptions is Canadair, (located in the province of Quebec) which contrary to the economic climate in Quebec has been hiring workers and in October 1979 began building a major new aircraft-assembly plant at Dorval.

This story started at Montreal St Hubert, where in 1911 Vickers Limited founded a Canadian subsidiary. In 1922 this engineering and shipbuilding works began assembling eight Viking six-seat amphibians for the RCAF, the final six being of increasingly local-built parts. Canadian Vickers was then joined by W T Reid, who had been chief designer at Bristol while Barnwell was in Australia; when Barnwell got bored (the biggest job he had to do was redesign the Avro 504 tailskid) and returned to Bristol, Reid had to move on and he chose to

give Canada its first design capability.

Reid's first offering was the best – 61 of various types of Canadian Vickers Vedette were delivered by 1930. It was almost a smaller Viking, and it led to various other indigenous designs which were mostly made in prototype form only, though there were small production runs of the civil and military Vancouver twin-engined flying-boat. What is especially interesting is that from the first order for Vikings a major duty of Canadian Vickers aircraft became forestry patrol and fire suppression (which in those days meant little more than fire spotting and the alerting of teams on the ground).

Canadian Vickers also made many aircraft under license, including Avro trainers, Fairchild FC-2 "bush" transports, 15 Fokker Super Universals, various Northrop Delta land- and seaplanes, and between 1938 and 1941 no fewer than 40 of the large and extremely useful Supermarine Stranraer

ocean patrol boats. In 1940–41 Canadian Vickers participated in Canadian Associated Aircraft which made 160 Hampden bombers, Vickers being responsible for fuselages. There followed a major war program which among other items included 600 PBY Catalina hulls and the assemblies and flight tests of 230 PBV-1A (OA-10A) amphibians and 149 similar Cansos for the RCAF, all at a very large new government plant at Cartierville on the west side of Montreal opened in 1942 and twice expanded.

In 1944 the Canadian government decided to increase the national – as distinct from foreign-owned – strength in planemaking, and after discussions with the parent Vickers Group bought Canadian Vickers and at the same time, in September 1944, decided to award the Cartierville plant a large contract for a Merlin-engined version of the DC-4 transport to meet the needs of the RCAF and Trans-Canada Air Lines. The new

Left: The Canadair Cartierville works in September 1968 comprised three plants – No 1 center foreground, No 2 center across field and No 4 right foreground in this picture; work began in October 1979 on building a big new aircraft-assembly works in Quebec Province.

Inset: Canadair's twin turbofan Challenger is a direct descendant of the Learjet LearStar and is being built in business, priority freight, airline and high-density commuter versions.

Right: One major Canadair antecedent was Canadian Vickers, which performed prodigious output feats during World War II; in this 1942 scene are two of the many women employed in the plant at the time, working on a Canso (Catalina) amphibian.

Crown company was registered in December 1944 as Canadair Limited; Benjamin W Franklin was appointed general manager. But then, in a startling reversal of the policy just agreed, Canadair was sold to the United States. John Jay Hopkins of the Electric Boat Company could see a vision of a giant industrial conglomerate, and the Canadian company was the first big acquisition. Soon Hopkins added mighty Convair and many other companies to form General Dynamics Corporation. This was good business strategy, but flew in the face of Canada's – and especially Montreal's – wish not to be completely owned from south of the 49th parallel.

H Oliver West was put in as president, and the American management assumed control from January 1947. The DC-4M program generated 70 aircraft, 45 of them pressurized, plus a C-5 with Double Wasp engines. But this was followed by two of the most cost effective manufacturing programs in aerospace history. In 1949 Canadair obtained a license for the F-86 Sabre and delivered 1815 of which 1341 were exported. The final 1025 had the Canadian Orenda engine, and by common consensus the last model, the Sabre 6, was the best dogfighter of its era. Next came a license for the Lockheed T-33 jet trainer; and despite the redesign, needed to fit it with the Nene (made a

few minutes away down Côte de Liesse Road by Rolls-Royce of Canada) everything went to schedule and 656 of the Canadair version, named Silver Star, were delivered by 1959.

In parallel an immense design effort took place in turning the British Britannia turboprop airliner into the CL-28 Argus ocean-patrol and ASW aircraft, the first of 33 flying in September 1957. Parent General Dynamics planned a mighty program based on the Britannia and thin-wing Bristol 187, involving Bristol, Convair and Canadair, but the British government managed to wreck this by cancelling the Orion engine. All Canadair could do was build a small batch of stretched Tyne-powered versions called CL-44.

The British also managed to foul up another program, the Canadair 540, an improved Convair 440 with Napier Eland turboprops. Rolls-Royce bought Napier, showed disinterest in the Eland, and the production 540s, called CC-109 Cosmo-

politans by the Canadian Armed Forces, had to be re-engined with American Allison T56s. But little went wrong with the Canadair-designed CL-41 Tutor jet trainer, with J85 engine made by Orenda at Toronto, of which 190 went to the CAF and 20 to Malaysia, nor to the massive participation in the F-104G program in which Canadair made 200 CF-104s for home use, 140 for NATO allies and many hundreds of major airframe portions for assembly elsewhere. With this experience it was not difficult to share license-production of 240 CF-5 and NF-5 fighters with Fokker, Canadair doing most of the work and all the assembly and flight testing.

There was little profit in the CL-84 VTOL research aircraft, but plenty in the CL-215, the only aircraft of the past 25 years to go into production with large piston engines. A multi-role amphibian intended chiefly as a firefighting water-bomber, it might have seemed outmoded but has never ceased to sell in increasing quantities, and the need to find more space for additional CL-215 tooling is one of the reasons for the new $25-million factory at the old Montreal airport at Dorval. Another is the heavy workload on parts for the Boeing 767 aft fuselage, the 747SP aft fuselage, and major parts for the F-15 and CP-140 Aurora. The main plant, now called Ville St Laurent, is full of the CL-600 Challenger program, the extremely successful business jet planned by Bill Lear and now also developed into the enlarged CF34-powered Challenger E (extended) with more room and longer range. Other programs include the CL-89, 227 and 289 surveillance RPV systems and a rapid-transit rail system located at Kingston, Ontario.

In 1944 Cartierville works took a big order for the Merlin-engined DC-4, which became the Canadair C-4 and was bought by both of the Canadian airlines and by BOAC, who operated 22 of them from March 1949 as the Argonaut class.

DH CANADA

In 1927 the board of de Havilland Aircraft took a positive decision to open associated companies overseas. Several orders for Moths had been received from Canada, and it appeared that business might be increased if a local assembly plant and overhaul facility were opened. What nobody thought for a moment was that little more than 30 years later the Canadian offshoot, together with a few other smaller overseas subsidiaries, would be the only remaining properties to bear the proud name – and they would no longer be owned by the original company.

An almost derelict warehouse was found at Mount Dennis, Toronto, which had the advantages of cheapness and proximity to a railroad spur. De Havilland Aircraft of Canada was formed as a limited company in January 1928. Eventually, by World War II, the authorized capital rose to $500,000, nearly all of which was purchased by Canadian investors. Moreover, top management was from the start Canadian. Business did indeed pick up, to such effect that

the old building was almost at once outgrown. In September 1929 a fine new factory was opened on a 70-acre plot at Downsview a few miles away, and there new Moths of many kinds droned away in all directions – 130 in 1929 alone. W D Hunter joined as director of engineering to make conversions for "bush" requirements such as cabin heaters and ski or float landing gear. The DH.61 flew in 1930 converted at Downsview to Pratt & Whitney power, and the local version of DH.83 Fox Moth had a pilot cockpit with a canopy and warm interior. Moths proliferated, and as World War II approached the Tiger Moth was ordered in unprecedented numbers. Downsview made 1520 from scratch, as well as 375 of locally developed versions of the Anson.

By far the largest wartime effort was the manufacture of 1032 Mosquitos, with Packard-built engines, which by 1945 were coming off a chain-driven mechanized assembly line in a monster plant rivalling those in the United States. How could such business continue? The local control com-

mittee, under chairman R A Laidlaw, studied the prospects for making the parent company's Dove, Vampire and other designs and instead voted to create aircraft for the Canadian market. This was an historic decision, and made up for an apparent lack of foresight by the parent. To provide a successor for the beloved Tiger seemed one objective; a utility bush transport better than the rivals seemed another. Hunter moved up to be a director, P C Garratt took over as managing director and the brilliant Pole W J Jakimiuk was appointed chief designer.

The homegrown designs got off on the right foot by being all-metal stressed-skin. The Tiger Moth successor was the DHC-1 Chipmunk, flown in May 1946. Downsview built 218, and would have built more had not the parent company decided to build it as well to the tune of 1014. The first

De Havilland's first essay into Canada, a hangar at the warehouse at Mount Dennis, Toronto, was set up in January 1928 to assemble and service DH.60 Moths.

bush transport was the DHC-2 Beaver. C H "Punch" Dickens, former bush pilot, was appointed sales director, and made sure the company got it absolutely right. The Beaver stayed in production from 1948 until 1967, the total being 1657 for 65 nations. Another 60 were built with turboprop engines. In December 1951 the DHC-3 Otter scaled up the Beaver formula to 600hp, and 460 were built for 36 countries. The DHC-4 Caribou of 1958 extrapolated the same formula to two much bigger engines and even more STOL performance, and

313 of these quite substantial machines were built. Throughout the 1950s boss Garratt flew himself to Downsview every morning in his Beaver amphibian, often not flying home until 10 at night. Another of the jobs he pushed through on time was license-production of 100 of the complex Grumman CS2F Trackers for the RCN, Brazil and Holland.

The three most recent DHC products are all still very much in production. At the time of writing the DHC-5 Buffalo twin-turboprop STOL transport has sold nearly

100, despite its highly specialized nature, and a civil version is being marketed as the Transporter. The smaller twin-turboprop Twin Otter, the DHC-6, first flew in May 1965, and has so far sold 698 in 77 countries. The latest, and by far the largest and most costly, of the company's products is the DHC-7 Dash-7, with its military 7R Ranger derivative, which flew in March 1975 and is notching up sales in ones and twos to customers who really need quiet-STOL performance, with 69 by late 1979. Thus DHC has never had a failure, a record few plane-makers can even approach. In 1962 it took over nearby Avro Aircraft and made DC-9 sections until the Malton plant was leased direct to Douglas Aircraft of Canada in December 1965. On 1 June 1974 de Havilland Aircraft of Canada was bought from Hawker Siddeley by the government of Canada. It would be sad if they changed the name.

Left: The current production scene at de Havilland Canada's plant features the DHC-5 Buffalo twin-turboprop assault transport, now also offered as a non-military Transporter version. The Canadian Armed Services' Buffalo, designated CC-115, has overall length increased by a nose radome and can carry up to about 40 equipped troops or 24 stretchers and their attendants.

Below: The DHC-7 Dash-7 continues the company's tradition of designing and building effective STOL aircraft. The Dash-7 adds two further attributes to the de Havilland Canada catalog – it is the biggest yet, providing for up to 50 passengers, and has been designed with four turboprop engines to provide quiet STOL performance to encourage operation from small airfields in built-up areas.

EMBRAER

Everyone knows Brazil is big, colorful and full of coffee. Its population, already 80 million, will double in a few years when the 40 million young people marry. Is it doomed to decline, as countless hungry mouths clamor at workless parents? Not if the local planemaker is any guide. EMBRAER – Empresa Brasilia de Aeronáutica SA – has only been in existence ten years but calculates it has now catapulted Brazil into sixth place among planemaking countries measured on sales turnover, now running at $200 million a year. There was never a success story like it.

Of course EMBRAER did not arise from a vacuum. The first man to fly in Europe, in 1906, was a Brazilian. The *Sao Paulo* monoplane flew at Osasco on 7 January 1910. Many other locally designed aircraft flew before the Muniz M-7 became the first series-produced type in October 1935. By 1938 Henrique Lage had delivered 130 HL-1, -4 and -6 trainers, and the Companhia Aeronáutica Paulista built nearly 500 aircraft from August 1942. In 1953 the Ministry of Aeronautics organized production of Fokker trainers, and in 1961 the stressed-skin Neiva Regente went into production, 120 being delivered, followed by 142 of the T-25 Universal. In 1962 Aerotec was formed, and since 1965 this company has delivered 155. But the government – perhaps showing more positive interest in aerospace planning than in some longer-established industrial societies – decided the nation could do better. It boldly decided to invent an aircraft industry, passing the appropriate law – Decree No 770 – on 19 August 1969.

Its terms of reference were simple: build everything that makes sense, or that Brazil can do as well as anyone else. The authorized capital was $Cr 200 million, about £40 million or US$90 million. At first it was all government-owned, but gradually 177,000 private and company shareholders have taken up 89.22 percent – though the government retains 54.42 percent of the voting shares. The company selected Sao José dos Campos, between Sao Paulo and Rio, as its location, where a swelling population which even then exceeded 300,000 already worked for General Motors, Ericsson, Kodak, Volkswagen and Petrobras – some

Above: The final assembly area of the EMBRAER works at Sao José dos Campos in 1979 shows mainly the company's staple product, the EMB-110 Bandeirante 12/19-seat feederliner. Second from camera is an EMB-111 maritime patrol version and three of the EMB-121 Xingu pressurized versions can be seen on the left.

Below: The very efficient-looking EMB-111 Patrulha, the maritime patrol version of the Bandeirante for the Brazilian Air Force. A photo-survey aircraft is another of the 13 variants so far built or projected.

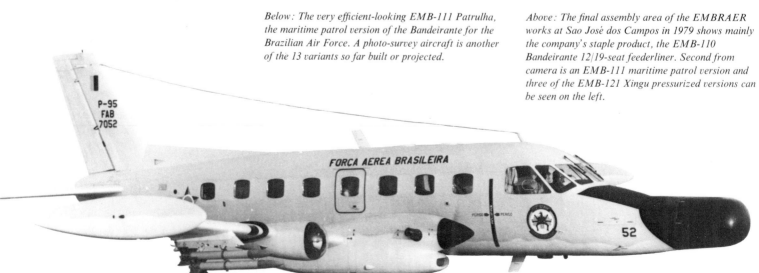

*The earliest of the indigenous Brazilian designs now
produced by EMBRAER, the EMB-200 Ipanema is a
single-seat agricultural aircraft. The prototype first
flew in July 1970 before EMBRAER started
planemaking, the airframe having been built by
Aerotec. Since that time several versions have been
developed, one of which, the EMB-201A, is illustrated.*

of the companies that scrambled to buy EMBRAER stock. The factory and offices were on virgin sites, but swiftly grew to 1.3 million square feet. The workforce, mostly young and 16 percent university graduates, grew at a steady 500 a year and today tops 4500 and is still growing – though carefully controlled. And the work has prospered.

Operations began in January 1970, and planemaking began a year later. The only product at first was a small twin-turboprop, the IPD/PAR-6504 Bandeirante, designed at the Centro Técnico de Aeronáutica by a new team led by the expatriate Frenchman Max Holste. The prototype flew on 26 October 1968. It was intended to replace the Twin Beech (C-45) in the FAB (Air Force), and the expectation that as many as 80 might be needed was a powerful factor in starting EMBRAER just down the road from CTA. But this was not the only iron in the fire. In 1969 design had begun on a modern agricultural aircraft, the EMB-201A Ipanema (name both of a famous Rio beach and of the Ministry farm where the prototype was tested in 1970). In May 1970 a license was signed with Aermacchi for the MB.326, subsequently produced as the multi-role AT-26 Xavante. In August 1974 EMBRAER signed a major agreement with Piper as a result of which the Brazilian company makes various Cherokee variants, includ-

ing the Cherokee Pathfinder (EMB-710C Carioca) made only by EMBRAER, as well as the Navaho Chieftain; the Seneca II is marketed and may soon be manufactured.

But the staple product has been the Bandeirante, which in August 1972 flew in an enlarged and generally redesigned form designated EMB-110. In all respects this is an aircraft to compete in the world market. Although early production was for Brazilian customers it has today been sold in large numbers in many countries including France, Britain and the United States as well as a host of less-developed nations. It has emerged in 13 major versions, not including the speedy pressurized T-tailed EMB-121 Xingu.

Yet another string to EMBRAER's bow is the EMB-312 advanced trainer, to fly by the time this book appears and powered by a single turboprop of the type used in the Bandeirante. Not yet announced is the EMB-120 Araguaia with four of the same engines and up to 30 seats instead of the 18 or 19 of the popular Bandeirante. On top of all this EMBRAER has, since 1976, been co-producing parts of F-5E Tiger IIs in an arrangement with Northrop. EMBRAER's 1000th aircraft was sold in December 1976 and its 2000th in December 1979. It helps, of course, to have a new plant, good management and a dedicated workforce. Whichever country brings EMBRAER into its next Mach 2 fighter project will not regret it.

FMA

*Argentina's aircraft industry produces mostly light
planes and small helicopters but FMA (Fàbrica
Militar de Aviones) is now embarked on production of
the IA 58 Pucará twin-turboprop counter-insurgency*

*aircraft for the Argentine Air Force. A Pucará takes
off at the 1978 Farnborough exhibition with weapons-
mounting points under fuselage and wings in view.*

Although neither the names Fuji nor Nakajima have ever been household words, except in Japan, the former is fast becoming one of the big names in general aviation while Nakajima was the No 1 builder of aircraft and almost No 1 in engines in Japan during World War II. The concern was also Japan's first planemaker, and built up such a reputation with warlike aircraft powered by single radial engines that by 1945 it was certainly in the top ten in the world, and ahead of any other company outside the superpowers. At the same time a substantial proportion of Nakajima's output was of other companies' aircraft; had Mitsubishi made all its Zeros, for example, the position of the two firms at the head of the league table would have been reversed.

During World War I Japan made increasing efforts to find out about military aviation. Observers were sent to Europe, having official status as Allies since Japan had declared war on the Central Powers on 23 August 1914. Among these observers was Lieutenant Chikuhei Nakajima or Seibei Kawanishi (or possibly both). Certainly by 1917 Nakajima, who though only 31 had qualified as an engineer (besides being a naval officer), had resigned his commission and gone into partnership with Kawanishi to form the first planemaking company in the Far East. Not unnaturally it was called Nihon Hikoki Seisakusho KK (Japan Airplane Manufacturing Company Limited), and it was registered on 6 December 1917. There is reason to believe that at about this time one of the partners also visited the United States, though their major problem was lack of finance. Curiously, no foreign manufacturing license appears to have been obtained.

The design office and factory was at Ota, in Gumma Prefecture. Nakajima himself appears to have done most of the initial design work, basing the first aircraft on the Curtiss JN-4 series and using OXX-5 or Hall-Scott engines. At least one design, the Nakajima 5, went into production after the Armistice as a general-purpose trainer and is said to have been the first home-produced aircraft used by the Imperial Army. But in the course of 1919 the partners quarrelled; possibly it was over the need to obtain foreign licenses. In December 1919 the company was dissolved and Kawanishi went off to form his own organization. By this time there were several other planemakers in Japan, but Nakajima was able to persuade the mighty Mitsui industrial empire to back him. In early 1920 he founded Nakajima Hikoki KK, and it soon became Number 1 in the country. Indigenous designs continued to appear, but by far the greater part of the output consisted of licensed designs such as the Nieuport 28 and 29, Hansa Brandenburg W 33 and Gloster Gambet. Engine production began with the Hispano HS 8 and really got into its stride with the Bristol Jupiter, named Kotobuki, around which a large new factory grew at Musashi. Growth of Nakajima was unrivalled by any competitor, and long before World War II the company had at least five plants and even had its own special-alloys production facilities. It was also increasingly

A line-up of Japan's best Army fighter of World War II, Nakajima Ki-84 Hayates ("Gale"), on Ustunomiya airfield with propellers removed in October 1945 after the Japanese capitulation.

Above: Another important World War II aircraft was the Nakajima B5N, which started life as a light bomber during the Japanese invasion of China and was later developed into the B5N1 "Kate" torpedo bomber, 40 of which took part in the Pearl Harbor attack. This B5N2, used mainly on antisubmarine duties in the later stages of the war, has been retouched with Japanese markings for recognition instruction.

Below: Successor to the Nakajima concern is Fuji, which got back into planemaking in 1953, started with licensed designs. The first Fuji design was the FA-200 Aero Subaru, a four-seater that first flew in August 1965 and is built in two basic versions.

involved in the production of licensed and indigenous designs of aircraft guns and probably other ordnance.

Unlike some rival companies in both Japan and the United States Nakajima was not an "Army" or "Navy" firm but mass-produced for both. Important Army designs included the Type 91 monoplane fighter, the Ki-27, the most important Army fighter between 1938 and 1942, and the chief Army fighters of World War II, the Ki-43, -44 and -84. Navy types included the A4N fighter, E8N seaplane, J1N1 twin-engine fighter, B5N and B6N torpedo carriers and C6N reconnaissance machine. The company also built the Ki-49, the Army's most formidable bomber of World War II, nearly two-thirds of Mitsubishi's Zero fighters and also designed and built the latter's floatplane versions. Between 1941 and 1945 Nakajima produced 28 percent of all Japanese aircraft, a total of 19,561, and over 37 percent of the nation's combat machines; engine deliveries totalled 36,440, or 31.3 percent. So important was this company that on 1 April 1945 it was put under national management with the title 1st Munitions Arsenal. Total aircraft deliveries from 1920 to 1945 were 29,760.

After the war a successor called Fuji Jukogyo KK (Fuji Heavy Industries Limited) was registered as a private company on 15 July 1953. It was inevitably a case of reverting to licensing, beginning with the Beech T-34 Mentor and Cessna Bird Dog. From the Mentor Fuji's own engineers developed a series of variants, and also gained experience which has been put to use in the very successful FA-200 lightplane

family and extrapolated up to the FA-300 twin, projected at the completely modern works at Utsonomiya City in 1971 and later developed as a joint project with Rockwell, which called it the Commander 700. Other licensing includes the Bell 204 and 205 "Huey" family of helicopters and the wings for Japanese P-3C Orions. The next major project is a twin-turbofan military trainer/attack aircraft. Employment at Utsonomiya has risen to over 3300, but about half are engaged on rail vehicles.

HAL

As far as the author can tell, the British Raj made no attempt to establish planemaking in India. This was left to William D Pawley, president of Intercontinent Aircraft of New York, whose business was exporting American aircraft. Normally the last thing such people want is aircraft manufacturers proliferating all over the importing countries, but in 1940 Pawley concluded successful negotiations with the government of the Indian State of Mysore and an Indian entrepreneur, Walchand Hirachand. As a direct result, Hindustan Aircraft Limited (HAL) was set up on a virgin site at Bangalore. Hirachand's interest is obvious, but Pawley's was probably based on the fact that India had more people than dollars, and that he could make more from part-ownership of an Indian factory than out of trying to sell American aircraft to a country where there was no home market and the airlines and Air Force were a British closed shop. His timing confirmed his belief that, once India had an aircraft works, it would be unlikely to want for work.

There seems to have been remarkable drive behind getting the operation launched in a country renowned for the complexity of its difficulties. Buildings were erected, shiploads of machine tools and aircraft-grade material imported (in a few more months everything was tightly controlled for the war effort) and a nucleus of skilled personnel trained at factories in the USA and even Britain. It was decided to make stressed-skin structures from the outset. A license was obtained to build the Harlow PC-5, a neat stressed-skin cabin trainer first flown in California in 1939. The first (US-constructed) PC-5 was assembled and flown at Bangalore in August 1941, and subsequently HAL was busy with assembly of various American types and production of major airframe sections for such aircraft as the Mohawk, Vengeance and C-47. From April 1942 HAL operated as an Indian national concern, Hirachand being bought out by the government in New Delhi, which in turn assigned operational control to the US Army, because they had people able to do the job. Bangalore soon shot past its original target of 5000 employees and made a significant contribution to Allied air power doing major overhauls and conversions, while also making a ten-seat glider from local materials.

After the war HAL almost wound down to a full stop. The US Army and the British departed, and the Indian government – which had no intention of letting HAL either close down or return to private hands – got a British mission to make recommendations. It also appointed Dr V M Ghatage

The first Indian domestic aircraft design was the Hindustan HT-2 basic trainer that first flew in August 1951. It was a stressed-skin aircraft with a Gipsy Major 10 engine in the prototype, but went into production with the Cirrus Major III engine.

leader of a newly formed design team. While C-47s were rebuilt as civil airliners and Prentices were at first assembled and then constructed under license for the new IAF, Ghatage designed the HT-2 basic trainer, HT-10 turboprop advanced trainer and the HT-11 Prentice successor. Only the HT-2 materialized, the first of 100 of these Chipmunk-like stressed-skin machines flying in August 1951. Meanwhile HAL organized comprehensive apprentice and educational courses, replaced the skilled Chinese who had been at Bangalore since 1941 with native Indians, and boldly embarked on license-production of the Vampire and its Goblin turbojet. A completely new factory was established for gas-turbine engines and in 1957 license-production started on the Folland Gnat and its Orpheus turbojet.

HAL's most difficult task was creating an Indian jet fighter. A special team was formed not under Ghatage but led by Kurt Tank, formerly of Focke-Wulf, and after flying a wooden glider in 1959 to test low-speed stability the prototype HF-24 Marut flew on 17 June 1961. By this time Ghatage's team had designed the HUL-26 Pushpak light aircraft, the HAOP-27 Krishak observation aircraft and the HJT-16 Kiran jet trainer, all of which were built in quantity. Subsequent designs include the HA-31 Basant ag-aircraft and HPT-32 trainer, while improved Maruts and the integral-tank Ajeet version of the Gnat have taken their place on the production line. Licensed types include the BAe 748, Alouette and a variant of the Lama called the Cheetah. The 748 operation was originally begun by the

IAF at its depot at Kanpur, assigning the Dart engine to HAL. To manage the operation a company called Aeronautics (India) was created in June 1964, and four months later this was taken over by HAL as its Kanpur Division, the title of HAL being changed to Hindustan Aeronautics Limited.

Two years previously the Indian government had taken the major decision to adopt the MiG-21 as its chief combat aircraft and build it under license. By October 1962 there was a busy traffic of Indians to Soviet establishments and training schools and Russians to India, and a completely new manufacturing MiG-complex was set up rivaling in size the existing HAL operation at Bangalore. An airframe plant was built at Nasik, an assembly line (with increasing local content of parts) to build the Tumansky R-11 engine was built at Koraput, and an electronics factory was established at Hyderabad. Production from Soviet components began in 1966, and subsequently HAL has increased local content to almost 100 percent on the airframe while progressing through five major MiG-21 sub-types.

In 1969 a Lucknow Division was formed to make a wide range of accessories, mainly licensed from Britain, the Soviet Union and France. This was then linked with Hyderabad Division to form an Accessories Complex. For the future a major program is assembly and later license-production of the Jaguar, licensing and local development of missiles such as the MiG-21's Advanced Atoll, and collaboration with Dornier on the LTA and with Aérospatiale on an ALH (advanced light helicopter). Total HAL employment in 1979 was 40,000.

The Hindustan HF-24 Marut fighter, designed under the leadership of Dr Kurt Tank, one-time Focke-Wulf technical director, flew for the first time in June 1961, to become the first supersonic aircraft designed in Asia outside the USSR, with a maximum speed of Mach

1.02. Mark 1 HF-24s entered service with the Indian Air Air Force in May 1964 and about 150, including this Mark 1T tandem-seat trainer starting in 1970, have been built, but projected Mark 2 and 3, possibly Mach 2, versions have not materialized.

All planemakers began with struggle, even if only against gravity; but none has a history remotely approaching that of Israel Aircraft Industries. Today it is just another of the world's great centers of high technology, a lot of edifices in glass and concrete where skilled modern people – 22,000 in fact – operate one of the biggest aerospace and advanced engineering businesses between Rome and Tokyo. But only 30 years ago this "dream" was an expanse of sand, and its realization was brought about by a series of furtive meetings in New York and other cities, unbelievable devices and subterfuges to outwit the FBI and a dozen other agencies, and the creation of an Air Force, an airline and an aircraft industry against amazing adversities.

The moving spirit behind many of these accomplishments was Al Schwimmer, who had worked on BT-13s at Vultee Field and been a flight engineer for TWA. In 1947 he bought an Air Force almost off American scrap heaps and got it to Israel, which hardly yet existed, under the cover of a no-cost airline for Panama, a place Schwimmer has avoided since. By 1951 he had Israel's future aircraft industry in a corner of a hangar at Burbank, California, and a sign at Lod airport (Lydda) proclaiming "Government Aircraft Overhaul Depot, Bedek Corporation, New York." It is typical of the irony of the new state's growing pains that not one building existed anywhere that Bedek could occupy despite the fact that the Middle East, like much of the world, was littered with derelict hangars and control towers. Making it all happen was the nearest thing since 1914 to the pioneer days of aviation, when individuals of strong character took decisions on the spot, projects begun in the morning were completed by nightfall, and often the workforce was so busy it failed to notice that wages had not appeared.

By way of overhauling L-4s, Stearmans, B-17s that were really flying heaps of scrap, and Spitfires that were usually meant to be delivered somewhere else, Bedek graduated by 1957 to license-manufacture of the Potez Magister jet trainer; the first flew on 7 July 1960. Later the whole Magister was made locally, and Bet-Shemesh Engines produced its Marboré turbojets. By 1960 Bedek looked after the Heyl Ha'Avir's Meteors, Mystères, Super Mystères, Vautours, Ouragans and their engines, and had flexed its design muscles by completely rebuilding cast-off C-97s and Stratocruisers as multirole swing-tail freighters and air-refuelling tankers. Small cells of design engineers began studying military electronics, ship-to-ship missiles and many other problems.

On 1 April 1967 Bedek was renamed Israel Aircraft Industries (IAI). It already employed 4000, and was a force in world aviation. Bedek Aviation's name continued as a division of IAI concerned with overhauls, modifications and (to take an example) the creation of the most sumptuous 707 executive aircraft in the world. IAI's Manufacturing Division is concerned with production, the chief aircraft being the Kfir, Arava and IAI 1124 Westwind and Sea Scan. All these aircraft were developed by IAI Engineering Division, the Kfir being derived from the French Mirage III and the 1124 being derived from the Jet Commander which Rockwell divested when it took over North American Aviation (and Sabreliner) to avoid anti-trust legislation.

The Electronics Division incorporates the former subsidiary company Elta and such other companies as MBT, Tamam and MLM. It has impressive capability in almost the complete field of airborne and surface electronics, navigation and weapon-aiming systems, the Gabriel naval missile, electronic passive defense systems and ECM. Combined Technologies Division again brings together numerous former companies and subsidiaries engaged in a wealth of precision engineering operations extending even to armored vehicles and fast patrol boats.

With the coming of peace to the Middle East the whole IAI outlook has softened and become reoriented towards going out into

Al Schwimmer, founder and president of Israel Aircraft Industries, one-time flight engineer with TWA, bought an air force for Israel by subterfuge and took the lead in building an advanced aircraft industry from scratch in a few years.

the world marketplace and winning work from outside. It has been planning for this world role, which it hopes will be mainly civilian, for many years, and is now looking for market openings sufficient to justify not only the proposed Arieh (Lion) tactical combat aircraft but also improved agricultural helicopters. In a decade IAI grew from 4000 to 23,000; it cannot expect to carry on like this, but with luck will not shrink.

Left: The IAI Arava twin-turboprop STOL light transport started with the 101, which first flew in November 1969, and continued with the military IAI-201 version that made its first flight in March 1972. The 201 can take up to 23 equipped troops or 2½ tons of freight and is stressed for rough-field work; it is in service with the armed forces of about ten countries. An improved (1979) IAI-202 is shown.

Below: Most advanced of the Israeli products is the Mirage-derived Kfir (Lion Cub) fighter, here seen in Kfir-C2 form at the Paris Air Show in 1979. The developed C2 version uses the basic Mirage 5 airframe with major changes to accommodate an afterburning J79 turbojet giving a maximum speed of over Mach 2.3 and is distinguishable by the fixed foreplanes just behind the air intakes.

KAWASAKI

Today the Kawasaki industrial empire is so vast and multi-faceted that it requires a real mental effort to picture the World War I era when, unlike most of the other warring powers, Japan – which was on the side of the Allies – had virtually no industry at all. What little it did have was centered at very few locations, such as the dockyard at Kobe where, in 1878, the Kawasaki Jukogyo Kabushiki Kaisha (Kawasaki Heavy Industries Limited) was established as the nation's first large shipbuilder. In 1917 it sent two engineers to France to learn about aircraft, and the resulting organization of an aircraft (Kokuki) department in February 1918 possibly represents the very beginning of commercial planemaking in Japan.

In common with the other departments and companies that soon grew around it, Kawasaki's Kokuki team was almost totally dependent on foreign engineers and even foreign hardware until well into the 1920s. (As is now well understood, this perfectly

One of the early Kawasaki designs developed out of experience with license-production of Salmson reconnaissance aircraft was this A-6 two-seat biplane intended to meet an Army requirement for a communications machine. It was not taken up by the Army but the newspaper Asahi Shimbun *bought it in 1934.*

natural situation, coupled with the Japanese government's occasional purchase of especially good foreign prototypes up to World War II, was used by most of the Western powers as a foundation for the belief that the entire Japanese aircraft industry existed by making copies of Western designs; indeed the copies were invariably held to be "inferior," presumably in materials or quality control, though for this additional belief there was no evidence whatever. The truth, that by 1935 Japanese design teams were very much to be reckoned with, was reported by several engineers who visited Japan in the late 1930s – and by troops on the receiving end in China, including American Colonel Claire Chennault – but for some reason these truthful reports were disbelieved or conveniently pigeonholed.)

Kawasaki's new team was at first based in the shipyard at Kobe, but before 1920 had moved outside the city into a purpose-designed factory with its own airfield at Akashi. Its first contract, received in January 1920, was for a batch of Salmson 2.A2 reconnaissance aircraft for the Army (the total requirement was 300, but it is doubtful that Kawasaki built all of them). Certainly Kawasaki-assembled Salmsons were flying by mid-1923, and in this year the company hired Dr-Ing Richard Vogt as chief designer. Vogt stayed until 1933 and not only designed at least 13 basic Kawasaki types but trained his successors led by Takeo Doi. (Subsequently he became better known as techni-

cal director of Blohm und Voss.)

Another event of 1923 was the establishment of a technical link with Dornier which two years later led to a license for the Do H (Falke) monoplane fighter and about a year after that for the Do N, which was very much like a landplane bomber version of the Wal. Kawasaki built 28 of the bombers, licensing the BMW VI engines under the designation Ha-9, the aircraft becoming the Imperial Army Type 87. The Akashi plant also built Dornier Komets, Merkurs and Wals, all with Ha-9s.

The most important of Vogt's programs were the Type 88 bomber and reconnaissance aircraft and Type 92 fighter; no fewer than 1114 of various versions of the former were built (all but 187 by Kawasaki) and 385 of the latter, which owed a little to the Falke. After Vogt's departure the company continued to work for the Army, producing 588

One of the effective Kawasaki aircraft of World War II was the Ki-45 Toryu (Dragon Slayer), codenamed "Nick," of which nearly 1700 were built. Fitted with a variety of weapons, the twin-engined Ki-45 was used as a night fighter and for ground attack throughout the Pacific and for home defense.

Ki-10s, the last Japanese biplane fighter, and 854 of the Ki-32 stressed-skin monoplane bombers. The Ki-10 was one of the first types to go into production at a large new factory at Gifu, outside Kagamigahara near Nagoya. Gifu expanded with government prodding and, though at least five further plants were added during World War II, Gifu became the largest company aircraft center after the 1937 decision to hive off the department as a separate subsidary company called Kawasaki Kokuki Kogyo KK. In 1939 Kawasaki engines were likewise put under a separate company, at Akashi. This left a sound basis for expansion and, though the wartime output of about 8250 completed aircraft and 10,000 engines

was modest, the types were all effective: the Ki-45 twin-engined fighter, Ki-61 and Ki-100 single-engined fighter, Ki-48 bomber and useful Ki-36 and Ki-55 tactical machines were the most important.

In 1953 the company again began aircraft work, not only overhauling US military types but building the Lockheed P-2

Neptune under license and developing the Kawasaki P-2J from it, the Boeing-Vertol 107 in various versions including Kawasaki developments, the Hughes 500-series helicopter, Lockheed T-33A jet trainer and Bell 47 helicopter. It also produced the Orpheus turbojet and makes its own versions of the Lycoming T53 turboshaft, as well as many parts for the F-4EJ, TriStar, F-15 and 747SP. Its own designs now include the C-1 military transport and, in partnership with MBB, the BK-117 helicopter. Structurally the arrangement goes back to 1918 with an Aircraft Group at Gifu, with 3200 employees, forming part of the giant Kawasaki Jukogyo KK.

Above: The Ki-61 Hien (Swallow) was odd-one-out in Japanese fighters in having a liquid-cooled engine, and was probably the more dangerous to the Allies in the early encounters for that reason. Codenamed "Tony" and used as a light bomber, the Hien started to appear with Japanese squadrons in the second half of 1942 and total deliveries were more than 2700.

Today one of the world's largest manufacturing companies, and bigger than any in Britain, Mitsubishi was another of the Japanese organizations that sent observers to France to learn about planemaking in 1917–18. In this case the chief emissary was Dr Kumezo Itoh (often spelt Ito), who among other things negotiated a manufacturing license with Nieuport for fighters and trainers. In early 1920 Mitsubishi Jukogyo KK formed a subsidiary to build aircraft, giving it the name Mitsubishi Naineki Seizo KK (Mitsubishi Internal-combustion Engine Company). Possibly as many as 200 Nieuports were built at Kobe, but while this program was still active the company established a new site at Oe-Machi, today written as Oye, near Nagoya. This remains the center of Mitsubishi plane-making to this day.

In February 1921 Mitsubishi NSKK invited Herbert Smith, designer from the recently defunct Sopwith Company, to bring a team of engineers to set up a design office at the Oye works. From the start the main customer was the Imperial Navy, which bought 128 1MF shipboard fighters, 159 of the 2MR two-seat reconnaisance version and 442 of the large and capable B1M bomber and torpedo-carrier. Before returning to England, Smith oversaw Dr Matubara's design of the 2MB1, one of the first locally designed aircraft, which was

adopted by the Army as Type 87. Several of Matubara's other designs (the S.81 and S.82 and their variants) owed much to a Martinsyde F.4 brought by the Sempill mission to Japan in 1921.

The next major program was the B2M, a metal-framed replacement for the wooden but otherwise excellent B1M; it was a Blackburn design and George Petty came out to supervise the program of 204 aircraft. In 1928 the company changed its name to Mitsubishi Kokuki KK (Mitsubishi Aircraft Company), but in 1934 it did an about-face and returned everything into divisions of the giant Mitsubishi Jukogyo. By this time it had nine lead designers, all Japanese, the most famous of whom were Joji Hattori, Fumihiko Kono (creator of the *Divine Wind*, the first Japanese aircraft to visit the West), Sueo Honjo (whose G3M bomber carried more bombs farther and for less fuel than the contemporary Wellington), Kiro Honjo, who had the peculiarly difficult task of meeting the Navy specification that led to the G4M strategic bomber (which almost tried to do a B-29's job with two engines), and one of the most famous fighter designers of all time, Jiro Horikoshi. Horikoshi's A5M was possibly the most agile of all monoplane fighters, while the A6M – universally known as the Zero – was not only a traumatic shock to the Allies but with its designer became

Right: This captured Zero fighter, an A6M5 Model 52 of early 1944, typifies the great fighter that was actually an obsolescent and very limited design but which, because of its range and maneuverability, and superiority over the even worse collection of aircraft available to oppose it in 1941–43, became synonymous with a myth of Japanese invincibility.

Below: One of the earliest native Mitsubishi designs, and the first Japanese aircraft to visit the West, was this second prototype of the Ki-15 series named Kamikaze (Divine Wind), which made a record flight to London in 1937 and is here seen at Croydon Airport.

synonymous with national invincibility.

During World War II Mitsubishi operated [and I am indebted to René Francillon for the list] airframe plants at Naguno, Takaoka, Suzuka, Kagamigahara, Inami, Obu, Tsu, Okayama, Yawata, Yokkaichi, Naruo, Mizushima and Kumamoto. There were also 11 engine plants, and together they produced 12,513 aircraft (17.9 percent of the national wartime total or 23 percent of the combat aircraft, and a weight of airframes that even beat Nakajima because of Mitsubishi's high proportion of large bombers)

and no less than 38 percent of all the country's engines, including impressive radials of 2500hp.

Operations began again in December 1952 when the Komaki South factory was built. Subsequently the original Oye site,

This partly built Mitsubishi J2M3 Raiden single-seat fighter was found in an underground assembly area at Atsugi without engines after Japan surrendered. The J2M, although from the same design team as the "Zero," was plagued with failures and production difficulties from its first flight in March 1942 and only about 500 were built.

Komaki South and North and Daiko were amalgamated into Nagoya Aircraft Works, a major Mitsubishi subsidiary, with Daiko responsible for engines. Among early overhaul contracts were several for the F-86, leading to license-production of 300 F-86F Sabres for the Air Self-Defense Force. Subsequently Mitsubishi manufactured 230 F-104 Starfighters in collaboration with Kawasaki, and the same team made 140 F-4EJ Phantoms and will handle the F-15CJ and DJ Eagle program terminating after 1982. Other license-production included

the Sikorsky S-55, S-58, S-61 and S-62 helicopters.

The company's chief home programs have been the MU-2 twin-turboprop, now expanded with the Marquise and Solitaire; the T-2 supersonic trainer and F-1 supersonic strike fighter; and the MU-300 Diamond I twin-turbofan business aircraft due for certification in 1980. Other Mitsubishi operations include major missile programs at Mitsubishi Jukogyo and other missile and space activities at Mitsubishi Electric.

OMNIPOL

Omnipol is the export organization for the aircraft industry of Czechoslovakia. About 29,000 are employed in factories which in 1945 were summarily thrown together in a single national group but today operate as three national corporations.

Czechoslovakia came into existence on 28 October 1918. After 300 years of Austro-Hungarian rule the easiest way of setting up an aircraft industry was to build Austro-Hungarian designs, but within a year three Czech companies had been formed – Aero, Avia and Letov – that between the wars out-performed all others in central Europe with nationally designed aircraft. The first, the Aero Tovarna Letadel, set up a production line at Prague-Vysocany in May 1919 building 100 Phönix D III scouts under the designation Aero 276. By 1923 Aero's own A 11 two-seater and nimble A 18 fighter were in production, the former being a prolific family that ran to over 440 aircraft with wheels, skis or floats and with no fewer than nine different types of engine

Czechoslovakia achieved prominence in the lightplane field in the 1930s through successive designs from the Benes-Mraz Company, in particular the Be-500 series which set world class records and led to the Mraz Sokol series still in production. This batch of new Be-50 two-seat trainers appear ready for delivery, circa 1937.

(too many types of engine was for many years a curse to the Czech Air Force and the airline CSA). Subsequently Aero made several hundred military and civil aircraft including 124 licensed Bloch 200 bombers and the mixed-construction A-204 passenger transport and A-304 reconnaissance bomber which were commandeered by the Luftwaffe and Bulgarian Air Force.

Most successful of all the Czech companies was Avia, the full title of which was "Avia" Akciova Spolecnost Pro Prumysl Letecky, set up in April 1919 as a subsidiary of the great Skoda group. It took over a derelict sugar refinery at Cakovice on Prague's east side, and quickly produced brilliant designs through the talents of P Benes and M Hajn, the designations having the prefix BH in consequence. The first to be built in quantity was the outstanding BH-3 monoplane fighter of 1921, and the last BH was the BH-33 of 1929, which had the distinction of being licensed to Yugoslavia and Poland.

The two designers then founded their own company, called Ceskomoravska Kolben Danek, at Prague-Karlin; it built the famous Praga series of lightplanes and engines. Avia's new chief designer was F Nowotny, whose B 534 fighter of 1933 was not only exceptional in all respects but

outnumbered the Luftwaffe with 445 in service at the time of the 1938 Munich crisis that put Czechoslovakia under the Nazi yoke. Avia also made trimotor transports, Fokker and Tupolev bombers and a batch of monoplane fighters for Bulgaria after the German occupation. After the Germans had left, Avia engineers gathered 500 sets of parts for Bf 109G fighters and completed 20 with the proper DB 605A engine and 480 with the Jumo 211F, resulting in the S 199 – rightly called Mezek (mule) by the Israelis, who took what they could get.

The Letov company, the Vojenska Tovarna Na Letadla "Letov," was formed from the Austro-Hungarian air arsenal at Prague-Letnany in November 1918. Its first task was repair and overhaul of former Austro-Hungarian machines for the new Czech Air Force, but under the design direction of Alois Smolik the company created a long series of military and civil aircraft up to the German occupation. The first was the Sm-1, later redesignated Letov S 1, a reconnaissance bomber flown in April 1920. Best-known was the S 328 of 1933, a machine very like the British Swordfish; 445 were built and after 1938 were passed to the puppet Slovak and Bulgarian Air Forces, as well as the Luftwaffe.

The only prewar Czech aircraft companies

The Avia B-34 pictured here was the prototype of the efficient B-534 fighter of 1933, of which several hundred were captured by the Germans when they overran Czechoslovakia in 1938–39. Most served the Luftwaffe as trainers but some were used as fighters on the Russian Front.

not located in the Prague area were both builders of lightplanes – Benes-Mraz at Chocen and Zlinska Letecka at Zlin. Under German occupation all the prewar factories were absorbed into the armament industry, Praga as the BMM (Böhmische-Märische Maschinenfabriken) and the others as part of the giant complexes administered by German aircraft companies. Letov, for example, was a major unit in the Junkers empire. In 1945, under Soviet authority, a national car and aircraft works administration was set up called Ceskoslovenské Závody Automobilové a Letecke. An office called Kovo Limited was created to handle sales, which in view of the attractiveness of such products as the Letov Lunak, Zlin Kmotr, Sohaj sailplanes and the powered Sokol, Junak, Trenér and Aero 45 light twin,

The principal current Aero product is the L-39 Albatros jet trainer/light attack aircraft, which first flew in November 1968. Production, against initial orders from Soviet, Czech and Iraqi Air Forces, started in 1973 and has now exceeded 1000 aircraft.

all available by 1949, grew rapidly.

By 1950 the industry was reorganized. Zlin was reconstituted as Moravan Národni Podnik in its original works, though the city of Zlin had become Gottwaldov. It is a world leader in piston trainer and aerobatic aircraft. Let Národni Podnik was established in 1950 at Uherské Hradiste (previously Kunovice) and produced the Aero 200 light twin (a standard aircraft throughout the Soviet Union), and twin-finned L 200 Morava, Z-37 Cmelák and L 60 Brigadýr agricultural and utility transports and more than 2600 of the world's most popular training sailplane, the all-metal L 13 Blanik. Its current product is the L 410 Turbolet twin-turboprop transport.

Third of the "companies," established in 1953, was Aero Vodochody Národni Podnik, located near Prague. This perpetuates the name but nothing else of the former Aero company. Its chief products have been the L-29 Delfin jet trainer, selected as standard for the Warsaw Pact (except Poland) in 1961, about 3600 being delivered, and its successor, the L-39 Albatros of which 1000 had been delivered by early 1980. The old Letov works was engaged in the 1950s in license-production of MiG jet fighters, while the new Let corporation built the Yak-11 advanced piston trainer. However, permission to build combat aircraft was revoked after the 1968 uprising; the last type was the MiG-21PFM.

PZL

The initials PZL have had two meanings, one for the old company which was obliterated in September 1939 and another for today's socialist enterprise which does surprisingly well under fairly obvious Warsaw Pact limitations. At all times Poland has shown a marked ability to produce outstanding aircraft capable of sustaining viable and profitable programs, and in this regard PZL has done better than most of the companies in western Europe.

In 1919 Poland, like Czechoslovakia, became a sovereign state that suddenly had its independence. A state organization called CWL (Centralne Warsztaty Lotnicze) was formed to handle aircraft repair and maintenance at Warsaw-Mokotòw, changing its name to CZL in 1924 (Centralne Zaklady Lotnicze) and in January 1928 to PZL (Panstwowe Zaklady Lotnicze or National Aviation Establishment). The paramilitary government of 1926 had urgently called for national capability in defense equipment, and PZL swiftly built up a design team – mainly with recent graduates from Warsaw Technical University – that appears to have been rather special. Leader of the team was the brilliant Zygmunt Pulaski.

From the proverbial clean sheet of paper Pulaski drew the P.1 fighter, L.2 four-seater, PZL.3 bomber, PZL.4 trimotor airliner and PZL.5 lightplane. The most important was the P.1, an excellent gull-wing monoplane from which stemmed the P.7 with PZL-built Bristol Jupiter and the P.11 with locally built Mercury. Both were extremely clean aerodynamically, entirely of stressed-skin construction, and the objective of good all-round performance and heavy armament (four guns) was met in

full. PZL made 150 P.1s from 1931 to 1933, and 225 P.11s from 1934 at a new factory at Warsaw-Okecie. Among many other military and civil types the P.23 Karaś attack bomber also stands out as significant in advanced structure, bomb load and numbers built (250, plus 54 of a more powerful export version). Chief designer of the P.23 was Stanislaw Prauss, who was one of those who succeeded Pulaski after the latter had been killed in a crash in 1931.

The story of how the PZL P.30 Zubr airliner was hastily turned into a structurally weak bomber has often been told, as has the even more distressing tale of how another Pulaski successor, Jerzy Dabrowski, led a team which in 1935 designed the greatest bomber of its era, the P.37 Loś, which was actually produced in numbers both at Okecie and at a much bigger plant at Mielec finished in 1939. This superb aircraft, with excellent reliability, high speed and a bomb load of 5568lb (2525kg), impressed everyone except the Polish general staff, who decided it was too radical, wholly unwanted and an embarrassment, and terminated production. Despite this the Air Force somehow received over 90, more than half of which gallantly went into action with untrained crews in the unexpected role of close support of troops overwhelmed by Panzer divisions. PZL had no chance to get into production with its new fighter and attack designs such as the Wyzel, Wilk, Sum, Jastrzab and Miś. Between 1941 and 1944 Mielec was a big slave-labor factory in the Heinkel organization.

In 1945 in the ruins of Warsaw, Tadeusz and Witold Soltyk and Eugeniusz Stankiewicz designed the Szpak-2 four-seat monoplane, the first of a profusion of lightplanes that appeared under a wealth of small organizations all part of the national ZPL (United Aircraft Industry). After many changes and reorganizations, though fewer than in western European planemakers, this has become the ZPL-PZL, in today's world signifying Polskie Zaklady Lotnicze (Polish aviation establishment), and the initials have even been turned into the phoneticized word Pezetel to identify the national aviation export organization.

Such an organization is needed because, unlike most European countries, Poland has built up a worldwide business in general-aviation aircraft (aircraft for purposes other than military, or commercial transport), a field assigned to Poland by the Soviet Union in 1959. With the home market of the entire Soviet Union and Warsaw Pact countries this has underpinned a business which today employs a remarkable 96,000 and since 1960 has produced 13,500 aircraft and 4750 helicopters – figures that possibly surpass all west European planemakers combined.

An organization called IL (Instytut Lotnictwa) handles research, and series-produces turbojets. CNPSL-PZL-Warsaw develops and makes lightplanes including the Wilga, Kruk and Koliber (licensed Socata Rallye). WSK-PZL-Mielec, the biggest factory, has delivered more than 8450 An-2 multi-role biplanes and about 550 TS-11 Iskra jet trainers, and is in production with the Soviet-designed An-28, the large and capable Dromader and M-15 ag-aircraft and many major parts for the Il-86 wide-body transport. WSK-PZL-Swidnik produces a growing family of twin-turbine helicopters.

Above: The PZL-Mielec An-2 is a 1947 Russian Antonov design now built in Poland after production of 5000 in the USSR up to 1950. Although antediluvian in concept and appearance, the An-2 is still selling well in seven or eight variants, including the 12-passenger airliner, five-seat executive, cargo/passenger, agricultural and others, to a score of countries. Polish deliveries now total well over 8000 aircraft. A PZL-Mielec An-2R agricultural version is illustrated.

Left: An outstanding Polish design of the interwar years was the PZL P.23 Karaś (Carp) attack bomber, which entered service in 1935 as an operational trainer and as a reconnaissance bomber in 1936. Over 200 were built for the Polish and Bulgarian Air Forces before Poland was overrun.

Right: Designed in Poland to joint Polish and Soviet requirements for a big agricultural aircraft, the PZL-Mielec M-15 is also a biplane and odd-looking, but as modern as the hour with tricycle landing gear, turbofan engine and excellent working conditions for a crew of three. After evaluation of prototypes deliveries against a substantial Soviet order started in 1976.

SHIN MEIWA

Neither the name of Shin Meiwa nor its predecessor, Kawanishi, are really familiar, except to military and aviation enthusiasts, who will probably agree that it built the best flying-boat of the World War II era and the best flying-boat of the modern era, and a host of other important machines. It also built a first-rate fighter, much more formidable than the Zero-Sen, that could have been a real menace had it been mass-producible from the start, as related later.

As outlined in the Nakajima (Fuji) story, Seibei Kawanishi went into partnership with Nakajima in 1917 and later walked out after a major difference of opinion. His Kawanishi Machinery combine started an aircraft (Kokuki) division in February 1920, and for the next 25 years concentrated on seaplanes and flying-boats under the expert direction of Eiji Sekiguchi. His first offering was the K.1, the first of a number of the division's aircraft to serve with another subsidiary, Japan Airline Company, directed by Ryuzo Kawanishi. Using mainly German watercooled engines the division produced ten basic types in its first seven years, most finding favorable publicity with various kinds of civil flying.

In 1928 the group began to expand,

finding new interest in building for the Imperial Navy. It was registered as Kawanishi Kokuki KK (Kawanishi Aircraft) and moved into a new and growing plant at Naruo near Osaka. The old works at Kobe was vacated, but after 1935 continued expansion resulted in a factory being built at Konan, between Kobe and Osaka, and a third at Himeji. Parts were produced by Takarazuka, near Naruo. No attempt was made to make anything but airframes, and from an early date these were almost entirely of light alloy.

Most successful of Sekiguchi's early types was the E7K biplane seaplane; about 530 various versions were built between 1933 and 1940. In 1936 the first H6K long-range four-engined flying-boat showed that Kawanishi could equal anything in the West; a major share in this famous ocean reconnaissance and transport machine was taken by Shizuo Kikuhara. When it was seen in World War II it was inevitably called "a copy of the Sikorsky S-42," but in fact it was dramatically superior, besides being much larger and heavier. What followed, the H8K, first flown in January 1941, was less-emphatically described as a reproduction of the Sunder-

land, but again there was no comparison. The H8K was a remarkable machine, the fastest flying-boat of its day, with the heaviest payload and most formidable armament which in some versions included five 20mm cannon. Naruo and Konan built 167 plus 215 of the earlier H6K.

Naruo also built 97 of the remarkable N1K1 seaplane fighter. From this was developed a landplane, the N1K1-J Shiden

The Kawanishi H8K flying-boat's similarity to the British Sunderland was only superficial. The Japanese boat, code-named 'Emily', was about 70mph faster at over 280mph and had a range of 4000 miles, about 1000 miles more than the Sunderland; it also had more defensive weapons and could carry twice the bombload at over 4000lb.

The Kawanishi N1K1 Kyofu (Mighty Wind), codenamed "Rex," had an excellent performance for a seaplane, which encouraged the designer to convert the basic design into a landplane, the N1K1-J Shiden ("George"), which also performed well but was very costly to maintain.

(Violet Lightning). Known to the Allies as "George," this was an outstanding fighter, but suffered from countless problems arising from its seaplane ancestry. Despite this, Naruo built 530 production Shidens and Himeji 468s before turning to the N1K2-J, a complete redesign with low wing, short and strong landing gear and about half the number of parts. To show how important this aircraft was, it was being built at Kawanishi, Mitsubishi, Showa, Aichi, Hiro, Omura and Koza when the war ended!

In 1949 the company was resurrected under the name Shin Meiwa Industry Company, gradually building up the old Konan plant and a second source at Itami. Managing director is Hajime Kawanishi, and the great Dr Kikuhara is still technical consultant. He played a major part in the design of the most advanced marine aircraft today, the PS-1 flying-boat and US-1 amphibian, both of which are serving with the Japan Maritime Self-Defense Force, the former mainly as an ASW platform and the amphibian as a search/rescue airplane. Shin Meiwa was a partner in NAMC (Nihon Airplane Manufacturing Company) which produced the YS-11 turboprop airliner family, and is a partner in CTDC (Civil Transport Development Company) which is helping Boeing produce the 767, with Japanese government finance. The company shares in the Mitsubishi T-2 and F-1 and license-built F-15 Eagle and Lockheed P-3C Orion programs and supplied the cargo handling system of the Kawasaki C-1.

Shin Meiwa was a partner in NAMC, the Japanese consortium that originated the YS-11 twin-turboprop short/medium-range airliner for up to 60 passengers. The YS-11 prototype flew in 1962 and entered airline service in 1965, and sold generally in small numbers to around 15 operators before production ended.

Born out of prolonged civil warfare and ever afterwards suspicious of most of the rest of the world, it is sad that so little is publicly known about the planemaking efforts of the Soviet Union. Admittedly there is a thousand times more to tell than can be set down here, but the author, at least, is still ignorant of such basic factors as how the prototypes developed by each design bureau (OKB) are evaluated (by flight personnel from the bureaus themselves, the State aviation ministry and the military or civil customers), how each design is allocated to particular production factories, and how the accounts are drawn up to provide some yardstick of financial return. It is proposed here to concentrate on the basics, only outlining in the most general way the types of aircraft involved. Since 1918 Russian designers have flown at least 350 distinct types of aircraft, of which something in excess of 180 have been built in more than development quantity; this explains the broad-brush treatment.

In Tsarist Russia planemaking was by no means confined to the well-known 'big names" such as Sikorsky, Anatra and Lebed; at least 21 companies were actually in production by 1917, some of them with several factories or workshops, and though more than half the output was of licensed foreign designs (or developments thereof) strenuous efforts were being made to build up national design capability. After the revolution in October 1917 planemaking was possible only in a few scattered locations, and many of the most talented and creative minds emigrated. Among those who stayed were Antonov, Beriev, Bratukhin, Chetverikov, Grigorovich, Ilyushin, Kalinin, Kamov, Lavochkin, Mil, Mikoyan, Myasishchev, Petlyakov, Polikarpov, Sukhoi, Tupolev and Yakovlev. All were aviation enthusiasts at the time of the revolution, though some were mere boys. [And to show how difficult it is to research the story, the date of Antonov's birth was undoubtedly 1906 yet there are detailed accounts of how he designed and tested a helicopter at the Lessner works in Petrograd in 1909–10! Perhaps there were two Oleg K Antonovs, father and son?]

It was natural for the Supreme Soviet to have a passion for State organization. To manage aeronautical research the TsAGI (central aerodynamics and hydrodynamics institute) was founded in December 1920 under the great Professor N Ye Jukovsky (like other Russian names this can be spelt in many ways). Nearly all the designers subsequently to be allocated bureaus of their own passed through this seat of learn- and research, which during the 1920s

outgrew its original Moscow building and today approximates the size of NASA. To look after design – an area fraught with suspicion, intrigue, political lobbying, severe punishment for "imperfect work," and even "unfortunate death after sudden illness" – technical staff were organized into OKBs located in city offices, on airfields or anywhere else, but usually not with an associated production plant. Mass production was the responsibility of a growing network of numbered State Aircraft Factories, backed up by a different numbered series of motor (engine) plants.

Among the earliest effective production programs, both initially centered at Factory No 1, previously the large Dux aircraft works founded in Moscow in 1910, were the R-1 (DH.9A) and U-1 (Avro 504K). Jukovsky supervised construction of a batch of TsAGI-designed large triplanes, called Komtas from the Commission for Heavy Aircraft, which were to be both transports and bombers, but they were not very good machines. At that time (1921–22) TsAGI was collaborating with other groups in attempting to replace traditional materials by metals, especially the new light alloy (almost identical to the German Dural) called Kolchug after the place where it was developed. The leading proponent of metal airframes was A N Tupolev, born in September 1888, who had so impressed Jukovsky that he had been appointed his deputy and, in 1921, head of the TsAGI design section. Within weeks of the latter appointment he had completed design of the ANT-1 (A N Tupolev Type 1) single-seater, with cantilever low wing. At least three were built, each with a different type of engine, with a greater proportion of

A group of aircraft designers seen at the 22nd Soviet Communist Party conference in 1961; left to right, A Yakovlev, S Tumansky, S Ilyushin and V Chernyshov.

Kolchug in each successive example.

By this time talks were being held with Germany which led to the 1922 Treaty of Rapallo and, among other things, the use of the Soviet Union as a location for an unfettered German aircraft industry. Put another way, the Germans sent at least 900 technical staff to help build a Soviet industry. The larger group came from Junkers, which occupied a newly built factory at Fili in the western suburbs of Moscow (not the former Russo-Baltic Wagon Works as often reported). There a succession of sound all-metal monoplanes proved both useful and technically instructive. One report states that the Junkers people were ousted in 1924 because "the Soviet authorities claimed that the Germans were . . . concerned solely with turning out excessively-priced and outdated aircraft." In fact the concession granted to the Junkers company was mutually beneficial, resulted in over 240 aircraft and was terminated by mutual consent on 1 March 1927; the Fili works became Factory 32.

Junkers technology assisted several Soviet design teams, none more than Tupolev's. His ANT-2 three-seater of 1924 was entirely made of Kolchug, using Junkers corrugated skin actually made on the imported rolling machine at Fili. From it stemmed such major types as the ANT-3 (most common service designation R-3), ANT-4 (TB-1) and ANT-5 (I-4). The -3 was a powerful biplane for reconnaissance; the TB-1, an outstanding twin-engined bomber, was also made as a torpedo-seaplane, transport and other

The big four-engined Tupolev ANT-6 (TB-3) first appeared in 1930 as a bomber. Typical of a number of Russian aircraft of the period it showed traces of the earlier Junkers assistance in founding the Soviet aircraft industry. The ANT-6 remained in production until the late 1930s and was used during the Hitler war mainly as a military transport, although a few were used as bombers in the early stages. The picture shows a party of Russian air notabilities on a visit to Paris in ANT-6s.

versions with the wing and possibly other parts assigned to deputy designer V M Petlyakov; the I-4 fighter was the first major project assigned to deputy designer P O Sukhoi. From 1925, Tupolev's bureau was the largest in the country, though its products were assigned to groups headed by the two designers mentioned, plus others such as A A Arkangelsky for high-speed bombers and the Pogosky brothers for flying-boats.

One area the "master" kept for himself was large landplanes, and here he was not only competent but a world leader between 1925 and 1940. The most important single design was the ANT-6 (TB-3) heavy bomber, first flown – with a hair-raising take-off due to mis-set trim and the absence of a throttle friction nut – on 22 December 1930. This great machine, a 2000hp four-engined cantilever monoplane considerably larger

than the Lancaster or B-17 of a decade later, failed to implant a belief in strategic bombing in the minds of the generals but did serve in large numbers, pioneered paratroop assault and airborne armor and led to many other designs. The wing was used in the five-engined ANT-14 airliner, while the smaller wing of the ANT-7 (R-6, Kr-6) was used in the ANT-9, virtually the standard Soviet airliner of between 1929 and 1936. Going sharply up the size scale Tupolev flew the monster ANT-16 (TB-4) and promptly outdid even this with the ANT-20 *Maxim Gorky*, flown in April 1934, with a span of 260ft (79.25m) and 7200hp! This was lost in a foolish mid-air collision, but the soundness of the design is shown by the production of 16 ANT-20bis, with six instead of eight engines but even greater gross weight, of which eight were still in daily transport service in 1945.

Pogosky creations included the ANT-8 (MDR-2) flying-boat with two engines, the ANT-27 (MDR-4) with three and the outstanding four-engined MTB-2 of 1937. This was the time of the Stalinist terror, and as someone had whispered that Tupolev was a traitor he was arrested and condemned to death. The splendid new flying-boat was thus called TsAGI-44 instead of ANT-44. The SB-2 bomber, produced earlier than Britain's Blenheim yet dramatically better in all aspects of performance, was built in larger numbers than any previous Tupolev type, and was also the first Soviet design licensed abroad (as the Czech Avia B-71). When, in 1940, the Soviet authorities decided to adopt a new aircraft designation system based on the leader of the design team rather than operational function, the SB-2 series became the Ar-2, and the TB-7 heavy bomber (once the ANT-42) was redesignated Pe-8 for Petlyakov. Tupolev's name was never mentioned but he had escaped execution and, along with many other creative workers, in fact spent several

Starting life in the middle 1930s as the ANT-42 because it came from the Tupolev bureau, and becoming the TB-7 heavy bomber, the Petlyakov Pe-8 was the only heavy bomber with which the USSR entered the war; it could take about a 9000lb load over a range of more than 2000 miles. The unusual manually operated gunner's position under the inboard engine nacelles is visible in this photograph of the Pe-8 that carried Soviet Foreign Minister Molotov to Britain in 1942.

Doyen of Soviet aircraft designers, A N Tupolev, in 1972.

years (in his case 1936–43) carrying on his work behind bars. His chief preoccupation during this period was a high-speed bomber originally called Samolyet (airplane) 103 but later ANT-58 – according to one story, because 58 was the number of Tupolev's cell in Butyryki prison! It was a brilliant success and not only won him his freedom but the designation Tu-2 and a Stalin (later called a Lenin) Prize.

One suggestion put forward as a reason for Tupolev's arrest was that he gave the Germans plans for the Bf 110 twin-engine fighter (an idea based on a supposed similarity between that aircraft and the Pe-2). This idea is so ridiculous it might even be true, were it not for the gross disparity between the two designs, the fact the Bf 110

was actually flying at Augsburg before the VI-100 (the project from which stemmed the Pe-2) had even been thought of, and the not entirely unrelated fact that both Tupolev and Petlyakov were arrested two years before the VI-100 plan was even drawn. In any case Petlyakov, like Arkangelsky, Myasishchev and Sukhoi, had by this time been allowed to form their own OKBs. Playing no small part in such decisions was Tupolev himself, appointed in 1932 to the administration board of the aircraft industry (the GUAP).

This was yet another job he managed from his cell, on top of which in October 1941 came the stupendous task of evacuating the entire industry to newly built plants east of the Urals. More than a million planemaking men and women were geographically relocated from 1000 to 6000 miles (1600–10,000km) farther east in a period of 19 weeks, in some cases arriving to find their first job was to dig the foundations of the factory. The hardships and difficulties surmounted are almost beyond belief. Frequently it was necessary to unload road vehicles and lift both them and their contents over impassable roads or places where the system had omitted to build a road. Almost everything went by rail, the trains being not so much a conveyance as a home for hundreds of complete families for weeks at a time. And it was afterwards calculated that within six months production was running at a rate greater than before the move. Since then the whole Soviet industry has been dispersed, with large complexes extending across to the Pacific coast.

In 1944 Tupolev gave his own OKB a task without parallel in history. It was to

dismantle a B-29 down to the last rivet, produce working drawings and specifications of all the materials and parts, and get into production. The result, achieved in under a year, was the Tu-4, which differed from the Boeing product only in such matters as the elimination of remote-control gun barbettes. Later Soviet remote-control armament systems were derived from the American one, and a Soviet copy of the bombsight. The overall result was a new foundation of technology on which was constructed the Tu-14, -16, -20, -22, -24 and -26 military bombers, reconnaissance and electronic-warfare aircraft (these are service designations) and the Tu-104, -114, -124,

Bottom: Considered among the best of Russian World War II aircraft, the Petlyakov Pe-2 earned a reputation for toughness and versatility; it saw service on all fronts as a light bomber, for reconnaissance and in general ground-attack and close-support roles.

-134, -144 and -154 civil transports. Andrei N Tupolev died on 23 December 1972. Today his son Alexei A Tupolev is chief designer Tu-144 and Dmitri Markov chief designer Tu-154 – both programs hit by prolonged troubles – and this OKB remains the chief source of large aircraft in the Soviet Union.

Petlyakov, like all Number 2s in the Soviet Union, got little public recognition of the large part he played in Tupolev designs right up to World War II. Like Tupolev he had been imprisoned in 1936, and actually designed the Pe-2 in a prison cell. But his release came earlier than his old boss's, probably in 1941, and he was all set for a major career when he was killed in a Pe-2 in early 1942. Later his bureau at Kazan was taken over by V M Myasishchev, who from 1929 had a major hand in Tupolev designs and especially in getting rid of the Junkers-inherited corrugated skin. Myasishchev's first wholly original design, initiated in 1939 when he too was in prison, was the DVB-102 (probably later designated Mya-1), an outstandingly advanced long-range bomber with pressurized crew compartments and intended to have 2500hp M-120 engines. He was out in the cold in 1946, but three years later was summoned by Stalin and ordered to create a large jet bomber. His offering, flown in 1953, failed to meet the extremely severe range requirement said to have been 16,000km (9942 miles); such a demand was far beyond what was possible with available engines, but under the Soviet system failure to comply could mean imprisonment in a forced-labor camp.

Nevertheless the West, which calls this aircraft "Bison," was thrown into a panic, and boosted output of Boeing bombers and tankers to try to close a mythical "bomber gap." The production Mya-4, or M-4, is still in service despite the severe loads borne by the structure, and it is probable that the fleet leaders have logged 15,000 hours each. The last M-series from Factory 23 was a

Below: After the war the Tupolev bureau was occupied mainly with the design of big jet transports and for a period of about two years between the grounding of the Comet I and the entry into service of the Comet 4 and Boeing 707 the Tu-104, which first visited London in March 1956, was the only jet in airline service. This picture shows the Tu-104A 70-passenger machine which quickly followed the original 50-seater into production.

Bottom: The Tupolev bureau is also responsible for a wide range of current military aircraft. The Tu-126 "Moss" airborne early warning and fighter-control aircraft is based on the Tu-114 220-seat long-range airliner, which itself was the passenger counterpart of the Tu-95 "Bear" bomber. The Tu-126's 36ft rotating radome serves a mass of electronics designed for long-range detection of enemy aircraft and communication with friendly aircraft; its four turboprops giving nearly 60,000hp provide a speed of up to 540mph and a maximum range of about 5500 miles. The picture was taken by a British F-4 Phantom; a US Navy F-4 is also in the picture.

monster supersonic bomber of 1957, the M-50, which despite prolonged tinkering was always deficient in range. Myasishchev became a professor at the Aviation Institute and died in October 1978.

Most successful of all Tupolev's protégés was Pavel O Sukhoi, born in July 1895. He was chiefly responsible for Tupolev fighters from the I-4 onward, as well as the record-breaking long-range ANT-25 of 1936. Sukhoi must in some way be suspect, because for some reason he was *not* imprisoned during the great terror. Instead he was given his own design bureau, the first mass product of which was the BB-1, later designated Su-2, tactical attack bomber. Subsequent prototypes were generally good, but for various reasons failed to enter production. The Su-6 *shturmovik* (assault) design was especially good, but the State chose the Il-10 because it could more easily succeed the Il-2. The Su-8 was a long-range *shturmovik* with 4000hp and four 45mm cannon, but the war was nearly over. The Su-15 had two Nenes mounted rather as in the British P.1, but the tailplane came off. The Su-10 was better than the generally similar British Sperrin, if figures are any guide, but the Tu-16 was better still. Sukhoi's bureau was closed in 1949.

After Stalin's death in 1953, Sukhoi was again reinstated (perhaps he knew too much for Stalin's liking). He chose Arkhip Lyulka's big AL-7 afterburning turbojet for the prototypes of 1956 which led to the swept Su-7 and delta Su-9. (He had previously had unsuccessful prototypes with the same designations, but Su-7 and -9 were service, not bureau, designations.) Neither had anything like adequate internal fuel capacity, but because they were large and easily developed very large numbers of both were produced. The Su-9 all-weather interceptor led to the Su-11 and today's twin-engined Su-15 series, while various subtypes of Su-7 led to the variable-sweep Su-17, -20 and -22. Since 1974 the most formidable tactical attack aircraft in the world, apart from the F-111, has been the Su-19, a large swing-wing bomber with tremendous capabilities. Sukhoi died in September 1975, but as is customary his OKB is still named after him.

Of the other leading Soviet designers who did not work directly for Tupolev, the most versatile was Alexander S Yakovlev. Born in March 1906, he began like Messerschmitt with simple gliders which were taken by train to meetings in the Crimea from 1923. Working as a mechanic at the Jukovsky academy he obtained Osoviakhim (shorter than the translation: association of societies dedicated to the promotion of defense and aero-chemical development) backing for a lightplane resembling a DH Moth. Yakovlev was a political animal, and thus knew how to survive in the Soviet Union. He called his firstborn the AIR-1, for A I Rykov, chairman of the council of people's commissars; when Rykov was shot he quickly redesignated it Ya-1. There followed a profusion of sportplanes, and graduation from the same academy where he had been a mere oily rag.

In 1931 he joined the TsKB (central design bureau) under Tupolev's only important contemporary, Nikolai N Polikarpov, who had managed the production of IM bombers before the revolution and in the period 1922–40 was the chief designer of fighters. Polikarpov had been given a bureau, the landplane department of Aviatrust (OSS), in 1926. In the same year he designed a little biplane which became the U-2, made in larger numbers than any other single type (at least 40,000) and later redesignated Po-2 in his honor. Polikarpov also designed the I-15 series of biplane fighters and I-16 monoplane, both outstanding for their era and both produced to the tune of 6500-plus. He died in 1944.

Below: An important contemporary of A N Tupolev was Polikarpov, who opened the bureau named after him with the design of the U-2 (later Po-2) basic trainer. It was built in large numbers (some 40,000) for many years and used on a wide variety of military and civil duties, even as an ambulance with stretchers carried on the lower wings. The Po-2s pictured are serving as trainers in the postwar Yugoslav Air Force.

Bottom: Also built in very large numbers (nearly 37,000) was the range of Yakovlev World War II singl single-seat fighters, which started with the Yak-1 before the German invasion and finished with the Yak-9 first produced in 1942. Here, Yak-1s enter large-scale production in a vast new plant, No. 153, a converted factory at Novosibirsk in the early war years.

The Yak-11 founded a class of simple training and general-purpose light aircraft that became standard equipment in the air forces of the USSR and its allies, and continued in successive marks of the Yak-18 into the 1980s. The Yak-11 (illustrated) is maintained in flying condition by a British owner.

Yakovlev chose to be a supervisor rather than a designer, so that he could "on the side" create lightplanes and have them made at the factory. He gave them all AIR designations, and in case anyone still thinks planemaking in the Soviet Union need not also make ulcers the AIR-7 is a case in point. This sporting speedster looked like a cabin version of the Boeing P-26, and of course was bright red. He demonstrated it before officials in mid-1932 when an aileron came off in flight, the aircraft making a forced landing. Yakovlev and his team were ordered out of the plant and carried on as best they could in a wooden hut. Then one day a superintendent came in and said to Yakovlev and his team, "There's been an order to keep you off the premises and to take away all your passes."

Eventually Yakovlev got audience with the mighty Rudzutak, chairman of the central commission, and poured out his troubles. Rudzutak told him to fly his new machine to his country house and give him a ride! This was actually accomplished, and the upshot was that a few days later Yakovlev was summoned by S P Korolev, head of the GUAP, who said "I have given orders for your bureau to be accommodated in a bed factory on the Leningradsky Prospekt; is that clear? Don't count on more. You may go. And don't go running about with your complaints." (To round off this tale, Korolev himself was behind bars three years later, but survived to lead the Soviet space effort and direct the design

of the *Vostok* spacecraft during the 1960s.)

The way things operated was for bed-making to be assigned to some other place and for Yakovlev to teach the former bed-makers how to build advanced aircraft. The same building is still occupied by the same OKB, but after emergence of the UT-2 and related trainers in 1935 Yakovlev soared in stature and saw the old workshops at Khimki replaced by a vast new plant where the Yak-4 twin-engine attack bomber and the first Yak-1 fighters were produced prior to the German invasion. In October 1941 Yakovlev was deputy commissar for the GUAP and on top of all his other problems had to organize the evacuation to the east. His own bureau moved to Kamensk-Uralsk and Novosibirsk where plants produced a total of 36,737 piston-engined fighters which in the Yak-1s were nearly all wood and in the Yak-9s were nearly all light alloy. Subsequently the bureau has tried almost everything, including STOL utility transports, complex radar-packed inter-

ceptors, piston and jet trainers, specialized aerobatic machines, supersonic attack and electronic-warfare platforms, tandem-rotor transport helicopters, jet VTOL naval aircraft and large civil jetliners. As this book goes to press Yakovlev is still very much alive, and his son Sergei Alexandrovich leads some of the design teams.

Yakovlev almost managed to eliminate one of his rivals by lending him a cabin monoplane in 1935 which crashed. The rival was Sergei V Ilyushin, born in March 1894 (and he said to Yakovlev "I have no grudge against you Alexander; it turns out that the engine will not work if the mechanic forgets the oil"). Apparently on his own initiative he organized the Avro production at the old Dux factory, then graduated from the Jukovsky academy and in 1931 was given his own OKB at the Central Airfield (later called Khodinka). There he managed two of the biggest-ever programs, one beginning in 1933 with the TsKB-26 and ending with 1528 DB-3 and 5256 Il-4

Yakovlev's early personal liking for designing small sportplanes has a modern parallel in the bureau bearing his name, which produced a fleet of Yak-50s in time to compete in the 1976 world aerobatic championships,

with devastating effect by taking first, second and three other places to win the team prize in the men's competition and the first five places in the women's championship.

One of Ilyushin's early designs was also rewarded with a huge building program that eventually completed over 36,000 aircraft. The famous Il-2 Shturmovik ground-attack aircraft started life as a single-seater (illustrated) but vulnerability to attack from the rear led to the addition of a rear-facing gunner's position, after which the Il-2 recorded the lowest loss rate of any Russian World War II aircraft.

bombers, and the other beginning with the TsKB-55 of 1938 and ending with no fewer than 36,163 Il-2 *shturmoviks* plus 4966 Il-10s and another 1200 Il-10s made in Czechoslovakia. From October 1941 Ilyushin was evacuated to Factory 18 at Kuibyshev, where slow resumption of production was described by Stalin as "an insult." He sent a scathing telegram, from which Ilyushin framed and hung on the wall the one sentence, "The Red Army needs the Il-2 as it needs air and bread."

After the war Ilyushin concentrated on powerful machines, flying a wealth of advanced prototypes as well as such bread-winners as the Il-12 and -14 piston-engined transports, the Il-28 jet bomber (which flew on British engines a year before the Canberra and has had a long and active career), the Il-18, -62 and -86 passenger liners and the Il-76 freighter. Ilyushin retired in 1970, and died in 1977. His son, Vladimir, is a test pilot for the Sukhoi bureau, and the OKB named for Ilyushin has since 1971 been directed by Genrik Novojilov (or, for those who cannot pronounce j except as in English, Novozhilov).

Another of the "old guard" still at work is Oleg K Antonov. Whether or not he really built a helicopter in 1909, he certainly built gliders in 1924 and by 1938 had by far the greatest reputation of any Soviet glider designer. In that year he was assigned to the Yakovlev OKB, but continued inter-

mittently with gliders including the KT (biplane wings and twin-boom tail that clipped onto a light tank), troop-carrying An-14 of 1944 and postwar A-series competition sailplanes. Copying the Fieseler Storch in 1939 gave him a taste for STOL utility transports and in 1947, a year after establishing his own bureau at Kiev, Antonov appeared to some observers to be behind the times in producing a large piston-engined biplane, the An-2. So unobsolete was this design that it has subsequently been made in larger quantity than any other single postwar aircraft type (about 6000 in the Soviet Union, 8600 in Poland and an unknown number much in excess of 1000 in China). It was followed by the big twin-turboprop An-8 of 1955, from which stemmed the larger four-engined pressurized An-10 and -12. The Kiev bureau also produced the giant An-22 Antei and a series of small STOLs of which the latest and best, the An-28, was assigned to Poland in conformity with the ruling that that country handles general aviation.

Another OKB whose products have sometimes been passed to Poland is that of Mikhail L Mil, born in November 1909 at Irkutsk and in 1931 a graduate of the newly formed Aviation Institute at Novocherkassk. After working on autogiros and helicopters at TsAGI he joined Kamov's group in the mid-1930s (Nikolai I Kamov was born in 1902, formed his own OKB in

1947 and died in 1973) and was allowed to form his own group in 1947 alongside that of Kamov; the latter concentrated on coaxial helicopters while Mil stuck to the conventional layout. One of Mil's greatest achievements was the Mi-4 of 1952, which looked like a Sikorsky S-55 (with which it was at first compared in the West) but was in fact much more powerful and capable even than an S-58. Subsequently Mil produced a series of helicopters much larger than any others in the world, his place on his death in January 1970 being taken by Marat N Tishchenko.

Georgi M Beriev, the leading postwar designer of Soviet flying-boats and amphibians, was born in 1906 and graduated from the Leningrad Polytechnic in 1928. He assisted the short-lived OKB of French-born P A Richard on the TOM-1 flying-boat, but neither this nor Grigorovich's designs met the need for a good naval flying-boat and the Italian SM.62 was built under license at a World War I plant at Taganrog. Beriev joined the central Aviatrust TsKB, was rapidly advanced in rank and by 1930 was head of the seaplane section. In 1931 he

After the war, thanks to British naivete in giving the Russians Rolls-Royce engines, Ilyushin developed several advanced jet aircraft, one of which, the Il-28 twin-jet bomber was flying with British engines a year before the Canberra. A squadron of Red Air Force Il-28s (a trainer nearest camera) is pictured just before withdrawal from East Germany in 1956.

Top: The USSR entered the field of wide-bodied airliners with the Il-86, which was first announced in 1971 and made its first flight in December 1976. After several different projections the Il-86 appeared with conventional four-jet configuration for up to about 350 passengers in a basic nine-abreast layout and a cruising speed of up to 590mph.

Above: Smallest of the current Antonov turboprop-powered transports is the An-28 light utility and general-purpose aircraft, one of which is pictured in Aeroflot livery. The An-28 has been developed over a fairly lengthy period to give STOL and rough-field capability generally to provide a modern replacement as maid-of-all-work for the An-2 biplane (picture on pp 238–39). Like the An-2, production of the An-28 is assigned to Poland.

Right: Looking very much like a Sikorsky S-55 but about twice as heavy and three times as powerful, the Mil Mi-4 helicopter of 1952 provided even greater load capacity than the S-58. It was the fourth design from the independent Mil bureau, which then went on to design a series of the world's most capable helicopters.

Left: One of the earliest designs by Beriev, who became
the leading Russian designer of marine aircraft, was the
Be-2 (MBR-2) which first appeared as a coastal
reconnaissance flying-boat in 1931. The MBR-2 was
also used on many other duties; Aeroflot used it as a
transport throughout the war years. More than 1300
were built.

Below left: A wartime photograph of S A Lavochkin,
whose bureau was also noted for a single class of
aircraft, stands in front of an La-5 fighter, his most
important design which first flew early in 1942. The
basic design was further developed into the La-7, La-9
and La-11, with ground-attack variants and an ultimate
speed well over 400mph; wartime production was more
than 22,000.

aviation if not in the whole world where
combat aircraft are concerned – MiG. Artem
I Mikoyan was born in Armenia in 1905
and toiled as a machinist and soldier before
graduating from the Frunze Military Academy and then the Jukovsky school. In
1937 he joined Polikarpov's OKB but a year
later took the unusual step of joining with
another Polikarpov designer, Mikhail I
Gurevich, to create the smallest possible
fighter in which the big AM-35 liquid-
cooled engine (Hispano-derived) could be
installed. In January 1939 they formed their
own OKB, and the I-200 prototype flew on
5 April 1940. From it stemmed the MiG-1
and -3 fighters which, though fast, had little
else to commend them. Despite this, 3422
were built when the program was terminated
in 1942.

In view of such limited success nobody
was prepared for the bureau's rise to global

designed the MBR-2 to replace the Italian
biplane and about 1300 of these tough
monoplane boats had been made when the
Taganrog works had to be evacuated in
1942. Subsequently the Be label has been
borne by many piston, turboprop and jet
boats, as well as by the Be-30 STOL local-
service airliner which lost out to the rival
L-410 from Czechoslovakia. Beriev's death
was reported in July 1979, and his bureau is
unlikely to continue.

Another once-great OKB that vanished
was that of Semyon A Lavochkin, born in
Smolensk in 1900. While studying at TsAGI
he worked on early Tupolev aircraft, then
joined Richard's bureau alongside Beriev
and in 1931 moved to Chizevsky's bureau
working on pressurized airplanes and
balloon gondolas. In 1935 he participated

in the Lavochkin-Lyushin heavy-cannon
fighter, but escaped the prison or firing
squad that awaited most of his colleagues in
what was known as the Kurchevsky bureau.
In fact he was at once appointed to the
GUAP, and in his spare time (!) worked
with Gorbunov and Gudkov on a new
wooden fighter which flew as the I-22
prototype in March 1939. From it stemmed
the LaGG-1, LaGG-3, La-5 family and
La-7, all important in World War II with
wartime output placed at 22,261. The postwar La-9 and -11 were outstanding, and of
course all-metal, but none of the 12 distinct
families of La jet designs achieved real production and Lavochkin's unrewarded
bureau was closed on his death in June 1960.

This virtually left the field free for what
must be the best-known word in Soviet

Above: Co-designer of the famous MiG series of fighters, A Mikoyan, in 1955.

Right: Among the first fruits of the epoch-making Mikoyan-Gurevich collaboration was the MiG-3 fighter. Seen here is a squadron of MiG-3s on duty in 1942. Although compact and fast, early MiG fighters were not particularly successful and the 3000 or so built were largely relegated to reconnaissance duties by the end of 1943, giving no hint of the fame to come.

Below: By far the most numerous swing-wing aircraft in the world are the various versions of interceptors (such as this example) and ground-attack aircraft designated MiG-23 or MiG-27. Simple, tough and well-equipped, they typify modern Russian engineering which concentrates only on essentials. Since the mid-1960s the world has been awaiting this famous bureau's next family of combat aircraft.

fame in the jet age. Its twin-jet 1-300, with BMW 003A engines, beat the rival from the Yak bureau into the air by one hour on 24 April 1946. While 500 of the production version, the MiG-9, came off the lines, a far more advanced all-swept fighter was created in weeks, swiftly modified to use the invaluable gift from Britain of the Nene turbojet, and flown on 2 July 1947. From this stemmed many thousands of the production MiG-15 which was such an unpleasant shock in Korea, and the re-designed MiG-17. The twin-jet MiG-19 of 1953 was Europe's first level-supersonic production aircraft, and advanced versions of this remarkably fine machine are still produced in China. There followed a series of combat aircraft of which the MiG-21, -23, -25 and -27 are the best-known, as well as several spectacular record-breakers.

Mikoyan died in December 1970 and Gurevich (who retired through ill-health in 1964) in 1976. Above all others this OKB perpetuates their names, though its new leaders are busy in their own right. Much of the world has been awaiting with some trepidation for the results of the past ten years' work.

DEVELOPMENT OF EUROPEAN AIRCRAFT MANUFACTURERS

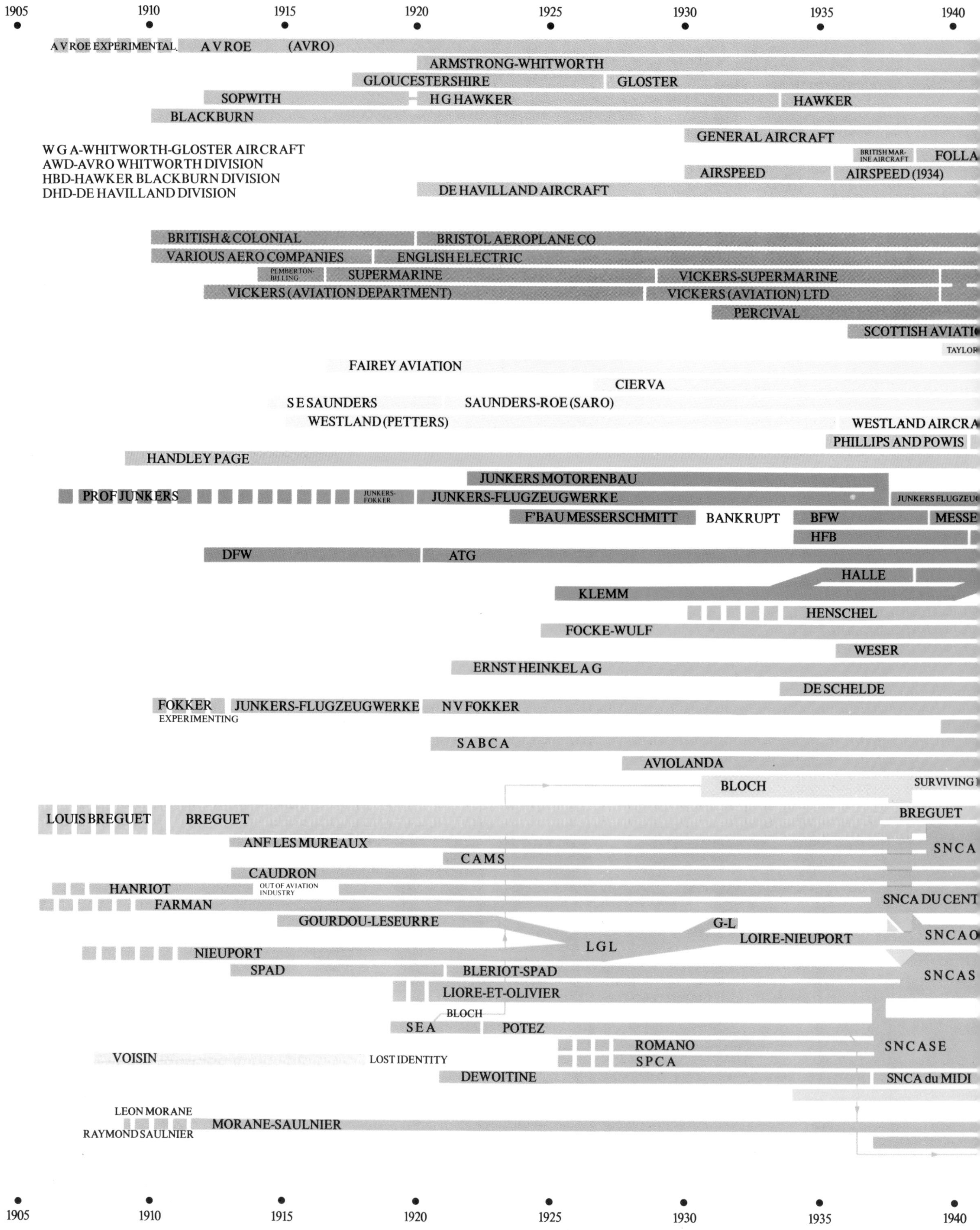

1905	1910	1915	1920	1925	1930	1935	1940

AVROE EXPERIMENTAL   AVROE   (AVRO)

ARMSTRONG-WHITWORTH

GLOUCESTERSHIRE   GLOSTER

SOPWITH   HG HAWKER   HAWKER

BLACKBURN

GENERAL AIRCRAFT

WGA-WHITWORTH-GLOSTER AIRCRAFT
AWD-AVRO WHITWORTH DIVISION
HBD-HAWKER BLACKBURN DIVISION
DHD-DE HAVILLAND DIVISION

BRITISH MARINE AIRCRAFT   FOLLA

AIRSPEED   AIRSPEED (1934)

DE HAVILLAND AIRCRAFT

BRITISH & COLONIAL   BRISTOL AEROPLANE CO

VARIOUS AERO COMPANIES   ENGLISH ELECTRIC

PEMBERTON-BILLING   SUPERMARINE   VICKERS-SUPERMARINE

VICKERS (AVIATION DEPARTMENT)   VICKERS (AVIATION) LTD

PERCIVAL

SCOTTISH AVIATION

TAYLOR

FAIREY AVIATION

CIERVA

SE SAUNDERS   SAUNDERS-ROE (SARO)

WESTLAND (PETTERS)   WESTLAND AIRCRA

PHILLIPS AND POWIS

HANDLEY PAGE

JUNKERS MOTORENBAU

PROF JUNKERS   JUNKERS-FOKKER   JUNKERS-FLUGZEUGWERKE   JUNKERS FLUGZEUG

F'BAU MESSERSCHMITT   BANKRUPT   BFW   MESSE

HFB

DFW   ATG

HALLE

KLEMM

HENSCHEL

FOCKE-WULF

WESER

ERNST HEINKEL AG

DE SCHELDE

FOKKER   JUNKERS-FLUGZEUGWERKE   NV FOKKER
EXPERIMENTING

SABCA

AVIOLANDA

BLOCH   SURVIVING

LOUIS BREGUET   BREGUET   BREGUET

ANF LES MUREAUX   SNCA

CAMS

CAUDRON   OUT OF AVIATION INDUSTRY

HANRIOT   SNCA DU CENT

FARMAN

GOURDOU-LESEURRE   G-L   SNCAO

LGL   LOIRE-NIEUPORT

NIEUPORT

SPAD   BLERIOT-SPAD   SNCAS

LIORE-ET-OLIVIER

BLOCH

SEA   POTEZ

ROMANO   SNCASE

VOISIN   LOST IDENTITY   SPCA

DEWOITINE   SNCA du MIDI

LEON MORANE
RAYMOND SAULNIER   MORANE-SAULNIER

1905	1910	1915	1920	1925	1930	1935	1940

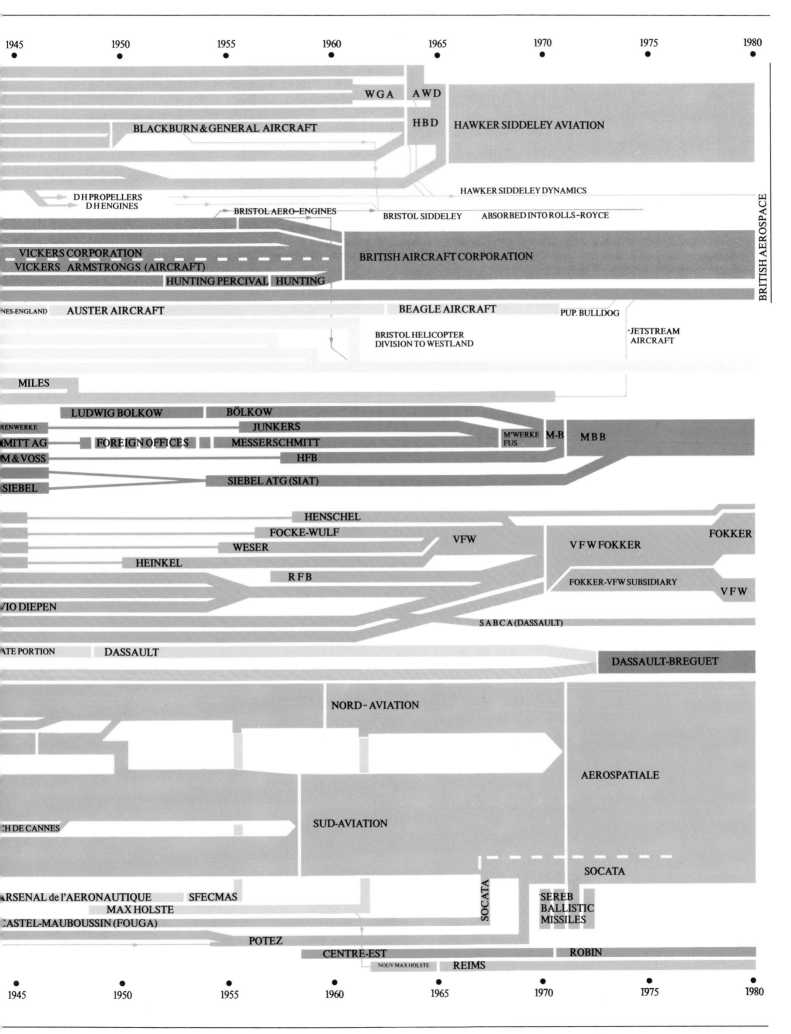

1945　1950　1955　1960　1965　1970　1975　1980

WGA　AWD

HBD　HAWKER SIDDELEY AVIATION

BLACKBURN & GENERAL AIRCRAFT

HAWKER SIDDELEY DYNAMICS

D H PROPELLERS
D H ENGINES

BRISTOL AERO-ENGINES　BRISTOL SIDDELEY　ABSORBED INTO ROLLS-ROYCE

VICKERS CORPORATION
VICKERS ARMSTRONGS (AIRCRAFT)

BRITISH AIRCRAFT CORPORATION

HUNTING PERCIVAL　HUNTING

NES-ENGLAND　AUSTER AIRCRAFT　BEAGLE AIRCRAFT　PUP. BULLDOG

BRISTOL HELICOPTER
DIVISION TO WESTLAND

·JETSTREAM
AIRCRAFT

MILES

LUDWIG BOLKOW　BÖLKOW

RENWERKE　JUNKERS

MITT AG　FOREIGN OFFICES　MESSERSCHMITT　M'WERKE
FUS　M-B　MBB

M & VOSS　HFB

SIEBEL　SIEBEL ATG (SIAT)

HENSCHEL

FOCKE-WULF

WESER　VFW　FOKKER

HEINKEL　V F W FOKKER

R F B　FOKKER-VFW SUBSIDIARY　VFW

VIO DIEPEN

S A B C A (DASSAULT)

ATE PORTION　DASSAULT　DASSAULT-BREGUET

NORD- AVIATION

AEROSPATIALE

CH DE CANNES　SUD-AVIATION

SOCATA

ARSENAL de l'AERONAUTIQUE　SFECMAS

MAX HOLSTE

CASTEL-MAUBOUSSIN (FOUGA)

SOCATA

SEREB
BALLISTIC
MISSILES

POTEZ

CENTRE-EST　ROBIN

NOUV MAX HOLSTE　REIMS

1945　1950　1955　1960　1965　1970　1975　1980

BRITISH AEROSPACE

ACKNOWLEDGEMENTS

Aeritalia: via Michael Hooks: 160 (center).
The Aeroplane: via Philip Moyes: 101.
Aérospatiale: 165 (bottom right), 168/169 (top 2), 170/171 (top 2), 172/173 (all 3), 174/175 (top 2); via Michael Hooks: 166 (bottom left), 178/179 bottom right); via Philip Moyes: 176/177 (bottom left).
Airbus Industrie: via Michael Hooks: 178 (bottom left).
Air Canada: 106 (center).
Air France: 164/165 (bottom), 187 (top); via Michael Jerram: 163 (center).
Air Portraits: 32 (top), 167 (top).
Associated Press: 242, 251 (top).
BAC Commercial Division: via Michael Hooks: 92/93, 111 (top).
BAC Preston: via Michael Hooks: 110.
BAC Weybridge: via Michael Hooks: 105 (center and bottom); via Philip Moyes: 104 (center); via Ann Tilbury: 106 (bottom).
Gordon Bain: 22/23 (top).
Beech Aircraft Corporation: 10/11 (bottom); via Michael Jerram: 11 (top), 12 (top).
Bell Helicopter Textron: 14 (both).
The Boeing Company: 16/17 (top); via Michael Hooks: 20 (top); via Philip Moyes: 16/17 (bottom 4), 20 (bottom), 21 (both); via Ann Tilbury: 18 (center), 19 (top).
Bristol Aeroplane Company: via Philip Moyes: 98/99 (bottom 2), 100 (bottom).
British Aerospace: 42/43 (center), 96/97; via Michael Hooks: 112 (top).
British Aerospace Weybridge-Bristol: 40/41 (bottom), 244/245 (center); via Ann Tilbury: 111 (bottom), 113 (bottom 2).
British Airways: 56/57; via Michael Jerram: 122 top).
British Hovercraft Corp: via Michael Hooks: 155 (top).
Britten-Norman Limited: 141 (top).
Charles Brown: via Michael Hooks: 100 (top).
Canadair: via Michael Hooks: 222 (major), 223 (bottom); via Ann Tilbury: 223 (top).
Canadian National Aeronautical Collection: 15, 26/27 (bottom).
Cessna Aircraft Company: 24 (bottom).
Curtiss-Wright Corp: via Philip Moyes: 30/31 (bottom 2).
Dassault-Breguet: 186 (bottom), 187 (bottom), 190; via Michael Hooks: 188 (center).
De Havilland: 124 (bottom).
De Havilland Canada: via Michael Hooks: 225 (top).
Dornier-Werke: via Philip Moyes: 191 (top and centre); via Brian Walters: 192 (bottom).
EMBRAER: 226 (bottom), 227 (top); via Michael Hooks: 226 (center), 218/219.
Fairchild Hiller Corp: 35 (bottom).
Fairchild Industries: 32 (bottom).
Fairchild Republic Company: 33 (bottom).
Fleet Air Arm Museum: 151 (top right).
Flight International: via Michael Hooks: 44 (top).
Ford Motor Company: via Philip Moyes: 36 (top).
General Dynamics: 6/7, 44/45 (bottom); via Michael Jerram: 42 (bottom).
GIFAS: via Michael Hooks: 176/177 (top and bottom right).
Grumman Corp: 51 (top).
Hawker Siddeley: via Michael Hooks: 119 (bottom); via Philip Moyes: 121 (top and center), 132 (center); via Ann Tilbury: 4/5, 127 (bottom right), 128 (bottom), 129 (top), 132 (top).
Hindustan Aircraft: via Philip Moyes: 230 (top).
Michael Hooks: Title page, 114, 124 (center), 134 (bottom), 156/157, 158/159 (bottom right), 191 (bottom), 208, 224, 236.

Stuart Howe: 13.
Imperial War Museum: via MARS London: 142.
Inter-Air Press: 19 (bottom), 22 (bottom), 34/35 (top), 49 (bottom), 50/51 (bottom), 54/55 (bottom), 58/59 (top left), 65 (bottom), 72 (bottom), 76 (top), 82 (center), 89 (bottom), 91 (center), 117 (bottom), 130/131 (bottom), 138, 141 (bottom), 146 (top), 152/153, 160 (bottom), 162/163 (bottom), 174/175 (bottom), 185 (top), 188/189 (top-center and bottom), 202/203 (bottom), 209 (bottom), 211 (center), 217 (top), 227 (bottom), 238/239 (top), 249 (top).
Israel Aircraft Industries: 231 (center); /Inter-Air Press: 231 (bottom).
Michael Jerram Collection: half-title, 12 (bottom), 18 (top), 24 (center), 25 (both), 36 (bottom), 38/39 (bottom right), 46 (bottom left), 47 (top), 48, 49 (top), 52, 56 (top left), 58 (bottom), 62/63 (top), 68 (top), 77, 78 (top), 80/81 (top 3), 86, 87 (top), 107 (center), 109 (bottom), 117 (top), 122/123 (bottom), 129 (bottom), 131 (center), 139, 166/167 (bottom), 170/171 (bottom), 184/185 (bottom), 186 (top), 188 (top left), 194 (bottom), 206, 209 (top), 213 (bottom), 217 (center), 221, 222 (inset), 225 (bottom), 231 (top), 237 (bottom), 239 (bottom), 247 (both), 249 (center).
Keystone Press Agency: via Philip Moyes: 33 (top), 69.
David Kingston: 46/47 (bottom).
J Lloyd: 38/39 (top).
Lockheed Aircraft Corp: 54 (top); via MARS London: 53; via Philip Moyes: 8/9, 55 (top and center), 59 (top).
Lockheed-California: via Ann Tilbury: 59 (bottom).
Lockheed-Georgia Company: via Michael Hooks: 60.
LTV Aerospace: via Michael Hooks: 91 (bottom).
Lufthansa: 215 (top); via Brian Walters: 192 (top), 199 (bottom), 200/201 (both), 203 (top), 205 (top).
Glenn L Martin Company: via Philip Moyes: 61 (top), 62/63 (bottom 2).
MBB: 205 (center), 207 (bottom); via Michael Hooks: 207 (top).
McDonnell Aircraft Corp: via Philip Moyes: 64/65 (top).
McDonnell Douglas Corp: 70/71 (all 3); via Ann Tilbury: 61 (bottom), 67 (both), 68 (bottom), 72 (center).
Ministry of Defence: 23 (bottom right), 132 (bottom), 245 (bottom); via Michael Hooks: 100 (center); via Philip Moyes: 198.
Philip Moyes Collection: Endpapers, 28/29 (bottom), 30 (top), 34 (bottom), 37 (both), 40 (top 2), 74, 80/81 (bottom), 88 (center), 90/91 (top), 94/95 (all 3), 99 (top), 104/105 (top 2), 107 (bottom), 108/109 (top 2 and bottom left), 113, 115, 116 (top), 118/119 (top 2 and bottom left 2), 120, 121 (bottom), 123 (top), 124/125 (top 3), 126/127 (center bottom and top right), 128 (center), 130/131 (top 2), 134 (top), 135, 136/137 (top 6), 140, 148 (top), 150/151 (bottom), 154/155 (bottom), 158/159 (top and bottom left), 161 (both), 165 (top right), 168/169 (bottom), 180/181 (all 4), 182/183 (all 3), 184 (top), 193, 197, 199 (top), 204/205 (top left and bottom), 212, 213 (top), 214 (both), 215 (center), 216/217 (left 3 and center bottom), 220 (bottom), 228/229 (all 3), 230, 232/233 (all 3), 234/235 (top and bottom left), 237 (top), 238 (bottom), 240/241 (all 3), 243 (both), 244 (bottom), 246 (both), 248 (both), 249 (bottom), 250 (both), 251 (center), 251 (bottom).
Naval Aircraft Factory: via Philip Moyes: 29 (top).
Northrop Corp: via Michael Hooks: 73, 75 (both), 76 (bottom).
Novesti Press Agency: 244 (top left).

NVKNV Fokker: 194/195 (top 2 and bottom right), 196 (top and bottom); via Michael Hooks: 196 (bottom).
Pan American: via Michael Jerram: 19 (center), 38 (bottom left), 87 (bottom).
Ted Pugh Collection: 143 (top), 162 (center).
RAAF: via Philip Moyes: 220 (top).
Rockwell International: 82/83 (top); via Michael Hooks: 79; via Michael Jerram: 83 (bottom).
Rolls Royce Limited: via Michael Hooks: 41 (top), 149.
Royal Aircraft Establishment Bedford: 136/137 (bottom).
Ryan Aeronautical Company: via Philip Moyes: 84/85 (both).
Saab-Scania: via Philip Moyes: 210 (both), 211 (top).
San Diego Harbor Department: via Philip Moyes: 27 (center).
Scottish Aviation: via Michael Hooks: 133 (bottom); via Philip Moyes: 133 (top).
Short Brothers: via Michael Hooks: 146 (bottom); via Michael Jerram: 145 (bottom), 146 (center); via Philip Moyes: 145 (top and center); via Ann Tilbury: 144 (both).
The Times: via Philip Moyes: 164/165 (center top).
USAAF: via Philip Moyes: 235 (bottom).
US Navy: 66, 88 (bottom); via Peter Kilduff: 82 (bottom), 91 (bottom); via Philip Moyes: 28 (top).
Vickers Limited: via Michael Jerram: 104 (bottom).
Vought Corp: via Jennifer Moore Personality Picture Library: 89 (top).
Brian Walters: 78 (bottom).
Westland Helicopters: via Michael Hooks: 148 (bottom); via Philip Moyes: 152 (top left).

INDEX